AF774275

'The global anti-money laundering system (AML) was designed by rich countries for rich countries, and yet this same system has now been spread to almost every country in the world. How have countries in Africa and the developing world more generally coped with having to adopt AML policy designed for very different circumstances? Despite the fact that the majority of the world's national AML systems now are in developing rather than developed countries, almost all the attention has been focused on Europe and North America. This volume is a long-overdue corrective to this fundamental bias in finally putting the AML experiences of developing countries at centre-stage. Both scholars and policy-makers need this book to properly understand how AML works, and often doesn't work, as a genuinely global system.'

Jason Sharman, *Sir Patrick Sheehy Professor of International Relations, Department of Politics and International Studies, University of Cambridge*

'Corruption and money laundering constitute serious obstacles to the development of developing economies. International instruments do not adequately reflect the challenges that less economically developed countries experience in ensuring compliance with their provisions. This book is timely and very important to the understanding of the efforts and constraints of developing countries to combat corruption and money laundering and to also comply with international legal provisions and standards. There is a dearth of academic literature on most of the issues covered in many chapters of the book. The publication is a major contribution to the understanding of money laundering and challenges encountered in combatting them in less developed economies. The contents of the book offer significant insight and will enlighten policy-makers, law enforcement personnel, financial institutions and scholars, and highly recommended.'

Etannibi E. Alemika, *retired Professor of Criminology and Sociology of Law, University of Jos, Jos, Nigeria, and currently Adjunct Professor at the Faculty of Law, Humanities and Social Sciences, Walter Sisulu University, Mthatha, South Africa.*

Global Anti-Money Laundering Regulation

This book explores the politics of money laundering and terrorist financing (ML/TF) regulation in several countries across Africa and the Small Island States. Developed countries created the Financial Action Task Force (FATF) to combat ML/TF globally. Expectedly, the FATF's standards mirror existing banking regulations within the G7 countries. Yet, the standards apply to all countries irrespective of the limited ML/TF risks they pose to the global economy, their weak pre-conditions for effective regulation and their non-involvement in the FATF's framing. Still, such countries, mainly within the Global South, have worked hard to amplify their compliance with the regime due to fears of the repercussions of their non-compliance. This collection demonstrates how the global ML/TF regulation is treated as an implicitly superior legal regime where the Global South must comply irrespective of their perception of the FATF's legitimacy challenges. It shows that beyond exogenous factors such as neo-colonialism, endogenous factors such as weak institutions and corruption undermine the compliance trajectory of the Global South. Furthermore, it analyses the unintended consequences of transplanting FATF standards into diverse legal and cultural contexts. The volume contributes to our understanding of the challenges of transplantation from the Global North and how the Global South is steering within the constraints created by the FATF. It advocates for a comprehensive understanding of the nuanced compliance challenges of developing countries. It further proposes practical solutions to address them, emphasizing the importance of risk-based understanding, accountability, capacity-building and coordination in achieving effective anti-money laundering and counter-terrorist financing measures. The collection will be essential reading for researchers, academics and policy-makers working in financial crime regulation and international economic law.

Nkechikwu Valerie Azinge-Egbiri is Lecturer in Business and Commercial Law at Lancaster University, England.

Nicholas Ryder is Professor in Financial Crime at the School of Law and Politics, Cardiff University, UK.

Ehi Eric Esoimeme, Esq., is Professor of Business Law and Ethics at James Hope University, Lagos, Nigeria; Rudolph Kwanue University College, Liberia; and Kennedy University of Baptist, United States.

The Law of Financial Crime

Series Editors:

Nicholas Ryder

Professor of Law, Cardiff University, School of Law and Politics, UK.

Dr. Lachmi Singh

Associate Lecturer, Bristol Law School, University of the West of England, UK.

Sam Bourton

Lecturer in Law, the University of the West of England, UK.

While a growing number of high profile financial crime cases have hit the headlines recently the topic of financial crime is also generating much attention amongst academics and practitioners. This series will be the first to be dedicated to the law of financial, or economic, crime and offers a platform for important and original research in this area.

Books in the series will cover traditional subjects of financial crime including money laundering, terrorist financing, fraud, market abuse, insider dealing, market manipulation, tax evasion, bribery and corruption. But broader legal and regulatory issues will also be covered as well as emerging areas of concern such as the risks to stability of the financial system posed by financial crime. Emphasis will be placed on comparative approaches to the subject considering legislation across a number of jurisdictions as well as international regulations where appropriate, giving the series a truly global outlook.

The titles in the series are primarily aimed at an audience of researchers, scholars and practitioners in the area but should also be of interest to policy makers, law enforcement agencies, financial regulatory agencies, as well as people employed within the financial services sector.

Available titles in this series include:

Anti-Money Laundering and the Law
Comparative Approaches to Countering Predicate Crimes
Engin Erken and Umut Turksen

Global Anti-Money Laundering Regulation
Developing Countries Compliance Challenges
Edited by Nkechikwu Valerie Azinge-Egbiri, Nicholas Ryder and Ehi Eric Esoimeme, Esq

For more information about this series, please visit: www.routledge.com/The-Law-of-Financial-Crime/book-series/FINCRIME

Global Anti-Money Laundering Regulation

Developing Countries Compliance Challenges

Edited by Nkechikwu Valerie Azinge-Egbiri, Nicholas Ryder and Ehi Eric Esoimeme Esq

Routledge
Taylor & Francis Group
LONDON AND NEW YORK

First published 2025
by Routledge
4 Park Square, Milton Park, Abingdon, Oxon OX14 4RN

and by Routledge
605 Third Avenue, New York, NY 10158

Routledge is an imprint of the Taylor & Francis Group, an informa business

British Library Cataloguing-in-Publication Data
A catalogue record for this book is available from the British Library

Library of Congress Cataloging-in-Publication Data
Names: Ryder, Nicholas, editor. | Azinge-Egbiri, Nkechikwu Valerie, editor. | Esoimeme, Ehi Eric, editor.
Title: Global anti-money laundering regulation: developing countries compliance challenges/edited by Nicholas Ryder, Nkechikwu Valerie Azinge-Egbiri, and Ehi Eric Esoimeme, Esq.
Description: Abingdon, Oxon [UK]; New York, NY: Routledge, 2024. | Series: The law of financial crime | Includes bibliographical references and index.
Identifiers: LCCN 2024032295 (print) | LCCN 2024032296 (ebook) | ISBN 9781032182889 (hardback) | ISBN 9781032182896 (paperback) | ISBN 9781003253808 (ebook)
Subjects: LCSH: Money laundering—Law and legislation—Developing countries. | Money laundering—Developing countries—Prevention.
Classification: LCC K1089 .G56 2024 (print) | LCC K1089 (ebook) | DDC 345/.1240268—dc23/eng/20240714
LC record available at https://lccn.loc.gov/2024032295
LC ebook record available at https://lccn.loc.gov/2024032296

ISBN: 978-1-032-18288-9 (hbk)
ISBN: 978-1-032-18289-6 (pbk)
ISBN: 978-1-003-25380-8 (ebk)

DOI: 10.4324/9781003253808

Typeset in Galliard
by Apex CoVantage, LLC

Contents

Contributors

Nkechikwu Valerie Azinge-Egbiri is a Lecturer in Business and Commercial Law at Lancaster University, England. Previously, she was an academic at the School of Law, University of Lincoln. Her research interest is in the field of financial services regulation, specifically on anti-money laundering and counter-terrorist financing (AML/CFT). Her research focuses on the relationship between global financial crime regulation and development, as well as the anti-money laundering compliance trajectory of emerging economies. Her interest in this area culminated in her recent book titled *Regulating and Combating Money Laundering and Terrorist Financing: The Law in Emerging Economies* (Routledge 2021). This book is the first of its kind that highlights the paradoxical implications of the global AML/CFT standards on emerging economies and challenges the justification for a uniform benchmarking framework. She is also a co-founder of the Global South Dialogue on Economic Crime, a multi-disciplinary platform for the advancement of dialogue and research on matters of financial crime as they affect Global South countries. She obtained her PhD in international financial crime regulation from the University of Warwick, United Kingdom. She also obtained her LLM in international economic law (with a distinction) from the same University. She holds an LLB degree from the University of Leicester and has been admitted as a Barrister and Solicitor of the Supreme Court of Nigeria.

Chinelo Bob-Osamor is a Barrister and Solicitor of the Supreme Court of Nigeria and a PhD student at the Law School, Cardiff University, UK. She is also a TV host, philanthropist and CEO of Ella-B Communication, which produces Discourse and Healthwise.

Jean-Pierre Brun is a member of the French judiciary. Since August 2008, he has worked at the World Bank Group and is currently Senior Financial Sector Specialist for financial market integrity (FMI) in the Finance, Competitiveness & Innovation Global Practice at the Bank. He is responsible for leading and conducting technical assistance and contributing to the policy dialogue related to the financial market integrity and the recovery of proceeds of corruption as part of the World Bank's FMI activities, as well as for the Stolen Asset Recovery Initiative (StAR), a partnership with the United Nations. He provides policy advice to countries on anti-money laundering and combatting the financing of terrorism (AML/CFT), asset recovery and building country capacity to conduct financial investigations and prosecute grand corruption cases. He specializes in the strategic, tactical and technical aspects of investigation, prosecution and legal analysis of AML/CFT and grand corruption cases. Previously, he was a Director of Investigations for Deloitte, worked as a Prosecutor specializing in AML/CFT and organized crime at the Tribunal of Paris, and had experience as a Government Auditor and an examining judge. A French national, he holds a master's degree in political science and law from Paris University and is a graduate of the French National School for Magistrates.

Egbiri Egbiri is a Barrister and Solicitor of the Supreme Court of Nigeria and an Attorney in New York State. He is currently Counsel in the Country Unit of the Legal Department at the International Monetary Fund (IMF). His role at the IMF includes advising member countries of the IMF on IMF's law and policies on lending, surveillance and technical assistance. He also participates in the IMF's Working Groups on different policy issues. Before joining the IMF, he was a Principal Legal Counsel with the Finance Division of the Legal Services Department of the African Development Bank Group (AfDB), where he advised on all aspects of AfDB's mobilization, investment and management of its financial resources and its borrowings in the international capital markets. He also negotiated, drafted and reviewed AfDB's ISDA master agreements and transaction confirmations with counterparties, and advised senior management on all aspects of finance law. He is an awardee of the ESQ Nigerian Legal Awards (2019) in the 40-under-40 (Nigerian Rising Stars) category. In 2019, he was ranked as one of the 100 Most Influential Young Nigerians (an honouree in the Law and Governance category).

Ehi Eric Esoimeme Esq is Professor of Business Law and Ethics at James Hope University (Nigeria), Rudolph Kwanue University (Liberia) and Kennedy University of Baptist (USA). Prof. Esoimeme is also concurrently the Founder and Managing Partner of E-Four and AAF, an Accredited Training Partner at the Global Academy of Finance and Management (USA) and the Editor in Chief of DSC Publications Ltd. (Nigeria). His area of specialism and expertise is in countering financial crime. This is categorized into regulatory law, substantive law, and professional compliance guidance in terms of strategic management of financial crime risks and vulnerabilities. Prof. Esoimeme's skill and knowledge in the field of the financial crime space are drawn from his many years of experience as a researcher and consultant in anti-money laundering laws and policies, counter-fraud measures, and anti-corruption strategies. So far, Prof. Esoimeme has authored more than 50 publications, including 12 books on financial crime compliance while his research on corruption and anti-corruption has been featured on

Harvard Law School's bibliography on corruption and anti-corruption. Prof. Esoimeme's second book titled "The Risk-Based Approach to Combating Money Laundering and Terrorist Financing" was rated as the #5 best money laundering book of all time by Financial Expert in its 2021 refresh of the rankings while Ehi's fifth book "Balancing Anti-Money Laundering/Counter-Terrorist Financing Requirements and Financial Inclusion" was named one of the best Banks books of all time by BookAuthority. On July 27, 2022, Prof. Esoimeme's Research Items on Financial Crime Compliance reached a new Milestone of 30,000 reads on ResearchGate. Prof. Esoimeme received a bachelor's degree in law from the University of Lagos and holds a master's degree in International Commercial Law with specialization in international banking law and anti-money laundering compliance from Cardiff University. Prof. Esoimeme holds the U.S. equivalent of a Juris Doctor in International Law and two PhD Degrees in International Public Law. He was admitted to the Nigerian Bar as a Barrister and Solicitor of the Supreme Court of Nigeria in 2010. Prof. Ehi Esoimeme is a member of the InstitutUniversitaire du Bénin (IUB) University, Board of Trusteeship, fellow of the International Institute of Certified Forensic Investigation Professionals Inc., United States, a fellow of the Global Academy of Finance and Management, a Lifetime Honorary fellow of the International Association for Quality Assurance in Pre-tertiary and Higher Education, a fellow of the Association of Enterprise Risk Management Professionals, a fellow of the Institute of Management Consultants, and a member of the Nigerian Bar Association.

Constance Gikonyo is an Advocate and a Lecturer by profession. She is a senior lecturer at the University of Nairobi, School of Law. Her research interests are in the areas of maritime law, anti-money laundering, asset forfeiture and the connection between money laundering and aspects of transnational organised crime. Further research interests are in illicit financial flows related to wildlife crimes and criminal justice strategies to combat wildlife crime. She has conducted trainings on the areas of anti-money laundering and asset forfeiture for various organisations. She has authored publications in her areas of research interests.

Jackie Harvey is an Emeritus Professor at Northumbria University's Newcastle Business School. She has had a varied career crossing from fiscal and macro policy economist, commercial banking and entering academia in 2000. She established her research reputation in the field of anti-money laundering, most recently being principal investigator on a UK FCDO–funded project examining beneficial ownership and corruption in Nigeria.

John Hatchard is a Barrister and Emeritus Professor at the University of Buckingham. He is currently a Visiting Professor at the United Nations International Anti-Corruption Academy in Vienna and a Visiting Scholar at

Arizona State University. He has held senior academic positions at universities in the UK, United States, Zambia and Zimbabwe. He has also served as the Chief Mutual Legal Assistance Officer at the Commonwealth Secretariat. He was also a Senior Fellow at the British Institute of International and Comparative Law and the Director of the University of Detroit–Mercy London Law Program. For many years he was Secretary-General of the Commonwealth Legal Education Association (CLEA) and now serves as a CLEA Vice-President. He has published well over 100 books and articles in the areas of corruption and money laundering, criminal law, criminal justice and evidence, constitutional law, good governance and human rights, with particular reference to the Commonwealth and Anglophone Africa. He has undertaken consultancy work for a wide range of international organisations, particularly in the field of good governance, combatting corruption and money laundering, and human rights.

Zakhele Hlophe, BA (Natal), MSc (Leicester), PhD (Kings College London), is a strategic adviser to the South African Parliament, particularly on the Portfolio Committee on Justice and Correctional Services and the Standing Committee on Finance. Previously, he taught criminal procedure at the University of KwaZulu Natal and was the course director for the post-graduate diploma in forensic investigations and criminal justice. He was a post-doctoral fellow at the University of Oxford–Princeton Global Leaders Fellow from 2014 to 2016. Prior to this, he did his PhD at Kings College, London, where his thesis titled 'Regulating Money Laundering in Developing Countries: A Critical Analysis of South Africa's Incorporation and Implementation of the Global FATF Standards' was published. He is a contributing author of *The Law of Evidence in South Africa* (OUPSA).

Simeon Igbinedion, LLB (Unilag); LLM and PhD (Gakushuin University, Tokyo); BL (Nigeria). Simeon was appointed an Associate Professor in the Department of Jurisprudence and International Law, Faculty of Law, University of Lagos in 2022. His research and teaching interests include but not limited to jurisprudence and legal theory, public international law, human rights law, international economic law, international criminal law, and diplomatic and consular law. He is a consultant on corruption, financial crimes and assets recovery. He also conducts training sessions in these areas for non-governmental organizations working in the field. He has presented papers and published a variety of articles and book chapters both locally and internationally on cross-border crimes, grand corruption, money laundering, assets recovery and repatriation of plundered but recovered assets to prior legitimate state owners. He has also co-edited a book on these thematic areas. Between 2021 and 2022, he was a consultant for Nigeria's primary anti-corruption agency, Independent Corrupt Practices Commission (ICPC), on illicit financial flows (IFFs).

Gosego Rockfall Lekgowe is an Attorney at Law before the High Court of the Republic of Botswana, a Notary Public and Conveyancer. He teaches commercial law at the University of Botswana including tax law, sale and credit agreements and negotiable instruments and banking law. He has also taught business law at Oxford Brookes University and equity and trusts at the University of Birmingham. He is interested in legal research on norms, synergies and interactions of legal orders. In 2011, he received the Barclays–FG Mogae award for a master's degree scholarship. At the LLM level, he studied WTO law, regional integration law, international investment law, international human rights and international humanitarian law. He acted as an Academic Assistant during the administration of the 2015 and 2016 WTO Regional Trade Policy Course. Amongst others, he has published chapters on socio-economic rights in Botswana and on public representation in SADC regional integration. He has a Certificate on Public Policy Analysis from London School of Economics and Political Science (LSE). He practices law part-time at Rockfall Lekgowe Law Group mainly in the areas of strategic litigation, labour law, construction law and general litigation. His law firm represented the applicants' cases that led to a change in dual-citizenship and LGBTQ rights in Botswana. He has sat as a member of the Law Reporting Committee of the High Court of Botswana.

Joy Malala is an Assistant Professor at Warwick University and an interdisciplinary researcher whose work is at the intersection of international law, public policy and global health. She has a special interest in researching financial regulation and supervision, the legal accountability of regulators, corporate governance and the regulation of financial innovation and technology. She researches financial sector reform through the consideration of the role of central banks, and systemically important financial institutions and their impact on emerging economies. She also researches the socio-legal and political landscape of FinTech in the Global South. She is the Co-Founder of the Global South Dialogue on Economic Crime, a multi-disciplinary platform for the advancement of dialogue and research on matters of financial crime as they affect Global South countries.

Donato Masciandaro is Full Professor of Economics, Chair in Economics of Financial Regulation, at Bocconi University. He is Director of the Baffi Centre for Applied Research on International Markets, Finance and Regulation, and Member of the Management Council of SUERF (Socièté Universitaire Europèenne de Recherches Financières). He is Associate Editor of the *Journal of Financial Stability*. His work has covered three main topics: central banking, financial regulation and supervision, and illegal financial markets. He is an op-ed columnist in the main Italian financial newspaper, *Il Sole 24Ore*.

Edefe Ojomo is a Lecturer in the Department of Jurisprudence and International Law at the University of Lagos, Nigeria. She has a Bachelor of Laws (LLB) from the University of Lagos; a Qualifying Certificate (BL) from the Nigerian Law School; a Master of Laws (LLM) in international and comparative law from the American University in Cairo; a Master of Arts (MA) in conflict, security and development from King's College London; and a JSD from NYU School of Law. Her JSD dissertation was titled 'Regionalism in West Africa: A Study of Remedial Governance Structure'. She has been a recipient of several fellowships and academic awards, including the African Graduate Fellowship at the American University in Cairo, the CSDG/ECOWAS Fellowship at King's College London, and several scholastic awards at the University of Lagos and the Nigerian Law School, where she graduated with First Class Honours. She also has certificates in research and specialized courses from several institutions and organisations, including the United Nations and the International Organisation for Migration. She has worked as an intern and a research fellow at the ECOWAS Commission, where she specialized in projects relating to peace building, mediation and the development of migration policies for the West African community. She has also trained government officials from West African countries on issues relating to integration and migration. Her research focuses on citizenship, migration and regional integration in Africa. She also provides research and program support to the Network of Migration Research on Africa (NOMRA).

Nicholas Ryder is Professor in Financial Crime, the School of Law and Politics, Cardiff University, UK. With an international reputation for excellence in policy-oriented research in financial crime, he has played advisory roles both nationally and internationally. His research has attracted funding (£1.6m) from Innovate UK, Economic and Social Research Council (ESRC), LexisNexis Risk Solutions, the City of London Police Force, the Royal United Services Limited, ICT Wilmington Risk and Compliance, the France Telecom Group and the European Social Fund. He has produced research of an international quality and created and edited Routledge's Financial Crime Series. Collectively, he has published monographs, edited books and articles in internationally recognised journals including *Legal Studies, Cambridge Law Journal, Journal of Business Law, Studies in Conflict and Terrorism* and *Contemporary Issues in Law*. He has been invited to consult by the media including Bloomberg News, the BBC, CNBC, the Sunday *Times*, the *Independent*, the *Wall Street Journal, Albawaba News, South China Morning Post*, the *Financial Times* and the *Telegraph*.

Emmanuel Oluwasina Sotande, MBA (Ahmadu Bello University, Zaria); PhD (University of Leeds). Emmanuel is an Assistant Director and Head, Federal Government Accounts Analysis and Reporting, Nigerian Financial

Intelligence Unit (NFIU). From December 2021 to June 2022, during the Covid-19 pandemic, he undertook a capacity-building assessment on combatting illicit financial flows in four countries in the Southern Africa Region: Madagascar, Mauritius, Mozambique and Zambia, a project funded by African Development Bank (AfDB). He conducted several anti-money laundering typologies studies for the Inter-Governmental Action Group Against Money Laundering in West Africa (GIABA). He has written several other academic articles majorly on combatting transnational organised crime, illicit financial flows and money laundering. This includes the study of Corruption and Money Laundering; Money Laundering and Terrorist Financing through Informal and Illegal Foreign Currency Exchange Service Providers in West Africa; Typologies on Money Laundering and Terrorist Financing Linked to Human Trafficking and Migrants Smuggling; The Regime against Money Laundering: A Call for Scientific Modelling; Financial Institutions Integrity, and; Related Impediments Affecting the Curbing of Illicit Financial Flows of Organised Crime in Developing Economies: Policy Implications.

Anastasia Sotiropoulou, LLB, LLM (Hons) (National Kapodistrian University of Athens, School of Law); LLM, JSD (Yale Law School); VRVS Graduate Program (Harvard Law School). She currently serves as a Legal Counsel at the Office of the Governor of the National Transparency Authority of Greece. She is an instructor at the American College of Greece-Deree College where she has been teaching courses at the Department of Sociology and the Department of Management and International Business since 2014. She is a member of the Athens Bar Association and has worked for the Greek Legal Council of the State and Greek law firms, while she has served as a consultant for the World Bank and as a Subject Matter Expert for Transparency International–Greece. Academically, she has contributed several papers to journals and edited collections and she is the co-author in two World Bank-StAR publications, *Public Wrongs, Private Actions; Civil Lawsuits to Recover Stolen Assets* and *Asset Recovery Handbook: A Guide for Practitioners* (second edition).

Peter Sproat is a research fellow at an investigative think tank which conducts forensic research and analysis on tax avoidance, tax policy, and tax law. Prior to that he was a senior lecturer in financial crime at Northumbria University and has extensive background in teaching aspects of financial crime, policing and politics at a number of universities in the UK. He has published numerous academic articles on anti-money laundering, asset recovery and the policing of fraud and organised crime.

Dominic Thomas-James, LLB(Hons) (Kings), MPhil, PhD (Cantab), Barrister is a Research Associate at Fitzwilliam College, University of Cambridge and a Global Justice Fellow at Yale University. He is a practising Barrister at Goldsmith Chambers, London, and is Director of Publications and Consultant to the International Chamber of Commerce FraudNet. He earned his PhD and MPhil from Queens' College, Cambridge, and read law at King's College London before being called to the Bar by Inner Temple. Dominic has consulted to various intergovernmental and international organisations, and is a Senior Organiser of the annual International Symposium on Economic Crime at Jesus College, Cambridge. He is author of the book *Offshore Financial Centres and the Law: Suspect Wealth in British Overseas Territories* (2021, Routledge).

Sue Turner is an Assistant Professor at Northumbria Law School with particular expertise in business and finance law and regulation. She leads numerous specialist modules across postgraduate, undergraduate and professional programmes and is a member of the Financial Crime Compliance Research Interest Group. Prior to joining Northumbria University, she was a banking and finance solicitor with a global law firm.

Tony Ward's interests as a legal scholar focus on the law of evidence and in particular expert evidence, including historical and philosophical perspectives on experts. He is also a criminologist specialising in state crime, such as violence and corruption by governments and officials. He is Co-Director of the International State Crime Initiative and one of the Editors-in-Chief of its journal *State Crime.* He is co-author with Penny Green of *State Crime: Governments, Violence and Corruption* (Pluto 2004) and *State Crime and Civil Activism* (Routledge 2019), and with Gerry Johnstone of *Law and Crime* (Sage 2010).

Figures

Tables

Foreword

The fight against illicit finance – the lifeblood of criminal organizations and terrorist networks – is a cornerstone of global security and economic stability. Yet, the current Anti-Money Laundering and Counter-Terrorist Financing (AML/CFT) regime presents a complex challenge, particularly for developing countries, small and fragile states. This book examines this complex landscape, exposing the unique hurdles that developing countries face in implementing effective measures.

The global AML/CFT framework, initiated by organizations like the Financial Action Task Force (FATF), sets a high bar for compliance by developing countries. Stringent regulations, while necessary, often disregard the realities of developing economies and the exogenous and endogenous factors that affect their ability to comply with the framework. These include limited resources, inadequate inter-agency collaboration, corruption, fragile financial systems and a vast informal sector. Compliance can be a costly burden, diverting funds from crucial development initiatives, whilst driving governments to be consumed by the implications of non-compliance on foreign direct investment, ignoring other domestic challenges.

Furthermore, the current "one-size-fits-all" approach often fails to address the specific vulnerabilities of developing countries. Criminal networks routinely exploit weaknesses in governance, weaknesses in data collection and management, porous borders and cash-based economies. Traditional financial institutions may coexist with a vibrant informal sector, making it difficult to track illicit flows. Financial institutions may also become risk-averse and heavy-handed in addressing issues with customers, with implications for the business environment.

This book examines these issues but goes beyond outlining the challenges. It proposes innovative solutions and calls for a more nuanced approach. Contextualizing the AML/CFT framework for developing countries is important whilst building capacity, knowledge sharing and targeted financing. Fostering regional cooperation and collaboration with developed nations is key to tackling cross-border threats. The book examines how regional approaches to AML/CTF standard setting and monitoring may address the capacity and legitimacy challenges that hamper compliance with the current framework.

The authors methodically analyse the challenges and opportunities presented by a more developing country–centred approach and offer practical recommendations for policymakers, financial institutions and international organizations. This book is a vital resource for anyone seeking to understand the complexities of the global AML/CFT regime and its impact on developing countries. It is a call for a more inclusive and effective approach, one that strengthens financial security while promoting sustainable development in the Global South.

Sope Williams
Stellenbosch University

Part I

Global Standards, Local Realities

1 The Challenges of the Global Anti-Money Laundering and Counter-Terrorist Financing (AML/CFT) Regime for Developing Countries

Nkechikwu Valerie Azinge-Egbiri, Nicholas Ryder and Ehi Eric Esoimeme

Introduction

Research on countries' compliance with the global anti-money laundering and counter-terrorist financing (AML/CFT) standards has often overlooked the nuanced challenges of developing countries. This edited book bridges that gap. It highlights that an amalgamation of endogenous factors, including weak laws and institutions, abuse of political powers, corruption and failing inter-agency collaborations have borne the blame for the inability of these countries to comply.[1] Likewise, exogenous factors, including colonialism, neo-colonialism, lack of legitimacy and mismatched transplantation have been implicated in the failings of developing countries to comply with the global standards.[2] Emphasizing both endogenous and exogenous viewpoints, this edited volume focuses on specific issues within developing countries to highlight their compliance challenges and the likely implications of failing compliance on their economy. This approach gives readers an insight into the underlying conflicts and ambiguities that trail the establishment and operationalization of the Financial Action Task Force (FATF) and the resulting legitimacy crisis that undermines the compliance trajectory of the jurisdictions in focus, while highlighting the internal issues that weaken compliance.

The inescapable questions that trail the book chapters are: Why are developing countries adopting the FATF's AML/CFT standards and are these standards contextually suitable when transplanted? What challenges do countries face with complying with these standards? What are the implications of failing compliance? And how can developing countries improve their compliance outcomes? While these questions are not particularly novel, this edited

1 Nkechikwu Azinge-Egbiri, *Regulating and Combating Money Laundering and Terrorist Financing: The Law in Emerging Economies* (Routledge 2022).
2 Nkechikwu Azinge-Egbiri, *Regulating and Combating Money Laundering and Terrorist Financing: The Law in Emerging Economies* (Routledge 2022).

DOI: 10.4324/9781003253808-2

book collates them to engage in a deeper analysis that draws lessons from research and practice. This approach unearths solutions that will encourage home-grown, contextual resolutions as opposed to the extant situation where non-compliance is constructed as a challenge based on internal incapacities and therefore assumes the superiority and expertise of the Global North to 'fix' developing countries.[3]

Each chapter takes either a doctrinal approach or mixed methods approach and draws on various sources with the implicit aim of telling a coherent narrative that contributes to the central theme. This text aims to encourage readers to engage in a thoughtful examination of certain contradictions, enabling them to make unbiased contributions to significant discussions concerning the global framework for addressing financial crime and its implementation in developing countries. However, a background of the FATF from a Global South perspective is critical to appreciate the analysis of the chapters.

'If You Are Not on the Table, You're on the Menu': A Global South Perspective of the Financial Action Task Force

At many Global South academic conferences, the words reverberate: *If you are not on the table, you are on the menu* – urging stakeholders to push for inclusion in Global North spaces. The phrase captures the thinking that unrepresented groups at decision-making meetings subsequently suffer financial vulnerability, get left out or worse yet, are on the *menu*. This is indeed the position of developing countries within the FATF.

Scholars from the Global South have consistently advocated for efforts aimed at decolonizing the study of law in its international context. They understand and acknowledge that international laws and the institutions they produce are mainly influenced by contemporary Eurocentric ideals and paradigms. This has often resulted in the perpetuation and reinforcement of those ideals on the rest of the world. Global South scholars also understand that the reductionist and judgmental assumptions made about their legal systems stand diametrically against the often inconsistent, contradictory application of Global North legal systems. This application sometimes results in evaluations and rankings. The recently abolished Doing Business reports provide an example. In this context where risks of doing business were evaluated according to Global North benchmarks, as Michaels states, lead to implicit legal superiority where countries in the Global South must comply.[4] In this vein, the incorporation of legal transplants within histories of colonial expansion demonstrates

3 Jemima Pierre, 'The Racial Vernaculars of Development: A View from West Africa' (2019) 122(1) American Anthropologist 1–13; Uma Kothari, 'Critiquing Race and Racism in Development Discourse and Practice' (2006) 6(1) Progress in Development Studies 1–7.

4 Ralf Michaels, 'Comparative Law by Numbers? – Legal Origins Thesis, Doing Business Reports, and the Silence of Traditional Comparative Law' (2009) 57 American Journal of Comparative Law 765–95.

the ways in which FATF governs developing countries. In this edited volume, we invite readers to explore perspectives from the Global South, which not only provide insights into how these countries are surviving Eurocentric framing but how they are attempting to challenge them and provide epistemologies that can promote a pluriversality of perspectives that emphasizes the significance of local norms as well as contextual factors.

Established in 1989 by the G7 in response to money laundering and terrorist financing threats, the FATF is a 'soft law', international standard-setting body for AML/CFT regulation.[5] Such 'soft law' classification is due to the nature of the FATF body, its standards and operational base. Unlike treaty bodies which originate from state-level agreements between countries and then become binding on countries that ratify the treaty, the FATF operates differently. Like other soft law bodies, the FATF was established through a regulatory alliance between countries represented by their Ministry of Finance and/or central banks. This subnational participation, exercised independent of national governments, gives the FATF its transgovernmental regulatory character.[6] Consequent on its nature, ratification is unwarranted for the applicability of the FATF standard on countries. Arguably, the FATF's soft law model allows for flexibility of the standards to react to situations that pose real-time threats.[7] However, the actual elasticity of the institution and its standards for developing countries is questionable.

Overtime, the FATF developed 40 recommendations on AML/CFT which it issues to countries to implement and comply with. The recommendations, backed by interpretative guidance and periodic updates, were developed on two fronts: prevention and enforcement.[8] Prevention is focused on regulation, supervision, reporting, consumer due diligence, sanctions, risk assessment and terrorist financing laws. Enforcement is designed to be more punitive, however, centred on investigation, confiscation, prosecution and punishment. The FATF standards are promoted as the minimum AML/CFT standards which countries are encouraged to comply with without force of compulsion. As such, the FATF's standards are depicted as 'non-mandatory', and countries may decide whether to implement a particular standard or strategy. However, core FATF documents have stated that 'should has the same meaning as must'.

5 Anne-Marie Slaughter, *A New World Order* (Princeton University Press 2004) 54.

6 Kenneth Blazejewski, 'The FATF and Its Institutional Partners: Improving the Effectiveness and Accountability of Transgovernmental Networks' (2008) 22 Temple International and Comparative Law Journal 1, 8.

7 Slaughter (n 5) 54; Kal Raustiala, 'The Architecture of International Cooperation: Transgovernmental Networks and the Future of International Law' (2002) 43(1) Virginia Journal of International Law 1, 26.

8 Eleni Tsingou, 'Global Governance and Transnational Financial Crime: Opportunities and Tensions in the Global Anti-Money Laundering Regime' (2005) 161(5) CSGR Working Paper 5 <https://wrap.warwick.ac.uk/1959/1/WRAP_Tsingou_wp16105.pdf> accessed 14 November 2023.

Therefore, the standards are indeed, requirements,[9] meaning that countries are mandated to comply with the FATF's standards. Without legally binding authority to sanction countries with weak compliance, the FATF publicly lists these countries. This 'soft listing' approach gains vitality from the FATF's linkages with the International Monetary Fund, the World Bank and the United Nations Security Council, alongside other related international institutions.[10] Arguably, the FATF's relationship with established supranational bodies have hardened its soft law nature, thereby allowing the institution to exert authority as the core body for setting and enforcing international standards.[11]

Many developing countries fall short on compliance largely due to endogenous and exogenous factors. Underlying these factors is the FATF's legitimacy deficit. Legitimacy in this context denotes 'the perception of actors on the acceptability of an institution'.[12] In other words, it is the process by which actors come to believe in the normative legitimacy of an institution.[13] Legitimacy is rooted in how countries perceive their input, throughput and output in an institution's processes and outcome. Global South countries have questioned the legitimacy of the FATF for various reasons. A key reason is the restricted membership band dominated by developed countries. Additionally, the institution's secretariat is located within the Organisation for Economic Co-operation and Development (OECD) with the implication that only OECD nationals are employed by the FATF. By implication, Global South countries are foreclosed from partaking in the development of recommendations and may only offer consultative input as discussions about the recommendation's content are usually made by the secretariat and debated during plenary sessions.[14] Their involvement in the consultation process is also limited as the experts involved are mostly drawn from developed countries.[15]

9 John Hatchard, *Combating Money Laundering in Africa: Dealing with the Problem of PEPs* (Edward Elgar 2020) 57–58.

10 Tsingou (n 8).

11 Dieter Kerwer and Rainer Hülsse, 'How International Organizations Rule the World: The Case of the Financial Action Task Force on Money Laundering' (2011) 2 Journal International Organization Studies 50, 53.

12 Ian Hurd, 'Legitimacy and Authority in International Politics' (1999) 53 (2) International Organization 379, 381; Chris Thomas, 'The Concept of Legitimacy and International Law' (2013) LSE Law, Society and Economy Working Papers 12/2013, 14 <http://eprints.lse.ac.uk/51746/1/__libfile_repository_Content_Law,%20society%20and%20economics%20working%20papers_2013_WPS2013-12_Thomas.pdf> accessed 10 November 2023; Julia Black, 'Constructing and Contesting Legitimacy and Accountability in Polycentric Regulatory Regimes' (2008) LSE Law, Society and Economy Working Papers 2/2008, 16 <www.lse.ac.uk/law/people/academic-staff/julia-black/Documents/black2.pdf>16 November 2023.

13 Thomas (n 12).

14 OECD Careers (OECD) <www.oecd.org/careers/apply/> accessed 20 October 2023.

15 FATF, *Consultation on Proposed Changes to the FATF Standards: Compilation of Responses from the Financial Sector (PART ONE)* (FATF 2012) <www.fatf-gafi.org/content/dam/fatf-gafi/public-consultation/First%20public%20consultation%20document%20responses%20financial%20sector%20part%201.pdf> accessed 12 November 2023.

The legitimacy challenge is further emphasized by the input challenge as the original recommendations were derived from existing banking practices in developed countries including France, Switzerland and the United States.[16] Undoubtedly, the FATF served as a springboard for private institutions in developed countries to tackle global issues relating to tax, drugs and inefficient AML/CFT rules.[17] Therefore, on AML/CFT issues where global convergence is required, only a select group of countries were privy to the decision-making process for the FATF standards.[18]Such undemocratic rule-making process is symbolic of 'regulatory imperialism', where powerful nations dictate the pace, process and content of the recommendations,[19] a challenge that undermines the FATF's authority and curtails the efficiency of its standards.[20]

The legitimacy challenges imply that the FATF's standards fails to recognize the varying nuances of developing countries yet holds unrealistic expectations from them to improve their AML/CFT framework to suit the requirements set by developed countries.[21] Without an option, developing countries transplant the FATF standards through model legislations that do not necessarily fit their national context. As a result, unintended consequences of transplantation have followed. For instance, the FATF recommends that funds to civil society organizations (CSO) be subject to increased scrutiny due to the terrorist financing risks they pose.[22] However, the impact of these recommendations is the overregulation of CSOs coupled with reduced funding for CSO activities due to the increased transaction costs they encounter. As a result, many CSOs, particularly human rights and women rights organizations, have failed to meet their project execution deadlines.[23] Moreso, the FATF recommendation has

16 This includes the United States 1970 Bank Secrecy Act, the UK and Switzerland KYC/CDD. France also mandated the inclusion of tax offences in the FATF's remit as a predicate offence as a requirement for its membership. Mark Pieth and Gemma Aiolfi, 'The Private Sector Becomes Active: The Wolfsberg Process' (2003) 10 (4) Journal of Financial Crime 359.

17 Mark Pieth and Gemma Aiolfi, 'Anti-Money Laundering: Levelling the Playing Field' (2003) Governance, Basel Institute on Governance 1, 9 <https://baselgovernance.org/sites/default/files/2019-06/WP01_Anti-Money%20Laundering.pdf> accessed 10 November 2023.

18 Kevin Shepherd, 'Guardians at the Gate: The Gatekeeper Initiative and the Risk-Based Approach for Transactional Lawyers' (2009) 43(3) Real Property, Trust and Estate Law Journal 1.

19 James Gathii, 'The Financial Action Task Force and Global Administrative Law' (2010) Journal of the Professional Lawyer 1, 9; Jose Alvarez, 'Hegemonic International Law Revisited' (2003) 97 American Journal of Comparative Law 873–87.

20 Frank Vibert, 'Reforming International Rulemaking' (2012) 3(3) Global Policy 391, 391.

21 Gathii (n 19).

22 FATF, 'Combating the Abuse of Non-Profit Organisations (Recommendation 8)' <www.fatf-gafi.org/content/dam/fatf-gafi/guidance/BPP-combating-abuse-non-profit-organisations.pdf> accessed 5 November 2023.

23 Duke International Human Rights Clinic, Women Peacemakers Program, 'Tightening the Purse Strings: What Countering Terrorism Financing Costs Gender Equality and Security' <https://law.duke.edu/sites/default/files/humanrights/tighteningpursestrings.pdf> accessed 10 November 2023.

been utilized to conscript CSOs as terrorist groups and subject them to the same treatment,[24] indicating that these countries are yet to attain the contextual reality of treating CSOs based on their risk classification. Another example of the unintended consequences is Kenya's attempt at complying with the FATF's digital identification guidance which raises both privacy and discrimination based on ethnicity as a concern.[25]

The highlighted challenges demonstrate that without representation, the resulting disproportionate standards that are applicable to all countries are simply an imposition of global standards that demonstrates that covenants of agency capture have overtaken the FATF's policy-making agenda.[26] Subsequent attempts to resolve the 'legitimacy crisis' through the creation of FATF-styled regional bodies (FSRBs) have been inadequate as primarily, these regional institutions were created due to external pressure on countries and reinforce compliance through the FATF's framework. Furthermore, during the recommendations review processes FSRBs noted that 'when making final decisions on recommendations, there are powers and opinions that supersede the others, with opinions from developed countries dwarfing others'.[27] The gaping disparity is also evident in the voting patterns and treatment of the FSRBs in comparison to FATF members. While the core FATF members were entitled to one vote each, each FSRB was collectively entitled to one vote.[28] Furthermore, while core members were (and are still) only subjected to peer pressure, FSRBs are subject to public listing. The implication is that the legitimacy crisis stifles any form of self-interest that propels proactive compliance and, rather, they set up developing countries to fail on compliance levels. As Chapter 4 demonstrates, these countries are more likely to be publicly listed by the FATF, a punishment that potentially subjects them to financial exclusion from the global market as it signals de-risking.

Structure of the Edited Book

For clarity of analysis, this book is portioned into 15 chapters that shed light on the challenges developing countries face in complying with the FATF recommendations. The chapters complement each other and, in some instances,

24 Emeka Njoku, 'The State and the Securitization of Civil Society Organisations in Nigeria' (2022) 51(1) Non-profit and Voluntary Sector Quarterly 190–215.

25 G Mutungu'u and I Rutenberg, 'Digital ID and Risk of Statelessness' (2020) 2(2) Statelessness and Citizenship Review 348; R Mosero, 'Analysing the Impact of Digital ID Frameworks on Marginalised Groups in Sub-Saharan Africa' 8–9 <https://journals.sagepub.com/doi/abs/10.1177/08997640211003256>.

26 Andrew Cornford, 'Basel II and Developing Countries' (2008) 2 Finance & Bien Commun 69, 69; Pieth and Aiolfi (n 16) 359; Gathii (n 19) 1, 9; Alvarez (n 19) 873–87.

27 Azinge-Egbiri (n 1).

28 Maria Machado, 'Similar in their Differences: Transnational Legal Processes Addressing Money Laundering in Brazil and Argentina' in Gregory Shaffer (ed) *Transnational Legal Ordering and State Change* (CUP 2013) 61.

reinforce arguments in their evaluation of the core theme. Of the 15 chapters contributed, we have three parts that will be briefly discussed.

Part I, themed '*Global Standards, Local Realities*' conceptually frames the book and is presented in four chapters. Chapter 1, the introductory chapter by Nkechikwu Valerie Azinge-Egbiri, Ehi Eric Esoimeme and Nicholas Ryder, highlights the endogenous and exogenous factors that affect the compliance trajectory of developing countries and the strong underlying role of legitimacy. Following this introductory note is Chapter 2 by Constance Gikonyo. This chapter uncovers the conflicts and ambiguities in international AML regime vis-à-vis African countries. The chapter examines the problematic assumptions, tensions, biases and contradictions in the global AML regime in relation to African countries. It argues that historically, African countries have been bystanders in the framing of the FATF governance regime and hence battle with compliance. Chapter 3 by Edefe Ojomo reinforces this position while also contending that regional organizations enhance the legitimacy of global actors. Specifically, the chapter examines how regional organizations like the West African FATF-styled regional body (GIABA) participates in standard setting, standard diffusion and standard implementation. Furthermore, the chapter explains how global, regional and national players interact to create an interconnected governance framework aimed at devising and enforcing standards that influence the operations of private actors within and across territories. The chapter's core argument is that regional actors like GIABA can be seen as governance brokers that build national actors' capacity and enhance global actors' legitimacy while fusing diverse interests. Chapter 4 by Nkechikwu Valerie Azinge-Egbiri, Joy Malala and Donato Masciandaro examines the extent to which public listing (blacklisting/greylisting) affects developing countries. The chapter interrogates the dominant assumption that the processes for evaluating and sanctioning countries for AML/CFT failings are infallible and amplifies countries' compliance. In so doing, it critiques the credibility of the FATF's listing, which disproportionately affects developing countries due to its implicit biases and legitimacy deficit. It concludes by arguing that shifting from biased listing to macro-risk listing is core to ensuring that public listing is contextual and focuses on the jurisdictions that present the most risk.

Part II takes a more practical approach as it focuses on *developing countries transplantation and compliance trajectory*. It is presented across 10 chapters with some having a single jurisdictional approach (Nigeria, South Africa and Botswana) and others focusing on Africa, Small Island Developing States or developing countries quite generally. Chapter 5 by Zakhele Hlophe examines South Africa's mis-implementation of the AML law in relation to the banking sector. Relying on evidence from South Africa's mutual evaluation report (MER) and data from the Financial Intelligence Centre and the Assert Forfeiture Unit, the chapter contends contrary to the FATF's de-risking expectations, banks unilaterally terminate customers' bank accounts to evade their own compliance obligations. It concludes that the unilateral closure of accounts based on the bank's reputational or business risks, done in the absence of court orders or law enforcement interventions, is unlawful and unconstitutional, and supplants the role of these institutions when combatting financial crime. Chapter 6 by Gosego Rockfall Lekgowe explores why Botswana is failing on its implementation and compliance. Specifically, it examines the implications of Botswana's legal culture for AML/CFT regime and prosecution of such offences. The chapter contends that Botswana's FATF implementation has been fraught with delays, hesitation and resistance due to the country's legal culture. While recognizing other factors that limit implementation and compliance, Lekgowe centres the chapter on the underlying role of 'legal culture', which includes the country's practices, values and traditions that can either facilitate or constrain legal change. Consequently, the chapter concludes with the argument that Botswana's lack of interaction with international law – which is symbolic of a legitimacy crisis – coupled with the culture of secrecy and poor citizenry consultation collide to undermine the country's compliance.

Chapter 7 by Ehi Eric Esoimeme and Chapter 8 by Emmanuel Oluwasina Sotande both explore Nigeria's compliance challenges with the FATF's standards. Focusing on mobile and internet banking transactions, Ehi Eric Esoimeme explores the national, legal, institutional and operational barriers hindering Nigeria's ability to utilize new technologies to combat money laundering and terrorist financing. The chapter argues that a shift in regulatory approaches and the provision of critical resources is core for ensuring that the country can better combat these crimes. Taking a more robust view of the issues raised by Ehi Eric Esoimeme, Emmanuel Oluwasina Sotande analyses the AML threats and vulnerabilities faced by financial institutions (FIs) in Nigeria. This chapter categorizes the challenges into four thematic areas; institutional and political impediments; key operational compliance challenges (including failure of customer due diligence; lack of a robust addressing system; challenge of new technologies; harassment of money laundering reporting officers by law enforcement agencies (LEAs); ineffective feedback mechanism between the Nigerian FIs, LEAs and Nigerian Financial Intelligence Unit; and deficit of record keeping within the Nigeria FIs); socio-economic AML challenges; and justified deficit of social justice. The chapter concludes that addressing these issues are core to combatting financial crime in Nigeria and across relatable countries.

The next set of chapters focuses on politically exposed persons (PEPs) and beneficial ownership. Chapter 9 by Chinelo Bob-Osamor questions why PEPs remain rife for laundering irrespective of the requisite transplantation. Utilizing case studies, the chapter illustrates that enforcement challenges in Nigeria coupled with lack of political will and other endogenous factors weaken the jurisdiction's compliance abilities. It concludes by recommending the need for establishing a prosecution review commission to check on the discretionary exercise of the Attorney General's prosecutorial discretion and argues for the limitation of constitutional immunity to civil and not criminal cases. Looking beyond Nigeria, Chapter 10 by John Hatchard locates African countries as victims of laundering of the proceeds of corruption by PEPs. This chapter offers a clear understanding of the architecture utilized by PEPs to conceal their beneficial ownership while continually laundering funds. However, taking a solution-driven approach, this chapter highlights ongoing developments to combat PEPs laundering through the introduction of beneficial ownership transparency laws. However, it acknowledges the challenges associated with the workability of the laws. Chapter 11 is written by Jackie Harvey, Peter Sproat, Sue Turner and Tony Ward with support from additional project members including Abdullahi Shehu, Abdullahi Bello, Petrus van Duyne, Sam Sittlington, Alan Doig, Jan van Koningsveld and Sinan Gonul. The chapter considers the tension between FATF's suggestion that countries maintain and share accurate and up-to-date information regarding the legal and beneficial ownership of companies and trusts (Recommendations 24 and 25) and its acknowledgement of the varying capacity of jurisdictions to live up to its standards – its 'low-capacity country' designation. The chapter does this by examining Nigeria's attempts to comply with these two recommendations which have evolved in the context of its anti-corruption regime. It argues that irrespective of the recently introduced laws aimed at ensuring beneficial ownership registers, the authorities will still face challenges in the creation of registers that meet the threshold of accuracy and reliability. The authors contend that such challenges arise from a cultural lack of transparency and tendency towards secrecy that compound systemic data deficiency within Nigeria's institutions, and an elaborate institutional landscape that masks its overall effectiveness, caused largely by a lack of inter-agency cooperation.

Chapter 12 by Dominic Thomas-James examines the compliance willingness of small island standards. The chapter highlights the dilemma of small island standards who have faced severe criticisms for becoming offshore financial centres, a trajectory they chose to ensure their economic sustainability. Underscoring the stigma faced by these countries due to their 'labelling' as offshore financial centres, this chapter builds on the author's earlier research to provide explanations as to the compliance successes and challenges of certain offshore jurisdictions – with reference to Commonwealth Caribbean nations and UK Overseas Territories. The chapter utilizes case studies to demonstrated how economic crime has destabilized some jurisdictions and their resulting legal and regulatory responses. The chapter also considers the impact of specific integrity-related initiatives, how this has translated to compliance, and the likely impact this may have for small states' longer-term implementation of global anti-financial crime norms. Chapter 13 by Simeon Igbinedion takes a detour to look specifically at terrorist financing. This chapter examines whether developing states can win the battle against terrorist financing. This chapter makes the critical argument that developing countries are currently unprepared to win the war against terrorist financing because the AML/CFT regime does not reflect their local peculiarities or circumstances. The chapter then provides some practical recommendations.

Chapter 14 by Jean-Pierre Brun and Anastasia Sotiropoulou is focused on assessing the successes and failures of asset recovery in developing countries. Taking a practitioner perspective, this chapter demonstrates that countries have made important progress in recovering stolen assets. However, drawing on existing experience, this chapter contends that there are still strategic and operational challenges that arise in the context of asset recovery efforts. As such, the chapter provides plausible alternatives to aid countries in achieving a more systematic and timely return of stolen assets.

Part III contains the concluding chapter – by Nkechikwu Valerie Azinge-Egbiri and Egbiri Egbiri. This chapter provides a simplified analysis of the extent to which robust understanding, accountability capacity building and coordination are critical to addressing the compliance challenges of developing countries. It argues that a practical approach to delisting requires strategic planning and dedicated resources tailored to understanding of pertinent AML/CFT risks within which countries operate.

Acknowledgement

As expected, putting together an edited book of this magnitude in this subject area has entailed a lot of work. This work has been compensated by the privilege of having inspiring exchanges with the contributors of the book who in our view are the most authoritative scholars in the area. Our contributors include expert academics, practitioners and legal professionals who have drawn from their expertise in academia, research institutions, international development, regulatory bodies and legal practice to write their chapters. We are indeed grateful to them for their stellar contributions, brilliant reflections, patience and readiness to make amendments where necessary. Indeed, thanks to their contributions, this book holds great importance in expanding the existing body of literature on AML/CFT, quite generally.

We are especially grateful to expert academics who offered critical comments on select draft chapters, particularly Dr. Steven Montagu-Cairns, Dr. Umut Turksen, Prof. Dr. Petrus C. van Duyne, Professor Colin King and Dr. Liliya Gelemerova. We also want to specially thank Adeola Adegbusi for her administrative support and the editorial and production team at Routledge for their time and understanding during the creation of this edited book.

Finally, our thoughts go to the victims of money laundering and terrorist financing in developing countries, to whom we devote this edited book. Some of these victims have had their future ripped from them by actions of leaders described as 'fantastically corrupt', and others have lost their lives in the pursuit of a society where integrity is enthroned. Today, across the developing world, individuals, researchers, institutions and civil society organizations alike are making bold steps not only to combat financial crime but to ensure that laws and frameworks are transplanted contextually to ensure that there are no more victims of the misapplication of the FATF standards or the endogenous and exogenous factors that occasion compliance challenges.

2 Uncovering Conflicts and Ambiguities in the International Anti-Money Laundering Regime Vis-à-vis African Countries

Constance Gikonyo

Introduction

In dealing with organised crime, terrorism, money laundering, and similar high-profile crimes, law enforcement strategies have focused on acquiring the financial benefit of the wrongdoers from their illegal activities. To achieve this, various international and regional organisations have been formed; for example, the Financial Action Task Force (FATF). The organisation oversees the implementation of anti-money laundering policies that aim to prevent the spread of money laundering activities and their predicate offences. The FATF has been successfully propagating its policies and seeking developed and developing countries to implement them.

These policies seem to work in developed countries; however, this is not the case in most African countries. The predominant view is that African countries are not keenly implementing the regime. Most have received less than satisfactory reports after the FATF-style regional bodies (FSRBs) mutual evaluation exercises. Consequently, there is a need to consider whether any underlying issues led to the extant situation. This chapter examines the presumptions, tensions, biases, and contradictions in the global anti-money laundering (AML) regime concerning African countries. It aims at increasing understanding of the problematic underlying issues affecting the AML regime and its transplantation from European to African countries. By evaluating these challenges, possible solutions that can foster effective implementation can be developed. The discussion will interrogate these issues under the following sub-headings: developmental and historical, institutional, cultural, economic, and implementation challenges. From the onset, it is essential to note that the various issues discussed herein should not be viewed in isolation in addressing the challenge of implementing AML systems in Africa. Instead, they should be considered as working in tandem towards achieving this inefficiency and ineffectiveness.

DOI: 10.4324/9781003253808-3

Conceptual and Historical Issues in Developing and Implementing the AML Regime

Development of the AML regulations and policies has predominantly been a developed nation's initiative with minimal, if any, involvement of the Global South. Development of the worldwide AML regime is generally credited as having been a G7 initiative, beginning at its summit in Paris in 1989.[1] However, there are contrary views on this aspect.[2] Some scholars hold that the American government propagated the AML initiative in its efforts to fight the drug trade surge.[3] It is advanced that the UN and the G7 were utilised to promote AML strategies that had been used in the United States. What is not contentious is the fact that developing countries were not involved in the forums working towards developing the AML policies. This is primarily because the process was undertaken through the G7 initiative and not the more inclusive forum of the United Nations. This has continued to be the case even as the global AML policies are reviewed.

Instead, ongoing initiatives have focused on creating FSRBs and getting African countries to adopt the standards as they are.[4] Consequently, as discussed herein, developing countries have implemented these policies due to coercion for fear of political and economic consequences. Moreover, consideration of the specific policies that were transferred shows that a one-size-fits-all approach is utilised instead of ensuring adaptation of the policies to suit the economic and social conditions prevalent in African countries.[5]

In analysing the developmental process of African countries adopting AML strategies, it is necessary to consider the following issues: Who are the agents of the AML policy transfer? How and when did the transfer take place? Answering these questions will provide insight into why African countries adopted AML like they did.

Broadly, policy transfer is the process of transferring knowledge about institutions, policies, or other aspects from one jurisdiction or institution to

1 FATF, 'History of the FATF' (2022) <www.fatf-gafi.org/about/historyofthefatf/#d.en.3157> accessed 25 July 2022.

2 Zakhele Hlophe, 'Regulating Money Laundering in Developing Countries a Critical Analysis of South Africa's Incorporation And Implementation of the Global FATF Standards' (Doctoral Dissertation, Kings College London 2013) 166–81; Rainer Hülsse, 'Creating Demand for Global Governance: The Making of a Global Money Laundering Problem' (2007) 21(2) Global Society 155; Michael Woodiwiss, 'Transnational Organised Crime: The Global Reach of an American Concept' in A Edwards and P Gill (eds), *Transnational Organised Crime: Perspectives On Global Security* (Routledge 2003).

3 Zakhele (n 2) 166–81.

4 Currently nine FATF-Style Regional Bodies have been established. See FATF, 'FATF Associate Members' (2022) <www.fatf-gafi.org/about/membersandobservers/#d.en.3147> accessed 25 July 2022.

5 See Emmanuel Sotande, 'The Regime against Money Laundering: A Call for Scientific Modelling' (2018) 21(4) Journal of Money Laundering Control 584.

another.[6] Either state or non-state actors can undertake this. For example, in relation to AML policy, diffusion has primarily been done by the FATF, a non-state actor. Different forms of policy transfer include copying, emulation, hybridisation, synthesis, and inspiration.[7] Of importance to this discussion is voluntary or coercive transfer. Voluntary transfer occurs when a government or agency seeks to learn from another government or agency. In contrast, coercive transfer occurs when governments are compelled to introduce policy changes.[8]

It is contended that the FATF's 40 Recommendations were copied from policies and experiences dealing with organised crime and financial regulation already operating in the US.[9] Accordingly, it has been claimed that the UN and the FATF were merely agents of transferring US policy.[10] The US brought these policies to an international forum through the G7. After adoption of the AML policies by developed nations, it was necessary to spread them to developing countries.

To ensure the adoption of these policies, the developed countries, through the FATF, utilised different mechanisms. This included coercion, declaring money laundering as a 'global problem', raising awareness campaigns of the ill effects of money laundering to non-FATF member countries, and characterising money laundering as a 'meta-crime'.[11] Consequently, the way to address this issue was advocated as the need for global harmonisation of rules under the leadership of the FATF. Appropriately, countries adopted these AML policies to protect themselves and their institutions from the vice because this was the right and necessary thing to do.

For countries that attempted to resist, coercion was employed. Coercion of developing countries to adopt AML policies was punctuated by the FATF's development of Non-Cooperating Countries and Territories (NCCT) blacklists.[12] Most countries placed on the NCCT blacklist were initially non-FATF

6 Mark Evans, 'Policy Transfer in Critical Perspective' (2009) 30 (3) Policy Studies 243, 243.

7 Mark Evans, 'Policy Transfer in Critical Perspective' (2009) 30 (3) Policy Studies. 243, 245. David Benson and Andrew Jordan, 'What Have We Learned from Policy Transfer Research? Dolowitz and Marsh Revisited' (2011) 9(3) Political Studies Review 366.

8 Evans (n 6) 243.

9 Zakhele (n 2) 166.

10 Zakhele (n 2) 166–67.

11 Zakhele (n 2) 184–86.

12 See FATF, 'About the Non-Cooperative Countries and Territories (NCCT) Initiative' (2022) <www.fatf-gafi.org/publications/high-riskandnon-cooperativejurisdictions/more/aboutthenon-cooperativecountriesandterritoriesncctinitiative.html?hf=10&b=0&s=desc(fatf_releasedate)> accessed 16 July 2022 for the NCCT lists. The NCCT blacklists are now categorised into two: High-Risk Jurisdictions subject to a call for action; Greylists, officially referred to as Jurisdictions Under Increased Monitoring. See Rainer Hülsse, 'Even Clubs Can't Do Without Legitimacy: Why the Anti-Money Laundering Blacklist Was Suspended' (2008) 2(4) Regulation & Governance 459 for further discussion on why the NCCT lists were stopped.

members.[13] According to Recommendation 22, these countries could have countermeasures imposed on them. The countermeasures entailed economic sanctions such as restricting their financial transactions with institutions based in G7 jurisdictions. Consequently, under duress, countries complied by implementing these standards.[14] Thereafter they were removed from this blacklist for having made progress. Accordingly, one can infer that, following the blacklists, other non-FATF countries that were not blacklisted engaged in 'pre-emptive compliance': adopting the standards to avoid blacklisting. This is a form of subtle coercion.

In certain instances, countries that ultimately refused to implement these standards suffered dire consequences. For example, Nauru did not enforce the FATF policies. Consequently, it faced a financial blockade by private institutions, primarily in developed countries. This led to a complete collapse of the country's financial system.[15] Fast-forward, and the country remained without a bank for over a decade.[16] Undoubtedly, the failure of a country's financial system can have disastrous effects on it and its economy. Upon seeing such outcomes, no government would argue about adopting the FATF policies. Instead, they would be coerced into complying to avoid such extreme effects. Moreover, African countries could have feared the competition ramifications their countries would have faced for failing to adopt the AML policies. As a result, this would have pushed a jurisdiction into adopting the FATF standards to ensure its banking sector remained competitive.

Further, to ensure compliance, a universal approach was adopted and using this approach generally leads to cultural misfits. The FATF policies were developed with the exclusion of developing countries, where most of Africa falls. This means that any opportunity to question and seek adaptation of the policies to the prevailing circumstances in African countries was not done. Nevertheless, since the countries had to adopt these measures, a universal approach was utilised. Countries implemented the measures blindly, leading to cultural misfits, that is, situations where implementation of the standards is complex or has led to problems because the measures are not suited to the socio-economic circumstances prevailing in a country.[17]

13 See FATF (n 12), for the lists from 2000 to 2007.

14 Hülsse (n 12) 459.

15 Jason C Sharman, 'Power and Discourse in Policy Diffusion: Anti Money Laundering in Developing Countries' (2008) 52 International Studies Quarterly 635, 645. See Kathryn L Gardner, 'Fighting Terrorism the FATF Way' (2007) 13(3) Global Governance 325.

16 Hülsse (n 12) 459, 462. About Nauru <http://naurugov.nr/government-information-office/media-release/nauru-gets-a-bank-again,-and-looks-back-at-two-years-of-progress.aspx> accessed 22 October 2021.

17 Nelson E Ojukwu-Ogba and Patrick C Osode, 'A Critical Assessment of the Enforcement Regime for Combatting Money Laundering in Nigeria' (2020) 28 African Journal of International and Comparative Law 85, 87; Nkechikwu Valerie Azinge, 'A Regulatory Misfit? A Closer Look at the Counter-Terrorist Financing Strategies in African States' (2019) 20(3) Journal of Banking Regulation 245.

When did the policy transfer occur? To appreciate the answer to this question and its implication for how African countries adopted AML policies, it is necessary to revisit the experience of most African countries in the 1980s. Starting then and throughout the 1990s, most African countries experienced structural adjustment programmes (SAPs). SAPs provided conditional lending to African governments and were supposed to assist countries in developing through liberalisation and privatisation.[18] Analysing the implementation of these policies by African countries highlights the fact that most had no choice but to accept and adopt them. Further, these policies mainly did not achieve what was intended at their inception. Instead, developed countries benefited from their implementation to the detriment of African countries.[19] Consequently, considering that African countries did not voluntarily adopt the AML policies, the coercion to implement them may be interpreted by some as a form of neo-colonialism. Moreover, this is reinforced by the fact that these countries were not engaged in the agenda-setting from the beginning.

Considering the debacle of the SAPs, African countries may view the imposition of the AML policies as a form of neo-colonialism. This is premised on the asymmetrical relationship involved in implementing these policies. African countries were never involved in the negotiation process; instead, they were boxed into a corner and had no option but to adopt these policies. This view is exacerbated by the continued direct or indirect control that former colonial powers still wield over developing countries. These are mainly governments in the north; large multinational corporations and organisations also based in the north continue to exercise indirectly over their former colonies or less developed states.[20]

Further, a review of the evaluation reports by FSRBs[21] shows that African countries are not given much flexibility to adapt the AML policies to suit their specific circumstances. Instead, they are expected to implement the policies as they are. This points to a situation where the relationship between the FATF and the African countries is skewed in favour of the FATF. Consequently, this can

18 Ralf M Mohs, 'Structural Adjustment Programmes in Sub-Saharan Africa' (1998) 23 Intereconomics 25–28.

19 See Franz Heidhues and Gideon A Obare, 'Lessons from Structural Adjustment Programmes and Their Effects in Africa' (2011) 50 Quarterly Journal of International Agriculture 55; Barry J Riddell, 'Things Fall Apart Again: Structural Adjustment Programmes in Sub-Saharan Africa' (1992) 30(1) The Journal of Modern African Studies 53; David Dollar and Jakob Svensson, 'What Explains the Success or Failure of Structural Adjustment Programmes?' (2000) 110(466) The Economic Journal 894.

20 See Mark Langan, *Neo-colonialism and the Poverty of 'Development' in Africa* (Springer 2017). Diana Haag, 'Mechanisms of Neo-Colonialism: Current French and British Influence in Cameroon and Ghana' (2011) International Catalan Institute for Peace, Working Paper No. 6; Ejike Ekwueme, 'Modulating Corruption and Money Laundering Through the Bretton Woods Institutions: The Case of Less Developed Countries (LDCs)' (2022) 25(2) Journal of Money Laundering Control 467.

21 The evaluation reports for a country can be accessed on the relevant FSRB website.

be inferred as a form of neo-colonialism through the continued advancement of foreign AML policies. Additionally, neo-colonialism can be inferred from the behaviour of international institutions such as the World Bank and International Monetary Fund, which have required African countries to seek their assistance to implement AML policies.[22] The perception of neo-colonialism reinforces the detached attitude of simply ensuring formal box-ticking compliance in implementing the AML regime by African countries.

Institutional Issues Impeding Effective and Efficient Implementation of AML Policies

Whereas in developed countries different systems are implemented, making accessing information relevant to the application of AML policies easier, the contrary is true in Africa. Instead, there is fragmentation or non-existence of these systems. These systems include immigration, customs, border crossing, tax authorities, land and vehicle registries, business and licencing registries, and civil records on marriage, death, children, and court records. These systems are not in place for various reasons. For example, the lack of legal requirement(s) to maintain such public registers and the cost of developing and maintaining these systems is prohibitive. There are also administrative and technical challenges.[23]

Nevertheless, in implementing AML policies, these systems are essential for undertaking customer due diligence (CDD) or 'know your customer' (KYC) measures. Consequently, though reporting institutions are required to undertake CDD, they are hindered from doing so effectively and efficiently.[24] Maintaining such registers would facilitate reporting institutions and investigatory agencies easy access to complete identification data regarding beneficial owners or other relevant information.[25] The unavailability of such records necessitates entities must utilise other means of establishing the information they require. Generally, this involves incurring expenditure in purchasing the relevant technology, time, and workforce resources.

The lack of effectively functioning public register systems is also evident within the criminal justice system (CJS). A functioning CJS is necessary for

22 See World Bank, 'Financial Integrity' <www.worldbank.org/en/topic/financialmarketintegrity> accessed 25 July 2022. Ekwueme (n 20) 467; Eleni Tsingou, 'Global Financial Governance and the Developing Anti-Money Laundering Regime: What Lessons for International Political Economy?' (2010) 47 International Politics 617, 623.

23 Brendan E Asogwa, 'The Challenge of Managing Electronic Records in Developing Countries: Implications For Records Managers in Sub Saharan Africa' (2012) 22(3) Records Management Journal 198.

24 Norman Mugarura, 'The Institutional Framework against Money Laundering and its Underlying Predicate Crimes' (2011) 19(2) Journal of Financial Regulation and Compliance 174.

25 Howard Chitimira and Sharon Munedzi, 'Selected Challenges Associated with the Reliance on Customer Due Diligence Measures to Curb Money Laundering in South African Banks and Related Financial Institutions' 2021 8(1) Journal of Comparative Law in Africa 42.

the detection, prevention, apprehension, and criminal adjudication processes of different crimes, including financial crimes.[26] Additionally, it is relevant that the CJS system captures and stores relevant data. Delays in the adjudicatory processes plague most African criminal justice systems due to judicial corruption, congestion of courts (with cases) and unnecessary reliance on technicalities.[27] Ultimately, these problems can lead to the collapse of the available infrastructure in the system. These problems are exacerbated by the fact that even where systems have been developed, there is a challenge in implementing and/or maintaining them. This is mainly due to inadequate resources, for example, lack of well-trained and sufficient staff to deal with money laundering cases.[28] This is from the point of detection, investigation, and prosecution. Moreover, systems should be maintained, and this calls for funds. Yet, in most instances, funds are lacking or inadequate.

The challenges facing the CJS affect the implementation of AML policies. The difficulties highlighted, such as prosecution delays, lead to the non-realisation of deterrence as a fundamental objective of criminal justice in a country.[29] This is a common scenario in many African countries and reinforces the belief that crime does pay.[30] This breeds a culture of impunity which is counterproductive in the fight against illicit financial flows. Additionally, when offenders walk freely in society, the impression created is that crime pays.[31] As a result, impunity has become the order of the day, leading to an upsurge of financial crimes, including money laundering.

The FATF recommendations show that information sharing is crucial to implementing the AML strategy. Specifically, 25 of the 40 Recommendations focus on this.[32] Information sharing cuts across various divides, public to public

26 National Council on Administration of Justice, 'Criminal Justice System in Kenya: An Audit' (2017) <http://kenyalaw.org/kenyalawblog/wp-content/uploads/2017/01/Criminal_Justice_Report.pdf> accessed 26 July 2022.

27 Maruf Adeniyi Nasir, 'The Viability of Recent Enforcement Mechanism to Combat Money Laundering and Financial Terrorism (AML/CFT) in Nigeria: An Overview' (2019) 22(3) Journal of Money Laundering Control 417, 418–19; Jessica Vapnek, 'Cultural Factors and Ethical Integrity' (2016) 39 Hastings International & Comparative Law Review 123, 124; Jamil Ddamulira Mujuzi, 'Investigating, Prosecuting and Punishing Corruption in Commonwealth East and Southern African Countries' (2019) 45(3) Commonwealth Law Bulletin 477.

28 Vapnek (n 27) 123, 124.

29 Peter J Henning, 'Is Deterrence Relevant in Sentencing White-Collar Criminals' (2015) 61 Wayne Law Review 27, 41.

30 Nasir (n 27) 417, 419.

31 Anna Markovska, Nya Adams, 'Political Corruption and Money Laundering: Lessons from Nigeria' (2015) 18(2) Journal of Money Laundering Control 169; Henning (n 29) 27, 58–59.

32 FATF, 'Consolidated FATF Standards on Information Sharing' updated November 2017 <www.fatf-gafi.org/publications/fatfrecommendations/documents/consolidated-fatf-standard-informationsharing.html> accessed 10 May 2022.

or public to private. This can also be domestically or across borders.[33] Examining the information sharing provisions highlights that the private sector is a much-needed ally in implementing the AML strategy.[34] This is because most of the entities classified under the Designated Non-Financial Businesses and Professions (DNFBPs) and financial institutions with reporting obligations fall within the private sector. Moreover, these entities are expected to engage in CDD and KYC. Effective implementation of the required measures calls for these private entities to install the appropriate systems and train personnel.

The challenge with relying on the private sector is it loads the sector with compliance costs, thus increasing their operating costs,[35] as well as saddling them with a 'gatekeeping role'. In ensuring compliance, these businesses also face conflicts of interest between fulfilling the expected AML obligations and fulfilling obligations owed to their customers. For example, lawyers and banks are forced to navigate the issue of complying with AML standards and abiding with the duty of confidentiality owed to their clients.[36] A further implication is businesses may fulfil the compliance requirements by engaging in defensive reporting, in which anything and everything is reported.[37] The ultimate result is overwhelming the financial investigation unit (FIU) with reports, thus reducing its effectiveness in identifying potential money laundering transactions.[38]

Overall, undertaking AML obligations such as CDD is a complex and tedious process that requires investment in technology, human resources, finances, and the resource of time.[39] Financial institutions and DNFBPs must invest in specific resources to enable them effectively and efficiently perform ongoing

33 Richard J Lowe, 'Anti-Money Laundering – The Need for Intelligence' (2017) 24 (3) Journal of Financial Crime 472–79; George Pavlidis, 'Financial Information in the Context of anti-Money Laundering: Broadening the Access of Law Enforcement and Facilitating Information Exchanges' (2020) Journal of Money Laundering Control 369.

34 FATF, 'Guidance on Private Sector Information Sharing' (2017) <www.fatf-gafi.org/publications/fatfrecommendations/documents/guidance-information-sharing.html> accessed 20 October 2021.

35 See Terence Halliday, Michael Levi and Peter Reuter, 'Anti-Money Laundering: An Inquiry Into a Disciplinary Transnational Legal Order' (2019) 4 University of California Irvine Journal of International, Transnational, and Comparative Law 1.

36 For further discussion see Constance Gikonyo, 'The Legal Profession in Kenya and its Anti-Money Laundering Obligations or Lack Thereof' (2019) 22(2) Journal of Money Laundering Control 247; Constance Gikonyo, 'Banks in Kenya and Anti-Money Laundering Obligations: The Conflicts of Interests Arising' (2021) 24(2) Journal of Money Laundering Control 427.

37 See Delphine Nougayrede, 'Anti-Money Laundering and Lawyer Regulation: The Response of the Professions' (2019) 43 Fordham International Law Journal 321; Viritha V Mariappan and Irfan Ul Haq, 'Suspicious Transaction Reporting: An Indian Experience' (2015) 18(1) Journal of Money Laundering Control 2.

38 See Constance Gikonyo, 'Detection Mechanisms Under Kenya's Anti-Money Laundering Regime: Omissions and Loopholes' (2018) 21(1) Journal of Money Laundering Control 59.

39 Rafael Pontes, Nick Lewis, Paul McFarlane and Patrick Craig, 'Anti-Money Laundering in the United Kingdom: New Directions for a More Effective Regime' (2022) (25) 2 Journal of Money Laundering 401.

screening of their clients. Moreover, firms must train their staff on AML obligations, ensuring compliance, and reporting any breaches that occur. This means an added expense for businesses. Big and well-resourced firms may have access to funds to apply these measures. But this poses a significant challenge for smaller firms. Further, to ensure the efficiency and effectiveness of the AML policy, an institution must undertake a risk assessment exercise. This, too, is a further cost for a firm. This exercise would enable an entity to determine its potential money laundering threats and adopt relevant counteractive measures.

From the preceding discussion it is evident the implementation of the AML policy leads to a crossover between the public and private boundaries of governance. This is because the AML strategies focus on the private sector for implementation. Most AML mechanisms require financial institutions and DNFBPs to play a key role as gatekeepers.[40] Hence, it is debated whether the government is passing its role to the private sector.[41] This interferes with how entities conduct their business and increases operation costs. This is because they must fund the different implementation mechanisms. Most of the time, these gatekeeping obligations require entities to incur costs of implementation and deal with the likely conflict of interest between the gatekeeper and the client.[42] This has exposed businesses to potential conflicts of interest situations, prosecution, or sanctions from the government for not fulfilling its mandate, as well as possible prosecution from clients for infringement of their rights. These problems extend internationally since these potential conflicts could arise due to different legal frameworks for data protection, privacy and secrecy laws affecting financial institutions.[43]

There are other institutional challenges that mainly affect the public sector and encourage corruption, which has a symbiotic relationship with money laundering.[44] These include low salaries paid to public administration employ-

40 See Chat Le Nguyen, 'Preventing the Use of Financial Institutions for Money Laundering and the Implications for Financial Privacy' (2018) 21(1) Journal of Money Laundering Control 47.

41 Karin Svedberg Helgesson, 'Public-Private Partners against Crime: Governance, Surveillance and the Limits of Corporate Accountability' (2011) 8(4) Surveillance & Society 471. Maria Bergström and Others, 'A New Role for for-Profit Actors? The Case of Anti-Money Laundering and Risk Management' (2011) 49 (5) Journal of Common Market Studies 1043; Joras Ferwerda, 'The Fight Against Money Laundering: A Public Task?' in Brigitte Unger, Daan van der Linde and Michael Getzner (eds), *Public or Private Goods?* (Edward Elgar 2017) 37–47.

42 See for example the debate between the advocates duty to their clients and implementation of the AML policy. See Nguyen (n 40) 47.

43 See Fabio Polverino, 'Data Protection, Anti-Money Laundering and Tax Evasion: Seeking An Equilibrium Between Public Policy and Fundamental Rights' (2018) 1(4) Journal of Financial Compliance 345; Jonida Milaj and Carolin Kaiser, 'Retention of Data in the New Anti-Money Laundering Directive – "Need to Know" Versus "Nice to Know"' (2017) 7(2) International Data Privacy Law 115.

44 See Norman Mugarura, 'The Effect of Corruption Factor in Harnessing Global Anti-Money Laundering Regimes' (2010) 13(3) Journal of Money Laundering Control 272; David Chaikin

ees, bureaucratic processes, lack of transparency, and accountability in public actions, too many controls that give too much discretion to the public official, too much centralisation and monopoly given to the public official, and the large size of the public sector.[45] Consequently, the public seeking these services bribes to speed up the service dispensation process. Interestingly, these practices by the public are, in certain instances, considered justifiable, acceptable, and even expected. These actions and perceptions relating to corruption are also linked to other cultural issues discussed herein that aid in making the AML regime ineffective in African jurisdictions.

Cultural Issues That Impede Application of AML Policies

The link between vices such as corruption that leads to the accumulation of illicit funds to be laundered and AML policies implementation is minimally explored, specifically in relation to African countries and the role culture plays in the fight against money laundering. An understanding of culture is relevant in comprehending the link between the two concepts. Culture is a learnt phenomenon that forms human identity and shapes one's assumptions, attitude, character, beliefs, and orientation.[46] Culture is passed on from generation to generation, and its acquisition is a result of the socialisation process. Generally, in Africa culture does not place a strong separation between private and public realms. Instead, public, family and wider community bonds are emphasised.[47] As such, a person does not operate in a vacuum, but from a cultural structure which informs their values. Consequently, cultural orientations come to bear even in our gestures, and people see and interpret realities from cultural windows.

Hence, understanding the complexity of social experience and cultural values is crucial when trying to understand the discourse of corruption.[48] That is, contextualising the cultural and social views of acceptable behaviour is required in understanding the behaviour of a person or people.[49] This too

and Jason C Sharman, *Corruption and Money Laundering a Symbiotic Relationship* (Palgrave Macmillan 2009); Sungyong Kang, 'Rethinking the Global Anti-Money Laundering Regulations to Deter Corruption' (2018) 67(3) International & Comparative Law Quarterly 695.

45 See Wisdom Okwuoma Otaluk, 'The Cultural Roots of Corruption: An Ethical Investigation with Particular Reference to Nepotism' (Doctoral thesis Kwa Zulu Natal University, 2017) 139–68.

46 Chinweuba, Gregory Emeka Chinweuba, 'Culture and Corruption: A Critical Analysis of the Basis of Nigerian Depraved Experience' (2018) 19(2) Unizik Journal of Arts and Humanities 112. See also the preamble of UNESCO Universal Declaration on Cultural Diversity, 'culture should be regarded as the set of distinctive spiritual, material, intellectual and emotional features of society or a social group, and that it encompasses, in addition to art and literature, lifestyles, ways of living together, value systems, traditions and beliefs'.

47 Vapnek (n 27) 123, 127–28.

48 Tone K Sissener, 'Anthropological Perspectives on Corruption' (2001) CMI Working Paper no. 5, 7 <www.cmi.no/publications/910-anthropological-perspectives-on-corruption>; Vapnek (n 27) 123, 126–27; Otaluk (n 45).

49 Sissener (n 48) 7.

should be applied in the discourse on corruption. Accordingly, this begs the question: What is the cultural perception of corruption in Africa, and what are the orientation and attitudes of individuals towards corruption? It is necessary to consider this question since corrupt activities generate a substantial amount of illicit financial flow in Africa.[50] Consequently, these funds can be targeted by AML policies for laundering purposes. Additionally, unless corruption is seen as unacceptable by its practitioners, implementation of reforms is difficult.

Generally, the definition of corruption, according to the law, is given from a Western point of view that focuses on the illegal nature of the act.[51] Sissener argues that people's own assessments of courses of action do not arise from a set of culturally universal, invariable norms that helps to decide if certain actions are to be classified as 'corrupt' or not.[52] Rather, what is seen as corruption varies from one context to another.[53] The role of networks in fuelling corrupt practices is closely associated with locally recognised norms of sociality. These social norms are enforced via normative constraints based on societal expectations, shame, guilt, peer pressure, and reputation.[54]

In the African context, individuals tend to justify illicit actions by automatically presupposing that corruption 'is simply the way things are done', that 'everybody else is doing it', 'get rich quick', 'it is our turn to eat', and that 'dishonest behaviour is necessary to get ahead'.[55] Additionally, in most African cultures practices of gift-giving between families and the use of solidarity networks to obtain goods and services is a common practice.[56] If an individual is in a position of authority, they are expected to help and give back to their community – for example, by getting funds allocated for a project or assisting fellow community members to secure employment. This is acceptable even if one engages in corrupt activities.

50 Christiaan Keulder, 'Africans See Growing Corruption, Poor Government Response, But Fear Retaliation If They Speak Out' (2021) Afrobarometer Dispatch No. 421 <www.afrobarometer.org/wp-content/uploads/migrated/files/publications/Dispatches/ad421-africans_see_growing_corruption-afrobarometer_dispatch-bh-24jan20.pdf>; Jorum Duri, 'Sub-Saharan Africa: Overview of Corruption and Anti-Corruption' (2020) at 4–7. <www.u4.no/publications/sub-saharan-africa-overview-of-corruption-and-anti-corruption> accessed 7 August 2021.

51 Jens Christopher Andvig and Others, *Corruption. A Review of Contemporary Research* (2001) 49–50 <https://nmbu.brage.unit.no/nmbu-xmlui/handle/11250/2473686> accessed 9 February 2022. See also Sissener (n 48) 4–5, discussing the problems of a legal definition of corruption.

52 Sissener (n 48) 1; Christopher Andvig and Others (n 51). See Otaluk (n 45) 64–117.

53 Sissener (n 48) 2.

54 Claudia Baez Camargo, 'Corruption, Social Norms and Behaviours: a Comparative Assessment of Rwanda, Tanzania and Uganda' (2017) 9 <https://baselgovernance.org/publications/corruption-social-norms-and-behaviours-comparative-assessment-rwanda-tanzania-and> accessed 12 October 2021.

55 Claudia Baez Camargo, 'Corruption, Social Norms and Behaviours: a Comparative Assessment of Rwanda, Tanzania and Uganda' (2017) 12 <https://baselgovernance.org/publications/corruption-social-norms-and-behaviours-comparative-assessment-rwanda-tanzania-and> accessed 12 October 2021.

56 Vapnek (n 27) 123, 127–28.

This illuminates how social interactions based on deeply held values, such as reciprocity and solidarity, can be conducive to the social acceptability of corruption.[57] Moreover, such corruption can be interpreted as a form of social security since it is considered taking care of one's community members.

Linked to this perception of corruption is that much of African society is moving from communal ownership to individualism, that is, towards materialism and wealth accumulation. This comes with the concept of wealth accumulation to show 'I have made it', that 'I am rich and hence worthy of respect'. Most African countries gained independence in the 1960s and 1970s. Before the enforcement of colonial rule in these countries, African cultural systems were utilised for governance in various aspects of life. These include political, social, and economic spheres. However, with the imposition of colonial rule these traditional systems were replaced by European governance systems. The traditional African systems were centred on the communal system of governance.[58] Accordingly, in matters such as property ownership, the focus was on communal proprietorship. The European system, on the other hand, focused on the individual concept of proprietorship. This led to erosion of the communal system and propagated capitalism and individualism.[59]

From then on, the concept of individualism began to take root in African societies. This led to African political leaders, the educated, public officials and those mainly in government being at the forefront in beginning the race to amass property. Gradually, this has developed into a culture of wealth accumulation. Moreover, the colonial system brought along the concept of capitalism and with this system the concept of wealth accumulation has continued to evolve. Ingraining the culture of wealth accumulation comes with the attitudes of 'get rich quick' or 'it is our turn to eat'. This orientation implies that when one is presented with an opportunity to acquire wealth, legally or otherwise, they should seize upon the chance. Consequently, there is a situation where those in positions of authority use these opportunities to amass wealth for themselves and their kin. Contrary to viewing this as an opportunity to serve, this behaviour is exacerbated by a culture of impunity and corruption.

These two elements work towards ensuring those who misuse or misappropriate public funds for a private benefit are not held accountable. Since the justice system is weak, issues arise in the prosecution of such cases. These include conducting poor investigations, interference with evidence, and interference with judicial officers. The outcome is inordinate delays in prosecution

57 Claudia Baez-Camargo and Nikos Passas, 'Hidden Agendas, Social Norms and Why We Need to Re-Think Anti-Corruption' 2017 Working Paper No. 22, 14; JP Olivier De Sardan, 'A Moral Economy of Corruption in Africa?' (1999) 37(1) The Journal of Modern African Studies 25.

58 Benon C Basheka, 'Indigenous Africa's Governance Architecture: A Need for African Public Administration Theory?' (2015) 50(3) Journal of Public Administration 466, 471–78.

59 Bruce Berman, 'Ethnicity, Patronage and the African State: The Politics of Uncivil Nationalism' (1998) 97 African Affairs 305, 314–15. George BN Ayittey, 'From Impunity to Accountability: Africa's Development in the 21st Century' (2010) 77(4) Social Research 1183.

or acquittal for lack of evidence. This bolsters the perception that one can evade accountability. Consequently, it is okay to use whichever means possible to acquire wealth. Hence, financial crimes such as money laundering are given an opportunity to thrive.

The culture of acquiring wealth at whatever cost is linked with the belief that economic wealth equates to political and social power. This is evident in the fact that most of the political candidates who are successful in elections are those that society perceives as being wealthy. Further, unlike Western states where the motivation is for public service, for some African leaders it is the contrary.[60] Consequently, those holding political power use this as an opportunity to amass wealth. Moreover, since they are in power, they can use it to ensure they are not held accountable.

There are other aspects linked to culture, specifically the patriarchal nature of society, that could help to explain the perception and handling of corruption and by extension other financial crimes in African and least developed countries. Different views abide on whether a patriarchal society is more prone to corruption. Proponents have concluded that a more patriarchal society, which most African countries are, is likely to be more corrupt. This is based on the view that men are more likely to be corrupt than women.[61] Hence, in societies where men are more in control, corruption is likely to thrive. Despite the existence of contrary views to this theory, the findings cannot be ignored. By implication, this leads to other financial crimes thriving, including money laundering.

Prevailing Economic Circumstances in Most African Countries

The level of societal development is another factor that encourages corruption.[62] Most African countries are classified as developing. This is based on, among other things, a significantly lower per capita national product, low labour productivity, a high illiteracy rate, and a high share of agricultural employment. These factors combined lead to poverty, slow economic growth, and unequal income and wealth distribution, which encourage corruption.[63]

60 Joseph Patrick Ganahl, 'Corruption, Good Governance, and the African State' (2012) Potsdam Economic Studies 137–38 <https://d-nb.info/1045780677/34> accessed 10 July 2022.

61 See Wang-Sheng Lee and Cahit Lee Guven, 'Engaging in Corruption: The Influence of Cultural Values and Contagion Effects at the Microlevel' (2013) 39 Journal of Economic Psychology 287; Alice Guerra and Tatyana Zhuravleva, 'Do Women Always Behave As Corruption Cleaners?' (2022) 191 Public Choice 173; Fernanda M Rivas, 'An Experiment on Corruption and Gender' (2013) 65(1) Bulletin of Economic Research 10.

62 See Vapnek (n 27) 123.

63 Vapnek (n 27) 123, 126–27. Joseph Ato Forson and others, 'Causes of Corruption: Evidence from Sub-Saharan Africa' (2016) 19(4) South African Journal of Economic and Management Sciences 562; Dominik Enste and Christina Heldman, 'Causes and Consequences of Corruption: An Overview of Empirical Results' (2017) Institut der deutschen Wirtschaft Report, No. 2 <www.econstor.eu/bitstream/10419/157204/1/IW-Report-2017-02.pdf> accessed 4 May 2022.

Other indirect effects arising are insufficient financial inclusion, unbanked masses, and financial illiteracy. This translates to various problems such as reliance on using cash as the primary means of exchange and underutilisation of the formal banking system, whereas an examination of the AML strategies shows that much implementation focus has been placed on formal financial systems such as banks in predominantly cash-based economies.[64] Ultimately this creates challenges in terms of effective implementation of the strategies.

Considering the socio-economic needs of Africa, financial inclusion is a major issue. Much of the African population is classified as unbanked and hence does not operate within the formal banking system.[65] Nevertheless, they actively utilise alternative forms of money/value transfer. These systems have also been classified as being prone to use for money laundering purposes.[66] The AML policies that have been developed do not take into consideration the uniqueness of the informal value transfer systems (IVTS); instead the formal AML policies are expected to operate on these systems as well. This makes implementation problematic for a variety of reasons. The IVTS systems cannot be 'upgraded' to have the features of and operate like commercial banks.[67]

Hence, applying formal sector instruments to informal systems of value transfer is problematic.[68] It leads to the poor in these countries suffering. For example, they are denied means of sending money that are affordable. Developing countries rarely have the capacity to fully enforce resource-intensive money laundering control measures such as suspicious transaction reports (STRs) and CDD in the formal sector.[69] So why expect that they can do it in an underground market? The attractiveness of using *hawala* is premised on factors such as its non-regulation under a formal system, affordability, the absence of formal sector alternatives, cultural context and sensitivity, familiarity, accessibility, efficiency and speed, anonymity, and having a predominantly cash-based society.[70] These characteristics make *hawala* popular due to its

64 Charles Goredema, 'Combating Illicit Financial Flows and Related Corruption in Africa: Towards a More Integrated and Effective Approach' (2011) Chr. Michelsen Institute U4 Issue 12, 18.

65 See Asli Demirgüç-Kunt and Others, 'The Global Findex Database 2021: Financial Inclusion, Digital Payments, and Resilience in the Age of COVID-19' (2021) <www.worldbank.org/en/publication/globalfindex/Report> accessed 26 July 2022.

66 See FATF, 'The Role of Hawala and Other Similar Service Providers in Money Laundering and Terrorist Financing' (2013) <www.fatf-gafi.org/documents/documents/role-hawalas-in-ml-tf.html> accessed 28 May 2022.

67 See Joana Trautsolt and Jesper Johnsøn, 'International Anti-Money Laundering Regulation of Alternative Remittance Systems: Why the Current Approach Does Not Work in Developing Countries' (2012) 15(4) Journal of Money Laundering Control 407.

68 See Halliday, Levi and Reuter (n 35) 1.

69 Quentin Reed and Alessandra Fontana, 'Corruption and Illicit Financial Flows: The Limits and Possibilities of Current Approaches' (2011) Chr. Michelsen Institute U4 Issue 2 (2011) 36; Sharman (n 15) 635, 642–43.

70 See Arya Harihan, 'Hawala's Charm: What Banks Can Learn from Informal Funds Transfer Systems' (2012) 3 William & Mary Business Law Review 273; Mathew J Rosenbaum 'A Paper Chase in a Paperless World: Regulating Informal Value Transfer Systems' (2012) 50 Columbia Journal of Transnational Law 169.

affordability, safety, reliability, and swift delivery, even to very remote areas, and they are cheaper compared to the formal money transfer systems. The qualities that make IVTS a desirable money transfer method are the same ones that also make it a favourable method for moving proceeds of crime. These characteristics include the anonymity involved, adaptability, lack of evidence, and its cultural context.

Moreover, a blanket assumption that IVTS systems are being used only for illegitimate purposes permits the one-size-fits-all application of the AML policies. This is highlighted by examining the content of the Special Recommendation VI and its interpretative note. It stipulates mandatory regulation across the board and criminalising IVTS operators who refuse to be licensed or registered. At the same time, attempting a risk-based approach would be more prudent. Where risks are assessed and depending on prevailing risks, an appropriate AML policy can be developed and implemented. The negative effect of over-regulation is that it most likely pushes IVTS operators further underground, thus having a counterproductive effect.[71] Ultimately, those seeking to use IVTS for illegal purposes such as money laundering are facilitated. Yet, the formal AML policies cannot address the situation.

Implementation of AML Policies

Focusing on formal systems leads to situations where relevant entities in implementing AML policies are excluded. For example, considering the high reliance on cash in most African economies,[72] it would be necessary to carefully consider which business entities deal with cash. Such businesses could be brought within the ambit of AML strategies. These entities include car dealers, liquor stores, nightclubs, art and antique dealers, car washes, restaurants, construction companies, supermarkets, beauty shops, and churches. This also means that it would be appropriate for each country to undertake a risk assessment to establish the risk level of these cash-intensive businesses to determine which ones should be included. This would ensure that the peculiarities of a particular country are carefully considered, thus avoiding a universal approach.

In terms of implementing the relevant AML regulations, financial institutions and DNFBPs are left on their own. In most instances, these entities do not receive guidance on how to do it. The development and implementation of the required processes and procedures is left to these entities. Hence, each has to hire private consultants to assist in developing systems to facilitate the implementation of the AML regime. These include manpower and the

71 See Nikos Passas, 'Fighting Terror with Error: The Counter-Productive Regulation of Informal Value Transfers' (2006) 45(4) Crime, Law and Social Change 315.

72 Joël Té-Léssia Assoko, 'Mastercard: In Africa, Our Biggest Competitor Is Cash' The Africa Report, 5 June 2020 <www.theafricareport.com/29360/mastercard-in-africa-our-biggest-competitor-is-cash/> accessed 19 July 2022.

appropriate technology.[73] Additionally, the requisite staff must be trained so that they are able to fulfil their AML roles effectively. Appropriately, these undertakings lead to an increase in implementation costs, which can be burdensome on an institution. Moreover, small and medium-sized entities may be unable to meet and/or mitigate these costs.

The costs of implementation can be mitigated if the relevant supervisory authority would assist in this process. However, the issue is, do the relevant supervisory authorities have the capacity to monitor and ensure enforcement by their members? For example, the law society in a particular country would qualify as a supervisory authority and it would assist in ensuring compliance of law firms. This is through training its members on their compliance obligations, developing guidelines, and assisting the FIU in ensuring adherence with the prescribed regulations.

Moreover, the pressure of potential sanctions to ensure compliance is likely to encourage entities to engage in 'formal compliance', which is not effective but simply for purposes of ticking boxes. For example, banks engage in defensive reporting by filing any STR reports without reviewing them. Additionally, implementing institutions are usually not given clear and helpful feedback by the relevant agencies to assist them in effective compliance.[74] Accordingly, there is need to build local capacity through training. This would assist in increasing the available manpower of individuals with the requisite local knowledge and hence can utilise it in ensuring effective implementation. This would seal the gap of having to continuously rely on expatriates. Moreover, providing clear incentives for effective compliance could be provided. This will give motivation to participating entities.

Another challenge of implementation relates to conducting KYC measures on potential clients. To engage in this process, clients must produce documents which can verify their identity and address. In most cases, this entails presenting a formal identification document, for example, a national identity card or utility bill. This presents a challenge because citizens in many African countries do not have formal identification documents for various reasons:[75] the government may not issue them, the process of getting one is slow and tedious, and cultural issues such as having a patriarchal society hinders females from seeking identification documents.[76] With regards to utility bills, these are

73 FATF, 'Guidance Politically Exposed Persons (Recommendations 12 and 22)' (2013) 14–18 <www.fatf-gafi.org/media/fatf/documents/recommendations/Guidance-PEP-Rec12-22.pdf> accessed 22 January 2018.

74 See Sisira Dharmasri Jayasekara, 'Challenges of Implementing an Effective Risk-Based Supervision on Anti-Money Laundering and Countering the Financing of Terrorism Under the 2013 FATF Methodology' (2018) 21(4) Journal of Money Laundering Control 601.

75 Abdullahi Y Shehu, 'Promoting Financial Inclusion for Effective Anti-Money Laundering and Counter Financing of Terrorism' (2012) 57 Crime Law Social Change 305, 315.

76 Alliance for Financial Inclusion, 'KYC Innovations, Financial Inclusion and Integrity in Selected AFI Member Countries' (2019) 30 <www.afi-global.org/sites/default/files/publications/2019-03/KYC-Innovations-Financial-Inclusion-Integrity-Selected-AFI-Member-Countries.pdf> accessed 18 July 2022; Shehu (n 75) 305, 316.

not commonly available documents. Because individuals may reside in informal settlements, proper geographic mapping has not been done; consequently, it is challenging to produce accurate address information and inadequate penetration of utility services; hence, no utility bills are given.[77] These examples highlight the challenges of utilising formal KYC identification processes and documentation in developing countries, whereas in developed countries, these challenges are not commonplace. The inference drawn is that innovative ways for undertaking KYC, applicable to the prevailing circumstances, should be developed for use in African countries.

Conclusion and the Way Forward

This chapter has shed light on the possible underlying issues that have hindered the effective implementation of the AML policies in African countries. The thesis is that utilisation of coercive methods instead of seeking positive policy adaptation that considers the environment in African countries has impeded successful implementation. Since the AML regime's inception globally, African countries were not involved in agenda-setting. After that, various coercive measures were utilised to ensure the adoption of the policies. Hence, African countries using the one-size-fits-all approach adopted the measures to avoid the negative consequences. However, this approach does not consider the existing social, cultural, and economic factors.

Undoubtedly, money laundering has adverse effects and measures should be adopted to address the problem. However, this must be done appropriately. Considering the challenges highlighted in this chapter, specific initiatives should be employed in African countries. Most importantly, the inclusion of African countries in the agenda-setting is needed.[78] This will allow these countries to present their views at the point these policies are being negotiated. Linked to this is avoiding the universal approach in policy development. Moreover, by including different countries in agenda-setting forums, countries with similar issues may come together in terms of policy transfer. African countries should consciously avoid the one-size-fits-all approach.[79]

Instead, they should embark on policy adaptation that incorporates self-reflection and examination. This requires a country to begin by examining how a policy was shaped by social, economic, political, and institutional settings in its country of origin. This will assist in explaining how the policy works in the country of origin. Appropriately, the borrowing country should consider the comparable policy situations between itself and the country of origin. This should also be accompanied by undertaking risk and regulatory impact

77 See Mugarura (n 24) 174.

78 See Jennifer Constantine and Alex Shankland, 'From Policy Transfer to Mutual Learning?' (2017) 36(1) Revista Novos Estudos 107; Noriaki Yasaka, 'Knowledge Management in International Cooperation for Anti-Money Laundering' (2017) 20(1) Journal of Money Laundering Control 27.

79 Ganahl (n 60) 83.

assessments.[80] This leads to an effective policy adaptation since the policy adaptation takes into consideration the unique aspects of the implementing jurisdiction. Moreover, it leads to developing systems that are enforceable using the feasible and available capacity in developing countries and can efficiently and effectively address the targeted challenge. To achieve what has been stated here, it is paramount that political will is demonstrated throughout this process.

80 See Julia Hertin, 'Making Government More Reflexive: The Role of Regulatory Impact Assessment' (Doctoral dissertation Wageningen University 2016). Although written from the perspective of environmental law, the discussion on the utilization of regulatory impact assessment in policy making is relevant to the discussion on general policy adoption.

3 GIABA

Combatting Money Laundering/ Terrorism Financing in West Africa

Edefe Ojomo[1]

Introduction

The Groupe Intergouvernemental d'Action contre le Blanchiment d'Ardent en Afrique de l'Ouest (GIABA) is one of the specialized agencies of the Economic Community of West African States (ECOWAS), a West African regional economic community (REC) comprising 15 member states.[2] GIABA is also an associate member of the Financial Action Task Force (FATF) as an FATF-styled regional body (FSRB).

GIABA is "responsible for facilitating the adoption and implementation of Anti-Money Laundering (AML) and Counter-Financing of Terrorism (CFT) in West Africa. It is also a FATF-Styled Regional Body (FSRB) working with its member States to ensure compliance with international AML/CFT standards".[3] It wears two hats as a regional governance institution: first, it is a limited participant in the global standard-setting process, where it also serves as a channel for the diffusion of global standards to its signatory states; and second, it is a regional institution charged with protecting the financial system under its jurisdiction and monitoring the implementation of AML/CFT standards in its signatory states. This situates GIABA as a governance broker that manages the relationship and interactions between global and national actors, leveraging the capacity and legitimacy of these actors. In this chapter,

1 I would like to acknowledge the contributions of Prof Benedict Kingsbury, Prof Richard Stewart, Thomas Streinz, and Aishani Gupta in developing and refining the ideas in this chapter. I bear full responsibility for any mistakes herein.

2 ECOWAS was established in 1975 with the main objective of promoting national and regional economic development within and amongst its member states. The current ECOWAS member states are the Republic of Benin, Burkina Faso, Cape Verde, Côte d'Ivoire, The Gambia, Ghana, Guinea, Guinea-Bissau, Liberia, Mali, Niger, Nigeria, Senegal, Sierra Leone, and Togo. In 1993, the establishment treaty was revised to expand its scope to cover political and security matters in a more robust and comprehensive regional integration exercise. West Africa has seen its fair share of civil wars, military coups, and socio-economic crises in the past few decades, and this has led to the region being one of the least developed on the continent and in the world. In a region with critically fragile state capacities, regional institutions are expected to play a particularly important role in advancing development efforts and strengthening state institutions.

3 <http://web.giaba.org/> accessed 19 November 2022.

DOI: 10.4324/9781003253808-4

I use the distributed administration framework, which is a system of global administrative law, to show how GIABA plays this role and the consequences of its position. In this first section, I provide an account of how GIABA was established, describing the circumstances and motivations that led to its creation. I also provide a brief explanation of the governance structure of GIABA to explain the various influences that determine its performance. In the second section, I explain the concept of distributed administration and describe the particular application of the three-level distributed administration to the role of GIABA as a governance actor. The third section provides concluding reflections on the discussions in the chapter.

The Establishment and Evolution of GIABA

GIABA was established by a decision of the ECOWAS Authority of Heads of State and Government (the Authority) in 1999,[4] and its Statute came into force in 2000. It was created to serve as the focal institution for AML regulation within the West African region, as well as to protect member states and their financial systems from the effects of money laundering and related financial crimes.[5] The rules governing membership of GIABA are not stringent, and the Statute simply states that membership is open to all member states of ECOWAS and African states that adhere to the Statute, upon approval by the Authority and the ECOWAS Council of Ministers (the Council).[6] Although GIABA was established as a specialized agency of ECOWAS, its establishment was not unrelated to global developments in AML at the time. The FATF was established in 1989 by the G7, eight other countries, and the European Communities.[7] These 16 founding members of the Task Force were driven by their expertise, experience, and growing concerns about the dangers of money laundering at the national and international level, and together, they produced a report of 40 Recommendations to combat money laundering.[8] The mandate of the FATF, its general interest in expansion, and a particular interest in Nigeria and West Africa were instrumental to the establishment of GIABA.

The 1990s saw an expansion in the FATF's membership and scope of activities. In 1996, the 40 Recommendations were revised to "take into consideration new trends in money laundering", and in 1998, the FATF committed itself to

4 Decision A/DEC.9/12/99 of the ECOWAS Authority of Heads of State and Government establishing the Inter-Governmental Action Group against Money Laundering in West Africa.

5 Article 2, GIABA Statutes.

6 Article 3 GIABA Statutes.

7 The eight other countries were Australia, Austria, Belgium, Luxembourg, the Netherlands, Spain, Sweden, and Switzerland. See Financial Action Task Force (FATF), Financial Action Task Force on Money Laundering: Report (1990).

8 The eight other countries were Australia, Austria, Belgium, Luxembourg, the Netherlands, Spain, Sweden, and Switzerland. See Financial Action Task Force (FATF), Financial Action Task Force on Money Laundering: Report (1990). This focus on expertise is considered as a legitimate basis for the exclusivity of the Task Force's membership. See Rainer Hülsse and Dieter Kerwer, 'Global Standards in Action: Insights from Anti-Money Laundering Regulation' (2007) 14 Organization 625.

building a worldwide network in AML by, inter alia, fostering the development of FSRBs. This was to extend the work of the FATF to regions where there was limited AML/CFT engagement. In 1999, the FATF opened its doors to new members, lifting the self-imposed moratorium on admissions placed during the first two years of its establishment.[9] The membership expansion was also expected to bring strategically important countries, particularly financial centres with significant influence in their respective regions, into the FATF. The FATF was interested in regions where it lacked representation, and this included West Africa.[10] In its 1998 and 1999 Annual Reports, the FATF expressed particular concern about money laundering trends in West Africa, especially among Nigerian organized criminal networks.[11] In 1999, the Authority of Heads of State and Government of ECOWAS adopted its decision to establish GIABA, and the FATF acknowledged this development in its 2001 report.[12]

GIABA took steps in 2006 to fulfil the conditions for becoming an FSRB, adopting relevant decisions by its institutions and making the necessary amendments to its Statute,[13] including acknowledging the increasing links between money laundering and the financing of terrorism.[14] Four years later, GIABA was recognized as an FSRB and became an associate member of the FATF. In 2013, it increased its membership to include Sao Tome and Principe and granted observer status to Comoros.[15]

As an FSRB, GIABA is entitled to attend FATF plenaries and other meetings, and it is entitled to representation at these meetings, although its member states do not attend FATF meetings in their national capacity but as representatives of GIABA. Within its internal processes, GIABA invites a small number of countries to attend FATF plenaries and meetings. Member states must sponsor their attendance at FATF meetings, so this may not be a priority for smaller states with bigger political and economic challenges and priorities.[16]

9 See the FATF Annual Report (1991) and FATF Annual Report (1999).

10 By this time, there were FSRBs in the Caribbean (the Caribbean Financial Action Task Force) and in Asia-Pacific (the Asia Pacific Group). See FATF Annual Report (1999). An FSRB was established for East and Southern Africa (the East and Southern Africa Anti-Money Laundering Group) in 1999. See FATF Annual Report (2000). This would be the first FSRB in Africa.

11 The 1999 Report contains a factual case study involving a West African citizen with suspicious business transactions and several assets in his home country and in Europe.

12 See FATF Annual Report (2001), 7.

13 At the 52nd Ministerial Meeting of the GIABA Ministerial Committee, the Ministers made a declaration to fulfil all the conditions for becoming an FSRB. See the preamble of the GIABA Statute.

14 This was in response to the FATF adopting 9 additional recommendations in 2003 to address terrorist financing, expanding the scope of the 40 recommendations. See the FATF 40 Recommendations (+9) (2003).

15 GIABA is one of the only ECOWAS institutions with non-ECOWAS representation.

16 Interview with GIABA official, January 2015. Note that this point is very important when considering the general cost of implementing many of these standards for smaller countries, which have limited resources and significant state building concerns. As Halliday et al. note, economic and financial costs are very important when considering the possibility of effectiveness in the implementation of these standards. Terrence Halliday et al., 'Global Surveillance of

GIABA's participation at the FATF includes its involvement in the development of methodologies and typologies, reviewing the 40 Recommendations, clarifying and revising aspects of the Recommendations, and defining the FATF's mandate. The FATF prides itself in providing a broad participatory space that engages governments, international organizations, corporations and other private institutions, and all stakeholders in its deliberations. The consultation space is indeed extensive and GIABA, as an associate member, has a seat at the table. However, the decision-making space is restricted to full members of the FATF.[17] So, after deliberations amongst all the stakeholders, the FATF's core membership decides on the mandate and plans of the Task Force. Usually, the deliberations are taken into consideration and adopted, making the deliberation process an important space for influencing the conduct and control of the Task Force. Nevertheless, the core membership has the power to approve or reject the decisions of stakeholders and to decide on sanctions mechanisms and targeted countries.

Being an FSRB has meant that GIABA ranks its success according to FATF perceptions, defined by FATF standards and methodologies. Not only is its organizational structure defined by the FATF, but its objectives and activities are limited by FATF requirements.[18] Nevertheless, its path is not necessarily unidirectional; GIABA plays an important role in the global, regional, and national framework for the regulation of AML/CFT. The internal (GIABA and member states) and external (GIABA, ECOWAS, and the FATF) engagements of the Organization provide ample opportunity for institutional innovation and orchestration. As I discuss herein, GIABA is positioned to act as an influential regional governance tool, with significant access to legitimacy and capacity pools that can foster this role.

Institutional Structure of GIABA: Internal and External Controls

As mentioned above, GIABA's institutional structure is designed to conform with the FATF-endorsed model. Although the Agency exists as a specialized agency of ECOWAS, it is also a part of the administrative framework of the FATF and must adhere to standards set by the latter regarding structural and operational issues. Consequently, there are two sets of controls and limitations GIABA must adhere to. The FATF High Level Principles and Objectives

Dirty Money: Assessing Assessment of Regimes to Control Money Laundering and Combat the Financing of Terrorism' (2014) Centre on Law and Globalization 48.

17 As Hülsse and Kerwer state (n 8), the current structure is a result of the FATF trying to strike a balance between legitimacy and effectiveness.

18 Although the FATF demands congruence among FSRBs, the Caribbean FATF, for instance, has been innovative in adopting its own standards that are not identical to the FATF's but are not inconsistent with them either. GIABA has not exactly done this. See Kenneth Blazejewski, 'The FATF and its Institutional Partners: Improving the Effectiveness and Accountability of Transgovernmental Networks' (2008) 22 Temple International and Comparative Law Journal 1.

for FATF and FATF-Styled Regional Bodies (FSRBs) define the relationship between the FATF and FSRBs as well as institutional requirements for FSRBs, and the internal structure of GIABA is derived from this. The FATF prescribes a structure that is similar to its internal structure so that FSRBs mirror its technical and political processes in the monitoring and implementation of its standards. This is one way to control the activities of the FSRB, by making sure that they are designed to follow a global script. The Principles require that FSRBs have a Secretariat, a Plenary as the highest technical body, a President or Chairperson, regular meetings of the Plenary and, where applicable, a ministerial body and a written procedure for meetings, and that they publish their proceedings transparently.[19] FSRBs are also expected to carry out mutual evaluations and report to the FATF on the result of those evaluations and on non-compliant states.

In addition to the above, the ECOWAS leadership performs a supervisory role that ensures that GIABA, as a regional agency, protects regional and national interests. As an agency of ECOWAS, GIABA's internal affairs are made subject to the authority of ECOWAS leadership. According to the GIABA Statutes, decisions of the Organization relating to membership, sanctions, implementation of measures, and revision of the Statutes are subject to the approval of the Authority and the Council.[20] Since GIABA's membership extends beyond ECOWAS, this means that signatories to the GIABA Statutes who are not ECOWAS members, like Sao Tome and Principe, are not represented in the top decision-making organs that have the final say in some of the affairs of GIABA.[21] GIABA membership is thus discriminately tied to implementation, meaning that members do not necessarily have a say in the

19 See the FATF (2012b), FATF High Level Principles and Objectives on the FATF and FATF-Styled Regional Bodies (FSRBs) 6–7 (2012) <www.fatf-gafi.org/media/fatf/documents/High-Level%20Principles%20and%20Objectives%20for%20FATF%20and%20FSRBs.pdf> accessed 19 November 2022.

20 Matters relating to membership (Articles 3, 5), sanctions (Article 6), implementation of measures (Article 12) and revision of the Statute (Article 17) are subject to the approval of the Authority and the Council. For example, Article 9(ii)(b) of the Statute provides that the Ad Hoc Committee of Ministers of GIABA is responsible for recommending the annual work plan for the approval of the ECOWAS Council of Ministers.

21 The statute provides that in order for states to qualify for membership of GIABA, they must adhere to the statute, which is recognized as meaning that they demonstrate commitment to the goals and objectives of GIABA. Interested states may apply to the Administrative Secretariat of GIABA for membership, and the application is considered by the GIABA Ministerial Committee (GMC), which forwards it to the ECOWAS Council of Ministers (the Council) for approval and recommendation to the ECOWAS Authority of Heads of State and Government (the Authority). The Authority confers membership of GIABA on applicant states, but this does not confer membership of ECOWAS on them. See, for instance, Decision A/DEC.1/02/13 Relating to the Granting to the Democratic Republic of Sao Tome and Principe Full Membership within the Intergovernmental Action Group Against Money Laundering in West Africa (GIABA) (February 2013).

political leadership of ECOWAS at the ECOWAS level, but they are committed to standards implementation by virtue of their membership.

The criteria for membership of GIABA are not as stringent as those imposed by the FATF. The GIABA Statutes provide that in order for states to qualify for membership, they must adhere to the Statutes, which is recognized as meaning that they demonstrate commitment to the goals and objectives of GIABA.[22] The FATF, on the other hand, conducts a two-step assessment and a comprehensive evaluation of prospective members in order to make a determination regarding their admission to membership.[23] This could take years. This marks a clear distinction between the rigorous process for becoming a member of a standard-setting body and that of joining a standard-implementing body. Countries that are admitted to set global standards are expected to meet qualitative and quantitative requirements and achieve specified levels of progress regarding the mandate of the FATF, whereas organizations like GIABA, whose main engagement with the global regulatory framework is to facilitate the implementation of standards, have less stringent requirements governing membership.[24] This shows how the FATF framework manages its balancing act of engagement and exclusion by focusing on effectiveness in engaging a class of countries in its "club" of regulators, while focusing on participation and commitment when inviting others to discuss and implement the standards set by the core group.[25]

GIABA's internal institutional structure comprises the Ad-Hoc Ministerial Committee, the Administrative Secretariat, the Technical Commission, and the Network of National Correspondents.[26]

The Ad-Hoc Ministerial Committee, generally referred to as the GIABA Ministerial Committee (GMC), is the highest decision-making organ of GIABA. The GMC comprises ministers from the line ministries of signatory

22 Interview with GIABA official. This has been interpreted to mean that states show their commitment by taking preliminary steps such as enactment of statutes or establishment of relevant institutions such as financial intelligence units (FIUs).

23 For a description of the FATF membership procedure, see www.fatf-gafi.org/about/membersandobservers/fatfmembershippolicy.html, accessed 19 November 2022.

24 The FATF (n 19) has a stringent two-stage process leading to membership, with evaluations and monitoring of substantive standards. See FSRB membership is extended to states that are usually not qualified for FATF membership. As we will see later, Nigeria has been working towards attaining FATF membership for over a decade, but it has been a member of GIABA for that long.

25 This clear-cut distinction, which may have existed in the 1990s after the FATF was just established, has been revised to provide for greater participation for those who were originally part of the system as standard implementers, partly because of concerns raised within those circles. For example, the Caribbean FATF set its own standards which it promotes within the region alongside FATF standards, and it contributed to the pressure on the FATF to adopt a more inclusive process for FSRBs in the former's decision-making. See Blazejewski (n 18). See also Hülsse and Kerwer (n 8).

26 Article 8.

states.[27] These ministers represent national and regional interests, and unlike the Plenary, which is a technical body, the GMC considers matters of policy and politics when making its decisions.[28] All decisions taken at the Plenary are referred to the GMC for approval. Where the decisions submitted to the GMC relate to matters that require the approval of the Authority or the Council, the GMC makes the requisite recommendation to the Council or the Authority, as needed. All signatory states have equal decision-making power in the GMC, making participation inclusive regardless of size, economy, expertise, or other considerations.

The GIABA Secretariat is located in Dakar, Senegal. It is responsible for the day-to-day operations of the Organization and for coordinating GIABA's relationship with its signatory states, the FATF, and other institutions. It is also responsible for organizing the meetings of the other organs of GIABA and planning GIABA's representation at FATF meetings. This is a particularly important role as it determines the involvement of signatories in the global policy-making process at the FATF. The staff of the Secretariat are not signatory state representatives, and they are expected to be committed to regional goals rather than pursue national interests.[29]

The Secretariat is also responsible for coordinating the activities of national correspondents. These national correspondents are regarded as focal persons for GIABA in their respective countries. They are responsible for implementing and supervising GIABA's national activities and interfacing with GIABA on all matters related to program and operational issues.[30] In 2012, all heads of financial intelligence units (FIUs) in member states were designated as national correspondents, in order to coordinate regional and national action. Since the FIUs, established pursuant to the FATF Recommendations, are responsible for preparing and implementing the national agenda for AML/CFT in their respective countries, the Secretariat liaises with them to ensure that national processes conform with regional activities and global standards.[31] GIABA, through

27 These are the Ministries of Finance, Internal Affairs, and Justice.

28 This dichotomy between politics and technical issues is recognized by the FATF in the High Level Principles, and it states that there must be a technical decision-making body in addition to a political decision-making body, but the latter, unlike the former, is not a compulsory structural requirement for FSRBs. See FATF (n 19).

29 Article 10, GIABA Statute. This is similar to provisions like Article 18, Revised ECOWAS Treaty (1993), and Article 100, UN Charter, establishing an international bureaucracy. One of the sanctions that can be taken by GIABA against member states is that their citizens will not be recruited to international posts in the Secretariat (Article 6, GIABA Statute) It is not clear how this would impact selection of staff to the Secretariat, especially if recruitment is tied to citizenship of signatory states.

30 Interview with GIABA official, January 2015.

31 Recommendation 29 of the Forty Recommendations (FATF (2012), provides that "Countries should establish a financial intelligence unit (FIU) that serves as a national centre for the receipt and analysis of: (a) suspicious transaction reports; and (b) other information relevant to money laundering, associated predicate offences and terrorist financing, and for the

the Secretariat, also provides technical assistance to member state institutions engaged in AML/CFT, such as relevant ministries and agencies involved in security, justice, and capital markets. In addition to this, the Organization provides assistance to financial institutions, designated non-financial institutions (DNFIs), and non-governmental organizations whose work involves AML/CFT.[32] The Secretariat is responsible for handling all these operational and administrative issues and liaising with the national, regional, and global partners of GIABA.

The Plenary of GIABA, its Technical Commission, meets twice every year, in May and November. These meetings provide an opportunity for members to discuss mutual evaluation reports and the follow-up reports for the period and to review typology reports prepared during that period. The Plenary comprises experts from member states, and they can be drawn from a wide range of institutions like the line ministries and other national institutions working in AML/CFT such as the central banks, securities and exchange commissions, and so on.[33] The mutual evaluation process is conducted by experts from signatory states and the process is administered by the Secretariat. External evaluators from the FATF or from the World Bank and International Monetary Fund (IMF) may be involved in the evaluation process.[34] Where the World Bank or IMF conducts an evaluation under any of their own programs, such as the Financial Sector Assessment Program (FSAP), GIABA can adopt these evaluations as suitable for its purpose, but this is subject to approval by the Plenary. The Plenary makes decisions regarding member state compliance with recommended standards and may recommend sanctions where appropriate. However, its decisions are not final and must be approved by the GMC.[35]

---

dissemination of the results of that analysis. The FIU should be able to obtain additional information from reporting entities, and should have access on a timely basis to the financial, administrative and law enforcement information that it requires to undertake its functions properly".

32 Having said this, it is important to note that there is limited engagement between GIABA and the private sector because the organization is an intergovernmental organization charged with facilitating AML/CFT amongst public sector institutions in member states. Nevertheless, GIABA tried to engage the private sector even outside the field of technical assistance. It facilitated the establishment of associations of Chief Compliance Officers in member states. These associations bring together the compliance officers in financial institutions and designated non-financial institutions for coordination of their efforts and information-sharing regarding implementation of the standards set in the Recommendations and related AML/CFT issues.

33 Although these ministries are listed as comprising the Technical Commission, in reality, the Commission is open to experts from different public institutions with preference given to the participation of the Central Banks of signatory states. Interview with GIABA official, January 2015.

34 For example, in 2009, the World Bank conducted the evaluation of Burkina Faso and the Off-Shore Group of Banking Supervisors (OGBS) conducted the evaluation of Ghana. See GIABA Annual Report (2009).

35 Article 6, GIABA Statute.

With these structures and controls in place, GIABA has been relatively successful in meeting its objectives, especially when compared to other ECOWAS agencies, many of which are adversely affected by financial, infrastructural, and political challenges that greatly undermine their efficiency.[36] In a region burdened with socio-economic and political challenges, the definition of success may vary at different levels, particularly depending on the interests being served. So, it is important to ask what the outcomes of the anti-money laundering governance framework mean for different actors. Next, I examine the governance role of GIABA by analysing the three-level distributed administration in which it operates.

The Three-Level Distributed Administration: Features and Consequences

The distributed administration is one of five systems of global administration employed by global standard-setting regimes to facilitate the diffusion and implementation of globally prescribed standards. It has been described as a system in which "domestic regulatory agencies act as part of the global administrative space . . . [and] take decisions on issues of foreign or global concern".[37] It is usually a two-level system in which national actors cooperate to develop, promote, and ensure the implementation of global rules. National actors, here, are more than just domestic actors in the implementation of global standards, but they are also participants in decision-making. The making and implementing of global standards usually has extraterritorial effect and as such places extraterritorial power in the hands of domestic institutions. So, these domestic actors not only apply global rules but they do so as part of the global system of governance by actively regulating the global administrative space.

The basic two-level distributed administration is concerned with how global regulatory institutions *and* national regulatory agencies interact to facilitate the processes of standard setting and standard implementation. These interactions do not necessarily involve independent institutions engaged in remote linkages based on similar goals and objectives but rather the distinction between levels can be tenuous in instances where one level is responsible for constructing the other and monitoring its internal processes as is the case with the FATF. The global institution may be responsible for establishing the

36 In 2013, ECOWAS institutions such as the Community Court of Justice, the West African Power Pool, the West African Monetary Agency, and the West African Health Organisation raised concerns about funding and infrastructural challenges, amongst other things. In the same year, GIABA was able to meet its funding requirements and achieve most of its objectives, experiencing little to no financial constraints in its operations. See ECOWAS Annual Report (2013).

37 See Benedict Kingsbury et al., 'The Emergence of Global Administrative Law' (2005) 68 Law & Contemporary Problems 15 at 21.

national or vice versa. This may involve state actors, non-state actors, or both. In a typical distributed administration, the aim is to engage standard setters and standard implementers in a comprehensive process of regulatory governance.[38] The exchange of capacity and legitimacy within these systems underlines their governance role, as this would affect the effectiveness of the regulatory system. The capacity of standard setters is usually determined by their expertise in the area of regulation, while the capacity of implementers is determined by expertise and resources necessary for applying the standards. Where standard setters are believed to have the expertise to define standards and make decisions, their capacity may not be called into question by standard implementers, but the capacity of standard implementers may affect their ability to comply. Legitimacy of the regulatory framework, on the other hand, may be defined by the expertise of standard setters or by the acceptance of the regulatory framework amongst its targets. In the first instance, participation in the regulatory system will usually depend on the belief in the validity of the purpose and content of the standards; thus standard setters will be those considered most capable of decision-making in the relevant field.[39] In the second instance, standard setting will be an inclusive process that involves standard implementers regardless of their capacity; thus, the standards will reflect the position of all implementers, regardless of their capacity.[40] The two-level distributed administration depends on its legitimacy for diffusion. This could be based on the expertise of standard setters or on the legitimacy of the regulatory framework.

In addition to a standard two-level distributed administration, capacity and legitimacy are spread out in a three-level distributed administration. Here, the global institution engages with a regional institution in the standard-setting process and the latter engages with national institutions for standard implementation. This could reduce transaction costs and promote engagement without compromising the effectiveness of the system. Although there is a layer of governance between standard setting and standard implementation, the representative nature of the global and the regional systems, amongst whom standard setting will take place, will determine the level of engagement and participation and the interaction between standard setting and standard implementation. This is one way to ensure that the legitimacy-effectiveness balance, which can be strewn in a two-level distributed administration, is maintained. However, the middle governance layer – in this case, GIABA – can play a

38 See Hülsse and Kerwer (n 8); Organizations and Nation States: New Perspectives on Conflict and Cooperation (Robert Kahn & Mayer Zaid eds. 1990).

39 This follows the more functionalist position of institutional and organizational theory, which focuses on productivity and consequences. Here, the legitimacy of institutions depends on their cost-benefit value. This is the view taken by institutionalists like North. See Douglass North, Institutions, Institutional Change and Economic Performance (1990); Hülsse and Kerwer (n 8); Kahn and Zald (n 38).

40 Hülsse and Kerwer (n 8), note that enhancing this kind of legitimacy tilts the balance in favour of legitimacy and sacrifices effectiveness.

dynamic role that sustains global and national systems while also constructing a potent governance framework.

The GIABA Statutes recognize the global, regional, and national focus of GIABA's activities. Among its objectives and functions recognized under the Statute, GIABA is expected to protect the financial systems of signatory states by promoting AML/CFT efforts and to promote regional efforts and concerns. Although the Statute does not contain an express regulatory function, the functions mentioned in the relevant Article 2 can be read broadly to cover a range of issues, including regional standard setting and regulation.[41]

GIABA can and does use the administrative rules set by the FATF to facilitate its regional activities. A good example is through the use of typology reports, which are part of the FATF brand.[42] They comprise research and analysis of money laundering and financing of terrorism methods and trends based on standards set by the FATF for the conduct of such research. Since its establishment, GIABA has published several typology reports on issues ranging from cash couriers to proliferation of small arms and light weapons (SALW).[43] Some of the issues covered under GIABA's typologies are globally relevant issues that are on the global agenda for AML/CFT, like the financing of terrorism. However, other issues covered in the typologies are matters peculiar to the West African region, and such important issues involve cash couriers (2007), the proliferation of SALW (2014), and informal and illegal currency exchange services (2021).

The 2014 Typologies report on the nexus between SALW and money laundering and financing of terrorism in the region addresses regional contextual elements. It notes the factors contributing to proliferation of SALW proliferation as

> porous borders between ECOWAS countries and the existence of large swathes of ungoverned or unmonitored territory. Compounding these

41 This is the section of the statute that states the objectives and functions of the Agency.

42 See High Level Principles, 8.

43 GIABA typologies include Typologies Report on cash transactions and cash couriers in West Africa (2007); Typologies of Money Laundering through the Real Estate Sector in West Africa (2009); Corruption and Money Laundering Nexus: An Analysis of Risk and Control Measures in Africa (2010); Threat Assessment of Money Laundering and Terrorism in West Africa (2010); Typologies Report on Laundering the Proceeds of Illicit Drugs and Narcotics and Psychotropic Substances in West Africa (2011); Tax Fraud and Money Laundering in West Africa: Human and Economic Development Perspective (2012); GIABA Typologies Report on Tax Crimes and Money Laundering in West Africa (2012); Typologies Studies on Money Laundering Arising from Electronic Counterfeiting and Intellectual Property Theft in West Africa (2017); The Nexus between Small Arms and Light Weapons and Money Laundering and Terrorist Financing in West Africa (2014); Money Laundering and Terrorist Financing Linked to the Extractive Industry/Mining Sector in West Africa (2019); Money Laundering and Terrorist Financing through the Informal and Illegal Currency Exchange Service Providers in West Africa (2021).

challenges are the weak – and often non-existent – capacities of law enforcement institutions and the largely informal and cash- based nature of economic transactions, which permits easy movement of money within and in between borders in West Africa.[44]

The proliferation of SALW in the region has posed significant challenges for regional peace, security, and development for decades. Civil wars, terrorist threats, and low-intensity conflicts in countries like Liberia, Sierra Leone, Mali, Niger, and Nigeria are recognized as having been intensified by the proliferation of SALW in the region.[45] In 2006, the Authority adopted a convention on SALW which was open for ratification by member states, and in 2014, only 10 of the 15 ECOWAS member states had ratified the Convention. One of the recommendations in the 2014 Typology on SALW was to urge the ECOWAS Commission to encourage member states to ratify the Convention and to prepare guidelines for its implementation.[46]

The Typology reports are prepared by consultants or working groups engaged by the Secretariat. The FATF may also collaborate with the GIABA Secretariat on the preparation of a typology report.[47] There is no direct collaboration with states on the preparation of the reports, although experts are drawn from signatory states to prepare the report. It is an independent process of the Secretariat, bringing together global and regional processes. Before any report is endorsed as a typology of GIABA, it must be approved by the Plenary.[48] This means that there is participation of the technical representation of member states in the adoption of typologies. GIABA does not monitor the implementation of typology recommendations in the same way that it coordinates state activity in relation to the FATF Recommendations.

The typologies, by focusing on regional matters, also bring pertinent regional issues to the attention of signatory states under a globally influential regime. GIABA, because of its relationship with the FATF, is strategically placed to influence member states in their domestic regulatory processes. It is able to sanction member states by suspending assistance to such states, refusing to recruit their citizens to the Secretariat, and suspending voting rights or,

44 GIABA, 'The Nexus between Small Arms and Light Weapons and Money Laundering and Terrorist Financing in West Africa' (2014) 3 <www.giaba.org/media/f/613_519_GIABA%20SALW%20Nexus-final.pdf> accessed 19 November 2022.

45 On security issues in West Africa, see Adekeye Adebajo and Ismail Rashid (eds), West Africa's Security Challenges: Building Peace in a Troubled Region (2004) <https://www.rienner.com/title/West_Africa_s_Security_Challenges_Building_Peace_in_a_Troubled_Region>.

46 GIABA (44) at 58.

47 A Typology report on Financing of Terrorism in West Africa was prepared by both organisations. See GIABA, Terrorist Financing in West Africa <www.giaba.org/media/f/632_TF-in-West-Africa.pdf> accessed 19 November 2022.

48 Interview with GIABA official, January 2015.

in the case of persistent default, revoking membership.[49] In addition to this, GIABA can use its influence in the FATF to demand higher sanctions at the global level for non-complying signatory states. This could include refusal by some of the financial centres of the world to do business with the country in question, which could have a devastating effect on the country's economy.[50] Therefore, as a specialized agency of ECOWAS, GIABA, through its global affiliation, is a useful tool for the enforcement of regional goals, which would otherwise be difficult to achieve with only regional resources.

Another area where GIABA can also promote regional interests is in border control, which is raised under the recommendations in many of the typologies. The porous borders in West Africa have been conduits for refugees, arms, cash couriers, and diseases. There is limited capacity to police the borders, and the migration program within ECOWAS is underequipped to handle the challenges of keeping the borders open and, at the same time, properly managed.[51] GIABA, which has a commendable budget history, can provide technical assistance in these areas. One of the mandates of GIABA is to provide technical assistance to signatory states in strengthen their AML/CFT capacities, and in 2011, the Agency met 99% of technical assistance needs of signatory states. Thus, where a nexus is established between any of the areas of regional concern and the Agency's globally sustained AML/CFT goals, the Agency can use its resources, including its global network, to address such regional issues.[52]

The experience of GIABA reveals that regional governance exists in a complex web of governance structures where the legitimacy and capacity of other governance structures can be harnessed and enhanced. Regional organizations can define their interests and pursue them by drawing from their environment, the governance order in which they operate. While their role is defined by their environment, they also have the capacity to define that environment.

The Role of Regional Governance Structures in Distributed Administration: A Hypothesis

Despite the somewhat benign picture painted in the preceding sections of the structural elements of the three-level distributed administration employed by

49 Article 6, GIABA Statute. GIABA can release – and has released – FATF press statements on a member state's failure to meet its AML/CFT obligations.

50 The FATF, through its influential membership, can recommend countermeasures against defaulting states so as to restrict the access of such states to the global financial system. See <www.fatf-gafi.org/topics/high-riskandnon-cooperativejurisdictions/more/moreaboutthe internationalco-operationreviewgroupicrg.html>, accessed 19 November 2022.

51 See Aderanti Adepoju, 'Migration in West Africa' (2003) 46 Development 37.

52 GIABA currently provides technical assistance in border control by providing cash machines at member state borders. This is one of the ways through which the Agency has implemented some of the recommendations contained in the typologies. Interview with GIABA official, January 2015.

the FATF, there are important points that can – and should – be raised about possible, and perhaps likely, consequences of this system.

Firstly, in a three-level distributed administration, collective decision-making, through the regional institution, can be used to pursue representation at the core, as has been the case with Nigeria in West Africa. In other words, limited engagement by the regional institution can be used to pursue full engagement by a particular state, and this can be seen as a means of promoting representation of other states within the region. GIABA provides an avenue for Nigeria to engage with the FATF in order to pursue its goal of full membership. Other members of GIABA see Nigeria as an influential regional instrument that can represent their interests at the global level, so they do not object to Nigeria's predominant role in GIABA. When Nigeria becomes a member of the FATF, its responsibility will be not just to its national constituents but also to regional constituents. Thus, this system facilitates cooperation at the regional level in order to advance representation at the global level.

Secondly, the arousal of interests at the global and national levels can lead to the establishment of new institutions for the diffusion of norms and standards. The reason behind the three-level administration is to place obligations on states without their actual participation in the process of defining and imposing obligations. Regional institutions can serve as a means of universalizing the interests of particular actors and placing obligations on third-party states through the interplay of power and proximity.[53] The use of regional institutions as middlemen can create an illusion not just of engagement but of consent.

Thirdly, the regional institution established to satisfy all these interests is usually the agent of at least two principals, one single principal at the global level and several collective principals at the national level. Where this institution is part of an already existing regional organization, as is the case with ECOWAS and GIABA, then we have a third single principal at the regional level. This means that the agent is expected to protect the interests of all these principals while acting within the confines of technical and political rules and institutions that serve as mechanisms of control. In the case of GIABA, the interests of all principals seem to be significantly aligned, but this is not an automatic occurrence. The goals of different principals might be misaligned, in which case, the agent would have to act based on its own preference. One example would be an instance where GIABA is forced to impose institutional obligations on a state that is overburdened with national and international

53 The power of the global institution is used to jump-start the power of a regional hegemon or other political actor who can, by reason of its geopolitical relationship with other states, facilitate global interests. However, in order for this to happen, the regional hegemon must have some interest that the global institution is able to address.

obligations and thus lacks the capacity to take on new obligations.[54] This would reveal a conflict between diffusion and contextualization, a situation that can be said to already exist in West Africa. So far, GIABA has consistently upheld global interests in a way that does not raise these questions, again implying some sort of absolute universalism in the global mission. While this might seem like an effective way to promote global standards, it can undermine the actual effectiveness of their implementation.[55]

Finally, agents have interests and preferences, and the regional middleman in the three-level distributed administration is no different. Therefore, it can use the influence and resources of its principals to pursue goals at different levels. This can facilitate contextualization, which can be done though the diversion of the resources of one principal to meet the goals of the agent or of other principals. In the case of GIABA, contextualization is not only positive; it is encouraged by both global and regional actors. However, it would require extra means of control by the principals to ensure that the agent does not undermine their interests. For instance, with the FATF, rules regarding non-derogation from the FATF Recommendations are meant to check contextualization. Nevertheless, real principal-agent problems exist and contextualization and diversion might undermine the goals and objectives of some or all the principals, depending on the circumstance.[56]

Concluding Reflections and Issues for Further Study

Before now, there has not been a comprehensive study of GIABA and the role it plays as a regional regulatory institution. This chapter has shown that GIABA – and other FSRBs – are poised to contribute to the global system of standard setting in AML/CFT while also serving as facilitators of standards diffusion and implementation. GIABA has pursued these objectives at different levels. It has also used its role as regional middleman to address regional issues that are peculiar to West Africa but absent from global regulatory concerns. The Agency constitutes a rather effective means of addressing such issues because it has the backing of a global regulatory system with the

54 On the nature and effect of obligation overload, Kevin Davis and Benedict Kingsbury explain that developing countries take on more external obligations than they can handle thus creating added strains to their already limited governance capacities. ***Obligation Overload: Adjusting the Obligations of Fragile or Failed States*** (unpublished paper, on file with author).

55 Contextualization, rather than universalism, can serve as a means of effective implementation, so that the focus is the achievement of goals rather than their widespread proclamation. See Daniel Barstow Magraw, 'Legal Treatment of Developing Countries: Differential, Contextual and Absolute Norms' (1990) 1 Colorado Journal of International Environmental Law and Policy 69.

56 See Andrew Cortell and Susan Peterson, 'Dutiful Agents, Rogue Actors or Both? Staffing, Voting Rules and Slack in the WHO and the WTO' in *Delegation and Agency in International Organizations 255* (Darren G Hawkins, ed. 2006).

resources to pass potent sanctions. In the same vein, it lends legitimacy to this global system which runs the risk of being regarded as a regime to "promote the objectives of dominant states and economic actors".[57] GIABA is thus an instrument to promote global, regional, and (some) national interests. So far, there has been no conflict between the interests it protects and promotes. The preceding analysis of the institutional structure of GIABA shows that there are opportunities for greater participation and accountability in the framework of the Agency, especially relating to its involvement with smaller states, non-signatory states, and private actors.

57 Richard Stewart, 'Remedying Disregard in Global Regulatory Governance: Accountability, Participation and Responsiveness' (2014) 108 AJIL 211.

4 Do Things Fall Apart? (Black) listing and Its Implications for Developing Countries

Nkechikwu Valerie Azinge-Egbiri, Joy Malala and Donato Masciandaro

Introduction

Extant literature critiques the legitimacy of the Financial Action Task Force (FATF)'s listing. Scholars contend that the FATF listing process is political,[1] biased against Global South countries,[2] and consequently, inconsistent in its outcomes.[3] This chapter contributes to this body of literature by utilising new data sets that demonstrate the inconsistencies of the FATF's listing outcomes. Employing a numerical aggregation of the FATF's assessment ratings of countries from 2010 to 2023, our research displays significant non-conformity with the FATF's listing requirements and raises questions about the technocratic basis of the FATF's listing.

The FATF's listing tool is a 'naming and shaming' strategy, adopted to combat money laundering and terrorist financing (ML/TF). The FATF evaluates countries to determine their extent of compliance and effectiveness with its global anti-money laundering and counter-terrorist financing (AML/CFT). Presumably, countries that fall short on compliance and effectiveness are listed to 'shame' them towards compliance by undermining their reputation and international status.[4] Naming and shaming tactics operate on the principle that making misconduct public and associating it with negative consequences deters others from engaging in similar behaviour. This is underpinned by the reputational cost theory, which at its core suggests that the inherent value

1 Nasir Sultan, Norazida Mohamed, Jamaliah Said and Azroz Mohd, 'The Sustainability of the International AML Regime and the Role of the FATF. The Objectivity of the Greylisting Process of Developing Jurisdictions like Pakistan' (2023) 27 JMLC 76–92; Guy Stessens, 'The FATF "Black List" of Non-Cooperative Countries or Territories' (2004) 14 (1) LJIL 199–207.

2 Nasir Sultan, Norazida Mohamed, Jamaliah Said and Azroz Mohd, 'The Sustainability of the International AML Regime and the Role of the FATF. The Objectivity of the Greylisting Process of Developing Jurisdictions like Pakistan' (2023) 27 JMLC 76–92; Guy Stessens, 'The FATF "Black List" of Non-Cooperative Countries or Territories' (2004) 14 (1) LJIL 199–207.

3 Katherine Long, 'Data Dive: FATF's Greylisting, Benchmarked' (*Vixio*, 5 July 2023) <www.vixio.com/insights/pc-data-dive-fatfs-greylisting-benchmarked> accessed 4 March 2024.

4 Jack Snyder, 'Backlash against Naming and Shaming: The Politics of Status and Emotion' (2020) 22(4) The British Journal of Politics and International Relations 644–53.

DOI: 10.4324/9781003253808-5

attached to a State's reputation is paramount and therefore the threat of public exposure serves as a potent deterrent against compliance.[5] Morse aligns with this theory, arguing that the FATF's listing is a powerful instrument that exerts market pressure to drive policy change within non-compliant countries.[6] Listed countries are assumed to suffer some ills as their non-listed counterparts restrict capital flows to them or delist their financial institutions. Given the assumed impact of listing, it is critical that the listing process is objective and expert based.

Several academics have argued that the FATF listing is expertise based and free from politics or bias. For instance, Morse contends that the FATF lists are drawn by an organisation that is highly technocratic and apolitical.[7] Earlier studies by Hülsse and Kerwer present the viewpoint that the FATF's listing is based on expert-led objective exercises.[8] Their postulations find credence in the FATF's 2003 report, which espoused the institution's focus on 'openness, fairness and objectivity' in the listing process and outcome.[9] These perspectives project a legitimate and non-arbitrary listing process that represents an objective assessment by neutral experts. As such, the scholars promote a hegemonic viewpoint of the FATF's infallibility.

Yet, extant literature and empirical data show significant inconsistencies between the evaluation reports and the listed countries. Riccardi[10] and Halliday et al.[11] argue that the FATF's evaluation ratings have room for subjectivity and are based on rationales that are difficult to understand. Furthermore, the link between the ratings and the lists are not clear-cut, as countries blacklisted in 2021 were never evaluated.[12] Even amongst evaluated countries, disparities existed amongst those with low ratings – as while some were listed, others were not.[13] Van Duyne et al. attribute these discrepancies to the unclear listing process, which is plagued with secrecy notwithstanding the potential harm it

5 Rachel Brewster, 'The Limits of Reputation on Compliance' (2009) 1(2) International Theory 323–33.

6 Julia Morse, 'Blacklists, Market Enforcement, and the Global Regime to Combat Terrorist Financing' (2019) 73(3) International Organization 511–45.

7 Julia Morse, 'Blacklists, Market Enforcement, and the Global Regime to Combat Terrorist Financing' (2019) 73(3) International Organization 511–45.

8 Dieter Kerwer and Rainer Hülsse, 'How International Organizations Rule the World: The Case of the Financial Action Task Force on Money Laundering' (2011) 2 Journal of International Organization Students 50, 53.

9 FATF, 'Financial Action Task Force, Annual Report 2003–2004' (*FATF*, 2 July 2004) <www.fatf-gafi.org/content/dam/fatf-gafi/annual-reports/2003%202004%20ENG.pdf> accessed 4 March 2024.

10 Michele Riccardi, *Money Laundering Blacklists* (Routledge 2022) 48.

11 Terence Halliday, Michael Levi and Peter Reuter, 'Anti-Money Laundering: An Inquiry into a Disciplinary Transnational Legal Order' 4 (1) UC Irvine Journal of International Transnational, and Comparative Law <https://scholarship.law.uci.edu/ucijil/vol4/iss1/3/> accessed 4 March 2024.

12 Riccardi (n 10) 51.

13 Riccardi (n 10) 48–52.

poses to countries.[14] Contrary to the FATF's contention on the openness of the listing process, van Duyne et al. contend that the volume of documents coupled with the depth of expertise required to address the evaluation questions significantly undermine the assessment process and its ability to generate objective listing.[15] This is because the questions are multidisciplinary and would require 'an almost utopian criminological and statistical sophistication and insight' on the state of affairs. As such, the reports that inform the listings rarely reflect accurate information, reliable statistics, and accessible databases.[16]

Global South countries bear the brunt of the FATF's listing inconsistencies. In comparison to developed countries, developing countries are more likely to be listed.[17] Sultan et al.'s qualitative study attributes this to assessor's pre-existing perceptions of developing countries and the political agenda of key actors (international institutions and the United States).[18] Global South countries are usually unable to exculpate themselves from the lists, as they are commonly carpeted and rendered voiceless at the plenary meetings reserved for them to raise issues concerning the ratings attributed to them. Rather, these meetings have remained an echo chamber for FATF members, who rarely change ratings allotted to developing countries.[19] Consequently, van Duyne et al. compare the FATF's listing approach to the indirect colonial rule approach used by the colonial powers of Great Britain and France.[20] These colonisers utilised local princes to engineer compliance, knowing that subjects would comply, in the knowledge that the imperial gunboat (blacklist) is near.[21] Arguably, these disputes demonstrated that underneath the surface of the listing process lies a complex interplay of power dynamics and differentials, reinforcing and at times exacerbating the existing inequality in its application,[22] and often leading to a rhetorical response.[23]

14 Petrus C van Duyne, Jackie H Harvey and Liliya Y Gelemerova, 'Learning More About the FATF: Knowing the Tree by its Fruits' in Petrus C van Duyne et al. (eds), *The Critical Handbook of Money Laundering, Policy, Analysis and Myths* (Palgrave Macmillan 2018) 141.

15 Petrus C van Duyne, Jackie H Harvey and Liliya Y Gelemerova, 'Learning More About the FATF: Knowing the Tree by its Fruits' in Petrus C van Duyne et al. (eds), *The Critical Handbook of Money Laundering, Policy, Analysis and Myths* (Palgrave Macmillan 2018)

16 Petrus C van Duyne, Jackie H Harvey and Liliya Y Gelemerova, 'Learning More About the FATF: Knowing the Tree by its Fruits' in Petrus C van Duyne et al. (eds), *The Critical Handbook of Money Laundering, Policy, Analysis and Myths* (Palgrave Macmillan 2018) 129.

17 Riccardi (n 10) 54–55.
Halliday, Levi and Reuter (n 11).

18 Sultan, Mohamed, Said and Mohd (n 1) 76–92.

19 Petrus C van Duyne (n 14) 141.

20 Petrus C van Duyne (n 14).

21 Petrus C van Duyne (n 14) 160.

22 Kishanthi Parella, 'Reputational Regulation' (2018) 67 Duke Law Journal 907; Keith A Petty, 'Beyond the Court of Public Opinion: Military Commissions and the Reputational Pull of Compliance Theory' (2011) 42 Georgetown Journal of International Law 1–54.

23 Brigitte Unger and Joras Ferwerda, 'Regulating Money Laundering and Tax Havens: The Role of Blacklisting' (2008) 8(12) <www.uu.nl/sites/default/files/rebo_use_dp_2008_08-12.pdf>

One may ask if the FATF listing can be biased yet objective. Can these contradictory perspectives be reconciled? Our empirical study cannot answer this question affirmatively. Rather, it contributes to existing literature by further exposing the listing's biases against developing countries, and arguing that these countries do not necessarily respond by amplifying their compliance – demonstrating a stigma paradox. Hence, our chapter postulates that the geographical concentration of the FATF listing illustrates that the instrument can be political and open to lobbying, and as such, is a grave political error with inherent contradictory consequences.

Our arguments are set out in four parts. The first part examines the concept of the FATF's listing as a tool for mandating AML/CFT compliance. Drawing on Katherine Long's data[24] on the FATF's listing inconsistencies, the second part will probe the listing biases against developing countries. The third part demonstrates that countries do not always respond to stigma by improving their compliance; rather, a stigma paradox may occur, when countries respond creatively in a way that challenges the tool's effectiveness. We conclude the chapter by emphasising prospective strategies for mitigating this bias.

The Financial Action Task Force (FATF) and Its Listing Tool

Established in 1989, the FATF is the foremost transgovernmental network responsible for issuing AML/CFT recommendations. Studies have shown that criminals take advantage of discrepancies in rules and arrangements across jurisdictions.[25] Hence, the FATF's recommendations have been targeted at harmonising countries' laws and arrangements, to hinder launderers from exploiting countries with weaker legal frameworks. Like other transgovernmental networks, such as the Basel Committee on Banking Supervision and the International Association of Insurance Supervisors,[26] the FATF is informal and lacks the legal authority or instrument to impose sanctions to prevent or combat ML/TF.[27] Rather, countries are only urged to adopt preventative measures that include legislative or regulatory changes.

accessed 4 March 2024; Gregory Rawlings, 'Taxes and Transnational Treaties: Responsive Regulation and the Reassertion of Offshore Sovereignty' (2007) 29(1) Law and Policy 51–66.

24 Long (n 3). We recognize, however, the challenges with Long's data, which includes its limited attention to the FATF's blacklisting requirements, and its failure to recognise the disproportionate weight given to each FATF recommendations in determine whether a country is listed.

25 Morse (n 6) 517.

26 Anne-Marie Slaughter, 'Governing the Global Economy through Government Networks' (*Carnegie Endowment for International Peace*, 23 May 2000) <https://carnegieendowment.org/2000/05/23/governing-global-economy-through-government-networks-event-164> accessed 3 March 2024.

27 Olga Balakina, Angelo D'Andrea and Donato Masciandaro, 'Bank Secrecy in Offshore Centres and Capital Flows: Does Blacklisting Matter?' 32 Review of Financial Economics 30–57; Doron Goldbarsht and Hannah Harris, 'Transnational Regulatory Networks: A Study in Compliance and Legitimacy in Counter-Terrorist Financing' 27 (3) Journal of Financial Crime <www.emerald.com/insight/content/doi/10.1108/JFC-01-2020-0013/full/html> accessed 2 March 2024.

To circumvent its informality challenge, the FATF has continually drawn support from powerful organisations, including the International Monetary Fund (IMF), the World Bank, and the European Union, amongst others. Such relationships allow the institution to compel countries to comply through listing, which assumably produces a stigma effect that puts listed countries under an intense pressure to comply.[28] However, the FATF has camouflaged its pressure on countries to comply by prefixing its recommendations with 'should'[29] – which is usually interpreted as 'may', and hence regarded as a suggestion. A closer examination of the FATF general glossary emphasises that 'should' and 'must' have the same meaning.[30] As such, the FATF recommendations are *mandatory* requirements.[31] By implication, when countries fall short on compliance with FATF standards, the institution can publicly list them. Countries are usually placed on the FATF blacklist or greylist. The blacklist is concerned with countries with significant AML/CFT failings, yet they are not actively engaging with the FATF to address deficiencies. With such countries, the FATF calls *on other countries to apply enhanced due diligence and countermeasures* in their dealings with them. The greylist is concerned with countries under increased monitoring that are actively working to address their highlighted deficiencies.

The FATF's adoption of the listing strategy is not novel, as other global institutions, albeit with varied levels of success, have used the naming and shaming strategy to combat issues such as tax governance,[32] air safety benchmarks, bank secrecy standards,[33] public sector corruption, and fraud.[34] The

28 Donato Masciandaro, 'Bank Secrecy in Offshore Centres, Capital Flows and Blacklisting: It Takes Two to Tango' (*SUERF Policy Note*, 19 May 2016) <www.suerf.org/policynotes/587/bank-secrecy-in-offshore-centres-capital-flows-and-blacklisting-it-takes-two-to-tango> accessed 3 March 2024.

29 FATF, 'The FATF Recommendations' (November 2023) <www.fatf-gafi.org/content/dam/fatf-gafi/recommendations/FATF%20Recommendations%202012.pdf.coredownload.inline.pdf> accessed 1 March 2024.

30 FATF, 'The FATF Recommendations' (November 2023) <www.fatf-gafi.org/content/dam/fatf-gafi/recommendations/FATF%20Recommendations%202012.pdf.coredownload.inline.pdf> accessed 1 March 2024.

31 John Hatchard, *Combating Money Laundering in Africa: Dealing with the Problem of PEPs* (Edward Elgar 2020) 57–58.

32 Katrin Eggenberger, 'When is Blacklisting Effective? Stigma, Sanctions and Legitimacy: The Reputational and Financial Costs of Being Blacklisted' 25 (4) Review of International Political Economy 483, 486.

33 Katrin Eggenberger, 'When Is Blacklisting Effective? Stigma, Sanctions and Legitimacy: The Reputational and Financial Costs of Being Blacklisted' 25 (4) Review of International Political Economy 483, 486. Many institutions use blacklisting to mandate compliance. For instance, Consolidated United Nations Security Council Sanctions List, the OECD and Transparency International amongst others have some form of public listings embedded in them.

34 Transparency International, 'Corruption Perception Index' (*Transparency International*, 2024) <www.transparency.org/en/cpi/2022> accessed 1 March 2024; The World Bank, 'Procurement – World Bank Listing of Ineligible Firms and Individuals' (The World Bank) <www.worldbank.org/en/projects-operations/procurement/debarred-firms> accessed 1 March 2024.

rationale for public listing is that the subjection of non-compliant entities to reputational damage with financial implications will for them supersede the benefits from non-compliance.[35] Additionally, shaming and listing acts as a low-cost enforcement tool. In some ways it is effective, because reputations are a valuable asset, and the widespread use of the public listing tool and its seeming accomplishments led to its adoption by the FATF.

To determine which countries to publicly list, the FATF conducts assessments to ascertain whether a country has poor AML/CFT compliance and effectiveness levels. Assessments are done periodically[36] in collaboration with the FATF's observer institutions (IMF and World Bank) or by regional bodies.[37] At each assessment, assessors rate each country's compliance level against each recommendation based on a scale: compliant, largely compliant, partially compliant, non-compliant, or not applicable. Countries may contest their eventual ratings at the FATF's plenary meetings; however, upgraded ratings are rare, as all member countries must agree to such changes.[38]

Countries' eventual compliance ratings culminate in a mutual evaluation report (MER). The MER (which also documents each countries' AML/CFT measures at the assessment period, alongside suggestions for improved compliance) is published and widely circulated.[39] When the MER documents significant deficiencies, the country concerned will usually be referred for review. Where such failings are unremedied within a year, the country will be grey-listed. Should the country fail to cooperate with the FATF, or adequately address a designated action plan, that country would slip into the blacklist.

The postulated implications of listing are dire. Researchers argue that, while listing is not synonymous with sanctions, the countermeasures have a similar effect.[40] For instance, financial dealings with listed countries will be carefully scrutinised for anything suspicious, host countries may reject subsidiary establishments,[41] and international organisations' outlook on the country or its credit lines may be altered or halted. As such, capital flows to the affected jurisdictions will significantly drop, and their competitive advantages will be eroded.[42]

35 Transparency International, 'Corruption Perception Index' (Transparency International, 2024) <www.transparency.org/en/cpi/2022> accessed 1 March 2024; The World Bank, 'Procurement – World Bank Listing of Ineligible Firms and Individuals' (The World Bank) <www.worldbank.org/en/projects-operations/procurement/debarred-firms> accessed 1 March 2024.

36 Every 4–5 years.

37 International Monetary Fund, 'Financial Sector Assessment Program (FSAP)' (IMF 2022) <www.imf.org/en/Publications/fssa> accessed 3 March 2024.

38 Morse (n 6) 517.

39 Goldbarsht and Harris (n 27) 861, 855.

40 Goldbarsht and Harris (n 27) 862.

41 Goldbarsht and Harris (n 27) 862; FATF Recommendation 19 calls on financial institutions to apply EDD measures to business relationships and transactions with natural and legal persons, and financial institutions; generally the FATF cautions other countries to ensure due diligence and increased countermeasures when relating with countries on the blacklist; this would most times lead to an increase in the cost of transnational business, and in extreme cases, economic ties are severed altogether.

42 Masciandaro (n 28).

Such actions are perhaps warranted, because transactions with blacklisted countries can occasion adjourning reputational effects. As such, scholars contend that the potential damage caused by the stigma effect has led international banks to avoid businesses with blacklisted countries.[43] Beyond banks, a much wider audience depends on the FATF blacklists to determine their interactions with countries based on integrity: market actors, governments, and even international institutions. To avert the risks of severe economic hardships, listed countries are urged to adopt measures to remove their detrimental rules and practices.[44]

Given the potential consequences of being listed for a country, one would assume that the factors that determine listing would be transparent. According to the International Co-operation Review Group (ICRG), which reviews the listing process,[45] countries are listed because they are adjudged to fail on some critical recommendations. These include the big six recommendations concerning (1) adequate criminalisation of money laundering and (2) terrorist financing, (3) implementation of targeted financial sanctions, (4) robust measures for customer due diligence and (5) record keeping, and (6) reporting suspicious transactions.[46]

Arguably, these recommendations are prioritised, as they serve as the building blocks upon which other recommendations rest. For instance, where a country is failing on recommendations (3) or (4) regarding robust criminalisation of ML/TF, the country's resulting AML/CFT structures and measures would be inadequate to combat financial crime. Furthermore, countries may also be listed where they are adjudged to be non-compliant or partially compliant to at least 20 recommendations.[47] Considerations for listing also includes an assessment of the country's effectiveness levels; where countries falter on these, there are repercussions.[48] Wider factors are also considered in listing countries: for instance, a country's engagement with the FATF or its regional bodies; the ML/TF threats perceived by the assessor; and the size of the country's financial sector. Countries with larger economies are assumed to pose more financial crime risks.[49] Once considered eligible for listing, countries have a 12-month period to engage with the FATF, or risk being listed.[50]

The challenge with the listing outcome is the geographical concentration of countries, which raises questions of bias. An examination of the lists from 2016 demonstrates African and Middle Eastern countries are more likely to be

43 Masciandaro (n 28).

44 Goldbarsht and Harris (n 39) 861.

45 FATF, 'High-Risk and Other Monitored Jurisdictions' (*FATF*, 2024) <www.fatf-gafi.org/en/publications/High-risk-and-other-monitored-jurisdictions/More-on-high-risk-and-non-cooperative-jurisdictions.html> accessed 5 March 2024.

46 FATF, 'High-Risk and Other Monitored Jurisdictions' (FATF, 2024) <www.fatf-gafi.org/en/publications/High-risk-and-other-monitored-jurisdictions/More-on-high-risk-and-non-cooperative-jurisdictions.html> accessed 5 March 2024; Masciandaro (n 28).

47 FATF (n 45).

48 FATF (n 45). So where a country has low or moderate level of effectiveness for 9 or more of the 11 immediate outcomes, with a minimum of two lows; or it has a low level of effectiveness for 6 or more of the 11 immediate outcomes.

49 FATF (n 45).

50 Morse (n 6) 512.

listed. Moreso, the distinctions between the black and the greylists also bear no weight on actual listing impact, due to the way the lists are communicated to the market.[51] However, these challenges are not new; they have plagued the FATF from the inception of its listing process in 2000, when the FATF introduced the Non-Cooperative Countries and Territories (NCCT) listing process, a predecessor of the ICRG review procedure that determined the listed countries. The listing process was centred on countries' technical compliance; the key aim was public shaming for countries that failed to implement and comply with FATF standards.

However, the IMF and the World Bank – the FATF's observers, from which it draws its legitimacy – were strongly critical of the FATF's initial blacklisting process.[52] Arguments abounded that the blacklists contravened the AML/CFT regime of voluntary participation and non-binding rules.[53] Furthermore, scholars contended that the instrument threatened sovereignty norms, due to the financial exclusion effect, and the double standard, as mainly non-member states were listed.[54] Other arguments centred on the seeming arbitrariness of the lists. For instance, Rawlings and Sharman contended that 'the methodologies used to compile the blacklists [were] opaque and [did not] follow any formal procedure'.[55] The informality persisted, irrespective of numerous documentations

51 Louis de Koker, John Howell and Nicholas Morris, 'Economic Consequences of Greylisting by the Financial Action Task Force' (*MDPI, Risks*, 25 April 2023) <www.mdpi.com/2227-9091/11/5/81> accessed 10 February 2024; Mizuho Kida and Simon Paetzold, 'The Impact of Gray-Listing on Capital Flows: An Analysis Using Machine Learning' (IMF Working Paper, May 2021) <www.google.com/url?sa=t&rct=j&q=&esrc=s&source=web&cd=&ved=2ahUKEwiH-t3DuM6CAxV8_7sIHUunBxYQFnoECA4QAw&url=https%3A%2F%2Fwww.imf.org%2F-%2Fmedia%2FFiles%2FPublications%2FWP%2F2021%2FEnglish%2Fwpiea2021153-print-pdf.ashx%23%3A~%3Atext%3DFor%2520empirical%2520execution%252C%2520we%2520use%2Cthe%2520country%2520is%2520gray%252Dlisted.&usg=AOvVaw1SveDYsPfMdc_Dnm1E0sYk&opi=89978449> accessed 14 February 2024.

52 MT Nance, 'The Regime That FATF Built: An Introduction to the Financial Action Task Force' (2018) 69(2) Crime, Law and Social Change 109–29.

53 T Doyle, 'Cleaning Up Anti-Money Laundering Strategies: Current FATF Tactics Needlessly Violate International Law' (2002) 24(2) Houston Journal of International Law 279, 298.

54 Jason Sharman, 'International Organization and Implementation by Blacklisting' (Paper presented at ISA Annual Convention, Chicago, 28 February–3 March 2007); P Reuter and EM Truman, *Chasing Dirty Money: Progress on Anti-Money Laundering* (Institute for International Economics 2004) 165–70; M Levi, 'Money Laundering and its Regulation' (2002) 582 Annals of the American Academy of Political Social Science 181, 182; V Mitsilegas, 'Countering the Chameleon Threat of Dirty Money: Hard and Soft Law in the Emergence of a Global Regime against Money Laundering and Terrorist Finance' in A Edwards and P Gill (eds), *Transnational Organised Crime: Perspectives on Global Security* (Routledge 2004); Kathrin Daepp, 'Le Regulation Selective de la Finance Internationale: L' Initiative Sur Les Pays Ou Territoires Non Cooperatifs du GAFI' Universite De Lausanne. Travaux De Science Politique (2006) Political Science Working Paper Series <www.unil.ch/iephi/files/live/sites/iephi/files/publications/TSP/28DaeppTSP.pdf> accessed 6 May 2015.

55 J Sharman and G Rawlings, 'National Tax Blacklists: A Comparative Analysis' (2006) 17(9) Journal of International Taxation 38–47; Unger and Ferwerda (n 23); C Tjalling, Koopmas Research Institute, Discussion Paper Series no. 08–12 <https://dspace.library.uu.nl/handle/1874/309681> accessed 15 February 2024.

on the FATF's listing criteria.[56] Additionally, findings show that the FATF originally determined listed countries by asking member countries for lists of suspected countries.[57] In essence, the listing was dependent on the subjective feeling of 'suspiciousness', rather than actual AML/CFT deficiencies – a challenge that occasioned its failure.[58] As a result, the 45 countries monitored for listing between June 2000 and February 2004 represented 8% of the global GDP, 15% of the total population, and 25% of foreign bank deposits in the world.[59] Unsurprisingly, those eventually listed were predominantly African and Middle Eastern countries, particularly repeat offenders like Myanmar, Nigeria, the Philippines, Indonesia, and Nauru. European countries were either not listed or increasingly de-listed, probably due to the need for stronger trade affiliations.[60]

In 2006, the blacklisting process was abolished, though the reasoning behind its abolishment was questioned. Sharman argues that it was eliminated because it had achieved its objective.[61] However, this argument is found wanting, as at the time of the elimination, the FATF's evaluation process was ongoing.[62] Additionally, countries that underwent the assessment process did not achieve full compliance on many ratings. Moreso, the process could not have achieved its objective – given that it was reintroduced in 2009,[63] and replaced by the ICRG alongside its regional review groups. Arguably, the consistent redesign of the FATF listing process demonstrates its underlying challenges that members were struggling to resolve.

Over time the FATF listings have evolved. For instance, following its reintroduction, the FATF list had three categories: the blacklists, the dark greylists and the light greylists. The blacklist included countries that had significant compliance challenges that occasioned the FATF to call on other jurisdictions to apply countermeasures. The dark greylist included countries that had significant deficiencies, yet no commitment to an action plan to address these – hence, the FATF called on countries to consider the risks arising from

56 J Sharman and G Rawlings, 'National Tax Blacklists: A Comparative Analysis' (2006) 17(9) Journal of International Taxation 38–47; Unger and Ferwerda (n 23); C Tjalling, Koopmas Research Institute, Discussion Paper Series no. 08 -12 <https://dspace.library.uu.nl/handle/1874/309681> accessed 15 February 2024.

57 J Sharman and G Rawlings, 'National Tax Blacklists: A Comparative Analysis' (2006) 17(9) Journal of International Taxation 38–47; Unger and Ferwerda (n 23); C Tjalling, Koopmas Research Institute, Discussion Paper Series no. 08–12 <https://dspace.library.uu.nl/handle/1874/309681> accessed 15 February 2024.

58 Unger and Ferwerda (n 23).

59 Donato Masciandaro, 'Money Laundering: The Economics of Regulation' (1999) 7 European Journal of Law and Economics 225–40.

60 Unger and Ferwerda (n 23).

61 Jason Sharman, *Havens in a Storm: The Struggle for Global Tax Regulation* (Cornell University Press 2006). Sharman argues that the removal of this process came head on with its rebuttal by the IFIs with whom the FATF sought partnership due to resource constraints, as it was against the nature of the fund's seemingly voluntary agenda.

62 Rainer Hülsse, 'Even Clubs Can't Do without Legitimacy: Why the Anti-Money Laundering Blacklist was Suspended' (2008) 2(4) Regulation and Governance <https://onlinelibrary.wiley.com/doi/full/10.1111/j.1748-5991.2008.00046.x> accessed 4 March 2024.

63 Morse (n 6) 518.

the identified deficiencies. Lastly, the light greylist included countries that had AML/CFT deficiencies but had an action plan of political commitment to address the identified deficiencies.[64]

However, from 2016, the light greylist was subsumed under the greylist, as the FATF noted that there was no call for countermeasures or enhanced due diligence to be applied against these jurisdictions; rather countries were enjoined to take the risks presented into account. Similar deficiencies exist with the updated lists, African and Middle Eastern countries are more likely to be listed. Furthermore, irrespective of the list where countries are placed, the implications are not radically different due to the way the lists are interpreted by the market.[65]

The listing biases are illuminated by our historicisation of the listing tool, which demonstrates the structural holdovers that layer onto the contemporary processes, highlighting the legitimacy challenges. The structural holdovers stem from what Nance says about the FATF's influence, which is that it reflects the power distribution among States, as well as sensitive assumptions about States' preferences. Drezner also asserts that the US and EU 'were able to cajole, coerce, and enforce a global anti-money-laundering standard into existence'.[66] As a result, the FATF framework is a 'powerful tool of global financial regulation that confirms states' continued dominance in a globalizing economy'.[67]

Who Is Listed: A Bias Against Developing Countries?

The FATF's listing methodology presents the illusion that its benchmark is sacrosanct, since it highlights the best practice attainable by countries. Hence, many developing countries strive to address salient points to avoid being publicly listed – and still, they fail. Far from being infallible, the listing process is fraught with legitimacy challenges, which undermines its ability to achieve its intended aim.

An examination of the composition and density of greylists unearths discrepancies between the MERs and the countries listed.[68] In Figure 4.1, we examine Katherine Long's data which detailed the technical and effectiveness compliance of the lowest scoring assessed countries from 2010 to 2023. The data demonstrates that although some countries recorded low technical compliance, they were never listed. Some countries, particularly Tonga, attained critically low technical compliance of 37 of 153 but have never been listed.[69] Yet Uganda, Senegal, and Nigeria (with scores of 70, 74, and 77, respectively) have been listed despite noted improvements. Figure 4.1 highlights other incidences of inconsistencies around the FATF ratings and the eventual listing.

64 de Koker et al. (n 51).
65 de Koker et al. (n 51); Kida and Paetzold (n 51).
66 DW Drezner, *All Politics is Global: Explaining International Regulatory Regimes* (Princeton University Press 2007).
67 Nance (n 52).
68 Riccardi (n 10).
69 Riccardi (n 10). For example, when FATF reviewed Madagascar in 2018, it was given an overall compliance rating of 46 out of 153 and an effectiveness score of 0, which is one of the worst scores the FATF has recorded. The country has made little progress since.

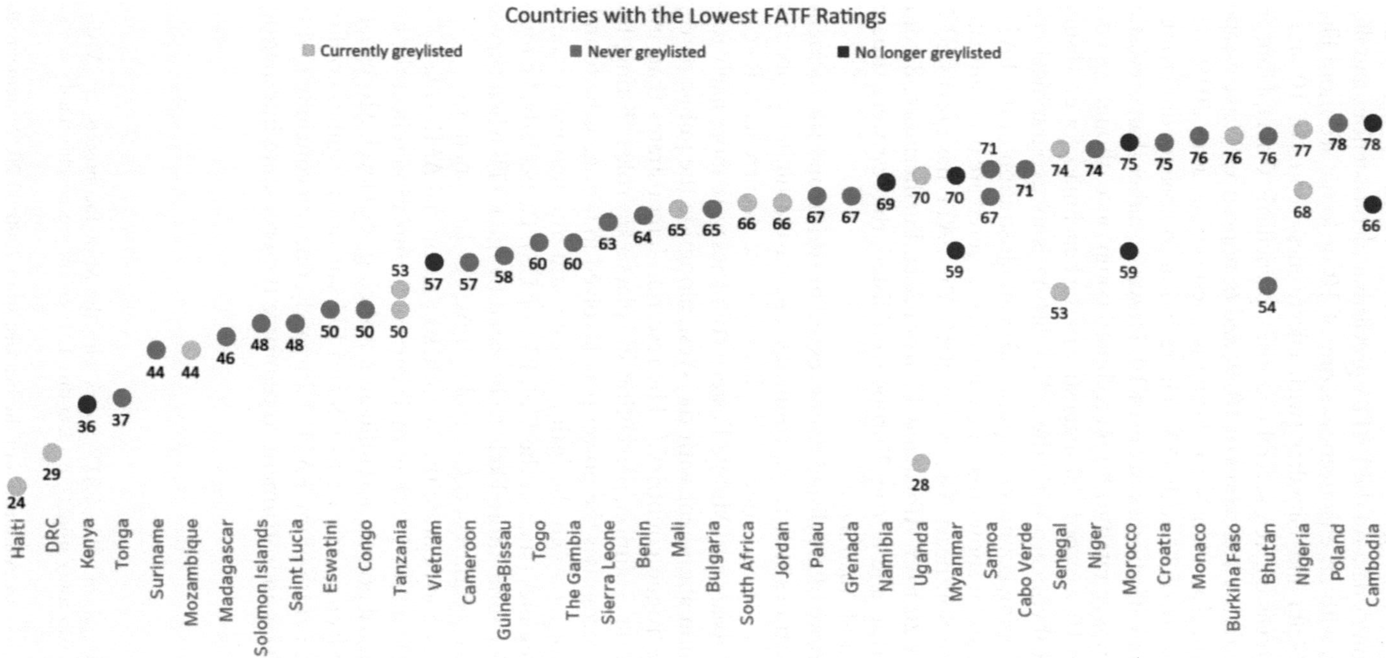

Figure 4.1 Countries with the lowest FATF ratings.[70]

70 Katherine Long, [Graph of] 'Countries with the Lowest FATF Ratings' (*Vixio*, 5 July 2023) <www.vixio.com/insights/pc-data-dive-fatfs-greylisting-benchmarked> accessed 4 March 2024.

As one might expect, irregularities trail the listings based on effectiveness. Figure 4.2 details Long's data on the FATF's greylisting inconsistencies and illustrates that countries with an effectiveness score of 10 or lower are more likely to be greylisted.[71] Malta and Gibraltar (with effectiveness scores of 10 and 9, respectively) were greylisted. Yet, several countries, particularly China, Hungary, and Bulgaria (with effectiveness scores of 10, 9, and 6, respectively) have escaped the greylist.[72] In particular, China's non-listing is questionable, as its 2019 MER recorded an overall score of 73, with 15% of its technical compliance displaying as non-compliant, and an effectiveness score of 10. However, rather than greylisting China, the country was re-rated to 86 on technical compliance, though its effectiveness remained on 10, a record still suggestive of the benchmark for greylisting.

Primarily, a critical concern with the FATF listing is its geographical concentration on developing countries. Figure 4.3 is an illustration of the FATF's greylist since 2010, and it shows that the countries targeted are predominately located in Africa and Southeast Asia. Since 2010, the FATF has greylisted 51 countries, including 20 from Africa and 11 from Asia. Furthermore, 8 countries from the Americas and 8 from Europe were listed; the rest were situated in the Middle East and Australasia.

In sum, the majority of greylisted countries are in Africa, and the incidence of re-listing demonstrates that these countries also have a higher probability of being greylisted more than once.[73] Explaining these occurrences, Riccardi argues that African, Asian, and Middle Eastern countries were more likely to be listed due to their non-alignment with the West, alongside the public perception of them being 'rogue countries'.[74] His research demonstrates that, even with the FATF's listing evolution, perception still plays a key role in listing. Furthermore, Riccardi recognises the power play involved in listing, as he found a significant correlation between the listing process and international organisations' sanctioning regimes (such as the UN, EU, or US). Particularly, he found that countries are five times more likely to be listed by the FATF when they are under the Office of Foreign Assets Control (OFAC) or EU sanctions.

Riccardi's findings corroborate the hypothesis that official AML (black)lists compiled by the EU and the FATF in their current formulation reflect the current balance of political powers and influence at their global level. Moreso, the fact that the public listings related to US and EU sanctions regimes confirms the Western-centric nature of the FATF. Ultimately, one can conclude that the FATF listing process is an instrument to reinforce the prevailing international sanctions regime.

71 Long (n 3).

72 Long (n 3).

73 Katherine Long, [Graph of] 'The FATF Scores with the Most Inconsistencies' (Vixio, 5 July 2023) <www.vixio.com/insights/pc-data-dive-fatfs-greylisting-benchmarked> accessed 4 March 2024.

74 Riccardi (n 10) 54–55. An examination of the blacklist from 2000 till 2022 augments Riccardi's findings. It demonstrates that African, Asia/Pacific and Middle Eastern countries are more likely to be listed than their European and American counterparts.

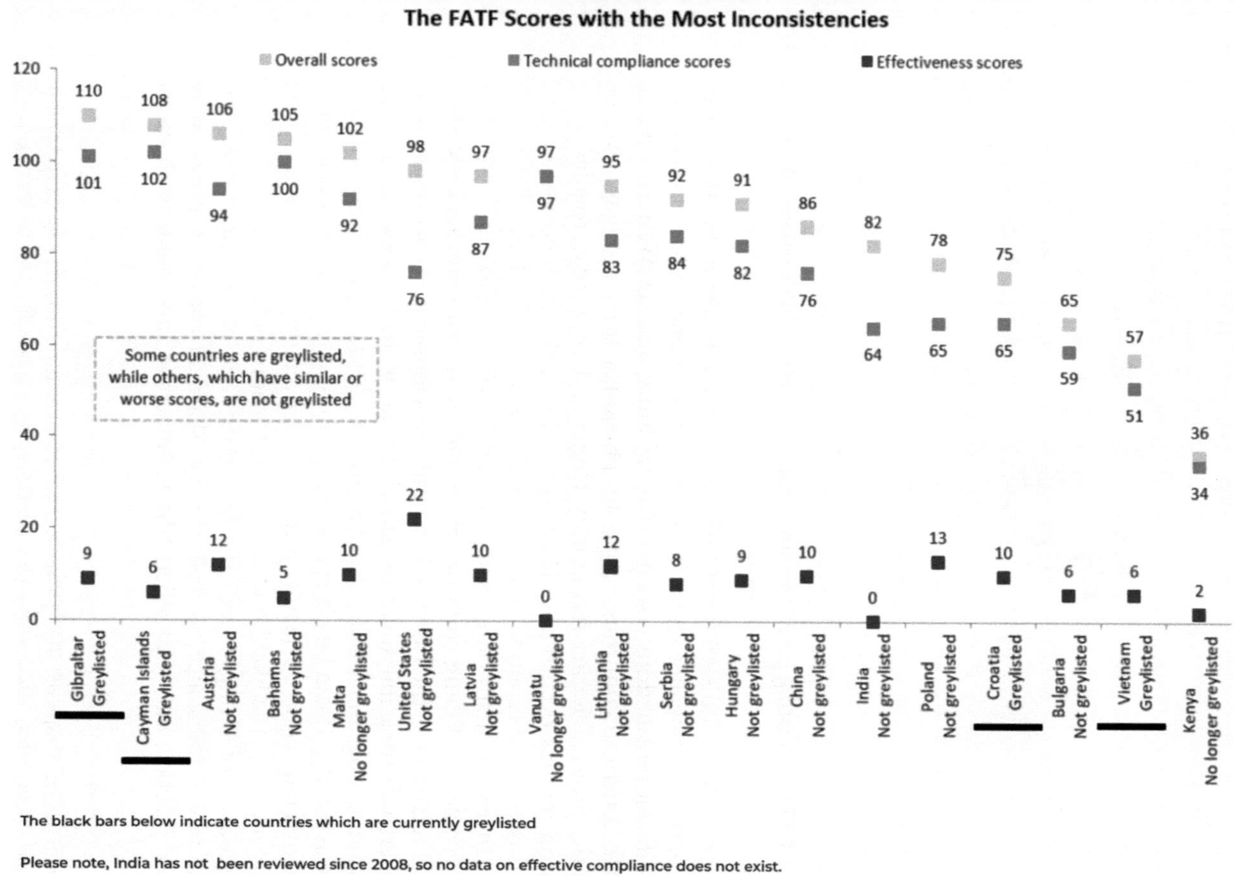

Figure 4.2 The FATF scores with most inconsistencies.[75]

75 Katherine Long, [Graph of] 'The FATF Scores with the Most Inconsistencies' (*Vixio*, 5 July 2023) <www.vixio.com/insights/pc-data-dive-fatfs-greylisting-benchmarked> accessed 4 March 2024

Figure 4.3 FATF greylisting predominantly situated in Africa and Southeast Asia.[76]

In essence, large and significant jurisdictions are unlikely to be listed, irrespective of their compliance and effectiveness scores. Long finds that economically significant jurisdictions – such as China, India, and key Western Europe and North American countries – have not previously been and may never be listed in the future.[77] Earlier research by Unger and Ferwerda provides some explanation for this occurrence. They contend that the high cost associated with halting trade or economic relations with big economies hinders their listing.[78] Furthermore, many developed countries engage in major trading deals as partners, while developing countries are usually of minor importance to their economic relations or their overall economic development. This explains why the Netherlands took initiatives to halt all financial transactions with Nauru following its listing, but would likely fail to take similar steps if, for instance, the US was listed.[79] It can be observed that political economy distortions have a detrimental impact on the listing process. Moreover, the absence of adequate disclosure increases the likelihood of these distortions occurring.

The paradox of listing unveils the bias embedded within the system, reifying the power imbalance, as well as what Sharman considers a process of politicised practice, that contradicts 'the technocratic and apolitical character

76 Katherine Long, [Graph of] 'FATF Greylisting Predominantly Situated in Africa and Southeast Asia' (*Vixio*, 5 July 2023) <www.vixio.com/insights/pc-data-dive-fatfs-greylisting-benchmarked> accessed 4 March 2024.

77 Long (n 3).

78 Unger and Ferwerda (n 23).

79 Balakina, D'Andrea and Masciandaro (n 27).

of the FATF as an expert body'.[80] Considering the ICRG listing requirement, which states that 'more significant financial sectors are prioritised for review',[81] one would expect countries with larger financial sectors or greater ML/TF risks to be listed.

Inversely, an interviewee documented by Azinge-Egbiri noted that 'the ICRG usually list developing countries. Whereas the money flows from these countries are much less than that from developed countries . . . it [the ICRG list] does not represent a totality of the countries not complying'.[82] By implication, this means that developed countries do not fear being listed – a challenge that potentially limits the effect of the lists. As such, this chapter postulates that the FATF threshold for listing is not necessarily geared at capturing narrow deficiencies with significant impact within developed countries. Rather, it seems to be more focused on non-compliance within developing countries, which are less connected with the global economy.

Aside from the possibility of being listed, developing countries are on the blacklist for a longer period than their Western counterparts. In Africa, for example, Nigeria was listed from 2001 to 2005, and then again in 2011 and 2012. Algeria was similarly listed from 2014 to 2015. These blacklisting patterns are even more heinous in the Asia-Pacific region, where Myanmar and North Korea have been blacklisted for 20 and 17 years, respectively. Iran, on the other hand, has been on the list for 15 years. This is in stark contrast to Western countries, which are barely listed despite their stronger ties to the global financial system, and the potentially graver consequences of their apparently 'insignificant' lapses. Western countries on the list, including Russia, Ukraine, Turkey, and Liechtenstein, stayed on the list for an average of two years. The rationale behind the variations in listing duration should be more explicitly and convincingly justified, to refute suspicion that political and economic factors hold greater significance than technical concerns.

The potential inconsistencies in the listing outcomes, as well as the bias against developing countries, suggest a significant disconnect between the FATF's assessment reports and listing. Perhaps one may construe the data irregularities as a contest to Morse's argument on the minimalised politics in the FATF listing process, as she argues that politics is secondary in the FATF's listing processes.[83]

However, the data findings give room for alternative interpretations for the reasoning behind the listing. We hypothesise that the public listing can be

80 Jason Sharman, 'International Organizations, Blacklisting and Tax Haven Regulation' (Paper presented at European Consortium of Political Research Joint Sessions, Uppsala, 13–18 April 2004).

81 For instance, USD 5 billion or more.

82 EENA4, Interview with Anonymous, 'Telephone Call' (2017) in Nkechikwu Azinge-Egbiri, *Regulating and Combating Money Laundering and Terrorist Financing: The Law in Emerging Economies* (Routledge 2022).

83 Morse (n 6) 518.

political and open to lobbying, based on the geography of the countries listed and the reasoning for protecting developed countries from being listed. This perspective can be further informed by the fact that, of the three countries blacklisted in 2022,[84] only Myanmar has undergone a mutual evaluation.[85] This prompts the question: from where did the FATF source its information to blacklist unassessed countries? Moreso, the compliance and effectiveness outcomes for several countries that have been delisted are not remarkably different, again calling into question the FATF's delisting criteria.[86] While appearing on these lists has severe consequences, the actual criteria for listing and delisting remain unclear and shrouded in secrecy.

While the FATF benchmark is assumed to be straightforward and unbiased, this section has highlighted that the listing process is flawed and lacks credibility. As a result, key actors, including international financial institutions and the marketplace, must exercise caution in their reliance on these lists, and, more importantly, in their interactions with 'listed countries'. It is especially important to investigate the consequences of being listed and how the listed countries respond to the situation. There are various theories that may help us understand this bias. For instance, the legal school Third World Approaches to International Law (TWAIL) emphasises the power imbalances, historical injustices, and the limitations of universal norms in the global legal order. In this case, FATF's recommendations, and uneven and inconsistent methodology in listing are manifestations of the power imbalances. TWAIL scholars such as Gathii[87] and Makau[88] have long argued that these power imbalances have led to differential impacts.[89] In doing so, they expose the limitations of universal norms, as this chapter has shown, as well as commonly held beliefs, such as the deterrent effect of listing countries. Yet, developing countries are still dealing with colonial era, power structures, and uneven development – all of which have contributed to differing vulnerabilities to illicit financing. This chapter calls for the centring of the periphery, just as in *Things Fall Apart* by Chinua Achebe:[90] shifting the narrative away from the FATF's implicit

84 Riccardi (n 10).
85 Riccardi (n 10).
86 Riccardi (n 10); Long (n 3).
87 James Thuro Gathii, 'TWAIL: A Brief History of Its Origins, Its Decentralized Network, and a Tentative Bibliography' (2011) 3 Trade, Law and Development 26.
88 Makau Mutua and Antony Anghie, 'What Is TWAIL?' (2000) 94 Proceedings of the Annual Meeting (American Society of International Law) 31.
89 Centre for Global Development, 'Unintended Consequences of Anti-Money Laundering Policies for Poor Countries' (*Centre for Global Development*, 2015) <www.cgdev.org/sites/default/files/CGD-WG-Report-Unintended-Consequences-AML-Policies-2015.pdf> accessed 1 March 2024.
90 Chinua Achebe, *Things Fall Apart* (Heinemann 1958); Chinua Achebe's, *Things Fall Apart* is a seminal work in African literature, first published in 1958. It is widely regarded as one of the most important books of the 20th century, offering a critical view of British colonialism in Nigeria from an African perspective. Achebe draws on the phrase "Things fall apart; the centre

bias – where their recommendations are universalised and imposed through coercion, demonstrating the power imbalance – and recentring the context of African countries, thus countering the hegemonic view of compliance. Chinua explores the external forces disrupting traditional structures, an allegory for the imposition of international financial regulations (like FATF standards) on African countries, potentially overlooking their specific contexts, and hindering their autonomy. We argue this coercion leads to a stigma paradox.

How Listed Countries Respond: A Stigma or Stigma Paradox?

An examination of how countries *respond* to being listed requires an interrogation of the implications of being listed. However, scholars are torn on the actual implications of listing countries. Empirical studies by Case-Ruchala and Nance,[91] Kudrle,[92] Farias and de Almeida,[93] and Collin et al.[94] find a limited or inconsistent effect of greylisting on cross-border bank liabilities, payments, and portfolio investments.[95] Their findings suggest that financiers' investment decisions are not determined by the FATF listing; this contradicts Morse's market enforcement hypothesis that listings have a statistically significant and negative effect on cross-border bank liabilities.[96]

---

cannot hold" from the poem 'The Second Coming' by WB Yeats, written in 1919. This line has been interpreted and discussed in various contexts because of its powerful imagery and the sense of chaos and disorder it conveys. Yeats wrote the poem in the aftermath of the First World War and during the beginning of the Irish War of Independence, reflecting a period of significant turmoil and transformation in society. The poem has been influential in literature and has found its way into various works, including being an inspiration for the title of Chinua Achebe's novel *Things Fall Apart*. Achebe's choice to title his novel after Yeats's line serves to underscore the themes of change, disintegration, and the clash between traditional and colonial forces depicted in the book.

91 Devin Case-Ruchala and Mark Nance, 'FATF Blacklists Don't Work the Way You Think They Do' (*Bahamas AML Conference*, 2020) <https://bahamasamlconference.centralbankbahamas.com/assets/images/pdf/conferences/2021/fatf-blacklists-dont-work-the-way-you-think-they-do-case-ruchala-and-nance.pdf> accessed 2 March 2024.

92 RT Kudrle, 'Did Blacklisting Hurt the Tax Havens?' (2009) 12(1) JMLC 33–49.

93 Maria Elisa Farias and Monica Arruda de Almeida, 'Does Saying Yes to Capital Inflows Necessarily Mean Good Business? The Effect of Anti-Money Laundering Regulations in the Latin American and the Caribbean Economies' (2014) 26 Economics & Politics 96–127.

94 Matthew Collin, Samantha Cook and Kimmo Soramaki, 'The Impact of Anti-Money Laundering Regulation on Payment Flows: Evidence from SWIFT Data' (2016) Working Paper 445, Center for Global Development.

95 Balakina, D'Andrea and Masciandaro (n 27) empirically evaluated the trend, magnitude and robustness of the stigma effect on capital flows, studying particularly the blacklisting effect on the relationship between international financial institutions and blacklisted banking systems. Their study, which focused on 126 countries from 1996 to 2014 found that the stigma effect does not exists. Donato Masciandaro False and Reluctant Friends? 'National Money Laundering Regulation, International Compliance and Non-Cooperative Countries' (2005) 20(1) European Journal of Law and Economics 17–30.

96 Morse (n 6).

According to Case-Ruchala and Nance, although Morse's findings indicate that listings occasion direct withdrawal of funds and loss of future investment opportunities, Morse's sample countries were limited to ten, thereby raising concerns about sample selection and generalisation.[97] Case-Ruchala and Nance broaden the sample countries to 47 and find that listing has a null effect on bank liabilities or portfolio asset investments.[98] Thus, they suggest that before countries are taken aback by the impact of greylisting, officials and scholars should reconsider the unjustified declarations of their purported impact.

Nevertheless, later studies align with Morse. For instance, a 2021 IMF Working Paper utilised inferential machine-learning to examine the impact of greylisting on all components of capital flows.[99] The IMF found that greylisting occasions a statistically significant reduction in capital flows on average of –7.6% of GDP.[100] Louis de Koker et al.'s determination of a significant correlation between the FATF listing periods and international development credits lends credence to the IMF's research.[101] As such, scholars contend that listed countries are less likely to access development credits, have declined market capitalisation, and depleted external reserves, alongside reduced GDP growth rates, thereby triggering a balance of payment crisis.[102] Collectively, both studies reveal that listing can have grave consequences for identified countries.

Given the potential consequences of listing, examining how countries respond to them is critical. Studies have found that listings cause reputational and other damages, and so they coerce countries into higher levels of compliance within a reasonable period.[103] In particular, Morse finds that initially listed countries are significantly more likely to adopt FATF-compliant laws on terror funding.[104] She supports her claims with the findings that 90% of listed countries adopted the FATF compliant laws on terrorist financing as of 2015, in comparison to 50% of non-listed countries. She compares this to 2009, where not one soon-to-be listed country had compliant laws.[105] Using Taiwan as a case study, Morse illustrates how market actors played a role in pushing for policy change following the country's 2010 listing. Long's findings align with Morse, illustrating that countries are more likely to introduce regulatory

97 Case-Ruchala and Nance (n 91) 1, 6–7.

98 Case-Ruchala and Nance (n 91) 19.

99 Kida and Paetzold (n 51).

100 Kida and Paetzold (n 51).

101 de Koker et al. (n 51) conducted a more robust study based on a sample of 177 countries from 2000 to 2020 and finds correlation between the FATF listing periods and declined international development credits, a challenge that continues post de-listing.

102 de Koker et al. (n 51). It is imperative to note that de Koker et al. contend that the correlation does not prove causation, as it may be that the FATF listing, and these variables are simply co-determined.

103 Morse (n 6). Jason Sharman, 'Power and Discourse in Policy Diffusion: Anti-Money Laundering in Developing States' (2009) 52 (3) International Studies Quarterly 635–56; de Koker et al. (n 51).

104 Morse (n 6).

105 Morse (n 6) 512.

changes in response to being greylisted.[106] At face value, these findings suggest that listings trigger a stigma effect – as countries and financial institutions, concerned about protecting their reputation and the need to access investments, comply with FATF standards. This then raises the question: do listed countries change their laws, and are those laws are sufficient to guarantee compliance?

Other empirical research outcomes demonstrate that various jurisdictions remain unperturbed by listing threats, and delay or fail to change their financial rules.[107] Some of these uncooperative countries are nevertheless delisted, even with insignificant changes on their compliance ratings.[108] Additionally, inefficient lawmakers may not always react efficiently to the listing pressure by drafting suitable laws.[109]

Moreover, it remains to be proven that legislative and regulatory reforms – hallmarks of formal compliance – are sufficient to guarantee actual compliance and decrease a jurisdiction's appeal for illicit funds. These are challenges that are symptomatic of a stigma paradox.[110] They may demonstrate that, while law is important in combatting financial crime, the robustness of laws can be largely dependent on other factors, which are sometimes internal to a country.[111] In the absence of these factors (which include a solid political, institutional, governmental, and financial system), the extent to which countries *can* comply with the law is questionable.

From this standpoint, our argument aligns with the widely recognised and significant differentiation between formal and substantive regulations, which is a prominent focus in the extensive and established body of literature on central bank autonomy.[112] Within this framework, scholars have initiated the process of constructing indices to comprehensively assess the institutional attributes specific to central banks.[113] The outcomes that are commonly referenced within this theoretical framework were generated by Alex Cukierman.[114] The key insights pertain to the notion that formal independence, as delineated in legal

106 Morse (n 6) 512.
107 Masciandaro (n 59).
108 Long (n 3).
109 Balakina, D'Andrea and Masciandaro (n 27); Masciandaro (n 28).
110 Balakina, D'Andrea and Masciandaro (n 27); Masciandaro (n 28).
111 Azinge-Egbiri (n 82).
Jack Snyder, 'Backlash Against Human Rights Shaming: Emotions in Groups' (2019) International Theory 1–24.
112 Donato Masciandaro, 'Independence, Conservatism, and Beyond: Monetary Policy, Central Bank Governance and Central Bank Preferences (1981–2021)' 122 Journal of International Money and Finance.
113 Robin Bade and Michael Parkin, *Central Bank Laws and Monetary Policy* (Department of Economics, University of Western Ontario 1985); Vittorio Grilli, Donato Masciandaro and Guido Tabellini, 'Political and Monetary Institutions and Public Financial Policies in the Industrial Countries' (1991) 13 Economic Policy 341–92.
114 Alex Cukierman, *Central Bank Strategy, Credibility, and Independence – Theory and Practice* (MIT Press 2003); Alex Cukierman, 'Central Bank Independence and Monetary Control' (1994) 104 (427) *Economic Journal* 1437–48.
Snyder (n 111).

statutes and regulatory frameworks, may deviate from the practical manifestation of independence. Even in situations where the rules remain consistent, such as when politicians' actions have a discernible impact on the decisions made by bureaucrats, they can influence the tangible outcomes of monetary policy actions. Returning to the subject at hand, it is worth noting that, while countries may be modifying their legislation to align with the technical requirements set forth by the FATF, the mechanisms in place to ensure the efficacy of these laws often remain inadequate. This inadequacy can be attributed to the presence of diverse factors that can give rise to disparities between the formally established rules and their actual impact.

Additionally, the compliance incentive of listed countries is also debatable. For some countries, their recognition as a weakly compliant jurisdiction can have beneficial effects,[115] which includes becoming a hotspot for the worldwide demand for non-transparent financial transactions.[116] A listed country can also be attractive for banking and non-banking institutions seeking to promote lightly regulated products and services to their wealthy or sophisticated clients. In essence, listing which is meant to be a 'stick' can turn into a 'carrot', occasioning the emergence of a stigma paradox: a desire to elude more prudent regulation. This undermines the very deterrence effect that listing aims to achieve.

This is in line with findings that countries with more economic freedom and lower levels of corruption are less attractive from investors who benefit less from them.[117] Such findings confirm that the desire to circumvent national laws and regulations can be a driver for the shifting financial assets abroad.[118] Compliant countries are also failing to comply effectively. For instance, when the Pacific island Nauru was listed for money laundering, threats of sanctions were

115 Andrew K Rose and Mark Spiegel, 'Offshore Financial Centers: Parasites or Symbionts?' (2006) 117(523) Economic Journal 1310–35; Balakina, D'Andrea and Masciandaro (n 27); Masciandaro (n 28).

116 Donato Masciandaro, 'Transparency Naming and Shaming: Are the Blacklists an Effective Tool?' in Funda Basaran Yavaslar and Johanna Hey (eds), *Tax Transparency* (EATLP Annual Congress Zurich, 7–9 June 2018) <www.ibfd.org/sites/default/files/2021-04/19_018_tax_transparency_final_web.pdf> accessed 2 March 2024.

117 Hisham Foad, 'The Determinants of Offshore Financial Centre Investment' (*SSRN*, June 2012) <https://deliverypdf.ssrn.com/delivery.php?ID=800100124064065088085090002073102081036046034042033020101002100072120068106093097095110003010016007048098010021085018019124011118055068037012101095114114093099110019079055064071065086074109126066094066067084071071126068112020102081025067089126078027&EXT=pdf&INDEX=TRUE> accessed 9 February 2024; Donato Masciandaro, 'Transparency Naming and Shaming: Are the Blacklists an Effective Tool?' in Funda Basaran Yavaslar and Johanna Hey (eds), *Tax Transparency* (EATLP Annual Congress Zurich, 7–9 June 2018) <www.ibfd.org/sites/default/files/2021-04/19_018_tax_transparency_final_web.pdf> accessed 2 March 2024.

118 Masciandaro (n 116).

not followed through by many state governments or multilateral institutions. Rather, only US banks took initiatives to halt transactions with banks in blacklisted countries (Nauru, Nigeria, and Myanmar).[119] Lastly, with the consistent statistics of 2%–5% of the global GDP laundered yearly[120] and the increasing rates of terrorism globally, can we credit the listing to have harnessed compliance?

Dismantling the FATF's Listing Effect: 'The Centre [Should] Not Hold'

As examined, recent scholarship has offered results supporting the perspective that the FATF's listing processes are inarticulate, and biased against developing countries. Still, market actors, government and other international organisations have doggedly relied on the listings to make decisions on financial investments into listed countries,[121] largely because the FATF is considered to be highly technocratic and apolitical. This assumption cannot be taken for granted.

The inconsistencies in the IMF's approach to the FATF's MER tell a different story. In 2021, the IMF stated that the compliance of countries is critical to the fund in relation to

> country surveillance, capacity development, forecast of demand for Fund Programs and estimates of capacity to repay . . . as the sudden loss of capital inflows after greylisting count lead to a loss of external reserves and for valuable countries, it would mean a balance of payment crisis and demand for an IMF program.[122]

Furthermore, the Fund emphasised that if the country has a fund program, '[greylisting] could mean delays in implementing agreed reforms or a need to recalibrate policy targets and timelines for achieving them . . . [or require] a call for closer monitoring'. This position demonstrates the IMF's strong reliance on the FATF's listing, and the likely implications thereof.

However, in 2022, the IMF's stance gradually deviated. For instance, the Fund extended a Precautionary and Liquidity Line for Panama, even as the country was greylisted.[123] However, the Fund denied Morocco funding in

119 Masciandaro (n 28).

120 UNODC, 'Money Laundering' (*UNODC*) <www.unodc.org/unodc/en/money-laundering/overview.html> accessed 8 February 2024.

121 Morse (n 6).

122 Kida and Paetzold (n 51).

123 International Monetary Fund, 'IMF Executive Board Approves US$2.7 Billion Precautionary and Liquidity Line for Panama to Address COVID-19 Pandemic' (IMF, Press Release No 21/19, 19 January 2021) <www.imf.org/en/News/Articles/2021/01/20/pr2119-imf-executive-board-approves-billion-precautionary-and-liquidity-line-for-panama> accessed 3 March 2024.

April/May 2022, due to greylisting, but extended a Flexible Credit Line in 2023, just after Morocco's delisting in February 2023. The IMF's inconsistency in extending lines of credit may cause one to question the extent of the institution's true reliance on the FATF's listing.

We argue that it could be more effective and fairer for the IMF to rely less on the FATF's biased standards, and more on its own findings. Of late, the IMF has demonstrated its recognition of the FATF's failings. Its September 2023 Nordic-Baltic Regional Report offers an insight into the institutions new AML/CFT strategic orientation.[124] In this report – contrary to the FATF's peer review methodology, which assesses the legal and regulatory framework of countries on nominally equal terms – the IMF took a macro-risk perspective, including financial flows and bilateral risks in its analysis of countries' vulnerabilities to and threat of money laundering. Furthermore, the IMF highlighted its focus on big financial centres, given its findings of the significant growth of financial flows to and from international financial centres – which, though they are involved in considerably complex financial crime cases, are not listed by the FATF.

In claiming to treat all countries equally, by examining their legal and regulatory framework, the FATF is instead subjecting listed countries to exposure and capacity building. Yet the notion of 'capacity building' indexes the assumption of White superiority and expertise and continues to depend on the construction of the incapacity of developing countries.[125] To date, the FATF seems to ignore the systemic inequality ingrained in its listing system, which is neither fair nor effective in countering financial crime. The Tax Justice Network likens the FATF's approach to a 'zero tolerance' policy in the fight against abuse, where the police focus on street dealers but not the underground godfathers or networks. As such, it is critical that the FATF's approach is displaced, in favour of a more centred approach – one that recognises that not all countries are equally responsible for financial crime, and developing countries are a small part of a wider problem. Yeats's poem critiques rigid systems and calls for change. This resonates with this chapter's argument that the FATF's universal standards are not suitable for all contexts, and as a result, 'the centre cannot hold'. Dismantling the listing effect calls for a decentralised system, which aligns with TWAIL's critique of power imbalances, and a need for alternative solutions that focus on collaboration with developing countries, rather than biased listing.

124 IMF, 'Nordic-Baltic Regional Report' (*IMF*, September 2023) <www.imf.org/en/Publications/CR/Issues/2023/09/01/Nordic-Baltic-Regional-Report-Technical-Assistance-Report-Nordic-Baltic-Technical-538762> accessed 2 March 2024.

125 Jemima Pierre, 'The Racial Vernaculars of Development: A View from West Africa' (2019) 122(1) American Anthropologist 1–13; Uma Kothari, 'Critiquing Race' and Racism in Development Discourse and Practice' (2006) 6(1) Progress in Development Studies 1–7.

Conclusion

Historically, many institutions have publicly listed countries, with the expectation that the reputational stigma will push countries to comply with their standards. As a soft law institution, the FATF adapted the listing methodology, and has since referred to it as the cornerstone of international efforts to checkmate money laundering and terrorist financing. However, this chapter argues that the listing approach is flawed, and risks bias against developing countries – which ironically are disproportionately more likely to be listed and spend more time on the list. Such an approach, based on the notion that all nations bear equal responsibility for financial crime, fails to adequately address the issue presented by major financial centres with significant money laundering and terrorist financing risks, which in turn pose systemic threats to the stability of the global financial system.[126] Given the likely implications of FATF listing, this chapter supports the perspective that the lists are misleading and flawed, as they can have grave consequences for affected countries. The chapter also recognises that the expected implications of listing do not always materialise; rather a stigma paradox may occur, where countries gain from being listed, demonstrating the limited effectiveness of the tool, and associated political error.

We have argued that things are falling apart and the 'centre should not hold', yet the FATF appears to be failing to learn from history. In over 30 years, it has consistently failed to rein in countries and achieve stellar compliance. Indeed, it is time to revisit its methodology and the associated political influences that affect its workability. It seems to us more effective and fairer to explore an alternative view, shifting towards the IMF's macro-economic approach, which focuses on large countries with the most material financial flows. We thereby argue that it is time for the IMF to shift from relying on the FATF standards, which are too weak to be effective; and such a shift will dismantle the FATF's continued biases against developing countries.

126 Markus Meinzer, 'IMF Challenges Ineffective FATF Approach to Money-Laundering' (*Tax Justice Network*, 12 September 2023) <https://taxjustice.net/2023/09/12/imf-challenges-ineffective-fatf-approach-to-money-laundering/> accessed 4 March 2024.

Part II

Transplantation Challenges and Compliance Trajectories

5 The Mis-Implementation of Anti-Money Laundering Laws and Regulations

A High-Level Review with Specific Focus on the Unilateral Termination of Customers' Bank Accounts in South Africa

Zakhele Hlophe

Introduction

South Africa has been implementing the anti-money laundering and counter-financing of terrorism (AML/CFT) laws and regulations since 2001. Recently, South Africa was greylisted by the Financial Action Task Force (FATF), joining a number of other countries[1] on the list, for failure to rectify some of its major deficiencies in implementing the global FATF standards.[2]

1 These countries are Albania, Barbados, Burkina Faso, Cambodia, Cayman Islands, Democratic Republic of the Congo, Gibraltar, Haiti, Jamaica, Jordan, Mali, Morocco, Mozambique, Nigeria, Panama, Philippines, Senegal, South Sudan, Syria, Tanzania, Türkiye, Uganda, United Arab Emirates, and Yemen. See Jurisdictions under Increased Monitoring – 24 February 2023 (fatf-gafi.org).

2 FATF (2023) Jurisdiction under Increased Monitoring – 24 February 2023, Paris. According to FATF, South Africa needs to implement the following action plan in order to be removed from the greylist: "(1) demonstrating a sustained increase in outbound MLA [Mutual Legal Assistance] requests that help facilitate ML/TF [Money Laundering/Terrorist Financing] investigations and confiscations of different types of assets in line with its risk profile; (2) improving risk-based supervision of DNFBPs [Designated Non-Financial Businesses and Professions] and demonstrating that all AML/CFT supervisors apply effective, proportionate, and effective sanctions for noncompliance; (3) ensuring that competent authorities have timely access to accurate and up-to-date BO [Beneficial Ownership] information on legal persons and arrangements and applying sanctions for breaches of violation by legal persons to BO obligations; (4) demonstrating a sustained increase in law enforcement agencies' requests for financial intelligence from the FIC for its ML/TF investigations; (5) demonstrate a sustained increase in investigations and prosecutions of serious and complex money laundering and the full range of TF activities in line with its risk profile; (6) enhancing its identification, seizure and confiscation of proceeds and instrumentalities of a wider range of predicate crimes, in line with its risk profile; (7) updating its TF Risk Assessment to inform the implementation of a comprehensive national counter financing of terrorism strategy; and (8) ensuring the effective implementation of targeted financial sanctions and demonstrating an effective mechanism to identify individuals and entities that meet the criteria for domestic designation."

DOI: 10.4324/9781003253808-7

While this chapter seeks to generally examine the challenges and weaknesses of South Africa's implementation of the AML/CFT standards, it specifically focuses on the regime's mis-implementation in the banking sector, particularly the practice by banks of unilaterally terminating customer's bank accounts under the guise of complying with AML/CFT or banking regulations, and safeguarding their reputation.

The central argument in this chapter is that banks in South Africa go further than is required by FATF standards, domestic laws, and regulations in implementing some of the AML/CFT requirements. By unilaterally terminating bank accounts of customers without law enforcement interventions or court orders, they arrogate to themselves law enforcement powers, which they do not have, and which are not prescribed by FATF standards, domestic laws, and regulations. In turn, they end up violating the very same standards, laws, and regulations, and even some of the constitutional rights enshrined in South Africa's Constitution. The implications of this are many, but the critical one is that banks could end up facing serious damages claims by aggrieved customers should they be found to be in the wrong by the courts.

The AML/CFT regulatory framework remains one of the crucial instruments in the fight against serious profit-driven crime, particularly corruption, tax evasion, and illicit financial flows. However, the deficiencies in South Africa's effective implementation of this regime exposes the country's fragile economy and fiscus to untold risks and implications. In the first part of this chapter, a short background is given to South Africa's incorporation of the global FATF standards. The second part analyses the statistics of South Africa's performance in achieving the main goals of the regime, which are to detect and seize the proceeds of crime. The last section looks at the perverse outcomes of implementation in the banking sector, particularly the unilateral termination of customer bank accounts based on perceived "reputational risk".

This chapter uses mainly data from the FATF mutual evaluation reports on South Africa, the Financial Intelligence Centre (FIC), and the Asset Forfeiture Unit (AFU) to show how South Africa has struggled to implement its regime. It also analyses the jurisprudence that is developing in South Africa concerning the unilateral termination of "bank-client relationships". I use the terms *FATF standards* or *AML/CFT standards or regime* interchangeably to mean the 40 + 9 Recommendations of FATF that have evolved since they were first adopted in the early 1990s following the formation of FATF by the G7 countries in 1989. I also use these terms to refer to domestic laws and regulations that emanate from FATF standards and related UN Conventions.

South Africa's Incorporation of the Global FATF Standards

South Africa started incorporating the global AML/CFT standards in the 1990s when it enacted the Drugs and Drug Trafficking Act of 1992, the Proceeds of Crime Act of 1996 (POCA), and the Prevention of Organised Crime Act of 1998. In 2001, it urgently enacted the Financial Intelligence

Centre Act to avoid being blacklisted by the FATF as a non-cooperating country.[3]

Again in 2004, it enacted the Protection of Constitutional Democracy Against Terrorists and Related Activities Act (POCDATARA), Act No. 33 of 2004, as many countries adopted counter-terrorism laws following the 9/11 tragedy in the United States in 2001. These laws focus on, among other things, tracing and taking away the material benefits from crime through seizing assets and monetary proceeds. The other focus of these laws is the regulation of businesses and professions to, primarily, monitor transactions taking place through them and report those that are suspicious or unusual and/or above a regulated threshold to the new breed of specialized "intelligence" organizations known as financial intelligence units (FIUs).

These laws have also led to the establishment of novel and specialized institutions within the criminal justice family. These are law enforcement, financial intelligence, regulatory, and asset forfeiture agencies at a domestic level. At a global level, there has also been a proliferation of "soft-law" regulatory institutions that play various roles in the regulation and dissemination of the AML/CFT regime such as FATF, FATF-style regional bodies (FSRBs), and the Egmont Group of Financial Intelligence Units (Egmont Group). South Africa domesticated these novel institutions such as the AFU and the FIC in 2003.[4]

South Africa was inducted into FATF membership after having largely adopted the policies, laws, and regulations that were required by FATF of its members, following a peer-review mutual evaluation in 2003.[5] However this peer-review mechanism of FATF did not only focus on member countries that established it, but all countries including non-members. South Africa, however, is fortunate to have been made a full member country, as it could participate and have a voice in FATF's deliberative processes after joining in 2003. Many other developing countries did not enjoy such luxury as they were merely bullied to adopt FATF standards through FATF's naming, shaming, and labelling of countries as Non-Cooperating Countries and Territories (NCCTs).[6]

3 Z Hlophe, 'Regulating Money Laundering in Developing Countries: Acritical Analysis of South Africa's Incorporation and Implementation of the Global FATF Standards' (Unpublished PhD Thesis, Kings College London 2013).

4 The Asset Forfeiture Unit (AFU) was established in May 1999 in the Office of the National Prosecuting Authority (NPA) to focus on the implementation of Chapters 5 and 6 of the Prevention of Organised Crime Act, Act No. 121 of 1998. The Financial Intelligence Centre was established and started operating in 2003 by the Financial Intelligence Centres Act, Act 38 of 2001. It is South Africa's Financial Intelligence Unit mandated to gather, analyse and disseminate financial intelligence. It was established to identify proceeds of crime, combat money laundering and the financing of terrorism.

5 See International Monetary Fund, *South Africa: Report on the Observance of Standards and Codes – FATF Recommendations for Anti-Money Laundering and Combating the Financing of Terrorism.* IMF Country Report No. 04/119 (International Monetary Fund, April 2004).

6 See Rainer Hülsse, 'Creating Demand for Global Governance: The Making of a Global Money Laundering Problem' (2007) 21(2) Global Society 155–78; DW Drezner, Globalisation,

To address democracy and legitimacy concerns, FSRBs were established throughout the world to give non-FATF countries some kind of quasi-membership in FATF.[7] Many scholars then viewed FATF as an undemocratic organization for demanding compliance with its standards from countries that had no voice in it.[8]

In this chapter I analyse South Africa's performance with seizing the proceeds of crime and detecting money laundering, starting with the data from the AFU.

Data from the Asset Forfeiture Unit

The 2021 South Africa's Mutual Evaluation Report by FATF noted the following in respect of South Africa's asset forfeiture regime:

> Whilst the authorities have demonstrated positive results for recovery of proceeds of crime in the area of fraud and economic crime including ML, efforts for recovery of assets from "State Capture" and proceeds which have been moved to other countries have been less successful to date due to the phenomenon of "State Capture" itself and resource constraints. . . . Overall, confiscation of proceeds of crime partially reflects South Africa's ML/TF risk and national AML/CTF policies and priorities.[9]

Harmonisation, and Competition: The Different Pathways to Policy Convergence' (2005) 12(5) Journal of European Public Policy 841–59; R Bosworth-Davies, Money Laundering: Towards an Alternative Interpretation – Chapter Two' (2006) 9(4) Journal of Money Laundering Control 346–64; JC Sharman, 'Power and Discourse in Policy Diffusion: Anti-Money Laundering in Developing Countries' (2008) (52) International Studies Quarterly 635–56; J Black, 'Contesting and Constructing Legitimacy and Accountability in Polycentric Regulatory Regimes' (2008) 2 Regulation and Governance 137–68.

7 See Rainer Hülsse, 'Creating Demand for Global Governance: The Making of a Global Money Laundering Problem' (2007) 21(2) Global Society 155–78; DW Drezner, Globalisation, Harmonisation, and Competition: The Different Pathways to Policy Convergence' (2005) 12(5) Journal of European Public Policy 841–59; R Bosworth-Davies, Money Laundering: Towards an Alternative Interpretation - Chapter Two' (2006) 9(4) Journal of Money Laundering Control 346 -64; JC Sharman, 'Power and Discourse in Policy Diffusion: Anti-Money Laundering in Developing Countries' (2008) (52) International Studies Quarterly 635 -56; J Black, 'Contesting and Constructing Legitimacy and Accountability in Polycentric Regulatory Regimes' (2008) 2 Regulation and Governance 137–68.

8 Rainer Hülsse, 'Creating Demand for Global Governance: The Making of a Global Money Laundering Problem' (2007) 21(2) Global Society 155–78; DW Drezner, Globalisation, Harmonisation, and Competition: The Different Pathways to Policy Convergence' (2005) 12(5) Journal of European Public Policy 841–59; R Bosworth-Davies, Money Laundering: Towards an Alternative Interpretation – Chapter Two' (2006) 9(4) Journal of Money Laundering Control 346–64; JC Sharman, 'Power and Discourse in Policy Diffusion: Anti-Money Laundering in Developing Countries' (2008) (52) International Studies Quarterly 635–56; J Black, 'Contesting and Constructing Legitimacy and Accountability in Polycentric Regulatory Regimes' (2008) 2 Regulation and Governance 137–68.

9 FATF, *Anti-Money Laundering and Counter-Terrorist Financing Measures – South Africa* (Fourth Round Mutual Evaluation Report, FATF 2021) <www.fatf-gafi.org/publications/mutualevaluations/documents/mer-south-africa-2021.html>.

Table 5.1 Freezing and Forfeiture Orders (2003–2021) (in ZAR)

Year	*Freezing Orders*	*Forfeiture Orders*	*Actual Recovery Into Criminal Asset Recovery Account or Victims*	*Number of Freezing Orders*	*Number of Forfeiture Orders*
2003	131,930,000	51,910,000	17,313,000	125	80
2004	222,616,000	86,741,000	35,737,000	228	148
2005	234,406,000	172,855,000	24,500,000	161	151
2006	344,129,000	106,748,000	18,823,000	252	221
2007	1,300,000,000	100,600,000	19,291,000	252	242
2008	394,000,000	127,322,000	45,564,000	226	223
2009	320,000,000	271,588,000	65,933,000	275	277
2010	491,000,000	184,960,000	51,657,000	280	275
2011	549,000,000	212,000,000	50,400,000	333	320
2012	553,000,000	164,000,000	131,100,000	318	300
2013	518,000,000	119,000,000	63,400,000	276	302
2014	701,000,000	296,400,000	182,900,000	363	390
2015	2,756,000,000	1,939,000,000	1,716,200,000	342	466
2016	778,900,000	349,600,000	444,200,000	326	418
2017	1,194,000,000	423,600,000	219,000,000	377	569
2018	4,400,000,000	350,950,000	415,500,000	324	563
2019	455,000,000	3,130,000,000	3,050,000,000	273	495
2020	1,950,000,000	455,000,000	160,000,000	326	417
2021	611,000,000	135,800,000	111,300,000		
Total	17,903,981,000	8,678,074,000	6,822,818,000	5,057	5857

Source: Compiled by author from National Prosecuting Authority Annual Reports (2003–2021).

This observation by FATF seem to reflect the situation in South Africa as shown by statistics from the AFU cases since its formation in 2001 until 2021. Between the financial years 2002/3 and 2020/21, the AFU was granted about 11,000 freezing/restraint and confiscation/forfeiture orders by the courts in South Africa.

Table 5.1 shows that from 2003 to 2021, the AFU has been granted freezing orders of R17,9 billion of alleged crime proceeds. (That is just over US $1.0 billion at the exchange rate of $1/R16,82 at the time of writing.) However, of that amount, only R8,6 billion had been made final orders by the courts in favour of the AFU by 2021. This means that of the amounts frozen, R9,2 billion worth of freezing orders between 2003 and 2021 had either been decided against the AFU or not finalized. From the R8,6 billion worth of final orders, only R6,8 billion was paid to the Criminal Asset Recovery Account (CARA), into which all confiscated and forfeit assets are deposited. Later I look at the statistics from the FIC and its contribution to detecting crime and forfeiture of its proceeds, comparing them to the above statistics from the AFU.

Financial Intelligence and Its Contribution

The FIC is the foremost regulatory authority on the country's AML/CFT regime. Its role is to ensure compliance with domestic laws and the global

FATF Standards and related UN Conventions.[10] It is also to produce the financial intelligence needed to fight money laundering and its predicate crimes, terrorism and proliferation financing. This financial intelligence is primarily based on the reporting of suspicious, unusual, cross-border, and threshold transactions of customers of banks and other regulated institutions.

FATF's mutual evaluations of South Africa in 2003, 2009 and 2021 have highlighted some challenges to South Africa's implementation of the AML/CTF regime, and some successes. The last mutual evaluation report of 2021 stated that:

> The use of financial intelligence plays an important part in addressing predicate crimes, ML, TF, and the identification of criminal assets. The FIC obtains a large number of obligatory reports and possesses tools and has access to additional information that allows it to analyse such reports and effectively produce operational financial intelligence.[11]

This intelligence is produced to aid the detection of crime and seizing its proceeds. When it was established in 2003, the FIC initially implemented only the suspicious transaction reports (STRs) regime. It added the cash transaction reporting (CTRs) obligation of cash amounts of R24 999 and above only in 2010.[12] Ever since then, the FIC receives millions of transaction reports (TRs) every year, most of which are CTRs, as shown in Table 5.2.

Evidence shows that STRs, which are reported on the basis of unusualness or suspicion, are mostly transactions which end up not being linked to criminal activity, if ever referred to law enforcement agencies (LEAs) and/or, at all, investigated. In a study[13] conducted in South Africa a decade ago, it was found that STRs often do not lead to many arrests and indictments as they end up not being linked to criminal activity, if ever referred to LEAs or investigated. This is confirmed by the findings of mutual evaluations reports released by FATF on South Africa in 2009 and 2021.[14]

However, this ineffectiveness of STRs to detect crime is not unique to South Africa, as several studies and enquiries conducted in Europe and America over the past two decades show that financial intelligence reporting has mostly not led to much crime detection.[15] Some have found that less than 1% of all

10 The United Nations Conventions related to the FATF Standards include the United Nations Convention Against Illicit Trade in Narcotic Drugs and Psychotropic Substances of 1998; United Nations Convention Against Transnational Organised Crime of 2000 (or Palermo Convention); United Nations International Convention for the Suppression of the Financing of Terrorism of 1999; and the UN Convention against Corruption of 2003.

11 FATF (n 9) 7.

12 FIC Annual Report, 2011.

13 Hlophe (n 3).

14 FATF (n 9).

15 The Clearing House, 2017, A new paradigm: redesigning the U.S. AML/CFT Framework to protect national security and aid law enforcement; M Gold and M Levi, *Money Laundering in the UK: An Appraisal of Suspicious-Based Reporting* (The Police Foundation, 1994); MH Fleming, *The UK Law Enforcement Use and Management of Suspicious Activity Reports: Towards Determining the Value of the Regime* (University College London 2005); Serious

Table 5.2 STRs and CTRs Received by FIC Between 2003 and 2021

Year	*STRs*	*CTRs*
2003	991	Not applicable
2004	7,480	Not applicable
2005	15,757	Not applicable
2006	19,793	Not applicable
2007	21,466	Not applicable
2008	24,580	Not applicable
2009	22,762	Not applicable
2010	29,411	Not applicable
2011	36,990	1,300,000
2012	53,506	5,531,058
2013	147,744	6,093,408
2014	355,369	6,169,985
2015	267,398	6,684,475
2016	180,363	9,134,339
2017	358,412	4,700,000
2018	330,639	4,884,417
2019	288,434	5,210,000
2020	299,256	5,930,000
2021	394,709	4,852,629
	2,855,060	60,490,311

Source: Compiled by author from FIC Annual Reports 2003–2021.

transactions reported to financial intelligence units around the world lead to any crime detection or recovery of proceeds.[16] This is much more true with threshold-based reports,[17] where cash amounts above a certain threshold must be reported, sometimes without any suspicion or unusualness. The FIC in South Africa receives an average of 5 million CTRs per year, as shown in Table 5.2.

Organised Crime Agency, *Review of the Suspicious Activity Reports Regime (The SARs Review)* (Sir Stephen Lander, March 2006); KPMG, *Money Laundering: Review of the Reporting Systems* (KPMG 2003); Z Hlophe, *Assessing the Effects of Anti-Money Laundering Regulations in the UK: Suspicious Transaction Reports and Their Effect in Detecting Money Laundering* (Unpublished MSc Thesis, Leicester University 2004).

16 The Clearing House, 2017, A new paradigm: redesigning the U.S. AML/CFT Framework to protect national security and aid law enforcement; M Gold and M Levi, *Money Laundering in the UK: An Appraisal of Suspicious-Based Reporting* (The Police Foundation, 1994); MH Fleming, The UK *Law Enforcement Use and Management of Suspicious Activity Reports: Towards Determining the Value of the Regime* (University College London 2005); Serious Organised Crime Agency, Review of the *Suspicious Activity Reports Regime (The SARs Review)* (Sir Stephen Lander, March 2006); KPMG, Money Laundering: Review of the Reporting Systems (KPMG 2003); Z Hlophe, *Assessing the Effects of Anti-Money Laundering Regulations in the UK: Suspicious Transaction Reports and Their Effect in Detecting Money Laundering* (Unpublished MSc Thesis, Leicester University 2004).

17 See Government Accountability Office, *Bank Secrecy Act: Increased Use of Exemption Provisions Could Reduce Currency Transaction Reporting While Maintaining Usefulness to Law Enforcement Efforts.* Report to Congressional Requesters, United States (Government Accountability Office, February 2008).

Since threshold-based reporting was introduced in South Africa in 2010, the FIC has received more than 60,4 million CTRs from regulated institutions, over 90% from banks and money service businesses (MSBs). This is simply because every cash transaction of R24,999 and above must be reported by regulated institutions to the FIC. While more objective than suspicious transaction reporting, threshold reporting is known for swamping the system with CTRs that are not useful for law enforcement purposes. That is why some jurisdictions do not place much value on them and have sought to exempt their reporting in particular instances.[18]

In South Africa, the threshold of R24,999 (or about US$1700 at the time of writing) has proven to be low, crowding the system with millions of reports of no immediate usefulness to law enforcement investigations or recovery of assets. This is to the extent that in 2019, the FIC released a discussion document where it was proposing to increase the obligatory threshold for CTRs to R49,999 and above (or about $3300 at the time of writing).[19]

Suspicious transaction reporting is known to be subjective as it depends on the opinion of the filer. For instance, in all legislation developed on AML/CTF in South Africa, there is no clear definition of the concept of "suspicious transaction". This leaves plenty of discretion to the filers because they may defend themselves that a particular transaction that was not reported did not raise any suspicion or grounds to suspect that it was linked to criminal or terrorist activities.

When it comes to unusual and suspicious activity reports, the FIC has accumulated over 2.8 million STRs since it was established in 2003, as shown in Table 5.2. Combined with CTRs which were reported for the first time since October 2010, the FIC is now sitting on a database of about 64 million TRs. The FIC has an objective in its strategic and annual performance plans to enhance the consumption of its financial intelligence products by LEAs. It measures that objective through the use of its financial intelligence products by the designated LEAs.

In this regard, it refers its financial intelligence products, which are primarily derived from STRs and CTRs, to the designated LEAs, which include foreign FIUs, for investigation. The FIC reports on the statistics of these referrals in its annual reports. Later we look at the statistics of these intelligence reports to determine the extent to which they have assisted South Africa to uncover the crimes for which they are being reported. Figure 5.1 shows that between 2003 and 2021, out of the 64 million TRs20 filed with the FIC, it proactively referred 13,989 intelligence reports to LEAs for investigation. On top of these, Figure 5.1 shows that the FIC referred 20,938 intelligence reports in response to requests by LEAs and partner FIUs across the world.

18 See Government Accountability Office, *Bank Secrecy Act: Increased Use of Exemption Provisions Could Reduce Currency Transaction Reporting While Maintaining Usefulness to Law Enforcement Efforts.* Report to Congressional Requesters, United States (Government Accountability Office, February 2008).

19 FIC Annual Report 2020/21, 21.

20 Transactions reports (TRs) are STRs and CTRs combined. The abbreviation "TRs" is used as shorthand and for convenience.

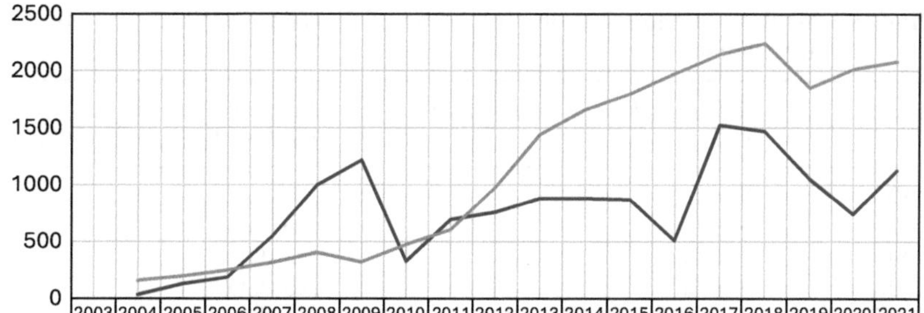

	2003	2004	2005	2006	2007	2008	2009	2010	2011	2012	2013	2014	2015	2016	2017	2018	2019	2020	2021
Referrals		36	134	191	549	1002	1221	331	697	761	883	883	870	511	1525	1470	1054	745	1126
Requests		161	199	250	318	406	323	476	607	980	1445	1661	1799	1979	2145	2243	1849	2017	2080

Figure 5.1 Intelligence reports referred to LEAs: 2003 and 2021.

Source: Compiled by author on statistics in the FIC Annual Reports.[21]

Both proactive and responsive referrals amounted to 34,918 intelligence reports/products that were referred to LEAs for investigation. These intelligence reports are supposed to assist LEAs in ongoing investigations. They also are instrumental in initiating new investigations or in applications to freeze and confiscate assets. All these close to 35,000 intelligence reports that were referred to LEAs by the FIC between 2003 and 2021 constitute far less than 1% (precisely 0.054 %) of all TRs filed with the FIC over the past 18 years by regulated institutions.[22] This means that 64 million TRs had to be made to refer only about 35,000 intelligence reports for investigations.

Commenting on a similar phenomenon on the ineffectiveness of TRs in detecting crime in the US, Lawrence Lindsey, a former member of the Board of Governors of the Federal Reserve System, said that:

> Between 1987 and 1995, the government collected 77 million currency-transaction reports, something on the order of 62 tons of paper. Out of that, it was able to prosecute *3,000* money-laundering cases. That is roughly one case for every *25,000* forms filed. In other words, entire forests had to be felled in order to prosecute one case. But it gets worse: Of the *3,000* money-laundering cases prosecuted, the government managed to produce only 580 guilty verdicts. In other words, in excess of *100,000* reports were filed by innocent citizens in order to get one conviction. . . . By any standard of cost-benefit analysis, we are asking for a lot of compliance to catch a few people.[23]

21 FIC Annual Reports, 2003/04 to 2020/21.

22 By regulated businesses/institutions, I loosely refer to all accounting and reporting institutions under the FIC Act which are regulated/obligated to file STRs and CTRs with the FIC. This includes banks, car dealerships, casinos, real estate agents, lawyers and other institutions listed in Schedule 1 and 3 of the FIC Act.

23 Lawrence B Lindsey, 'The Money-Laundering Conundrum: Mugging Privacy in the Assault on Crime?' CEI Conference on Financial Privacy, 30 November 1999.

Table 5.3 Section 34 Interventions and Value of Proceeds in Which the FIC Provided Intelligence

Year	*Amounts Frozen in Terms of Section 34*	*Value of Proceeds Recovered Where the FIC Provided Intelligence*
2003	No data	No data
2004	No data	No data
2005	No data	No data
2006	No data	No data
2007	R1,550,000	No data
2008	R2,700,000	No data
2009	No data	No data
2010	R128,000,000	No data
2011	R6,700,000	No data
2012	R17,200,000	No data
2013	R334,800,000	R1,171,000,000
2014	R76,931,255	R411,983,587
2015	R181,012,218	R2,296,768,045
2016	R184,600,000	R477,600,000
2017	R149,000,000	R443,900,000
2018	R55,000,000	R3,028,379,892
2019	R53,600,000	R2,143,200,000
2020	R70,700,000	R2,973,180,000
2021	R613,200,000	R3,398,710,000
Total	**R1,874,993,473**	**R16,344,721,524**

Source: FIC Annual Reports 2003 to 2021.

It is unclear how many of the referrals end up initiating new investigations or assisting in ongoing investigations, leading to arrests, convictions, and asset forfeiture, as the FIC has over the years not kept or reported clear statistics in this regard.

However, the FIC in its annual reports does attempt to report some of this data, although with some inconsistencies and gaps that need to be filled, as shall be shown later. In this regard, the FIC may need to commission an independent study that will trace the contribution of its financial intelligence in law enforcement efforts since its establishment. Data sourced from the FIC between the 2003/4 and 2020/21 annual reports, as shown in Table 5.3, shows that the FIC has used its section 34 intervention, which allows it to proactively freeze suspected proceeds of crime in bank accounts, to freeze more than R1,8 billion.[24] It is, however, important to mention that freezing orders are no guarantee of asset forfeiture. In many instances freezing orders are challenged in court successfully and set aside as discussed earlier above in the analysis of Table 5.1.

24 Section 34 of the Financial Intelligence Centre Act enables the FIC to freeze suspected funds in bank accounts for a period of up to 10 days to allow law enforcement agencies to bring applications for its restraint/freezing and confiscation/forfeiture.

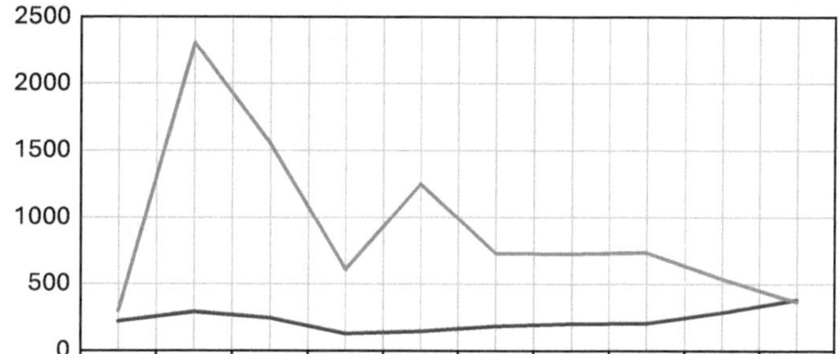

	2012	2013	2014	2015	2016	2017	2018	2019	2020	2021
FIC	220	292	246	130	145	186	202	205	287	381
Supervisory Body	300	2307	1556	610	1251	727	726	737	537	368

Figure 5.2 Number of compliance inspections conducted 2012–2021.

Source: Compiled by author from data in the FIC Annual Reports 2011/12–2020/21.

From data reported only from 2012/13 in its annual reports, as shown in Table 5.3, the FIC claimed to have assisted in the recovery of close to R16,3 billion in proceeds of crime. This figure is too high, however, and therefore inconsistent, when compared to the confiscation and forfeiture orders won by the AFU between 2003 and 2021, which amount to only R8,6 billion (see Table 5.1). Over the same period (between 2013 and 2021) in which the FIC claims to have assisted in the recovery of R16,3 billion, the AFU achieved freezing orders worth R13,3 billion. It is therefore unclear how the FIC claims to have assisted in recovering R16,3 billion over the same period. This is one of the gaps and inconsistencies in the statistical data reported by the FIC in its annual reports.

Compliance Inspections and Administrative Fines

The AML/CFT regime has been hard at work when it comes to compliance, conducting thousands of inspections on regulated institutions and dishing out fines or remedial sanctions for non-compliant regulatees. As shown in Figure 5.2, in the 2011/12 financial year, the FIC established the compliance enforcement system whereby all regulated institutions could be inspected for compliance by their industry supervisory bodies and the FIC and be sanctioned for non-compliance.[25] In that year, the FIC and supervisory bodies conducted 520 compliance inspections: 220 by the FIC and 300 by supervisory bodies.[26]

Over the past 10 years, as shown in Table 5.4, there were even more compliance inspections (11,413) than proactive financial intelligence product

25 FIC Annual Report 2011/12, 21.
26 FIC Annual Report 2011/12, 21.

Table 5.4 Financial Penalties for Non-compliance With the FIC

Name of Bank	*Administrative Sanction*	*Year*
Absa Bank Limited (ABSA)	R10,000,000	2014
FirstRand Bank Limited (FNB)	R30,000,000	2014
Nedbank Limited (Nedbank)	R25,000,000	2014
Standard Bank of South Africa Limited (Standard Bank)	R60,000,000	2014
Capitec Bank Limited (Capitec)	R5,000,000	2015
Deutsche Bank AG (Deutsche)	R10,000,000	2015
GBS Mutual Bank (GBS)	R500,000	2016
Habib Overseas Bank Limited (Habib)	R1,000,000	2016
Investec Bank Limited (Investec)	R20,000,000	2016
Standard Chartered Bank (JHB Branch) (Standard Chartered)	R10,000,000	2016
South African Bank of Athens Limited (Bank of Athens)	R3,000,000	2016
Société Générale (JHB Branch) (Socgen)	R2,000,000	2016
Absa Bank Limited	R10,000,000	2016
VBS Mutual Bank (VBS)	R2,500,000	2017
China Construction Bank (JHB Branch) (CCB)	R75,000,000	2018
HSBC Bank Plc (JHB Branch) (HSBC)	R15,000,000	2018
Bidvest Bank Limited (Bidvest)	R5,250,000	2019
Sasfin Bank Limited (Sasfin)	R500,000	2019
Bank of Baroda	R400,000	2019
Standard Bank of South Africa Limited	R30,000,000	2019
Bank of China	R2,000,000	2019
GroBank Limited (formerly known as South African Bank of Athens Limited) (GroBank)	R5,000,000	2019
Ubank Limited (Ubank)	R500,000	2019
HBZ Bank Limited (HBZ)	R0	2019
Deutsche Bank AG (JHB Branch)	R38,000,000	2021
Total	R360,650,000	

Source: FIC Annual Reports 2013/14–2020/21.

referrals (9,828) to LEAs. This may suggest that the FIC prioritizes compliance inspections more than referring money laundering and related activities' investigations to LEAs. Compliance inspections also come with sanctions in instances where non-compliance is found, as shown in Table 5.4.

Since the compliance inspections and sanctions regime was introduced in 2012, the South African Reserve Bank (SARB) has imposed fines to the tune of R360 million on non-compliant banks operating in South Africa, including against the so-called big-four banks (Absa Bank Limited [ABSA], Standard Bank, FirstRand Bank Limited [FNB], and Nedbank) and some branches of international banks.

However, there seem to be challenges with the consistency of these fines. For instance, in 2014, ABSA and FNB were fined for similar violations of sections 21, 22, and 42 of the FIC Act, but the financial penalty was R10 million for ABSA and R30 million for FNB.[27] On another case, the Bank of Baroda (BOB) was fined R11 million, which was reversed to R400,000 on appeal to the Appeal Board of the Financial Intelligence Centre Act in 2019.[28]

Banks in South Africa seem to be influenced by these fines when they make decisions to terminate bank accounts of some of their so-called high-risk clients in recent times. They have argued that some of these clients expose them to "reputational" or "business" risk, therefore justifying their un-banking.[29] The termination of bank-client relationships cases currently decided in the courts in South Africa were badly pleaded by the victims, however. This then led, in my view, to the development of wrong jurisprudence, which views the issue of unilateral termination of bank-client relationships as a private law of contract issue. As shall be discussed later below, confining the analysis of bank-client relationships as merely contractual fails to appreciate that such relationships are now also intermediated by statute, particularly the FIC Act, and the Bill of Rights in the Constitution of South Africa. The termination of bank accounts is related to the implementation of the AML/CFT statutory and regulatory provisions of the FIC Act and related legislation, which imposes certain duties on banks and other regulated institutions, as shall be discussed later.

Unilateral Termination of Bank-Client Relationships

The remainder of this chapter argues that the practice of banks of unilaterally terminating the bank accounts of customers without the involvement of LEAs and the courts offends the very same AML/CFT laws, regulations, and related legislation against corruption and terrorism financing that banks purport to be complying with when they unilaterally terminate their bank-client relationships. This practice of unilaterally terminating bank accounts may further violate many rights in the Constitution. I argue that this practice amounts to the mis-implementation of the AML/CFT regime, which then leads to some unintended and undesirable consequences.

It is important to highlight that this is not the first time that the implementation of the AML/CFT regime is found to conflict with the public interest when implemented haphazardly in developing countries. When the regime was initially implemented, some studies found that the aggressive implementation of Know Your Customer (KYC) or Customer Due Diligence (CDD) prescripts of the FATF standards led or could have led to financial exclusion in developing countries, particularly in instances where customers of regulated institutions could not comply with the proof of address requirements

27 See FIC Annual Report, 2014/15.

28 See *South African Reserve Bank v Bank of Baroda* (South Africa) (A267/2018) [2019] ZAGPPHC 218; 2019 (6) SA 174 (GP) (2 April 2019). See also *Bank of Baroda (South Africa) v South African Reserve Bank*, Appeal Board of the Financial Intelligence Centre Act.

29 *Annex Distribution (Pty) Ltd and Others v Bank of Baroda* (52590/2017) [2017] ZAGPPHC 608; 2018 (1) SA 562 (GP) (21 September 2017).

and would therefore be excluded from accessing basic bank accounts.[30] In this regard, FATF had to intervene and clarify that its standards were not aimed at excluding customers from accessing financial services.[31]

It is my view that FATF should intervene again on this issue of unilateral termination of bank accounts, to ensure that banks do not misinterpret nor mis-implement FATF standards. Local regulators should also intervene to ensure that domestic AML/CFT laws and regulations are not mis-implemented, as this could have dire unintended and undesirable consequences. These consequences include the negation of the fight against crime; the supplanting of the role of LEAs, including the courts, by banks; public interest considerations including loss of jobs and financial exclusion, and violation of constitutional rights – violations which result in or perpetuate unfair discrimination and harassment.

In most high-profile unilateral bank account terminations that have been on the news in South Africa, which I shall discuss, it has never been alleged that banks are unilaterally terminating existing banking relationships because customers hadn't complied with their KYC/CDD obligations. In fact, banks shut down bank accounts of some prominent customers whose CDD has been conducted to the extent of having granted such customers long-term credit such as mortgage and business loan facilities, as shall be shown later. Unless such customers are fraudsters, banks would be reckless even to advance credit to such customers without the necessary credit risk assessment and CDD.

AML/CFT Laws Do Not Prescribe Termination of Bank Accounts

It is only when customers fail to comply with the KYC provisions where regulated institutions are obliged by the FIC Act not to enter bank-client relationships or to terminate existing business relationships.[32] Once banks

30 See Genesis, ***Implementing FATF Standards in Developing Countries and Financial Inclusion: Findings and Guidelines*** (Hennie Bester, Doubell Chamberlain, Louis De Koker, Christine Hougaard, Ryan Short, Anja Smith and Richard Walker. Final Report, February 2008), First Initiative, on this point. See also L De Koker, 'Money Laundering Control and Suppression of Financing of Terrorism: Some Thoughts on the Impact of Customer Due Diligence Measures on Financial Exclusion' (2006) 13(1) Journal of Financial Crime 26–50.

31 On learning of the perverse outcomes of customer due diligence in developing countries, FATF published a guidance note in 2008 to guide countries on the implementation of Know Your Customer standards in low capacity countries. See P Vlaanderen, 'The Fight against Money Laundering and Terrorist Financing in Low-Capacity Countries' Speech by FATF President Paul Vlaanderen at the ESAAMLAG 9th Council of Ministers Meeting, Maseru, Lesotho, 21 August 2009. See also FATF, ***Guidance on Capacity Building for Mutual Evaluations and Implementation of the FATF Standards within Low Capacity Countries*** (FR: FATF/OECD 2008).

32 P Vlaanderen, 'The Fight against Money Laundering and Terrorist Financing in Low-Capacity Countries' Speech by FATF President Paul Vlaanderen at the ESAAMLAG 9th Council of Ministers Meeting, Maseru, Lesotho, 21 August 2009. See also FATF, ***Guidance on Capacity***

have profiled or "KYC'd" their customers, they really have no justification or excuse under the AML/CFT laws and regulations to terminate customers' bank accounts. The FIC Act permits them to freeze such bank accounts when instructed by the FIC through its section 34 intervention or through court orders brought in terms of POCA and related legislation aimed at freezing and confiscating proceeds of crime. Even then, the requirement is for them to freeze bank accounts pending whatever investigative or judicial processes that may have been initiated by LEAs, not to terminate.

Law Requires Monitoring and Reporting of Transactions, Not Termination

What the AML/CFT standards require of banks is for them to monitor their customers' bank accounts so that they can be able to identify any transactions that are unusual or suspicious or above a certain regulated cash threshold.[33] Another role linked to monitoring transactions is the obligation to report the prescribed transactions to the FIC.[34] The fact that banks have reported transactions to the FIC does not entitle them not to proceed with those transactions or to terminate customers' bank accounts. Section 33 of the FIC Act states clearly that a regulated institution

> required to make a report to the Centre in terms of section 28 and 29, may continue with and carry out the transaction in respect of which the report is required to be made unless the Centre directs the . . . institution or person in terms of section 34 not to proceed with the transaction.

Simply terminating a relationship based on suspicion or based on having made a report to the FIC could instead amount to a criminal offence of "tipping-off" under the FIC Act (see section 29(3) of the FIC Act), as shall be discussed later.

Bank-Client Relationships Merely a Contractual Issue?

It is my view that the decided cases in South Africa have not only been badly pleaded by those who sought to interdict the unilateral termination of their bank accounts but have mainly, if not only, been pleaded on the basis that the bank-client relationship is merely a contractual issue. In *Bredenkamp and*

Building for Mutual Evaluations and Implementation of the FATF Standards within Low Capacity Countries (FR: FATF/OECD 2008).

33 See sections 28, 29, 30, and 31 of the FIC Act, which respectively place a duty to report CTRs, STRs, cross-border conveyance of cash in and out of South Africa, and electronic transfers of money to and from South Africa.

34 See sections 28, 29, 30, and 31 of the FIC Act, which respectively place a duty to report CTRs, STRs, cross-border conveyance of cash in and out of South Africa, and electronic transfers of money to and from South Africa.

Others[35] and *Annex Distribution and Others*,[36] the litigants sought to interdict and set aside the unilateral termination of their bank accounts by banks. However, they limited their pleadings to the bank-client relationship being a contractual issue, not considering that it is now also mediated by statute, particularly the FIC Act, and the Constitution. Except for the *Sekunjalo* litigation in the Equality Court and the Competition Tribunal, they have also hardly pleaded the violation of constitutional rights which are impacted by the bank-client relationship.[37] *Sekunjalo* took the argument even further in the Competition Tribunal by arguing anti-competitive practices which violate the competition laws of South Africa.[38]

In *Annex Distribution and Others*,[39] 20 companies linked to the "Gupta family" took the Bank of Baroda (South Africa) to the North Gauteng High Court

35 *Bredenkamp and Others v Standard Bank of SA Ltd (599/09) [2010] ZASCA 75; 2010 (4) SA 468 (SCA); 2010 (9) BCLR 892 (SCA); [2010] 4 All SA 113 (SCA) (27 May 2010).*

36 Annex Distribution (n 29).

37 According to the court papers filed in the Equality Court in Cape Town, the Sekunjalo Group of Companies (Sekunjalo) is a group of companies whose accounts are being unilaterally terminated by banks in South Africa. This includes the accounts of Independent Newspapers, a global media brand, which is largely owned by Sekunjalo in South Africa. Sekunjalo filed an application for an interdict in the Equality Court to stop the banks from unilaterally terminating its bank accounts. They also seek a declaration of this practice as unconstitutional and amounting to unfair discrimination and harassment in terms of the Promotion of Equality and Prevention of Unfair Discrimination Act (PEPUDA), Act No. 4 of 2000. The main application has not been heard by the Equality Court, but an interim interdict was granted by the Equality Court, stopping one of the banks, Nedbank, from closing the bank accounts and ordering Nedbank to re-open those that it had already closed pending the finalization of the main application. The interim interdict was granted on 17 June 2022 in a judgment delivered by Judge Dalamo. See *Surve and Others v Nedbank and Others, 2022,* Equality Court, Western Cape, EC02/2022, 17 June 2022.

38 See *Surve and Others v Nedbank and Others, 2022,* Competition Tribunal of South Africa, Case No:IR153Dec21, 16 September 2022, The Competition Tribunal (comptrib.co.za). In the Competitional Tribunal, *Sekunjalo* argued that the termination of its bank accounts or refusal to provide such amounted to abuse of dominance, or collusion, or coordinated conduct which lessened competition in contravention of the Competition Act. *Sekunjalo* further argued that without access to banking and payment services, *Sekunjalo* would cease to operate, thus eliminating effective competition in various markets in which *Sekunjalo* operated. In granting interim relief to Sekunjalo, in a judgment handed down on 16 September 2022, the Competition Tribunal found that, among others, Sekunjalo had established prima facie that the banks engaged in a concerted practice involving a concerted refusal to supply banking services to Sekunjalo amounting to a restricted horizontal practice in terms of section 4(1)(a) of the Competition Act, Act 89 of 1998 (South Africa). The Tribunal said that banking plays a central role in the economic life of society and no commercial transaction of substance and scale is possible without banking services. It further said that Sekunjalo had established a *prima facie* case that the conduct of the banks has the effect of impeding or preventing Sekunjalo from participating in or expanding within the markets in which the Group operates and thereby substantially lessening competition. The interim interdict by the Tribunal ordered some banks to restore banking services to Sekunjalo that had been terminated and interdicted others from doing so pending the finalisation of the main application.

39 Annex Distribution (n 29).

to interdict it from closing their transactional and other facilities. In this case, Fabricius J confirmed the principles set out in *Bredenkamp*[40] by the Gauteng High Court and the SCA, on appeal, in 2010. In summary, *Bredenkamp* set out that the banker-client relationship is contractual in nature, and a decision to terminate that relationship is governed by the ordinary rules of contract.[41] It went further to say that banks can unilaterally terminate bank accounts without even giving the customers a right to be heard or reasons for such terminations.[42]

In my view, this position fails to show that the bank-client relationship has evolved and is now regulated by the FIC Act and the Constitution. At para 21 of *Annex Distribution and Others*, Fabricius J stated:

> Applicants acknowledge, and it is indeed so, that the relationship between the parties hereto is contractual in nature. As a result, a decision to terminate that relationship is governed by the ordinary rules of contract. I may just add at this stage that as far as considerations of the balance of convenience are concerned, I will keep in mind that Respondent (Bank of Baroda) is subject to a number of statutory obligations, which are aimed at the integrity of the banking system and to prevent dishonesty and corruption among others.

While Fabricius J was correct to state that banks are subject to statutory and regulatory obligations, the reality is however more than that. The AML/CFT laws and regulations have become a material aspect of the bank-client relationship. When interdicting and seeking to set aside the unilateral terminations, litigants need to plead for the development of the common law in this area. At para 29 of *Bredenkamp*, Harms DP noted that the appellants sought to set aside the termination of business relationships, "[saying] before us that they do not suggest that the common law had to be developed." This, in my view, was a huge mistake.

Litigants should have raised this issue more sharply in their pleadings. They should have argued that in the light of the FIC Act and its regulations mediating the bank-client relationships, particularly the onboarding and continuous monitoring and reporting of customer transactions, the courts are obliged to interpret the objectives and provisions of the FIC Act and related legislation. The courts would also need to determine if any constitutional values and rights are violated by such terminations. The courts would then determine that banks are neither expected nor encouraged by the AML/CFT and related laws and regulations to terminate the facilities of customers. They are merely

40 *Bredenkamp and Others v Standard Bank of SA Ltd (599/09) [2010] ZASCA 75; 2010 (4) SA 468 (SCA); 2010 (9) BCLR 892 (SCA); [2010] 4 All SA 113 (SCA) (27 May 2010).*

41 *Bredenkamp and Others v Standard Bank of SA Ltd* (599/09) [2010] ZASCA 75; 2010 (4) SA 468 (SCA); 2010 (9) BCLR 892 (SCA); [2010] 4 All SA 113 (SCA) (27 May 2010).

42 *Bredenkamp and Others v Standard Bank of SA Ltd* (599/09) [2010] ZASCA 75; 2010 (4) SA 468 (SCA); 2010 (9) BCLR 892 (SCA); [2010] 4 All SA 113 (SCA) (27 May 2010).

required to not turn a blind eye and to report customer transactions that are prescribed by the FIC Act and related laws.

Courts in South Africa would eventually need to clear things up when it comes to the circumstances under which banks can unilaterally terminate relationships by interpreting the global FATF standards, the domestic statutory and regulatory provisions, the common law of contract, and the constitutional rights that are affected by such unilateral terminations.

Relationship Between the Constitution and Common Law

It is important to highlight the relationship between the Constitution and statutes on the one hand, and common law on the other, in South Africa. South Africa's common law "is not sacrosanct, untouchable or protected from constitutional scrutiny".[43] The Constitutional Court of South Africa has stressed that courts are obliged to develop the common law in line with the Constitution, which enjoys the status of supremacy above all law in the country. In *Carmichele*,[44] the Constitutional Court stated that South African courts have an obligation to develop the common law. At para 33 it stated:

> Section 173 of the Constitution gives to all higher courts, including this Court, the inherent power to develop the common law, taking into account the interests of justice. In section 7 of the Constitution, the Bill of Rights enshrines the rights of all people in South Africa, and obliges the state to respect, promote and fulfil these rights. Section 8(1) of the Constitution makes the Bill of Rights binding on the judiciary as well as on the legislature and executive. Section 39(2) of the Constitution provides that when developing the common law, every court must promote the spirit, purport and objects of the Bill of Rights. It follows implicitly that where the common law deviates from the spirit, purport and objects of the Bill of Rights the courts have an obligation to develop it by removing that deviation. [References omitted]

The bank-client relationship as understood at common law now deviates from the spirit, purport, and objects of the Bill of Rights. It does this by permitting banks to violate the rights of customers through the practice of unilaterally terminating their bank accounts. Although there is no right in the Bill of Rights of access to financial services in South Africa, there are many other implied rights that are protected that cannot be meaningfully exercised or enjoyed without access to banking facilities.

43 C Botha, *Statutory Interpretation: An Introduction for Students* (5th edn, Juta 2012) 43.

44 *Carmichele v Minister of Safety and Security* (CCT 48/00) [2001] ZACC 22; 2001 (4) SA 938 (CC); 2001 (10) BCLR 995 (CC) (16 August 2001).

Constitutional Rights Affected by Unilateral Termination of Bank Accounts

The constitutional rights that are affected by the unilateral termination of bank accounts include the right of freedom of trade, occupation, and profession (section 21); housing (section 26); health care, food, water, and social security (section 27); education (section 29). The right to equality and human dignity may also be added to the list in instances where regulated institutions treat customers differently depending on an unclear criterion which may raise perceptions of unfair discrimination and harassment.[45] The litigants failed to plead these issues in *Bredenkamp* and pleaded the issue of fairness citing *Barkhuizen v Napier*[46] as authority, which was dismissed by the Court. As a result, there was no constitutional analysis on how the unilateral terminations could have violated constitutional rights in *Bredenkamp*.[47]

In the current *Sekunjalo* matter that is before the Equality Court, the interveners[48] are arguing that without access to transactional accounts, businesses and individuals are unable to receive payments or to pay for goods and services in the formal sector of the economy. This violates their section 21 rights/freedoms in the Constitution. With regards to housing (section 26), banks and estate agents require bank statements to assess customers for mortgage or rental lease agreements. Without these, the right to housing cannot be meaningfully enjoyed.

For access to medical aid insurance, medical health companies require to debit subscriptions from bank accounts. This is the same for short- and long-term savings or investments. Unilateral termination of bank accounts of customers deprives customers from enjoying these rights, as they ultimately become "red-listed" by other financial service providers when their bank accounts get terminated by others.

The example of this phenomenon can be found in the *Sekunjalo* application, where its companies went to several other financial services providers to try and open bank accounts and were unsuccessful or were turned down.[49] Had

45 This is the argument that is being advanced by the Sekunjalo Group of Companies in the Equality Court in the Western Cape.

46 *Barkhuizen v Napier 2007 (5) SA 323 (CC) [2007] ZACC 5; 2007 (7) BCLR 691 (CC).*

47 It is important to state that based the facts in *Bredenkamp*, even if constitutional issues were raised, Bredenkamp would have had his accounts closed because he had been blacklisted by the Office of Foreign Assets Control (OFAC) in the US. OFAC is however a statutory body of government (the US Treasury) which derives its mandate from statute.

48 These are the parties that have been admitted by the Equality Court in the Western Cape to join *Sekunjalo* in its litigation of unfair discrimination and harassment.

49 A confirmatory affidavit of Mr Wakeel McLachlan dated 1 February 2022 was filed at the Equality Court, a Group Executive: Investments for Ayo Technology Solutions Limited ("Ayo"), a public company listed in the Johannesburg Stock Exchange, and is part of the Sekunjalo Group of Companies. This affidavit explains in detail how Ayo tried to get alternative banking facilities when FNB closed its accounts in 2020 and 2021. All those attempts were fruitless as Ayo and other companies within the Sekunjalo Group were denied access to such banking facilities. In the Competition Tribunal decision on the interim interdict, the Tribunal narrated the story of

they not been taken to court, the Sekunjalo Group would probably be out of business by now, and this is not far-fetched. The Oakbay Group of Companies was taken out of business when its accounts were unilaterally terminated by all the major banks in South Africa. The story of the Oakbay Group bank account terminations is covered in the Zondo Commission of Inquiry.[50]

Recent De-risking and Regulatory Avoidance/Evasion Studies

Banks can and do unilaterally terminate bank accounts of customers because they want to avoid/evade their regulatory obligations. This is what has become known as de-risking. The FATF defines de-risking as

> the phenomenon of financial institutions terminating or restricting business relationships with clients or categories of clients to avoid, rather than manage, risk.[51]

This phenomenon has been taking place in many countries since the introduction of AML/CFT laws and regulations. In 2015, the Financial Conduct Authority of the UK commissioned a study to examine the nature and scale of de-risking in the UK.[52] This study found that there was de-risking by banks in the UK which was "partly a result of the higher costs of compliance . . . and partly a response to criminal, civil and regulatory actions. These include regulatory settlements, including Deferred Prosecution Agreements (DPAs), especially those reached in response to AML/CFT failings."[53]

The World Bank Group has also conducted surveys on this phenomenon from a global perspective, focusing on money transfer operators (MTOs)[54] and correspondent banking relationships (CBRs). The surveys were commissioned by the G20's Global Partnership for Financial Inclusion.[55] They confirmed that de-risking is taking place with banks closing accounts of MTOs and

one of Sekunjalo Group companies, Puleng Technologies (Pty) Ltd. (Puleng). Puleng, a company with a turnover of R300 million, had to be sold by Sekunjalo for a loss after its bank accounts were unilaterally terminated. Some customers, including Discovery, a large medical scheme and financial services provider in South Africa, terminated its contract with Puleng on the basis that it no longer had a bank account and could not pay Puleng by using third-party payment options. See paras 259 to 260 of *Surve and Others v Nedbank and Others*, Competition Tribunal (n 38).

50 Judicial Commission of Inquiry into State Capture Report: Part VI, Vol.1: Vrede Dairy Project/Estina and Closure of Gupta Bank Accounts, Johannesburg, South Africa.

51 The World Bank Group, *Report on the G20 Survey on De-risking in the Remittance Market* (World Bank Group 2015) 1.

52 See D Artingstall et al., *Drivers and Impacts of Derisking*: A Study of Representative Views and Data in the UK (H John Howell & Co. Ltd. 2016) for the Financial Conduct Authority, Surrey, UK.

53 See D Artingstall et al., *Drivers and Impacts of Derisking*: A Study of Representative Views and Data in the UK (H John Howell & Co. Ltd. 2016) 7 for the Financial Conduct Authority, Surrey, UK.

54 MTOs are remittance services providers which provide cross-border money transfer services.

55 The World Bank Group (n 51).

terminating corresponding bank relationships with small banks in developing countries or high-risk jurisdictions.[56]

Cenfri, a research institute operating in Africa and based in Cape Town, South Africa, published a study in 2020 which looked into the phenomenon of de-risking in Africa and the impact that it had on capital flows, regional trade, and industrial development.[57] This study found that AML/CFT practices shaped de-risking activities of financial institutions, which in turn affected capital flows.[58] The FSARB of Eastern and Southern Africa, known as the Eastern and Southern Africa Anti-Money Laundering Group (ESAAMLG), also published a report[59] which looked at the phenomenon of de-risking in its region. This study confirmed that de-risking in these countries was taking place where banks were terminating corresponding relationships with each other across the region and were terminating accounts of customers.[60]

It said that 40% of the surveyed banks had been impacted by de-risking through termination and/or restriction of corresponding bank relationships, citing remittance products in USD, EUR, AUD and GBP currencies being the most affected.[61] It also found that "80% of financial institutions that were surveyed have terminated relationships with customers who were viewed as being high risk . . . from high risk countries and customers who do business with high risk countries."[62]

FATF has stated categorically that it is not the objectives of its regime to exclude ordinary citizens and businesses of countries it regulates from accessing the financial system and services. In a Note it published on 23 October 2015 titled "FATF Takes Action to Tackle De-risking", it stated:

> Derisking is having a significant impact in certain regions and sectors in particular and, although there is currently no evidence that de-risking is adversely impacting global financial stability, the international community continues to study this issue. . . . This is a serious concern for FATF and the FATF-style regional bodies to the extent that de-risking may drive financial transactions underground which creates financial exclusion and reduces transparency, thereby increasing money laundering and terrorist financing.

56 The World Bank Group (n 51).

57 Cenfri, *De-risking and Illicit Financial Flows: The Role of Regional Economic Hubs* (Cenfri 2020).

58 *Cenfri, De-risking and Illicit Financial Flows: The Role of Regional Economic Hubs* (Cenfri 2020).

59 ESAAMLG, Report of the survey to assess the existence, causes, and impact of de-risking within the Eastern and South Africa Anti-Money Laundering Group Region. Working Group on Risk, Compliance and Financial Inclusion (WG-RCFI) 2017.

60 ESAAMLG, Report of the survey to assess the existence, causes, and impact of de-risking within the Eastern and South Africa Anti-Money Laundering Group Region. Working Group on Risk, Compliance and Financial Inclusion (WG-RCFI) 2017, 66.

61 ESAAMLG, Report of the survey to assess the existence, causes, and impact of de-risking within the Eastern and South Africa Anti-Money Laundering Group Region. Working Group on Risk, Compliance and Financial Inclusion (WG-RCFI) 2017, 66.

62 ESAAMLG, Report of the survey to assess the existence, causes, and impact of de-risking within the Eastern and South Africa Anti-Money Laundering Group Region. Working Group on Risk, Compliance and Financial Inclusion (WG-RCFI) 2017, 66.

> The drivers of de-risking are complex and include: profitability; reputational risk; lower risk appetites of banks; and regulatory burdens related to the implementation of anti-money laundering and counter-terrorist financing (AML/CFT) requirements, the increasing number of sanctions regime, and the regulatory requirements in the financial sector."[63]

On 27 October 2021, FATF published another Note titled "High-Level Synopsis of the Stocktake of the Unintended Consequences of the FATF Standards", where it again addressed the issue of de-risking. It stated that de-risking and financial exclusion remained challenges for many sectors and was contrary to its AML/CFT risk-based approach to compliance.[64] It described de-risking and financial exclusion as unintended consequences of the implementation of its standards.[65] It also said that sometimes these challenges are caused by the "incorrect implementation" of its standards.[66]

The FIC, in its 2016/17 Annual Report following the enactment of amendments to the FIC Act that introduced the concept of politically exposed persons (PEPs) (or what South Africa refers to as domestic and foreign prominent influential persons [PIPS]), warned that the introduction of this concept in South African law does not assume that PEPs/PIPs are involved in financial crime.[67] It further warned that the amendments to the FIC Act did not empower the FIC or banks to investigate financial crimes or participate in criminal prosecutions.[68]

It also warned that the FIC Act does not give regulated institutions powers to "invade the privacy and dignity of customers".[69] Lastly and most importantly, it warned that the FIC Act "does not require financial and other institutions to avoid doing business with any category of customers or to end their relationships with customers".[70] However, these warnings may have been a little too late, as South African banks had already started to implement the PEPs/PIPs framework, in the case of *Oakbay*, before even the 2017 FIC Amendment Act was passed or signed by the President.

63 FATF, 'FATF Takes Action to Tackle De-Risking' 23 October 2015 <www.fatf-gafi.org/publications/fatfrecommendations/documents/fatf-action-to-tackle-de-risking.html>

64 FATF, 'High-Level Synopsis of the Stocktake of the Unintended Consequences of the FATF Standards' 27 October 2021, 1 <www.fatf-gafi.org/media/fatf/documents/Unintended-Consequences.pdf>.

65 FATF, 'High-Level Synopsis of the Stocktake of the Unintended Consequences of the FATF Standards' 27 October 2021, 1 <www.fatf-gafi.org/media/fatf/documents/Unintended-Consequences.pdf>.

66 FATF, 'High-Level Synopsis of the Stocktake of the Unintended Consequences of the FATF Standards' 27 October 2021, 1 <www.fatf-gafi.org/media/fatf/documents/Unintended-Consequences.pdf>.

67 FIC Annual Report, 2016/17, 11.

68 FIC Annual Report, 2016/17, 11.

69 FIC Annual Report, 2016/17, 11.

70 FIC Annual Report, 2016/17, 11.

FATF Standards Do Not Require Termination of Customer Relationships

When all of the above-mentioned studies and Notes are considered, it should be clear by now that the AML/CFT laws and regulations were never enacted to encourage the termination of bank-client relationships. If they do so, this is an unintended and undesirable consequence of their mis-implementation. Banks or any other regulated institution should not turn around and claim that the AML/CFT standards and laws made them do it.

In *South African Petroleum Energy Guild*,[71] Sutherland J had to decide whether the bank had a duty to freeze a customers' account on suspicions of money laundering. At para 27, he said:

> It seems to me that the obligations of a bank to initiate action about money laundering are wholly regulated by statute. There is no space, and indeed no need that is discernible in this regard, to imply additional duties on the bank into its contracts with its clients. . . . The respondent's role in combatting money laundering is already spelt out in the legislation: in essence to be vigilant about possible unlawful activity and report it when it is noticed and if lawfully instructed to put a hold on funds, to do so. There is no scope to develop a role for what would be a cousin of the Lex Commissoria to add to the battalions arrayed against rich crooks.

At para 28, Sutherland J explained further:

> Moreover, the term sought to be imputed and its radical intrusion on the rights of a client far exceed what FICA authorises the [FIC] to do. What is sometimes overlooked is that even criminals have rights; the more basic of which is to be convicted before being punished. With the sole exception of the process of asset forfeiture provided for in chapter 6 of POCA, our law adheres to this order of things.

The reasoning of Sutherland, in my view, is one of the correct positions to follow in these matters. Bank should not seek to exercise functions and powers they do not have. They should do what is prescribed by the relevant laws and regulations. Even the recently released Zondo Commission report,[72] referred to earlier, noted at paras 794–96 that:

> 794. . .. In Bredenkamp and Others v Standard Bank of SA Ltd the Supreme Court of Appeal decided that a bank was not obliged to hear its client's side of the story before the bank could terminate the relationship.

71 *South African Petroleum Energy Guild (NPC) v RMB Private Bank* (2014/27890) [2014] ZAGPJHC (5 December 2014).

72 Judicial Commission of Inquiry into State: A Capture Report: Part VI, Vol. 1 (n 50) 263–64.

> It seems that the Supreme Court of Appeal's basis for this decision was that the relationship between a bank and a client is a contractual one.
>
> 795. Representatives of Banks who testified before this Commission revealed that the banking industry is regulated or is subject to many laws. Banks possess an enormous amount of power. This would become very clear if all the banks were to refuse that you hold an account with them. You would not be able to run any serious business without being able to open a bank account. If you already had a bank account and all the banks in which you have accounts terminated their relationship with you, that would be devastating. If you were running a serious business, you would need to close down that may result in job losses. Depending on the size of the business one may be talking about hundreds or thousands of people who would lose jobs. The workers would have to suffer serious consequences even though they may not have done anything wrong themselves.
>
> 796. The fact that the relationship between a bank and a client may be contractual is neither here nor there because there are other relationships which are or were at some stage contractual in nature and Parliament intervened in order to infuse the notion of fairness in the relationship.

After these observations, Chief Justice Zondo recommended that "relevant existing legislation governing banks be amended to introduce this requirement of fairness or, if warranted, a new piece of legislation be enacted which will make this a requirement."[73]

Unilateral Termination Amounts to "Tipping-Off"

There is space to develop the common law in line with statutes regulating money laundering and counter-financing of terrorism, market conduct, and the Constitution in South Africa. The provisions of these laws merely require regulated institutions to identify, monitor, and report suspicious and unusual activities. When they terminate relationships unilaterally, they are actually violating some provisions of these AML/CFT laws, such as the "tipping-off" provisions found in section 29(3) of the FIC Act. What will be important to ensure in the future is that when banks require to terminate accounts unilaterally, they should apply for a court order which authorizes them to unilaterally terminate such bank accounts upon convincing the courts that such customers have offended the laws which the banks seek to comply with.

There must also be mechanisms put in place to ensure that unilateral terminations do not rely on non-legal concepts such as "reputational risk", as this could result in actual or perceptions of unfair discrimination and harassment. Reputational risk could be used as an excuse for any form of discrimination,

73 Judicial Commission of Inquiry into State: A Capture Report: Part VI, Vol. 1 (n 50) para 798.

especially in a country that has just emerged from the vestiges of apartheid. It could also be abused to target political opponents by those in power. Already politicians have entered the debate with regards to these unilateral terminations.

In a press briefing held in early December 2022, the leader of the third largest political party in South Africa, the Economic Freedom Fighters (EFF), Mr Julius Malema, accused banks of being selective in unilaterally shutting down bank accounts of political opponents of the current President of South Africa, Cyril Ramaphosa.[74] In this press briefing, he questioned why banks had not shut down the bank accounts of Ramaphosa, who recently was alleged to have kept millions of US dollars (foreign currency) under mattresses in his Phala Phala farm in Limpopo, South Africa.[75]

This is a legitimate question if banks are genuine about reputation risk. President Ramaphosa has received a lot of negative press because of the Phala Phala saga, including for his presidential campaign (known as CR17) donations to become the president of the ruling party, the African National Congress, in 2017. However, none of the banks has been reported to have closed his bank accounts.

In the Equality Court and the Competition Tribunal, in the ongoing *Sekunjalo* matters, banks are struggling to justify why bank accounts of some businesses have not been terminated despite those businesses having admitted to or having been found guilty of serious unlawful activities. Some of these are well known international and local organizations such as Glencore, Steinhoff, Tongaat Hullets, Bain & Co, EOH, and KPMG. At paras 210–12 of its reason for decision, the Competition Tribunal noted "that a selective approach to closing down accounts of disfavoured firms while keeping accounts of favoured firms open by the Respondent Banks", showing that the concept of reputational risk is not applied in an unbiased manner by the banks in South Africa.[76]

Conclusion

In conclusion, there is a need for more research and debates on this issue of the unilateral closure of bank accounts by banks in South Africa, and elsewhere. This chapter has only covered those prominent bank account terminations

74 Siyabonga Sithole, 'Malema Slams Banks for Being Selective in Closing Down Accounts of Enemies of White Monopoly Capital' (*Independent Online*, 6 December 2022). Malema slams SA banks for being selective in closing down accounts of enemies of white monopoly capital (https://iol.co.za).

75 Siyabonga Sithole, 'Malema Slams Banks for Being Selective in Closing Down Accounts of Enemies of White Monopoly Capital' (*Independent Online*, 6 December 2022). Malema slams SA banks for being selective in closing down accounts of enemies of white monopoly capital (https://iol.co.za).

76 *Surve and Other v Nedbank and Other* (n 37).

that were in the news at the time of writing or that had been litigated. It is possible that many South Africans and businesses have had their bank accounts terminated unilaterally. It would therefore be difficult to know the scale and extent at which these unilateral terminations have been taking place simply because bank-client relationships are confidential. The public generally gets to hear about these when affected parties are engaged in litigation, such as the *Oakbay* and the *Sekunjalo* matters discussed herein.

The issue is complex, however, and requires a delicate balance between the objectives of the AML/CFT requirements, the extent of the banks' rights to unilaterally terminate customer relationships under the common law of contract, and the interplay between such and the constitutional rights of customers, which in South Africa can be limited through law of general application as provided for in section 36 of the Constitution.

Judging by the interim interdicts granted in favour of *Sekunjalo* in the Equality Court and the Competition Tribunal, and the reasoning of the judges, banks face a mammoth task in convincing the courts that *Bredenkamp*, an SCA judgment which they have heavily relied upon in unilaterally terminating customer bank accounts, will protect them. It is my view that legal and regulatory mechanisms should be put in place to ensure that the implementation of AML/CFT laws and regulations does not result in the undesirable and unintended consequences. Regulators and the courts (through their judgments) should also give guidance in instances where FATF standards, laws, and regulations are being incorrectly implemented. Banks, however, do face serious compliance dilemmas and may face serious damages claims in instances where they violate constitutional rights and get litigated against.

6 Implications of Botswana's Legal Culture in the Implementation of the AML/CFT Regime and Prosecution of Money Laundering/Financial Crimes

Gosego Rockfall Lekgowe

Introduction

The 2007 Mutual Evaluation Report (2007 MER)[1] for Botswana called for radical reforms in Botswana's criminal system on a scale the country had never undertaken. In implementing the 2007 MER, Botswana faced an array of constraints and challenges. Not only did these challenges surface in the implementation of the 2007 MER, but they also reared their heads in the prosecution of money laundering (ML) crimes.

Through the lens of legal culture, this chapter examines the legal change brought about by the Anti-Money Laundering/Countering the Financing of Terrorism (the AML/CFT Regime) in Botswana. It focuses on the constraints and challenges experienced by Botswana in implementing this regime. In this chapter, AML/CFT Regime refers to the international regulatory standards brought about by the Financial Action Task Force (FATF). Legal culture can spark, facilitate or constrain legal change. Thus, this analysis puts Botswana's legal culture under the microscope and contends that the constraints and challenges that Botswana experienced stemmed from her legal culture. These challenges are also observed in the prosecution of ML crimes. Botswana's ambivalent attitude towards international law, her culture of secrecy, poor consultation of the citizenry on new laws and poor institutional coordination are placed at the centre as the causes of these constraints and challenges.

The chapter begins with an assessment the concept of legal culture. It then discusses aspects of Botswana's legal culture that are identified as the causes of Botswana's constraints and challenges. These cultural elements are Botswana's ambivalence towards international law, culture of secrecy, weak model of consultation and education on law-making and poor institutional coordination. The last two sections examine Botswana's implementation of AML/CFT laws and prosecution of ML crimes in two cases.

1 Eastern and Southern Africa Anti-Money Laundering Group (ESAAMLG), *Anti-money Laundering and Counter-Terrorist Financing Measures – Botswana, Second Round Mutual Evaluation Report* (ESAAMLG 2007) <www.esaamlg.org/reports/me.ph> accessed 13 March 2022.

DOI: 10.4324/9781003253808-8

The Meaning of Legal Culture

The AML/CFT Regime called for significant reforms in Botswana's legal environment. In the course of implementing this legal change, Botswana experienced constraints and challenges. This chapter argues that the constraints and challenges that Botswana experienced can be explained through Botswana's legal culture. Legal culture is the legal system's way of doing things: it entails the habits and behaviour of the legal system. These habits and behaviours may constrain legal change or facilitate it. According to Friedman, legal culture consists of three components: the structural component, the cultural component and the substantive component.[2] The structural component entails the institutions, their shape, form and processes. The cultural component consists of the "values and attitudes which bind the system together and which determine the place of the legal system in the culture of the society as a whole."[3] The laws, rules, doctrines, statutes and decisions are the substantive component. Thus, under the lens of legal culture, the legal system is conceived as the collisions and interactions of these three components. These components can be identified in Botswana's legal culture and then be used to explain the constraints that Botswana faced in implementing the legal change required by the AML/CFT Regime.

These components can be further divided into sub-systems. This sharpens the lens so that more knowledge can be gained about a legal system. The legal system can be seen as a set of structures that processes inputs (demands and resources) from an environment, sends its outputs (functions) and receives feedback from that environment. The legal system has three core components.[4] Firstly, it entails the social and legal forces which press in and make the law. Secondly, the law itself is a component of the system and is also the output of the system. The last component is the impact of the law on behaviour in the outside world. To achieve depth and detail, variations within legal cultures exist as the internal and external culture. The ideas and practices of legal professionals form the internal culture, whilst the opinions, interests and pressures brought to bear on law by wider social groups form the external culture. Legal culture can exist at the micro-level, in the court or lawyer's office, and at the macro-level, that is, membership of the families of legal systems. Together these ontological components can be applied to extract inferences about the nature of society.

In evaluating a country's legal culture, various indicators can be used. These indicators include goal attainment of public administrations, degree of legalization of state activities and frequency of illegal (corrupt) behaviour of public

2 Lawrence M Friedman, *The Legal System: A Social Science Perspective* (Russel Foundation 1975) 16.

3 Lawrence M Friedman, 'Legal Culture and Social Development' (1969) 4(1) Law & Society Review 29, 34.

4 Lawrence M Friedman, 'Legal Culture and Social Development' (1969) 4(1) Law & Society Review 14.

officials. The character of the population is also relevant, such as knowledge of law in the general population, attitudes towards state regulation and preferences for formal versus informal dispute resolution. Other vital factors include the ideological position of judges,[5] the extent to which the legal system is led by the state or by the party, the number and power of courts, the nature of the legal profession, the importance of the judiciary, and the nature and extent of legal training, as well as ideas about what law is for, where it is to be found, and how regulation and dispute resolution should take place. These factors are detectable, concrete and tangible behavioural and attitudinal indicators.

Legal culture can stimulate, drive or stifle legal change.[6] Nonetheless, like many conceptual frameworks, it has some blind spots and has been a subject of considerable debate. Even though a description of legal culture has been preferred above, the meaning of legal culture is still contested and vague, and this may endanger its explanatory value. Cotterrell claims that the concept brings nothing to the table since everything about the law needs to be understood in relation to the social conditions which have produced it.[7] Also, identifying indicators of legal culture is not an enterprise – one risks injecting what one wishes to see into legal culture. Others[8] argue that the separation of internal and external culture creates a homogenous and static concept of culture. Moreover, the theory's underlying assumption that culture influences the law is said to be problematic in that it ignores that the law also influences culture. To these methodological challenges, Nelken[9] offers a helpful remedy. He recommends that the following be made explicit: (1) the kind of facts that are thought to make up legal culture; (2) the chosen approach within which the concept is deployed; and (3) the normative aspects of the inquiry. This remedy brings rigor and clarity to the framework. Not surprisingly, other scholars have employed this remedy. To adopt Nelken's remedy, the facts that constitute culture in this chapter are the values, opinions, attitudes and beliefs about law. The focus is on how challenges experienced by Botswana in implementing the AML regime can be explained by the values, opinions, attitudes and beliefs of relevant actors about law. Thus, legal culture is being used a causal explanation for the challenges. Normatively, legal culture is used in the sense of a "culture of legality" but as an assessment of the context in which the AML regime was received and what constraints and challenges Botswana faced in prosecuting crimes under the law.

5 Volkmar Gessner, 'Global Legal Interaction and Legal Cultures' (1994) 7 Ratio Juris 132, 135.

6 Ian Watson, 'Legal Change: Sources of Law and Legal Culture' (1983) 131 University of Pennsylvania LR 1121, 1154.

7 Roger Cotterrell, *The Sociology of Law: An Introduction* (rev edn, Butterworth 1992).

8 Reinmann Mathias and Reinhard Zimmermann, *The Oxford Handbook of Comparative Law* (2006; online edn, Oxford Academic, 18 September 2012) <https://doi.org/10.1093/oxfordhb/9780199296064.001.0001> accessed 15 October 2022.

9 David Nelken, *Comparative Legal Research and Legal Cultures: Facts, Approaches, and Values* (Annual Review of Law and Social Science 2016) 45.

As a conceptual framework, legal culture holds an enduring appeal[10] owing to its epistemic outcomes. It "points to differences in the way features of law are themselves embedded in larger frameworks of social structure and culture which constitute and reveal the place of law in society."[11] Thus, it allows focus on a study of legal action that is not confined to legal texts, roles and performances. It emphasizes "the role of taken-for-granted and tacit actions that operated on and within the interactions of thé legal system and its environment"[12] Furthermore, it combines the micro level (the individual) and the macro level (the structure), which allows for a wholesome study of phenomena. Consequently, it locates the constraints and challenges of implementation within the legal system – the legal system and the culture and institutions around it constitutes the epistemic sites for interrogation.

Legal Culture in Botswana

Applying the concept of legal culture described earlier, Botswana's legal culture consists of the values and attitudes of the internal and external actors, the laws, rules, doctrines, statutes and decisions of the courts – all of which can be summed up to the structural, cultural and substantive components. This section evaluates aspects of Botswana's legal culture that explain the constraints and challenges that Botswana faced in the implementation of AML/CFT legal changes: the ambivalent attitude of Botswana towards international law, its culture of secrecy or lack of transparency, and lack of expertise in financial crimes.

Ambivalence Towards International Law

Botswana's attitude towards international law is an integral component of her legal culture. As a dualist state, international law in Botswana has no legal effect[13] unless it is incorporated into domestic law. The power to conclude international treaties is the prerogative of the Executive, which is headed by the President. The Constitution[14] entitles the President to use his deliberate judgment in exercising his Executive powers, and in doing so, he is not obliged to consult anyone. Generally, Botswana's attitude on international law can be characterized as one of ambivalence. There is an observable tendency to sign or ratify treaties only when Botswana's material interests are in jeopardy. Rarely

10 Sally Engle Merry, 'What Is Legal Culture – An Anthropological Perspective' (2010) 5 Journal of Competition Law 40.

11 David Nelken, 'Towards a Sociology of Legal Adaptation' in C Nelken and Johannes Feest (eds), *Adapting Legal Cultures* (Hart Publishing 2001) 25.

12 Susan S Silbey, 'Legal Culture and Cultures of Legality' in John R Hall, Laura Grindstaff and Ming-Cheng Lo (eds), *Handbook of Cultural Sociology* (Routledge 2010) 470.

13 This has been used to generally mean that the rights and obligations arising from such treaties cannot be enforced in Botswana courts. However, such treaties have frequently been used.

14 Constitution of Botswana 1966, s 47.

are treaties signed for purely ideational ones. This is shown by three trends. First is Botswana's reluctance to ratify or accede to some critical international human rights treaties – she has only signed a few treaties.[15] Secondly, where treaties are ratified, they are hardly ever incorporated into Botswana's domestic law so much that non-incorporation has become the norm. Lastly, Botswana has refused to abide with a decision of the African Commission.[16] Considering that Botswana has been labelled the African miracle, this attitude is surprising.[17] This legal culture – one of ambivalence towards international law – can be seen in Botswana's journey in implementing the AML/CFT Regime.

Culture of Secrecy or Lack of Transparency

Botswana maintains a culture of secrecy. A survey by the African Platform on Access to Information (APAI) conducted in 2013 found that State held information is hardly accessible, government institutions are secretive.[18] The MISA Transparency Assessment conducted in 2017 concluded that

> Botswana is a very secretive country – out of eight organizations surveyed, only four responded to the information requests. Release of information by public organs is regarded as a favour to the public. Despite the recognition of the right to information by Section 12 of the Constitution and other public policy pronouncements, government bodies view any unsolicited request for information with suspicion.[19]

Despite these negative reports, there is still no law on freedom of access to information in Botswana. Pegg[20] observes that "Botswana's democracy is

15 Bugalo Maripe, 'Giving Effect to International Human Rights Law in the Domestic Context of Botswana: Dissonance and Incongruity in Judicial Interpretation' (2014) 14(2) Oxford University Commonwealth Law Journal 251. Some of the treaties that Botswana has not ratified include the International Covenant on Economic, Social and Cultural Rights, the Optional Protocol of the Convention against Torture and Convention for the Protection of All Persons from Enforced Disappearance.

16 *John K. Modise/Botswana* [1993] ACHPR and *Kenneth Good/Republic of Botswana* [2010] ACHPR 106.

17 Amelia Cook and Jeremy Sarkin, 'Is Botswana the Miracle of Africa? Democracy, the Rule of Law, and Human Rights Versus Economic Development' (2010) 19 Transnational and Contemporary Problems 453. See N de Jager and D Sebudubudu, 'Towards Understanding Botswana and South Africa's Ambivalence to Liberal Democracy' (2017) 1 Journal of Contemporary African Studies 15.

18 APAI Secretariat, *Access to Information in Africa: Examining Progress since the APAI Declaration* (APAI Secretariat, Windhoek, 2013) <https://action-namibia.org/wp-content/uploads/2017/10/ATI-in-Africa-Infographics.pdf> accessed 21 February 2017.

19 Media Institute of Southern Africa, *MISA Transparency Assessment: The Citizens' Analysis of Government Openness in Southern Africa* (MISA Regional Secretariat, 2017) 8–12.

20 Scott Pegg, 'Presidential Succession and Academic Freedom: Botswana Deports Leading Political Scientist Kenneth Good' (2005) 38 Political Science & Politics 829.

highly elitist, power is excessively centralized in the presidency, secrecy and non-accountability in government are pervasive, and there is growing autocracy." Preventing, detecting, disrupting, investigating and prosecuting ML/FT crimes requires effective information disclosure and sharing. In a country such as Botswana, where secrecy is a culture, implementing the AML/CFT Regime became a daunting challenge.

Law-Making: Minimal Consultation and Education

Parliament is the law-making authority in Botswana.[21] This power is exercised through Bills passed by the National Assembly.[22] Even though the Constitution does not explicitly make it a requirement, the National Assembly publishes Bills in the Government Gazette. Whilst Members of Parliament are expected to consult their constituencies on Bills before Parliament to educate them on the laws and illicit their views, the lack of skills to understand complex and novel laws such as AML/CFT legislation presents a challenge. In addition, as Bills are published in the Government Gazette, members of the public have access to study, interrogate and make their views known. As AML/CFT legislation is normally drafted in complex language, not many people are able to read and understand it. The absence of a law revision commission compounds the matter. This means there are no institutions regularly consulting members of the public on the need for laws and the operation of the existing ones. Educating the members of the public, including stakeholders, on legislation is also not the norm in Botswana. Normally, Bills are debated in Parliament, made into laws, and the members of the public are expected to comply. As a result, a weak model of public consultation and public participation in law-making exists.

Institutional Coordination and Poor Prosecution Record

The four key legal institutions responsible for investigating or prosecuting ML suffer from an acute lack of coordination. These are the Botswana Police Service (the BPS), the Directorate on Corruption and Economic Crime (DCEC), the Directorate of Intelligence and Security Services (the DISS) and the Director of Public Prosecutions (DPP), which is constitutionally mandated to handle criminal prosecution.

Due to the broad provisions governing their mandates, the three institutions have overlapping mandates. This has become a source of constant tension. The BPS exists to "to protect life and property, prevent and detect crime . . . apprehend offenders, bring offenders to justice, duly enforce all written laws with which it is directly charged and generally maintain the peace."[23] One of the

21 Constitution of Botswana 1966, s 86.
22 Constitution of Botswana 1966, s 87.
23 Botswana Police Act, Act 29 of 1978, sec 6(1).

functions of the DCEC is to "to investigate any alleged or suspected contravention of any of the provisions of the fiscal and revenue laws of the country."[24] On the other hand, the DISS operates under the Intelligence and Security Services Act.[25] Its main statutory objective is to protect the national security interests of Botswana by detecting and identifying any potential or actual national security threats. The definition of "national security threat" includes any threat or act of violence or unlawful harm that is directed at or intended to achieve, bring about or promote any constitutional, political, industrial, social or economic objective or change in Botswana and includes any conspiracy, incitement or attempt to commit any such act or threat.[26] The DPP is constitutionally mandated to handle criminal prosecution. There are no systems for coordinating these bodies. The DISS has been accused of interfering with other agencies. In February 2022, the Chairman of the Law Society of Botswana complained about the sweeping powers of the DISS which have allowed it operate above the law and usurp the mandate of other law enforcement agencies.[27] The DCEC investigates cases and transmits them to the DPP for prosecution. It has condemned the DPP for not prosecuting cases that are transmitted to it. In March 2021, the Law Society of Botswana called for the resignation of the DPP alleging that the DPP was prosecuting matters on dictation from the DISS.[28]

Furthermore, there are concerns on the independence of the DPP and the DCEC. The DPP is appointed by the President and is administratively accountable to the Attorney General, the government's principal legal advisor. The Director of the DCEC is appointed by the President. The Director has no security of tenure. The DCEC is controlled by the Office of the President. The President of the Botswana Congress Party, one of the main opposition parties, has called for reform of the DCEC and proposed enhanced security of tenure for the Director General of the DCEC, removing the DCEC from the control of the Office of the President, ensuring that the appointment of the Director General is subjected to a transparent process that is aimed at identifying the most competent applicant, removing from the DCEC law clauses that allow the President to interfere with the DCEC investigations, and further, that the DCEC be subjected to parliamentary oversight.[29]

24 Corruption and Economic Crime, Act 13 of 1994, s 6(c).

25 Intelligence and Security Services Act 16 of 2007.

26 Intelligence and Security Services Act (n 25) s 2(c).

27 Tefo Pheage, 'Protect Police from DISS Abuse – LSB' (*The Botswana Gazette*, 2 February 2022) <www.thegazette.news/news/protect-police-from-diss-abuse-lsb/> accessed 19 October 2022.

28 Tefo Pheage, 'DPP Must Resign: Law Society' (*The Botswana Gazette*, 31 March 2021) <www.thegazette.news/news/dpp-must-resign-law-society/> accessed 19 October 2022.

29 The Administrator, 'Statement on Directorate on Corruption and Economic Crime by Saleshando' (*The Botswana Gazette*, 14 September 2020) <www.thegazette.news/news/statement-on-directorate-on-corruption-and-economic-crime-by-saleshando/> accessed 19 October 2022.

Linked to poor institutional coordination is a poor record of prosecution of corruption and economic crimes. Since the establishment of the DCEC, no politically exposed person (PEP) has been convicted for offences in the Corruption and Economic Crimes Act, notwithstanding many indictments. In such cases, lawyers were engaged and the DPP lost the cases on technicalities before the cases could proceed to trial stage. This raises questions about the effectiveness of the Act and does not augur well for effective investigation and prosecution of crimes. Most of those indicted were ruling party members and former Cabinet members. Generally, there is no culture of actively prosecuting economic and financial crimes. Alternatively, there is no political will by the DPP to see these cases through as most of them involve ruling party elites. This may be due to the lack of independence of these agencies.

Implications of Botswana's Legal Culture in the Implementation of the AML/CFT Standards

The aspects of Botswana's legal culture discussed earlier can be seen as some of the causes of the challenges and constraints experienced by Botswana in implementing the 2007 MER recommendations and in the prosecution of ML crimes. In other words, these constraints and challenges can be seen as effects of Botswana's legal culture – the interaction of the structural, cultural and substantive components. To expose this interaction of the structural, cultural and structural components of Botswana's legal culture, this section traces the trajectory of Botswana's implementation of the AML/CFT Regime from the 2007 MER.

2007 MER

Botswana's journey with the AML/CFT Regime begins with the 2007 MER. The 2007 MER noted a few positive features of Botswana's legislative scheme. It found that key fundamental components of the AML regime were in place. There was criminalization of the offence of money laundering, confiscation of proceeds of crime, preventive measures and suspicious transaction reporting. In addition, Botswana was a signatory of the United Nations Convention on the Suppression of the Financing of Terrorism.[30] However, there were implementation challenges. Firstly, although enacted in 1990, by 2007, there had not been any single prosecution under Botswana's key AML/CFT law, the Proceeds of Serious Crime Act.[31] There was also a low number of suspicious transaction reports (STRs).[32]The law had no civil forfeiture regime. The prosecution focused exclusively on predicate offences. No reasons were

30 Adopted by the General Assembly of the United Nations in resolution 54/109 of 9 December 1999.

31 Proceeds of Serious Crime Act, Act 19 of 1990.

32 Eastern and Southern Africa Anti-Money Laundering Group (ESAAMLG) (n 1) 7.

provided for this exclusive focus on prosecuting predicate offences. One can only make reasonable inferences. This is likely an indication of the lack of skilled prosecutors at the prosecuting authority. This deficiency was only picked in the 2007 MER. Primarily, the failure to recognize this deficiency earlier and provide for corrective measures points to the lack of policy monitoring and evaluation. This may also explain why no national risk assessment was carried out.

Secrecy was manifest. There were no systems for establishing beneficial owners, even when registering companies. Establishing beneficial owners could expose the elites who may have obtained their funds and assets improperly. There were no due diligence requirements on designated bodies and banks for PEPs. There was no law regulating trusts – instruments used mostly by the elites. Lastly, notwithstanding that Botswana had signed the United Nations Convention on the Suppression of the Financing of Terrorism, the crime of terrorism had not been criminalized, which aligns with Botswana's attitude of ambivalence towards international law.

2017 MER[33]

By 2017, in response to the 2007 MER, Botswana had enacted three legal instruments: the Financial Intelligence Act[34] (FIA, 2009); the Proceeds and Instruments of Crime Act[35] (PICA, 2014) and the Counter Terrorism Act[36] (CTA, 2014). A new AML/CFT legislative scheme was in place for Botswana. The DPP established an Asset Forfeiture Unit (AFU) in September 2015 to target proceeds and instrumentalities of crime and ensure that ML is prosecuted.

Implementation was still a struggle and was marred with inordinate delay and material omissions. Although enacted two years after the 2007 MER, the FIA, 2009 only went into operation five years later in 2014. The other two pieces of legislation were enacted seven years after the 2007 MER. Still, as was the case in 2007, the country had not carried out an AML/CFT national risk assessment. The ambivalence of Botswana towards international law presented challenges. The new legislation, the PICA, 2014, was deficient as it failed to domesticate all offences set out in the Vienna, Palermo and Terrorist Financing Conventions.[37] Furthermore, secrecy was maintained. There was apparent resistance by the

33 **Eastern and Southern Africa Anti-Money Laundering Group (ESAAMLG),** *Anti-money Laundering and Counter-Terrorist Financing Measures – Botswana, 1st Enhanced Follow-up Report & Technical Compliance Re-Rating* **(ESAAMLG 2019) <www.esaamlg.org/reports/me.ph> accessed 13 March 2022.**

34 Financial Intelligence Agency Act, Act No 11 of 2019.

35 Proceeds and Instruments of Crime Act, Act 28 of 2014.

36 Counter Terrorism Act, Act 24 of 2014.

37 The offences of illicit arms trafficking; hostage-taking; individual terrorist; proliferation of weapons of mass destruction; and kidnapping have not yet been criminalized as required by the Conventions, limiting international cooperation which can be provided where dual criminality is required.

policymakers in implementing AML/CFT standards in some industries. The FIA, 2009 designated AML/CFT supervisory bodies for all financial institutions (FIs) and Designated Non-Financial Businesses and Professions (DNFBPs) and left out dealers in precious metals. There was no requirement to collect information on beneficial ownership, cross-border wire transfers and PEPs.

Insufficient consultation and education on the new legislation caused some constraints in proper implementation of the AML legislation. The market and society had not been adequately educated on the legal requirements of the AML legislation. The MER noted that there generally was a low understanding of ML/TF risks in Botswana, and stakeholders were still familiarizing themselves with the requirements of the law. Even officers who had received training were not using the training to pursue ML investigations – legal action was still concentrated on predicate offences. Still, there was no record of any case on ML/TF that had been successfully investigated and prosecuted using the PICA, 2014. DNFBPs have no understanding of their AML/CFT obligations and ML/TF facing them. The DPP was not adequately resourced – there were no experienced prosecutors to deal with AML cases.

Notwithstanding that some laws had been amended to address deficiencies raised in the 2017 MER, ingrained in the amendments were policy, institutional and attitudinal choices aligned with the components of the Botswana's legal culture. In the 2019 Follow Up Review (2019 FUR),[38] Botswana had finally carried out its National Risk Assessment (NAR). However, the assessors noted that Botswana had still not identified its ML/TF risks.[39] Policy deficiency remained a problem. Botswana had not yet come up with AML/CFT policies informed by identified risks. Further, no mechanisms had been put in place to enable policymakers and competent authorities to cooperate, coordinate and exchange information domestically concerning development and implementation of policies and activities. No policies had been enacted to assist authorities to facilitate evaluation of FIs' risk assessments, policies and procedures in relation to new products and new business practices. Botswana had also not yet introduced measures that address virtual assets and virtual asset service providers.

Resistance to transparency remained a problem. The definition of beneficial owner in the FIA, 2019[40] in relation to life insurance policies and trusts did not include a natural person who controls a customer and on whose behalf a transaction is conducted. In addition, whilst there was a requirement for FIs to establish the nature of customer's business and its ownership or control, there was no legal requirement for FIs to verify the identity of a beneficial owner through the identity of the settlor, trustees or other persons exercising ultimate effective control.[41] As regards implementation of international law, the country still had no mechanisms for identifying targets for designation, based

38 Eastern and Southern Africa Anti-Money Laundering Group (ESAAMLG) (n 33).
39 Eastern and Southern Africa Anti-Money Laundering Group (ESAAMLG) (n 33) 42.
40 Financial Intelligence Agency Act (n 34) s 2.
41 Financial Intelligence Agency Act (n 34) ss 10, 11.

on the designation criteria set out in the relevant United Nations Security Council Resolutions (UNSCR).

Investigation and Prosecution of AML/CFT Cases in Botswana

This section turns to the constraints and challenges in the investigation and prosecution of ML crimes in Botswana. Some of the aspects of Botswana's legal culture are responsible for causing constraints and challenges in the investigation and prosecution of AML/CFT cases. Poor institutional coordination and lack of education on the requirements of the law appear to be the dominant ones here. This is demonstrated in the cases of *Kgori Capital* case[42] and the infamous *Butterfly* case,[43] both of which are discussed below.

The **Kgori Capital** *Case (2019)*

In the *Kgori Capital case*, the High Court had found that Kgori Capital Pty Ltd (Kgori Capital) and its directors had benefitted from SCRA and assessed the value of the benefit to be BWP 10 515 768.79 (equivalent to £698 598.76). Kgori Capital and its directors were ordered jointly and severally to pay to the Government a civil penalty equal to that amount. Kgori Capital appealed the judgment to the Court of Appeal. The *Kgori Capital* case reveals some of these challenges. Notwithstanding that the case involved such a huge sum of money that the DPP believed to have been obtained fraudulently from the government, its investigation and prosecution strategy is replete with serious lapses in judgment. The DPP appears to not have carried out adequate legal research on the matter. Here is what the Court of Appeal said about the DPP's legal arguments – demonstrating that little research was carried out on the case: "The heads of argument were rather laconic and the oral argument was somewhat different from what had been the case until then."[44] Commenting on the quality of the evidence adduced by the DPP, the Court said:

> The DPP chose to file a number of lawyerly affidavits dealing with the documents and their interpretation. The deponents also made allegations of which they have no personal knowledge and did not explain why they could not produce witnesses.[45]

In some cases, the DPP failed to deal with the evidence of Kgori Capital's key witnesses. The Court of Appeal noted that the DPP failed to deal with the evidence of the Director and Chief Operations Officer, who was a signatory

42 *Kgori Capital Pty Ltd v Director of Public Prosecutions and Attorney General*, Court of Appeal Criminal Appeal No. CLCGB 033–19 (26 July 2019), unreported.

43 *Director of Public Prosecutions and Attorney General v Welheminah Mphoeng Maswabi*, Court of Appeal Civil Appeal No. CACGB 212–21 (5 August 2022), unreported.

44 *Kgori Capital Pty Ltd v Director of Public Prosecutions and Attorney General* (n 42) para. 43.

45 *Kgori Capital Pty Ltd v Director of Public Prosecutions and Attorney General* (n 42) para 44.

to the interim mandate.[46] This meant that the DPP was bound by the answers she proffered. In relation to the charge of obtaining by false pretences, "On a question as to who had been deceived by Kgori Capital, counsel for the DPP gave no answer because there was no answer."[47] In the Court of Appeal's view the DPP sought to escalate what essentially was a contractual dispute as to interpretation into a criminal matter.

The **Butterfly** *Case (2019)*

In October 2019, the DPP charged an intelligence officer, Welheminah Maswabi (code-named Butterfly) of financing and facilitating the commission of acts of terrorism in violation of the Counter Terrorism Act,[48] possession of unexplained property[49] and false declaration.[50] It was said that she had transferred an amount of USD 2,950,000.00 to Isaac Kgosi, former head of the Directorate of Intelligence and Security Services, who had threatened to commit acts of terror against the Republic of Botswana. Butterfly was then arrested and detained for more than a month on the basis that she was a threat to the State.

The investigations were carried out by DCEC, the BPS and the DISS. The State's case was set out in an affidavit by a DCEC's investigator.[51] He indicated that he had received information that under the instructions of the Former President of the Republic of Botswana, Seretse Khama Ian Khama, and former Director General of Intelligence and Security Services, Isaac Seabelo Kgosi created three Special STX Unit Accounts held in South African banks. It was alleged that this was done without the knowledge of the Accountant General and as a scheme to misappropriate the funds by the former President and Director.

On Butterfly's first attempt, she was denied bail by the High Court. She was granted bail on her second application on the basis that the State had fabricated evidence. In her affidavit supporting her application for bail, she produced an affidavit by Seretse Khama Ian Khama denying that he had ever issued instructions to officers of the Bank of Botswana. There was no evidence of the existence of the accounts from Bank of Botswana. Butterfly also produced documentary evidence from the named South African banks indicating that they held no such accounts. The DPP chose not to respond to the allegations. In June 2020, the DPP engaged Advocate Gerrie Nel of the AfriForum to assist with the prosecution and pursuing the request for mutual support from South Africa. After 11 months with no response, in August 2020, AfriForum filed an application in South Africa to compel the South African government to respond to the mutual support request. In November 2020, the

46 *Kgori Capital Pty Ltd v Director of Public Prosecutions and Attorney General* (n 42) para 55.
47 *Kgori Capital Pty Ltd v Director of Public Prosecutions and Attorney General* (n 42) para 60.
48 Counter Terrorism Act (n 36) s 5(1)(f)(ii).
49 Corruption and Economic Crimes Act (n 24) s 34(1)(b).
50 Penal Code, Law 2, 1964, s 315.
51 These events are narrated in the High Court judgment.

DPP withdrew the financing of terrorism count. The accused filed an application for review to set aside the other two charges at the High Court. Yet again, with no explanation, the DPP failed to oppose the application, and Butterfly succeeded.[52] The DPP appealed. In August 2021, the DPP withdrew all the charges against Butterfly citing lack of evidence as a basis.[53]

Analysis and Findings

Various explanations may be furnished for the DPP's failures in these cases. Firstly, Botswana has no culture of active prosecution of financial crimes. The externally enforced nature of the AML/CFT regime, together with the undesirable EU blacklisting, is the primary motivation for the DPP's enthusiastic litigation in the AML/CFT area. Thus, the motivation to prosecute AML/CFT cases is generated externally. The very fact that the prosecution of financial crimes is a novel feature of the criminal system means prosecuting these crimes will be for a long time be a Sisyphean task for the DPP. As argued in this study, that is due to the interaction of the structural, cultural and substantive factors of what constitutes aspects of Botswana's legal culture.

Secondly, since they usually involve serious layers of transactions, AML/CFT can be difficult to investigate and prosecute.[54] They make new demands on Botswana's legal institutions and legal personnel because the cases arise out of new laws and require specialist evidence. Combined with the fact that legal education in Botswana does not cover AML/CFT laws, lack of expertise in these matters is a major problem as the majority of lawyers were not taught AML/CFT laws at law school. The engagement of a foreign advocate in the *Butterfly* case demonstrates the lack of expertise by both DPP and external lawyers in these matters. This is made worse by the small number of lawyers at the DPP due to financial constraints.

Thirdly, AML/CFT is a combination of criminal and civil proceedings. Civil proceedings are not a dominant feature of litigation in criminal prosecution, the province of the DPP lawyers. The litigation culture of the DPP is dominated by criminal cases, thus, the failure to appreciate the procedural rules of civil procedure may be due to this new litigation territory. In *Kgori Capital*, it does appear that motion proceedings were not well appreciated by the lawyers representing the DPP.

Fourthly, both cases demonstrate a failure of proper investigations and analysis of the evidence. This may be borne out of the lack of expertise, the lack

52 *Welheminah Maswabi v Director of Public Prosecutions and Attorney General* MCHGB 000028–21. (Judgment delivered on the 23 August 2021.)

53 Lawrence Seretse, 'We Have No Evidence, Free Butterfly' (*The Botswana Gazette*, 4 August 2021) <www.thegazette.news/news/we-had-no-evidence-free-butterfly-dpp/> accessed 19 October 2022.

54 Bonnie Buchanan, 'Money Laundering – A Global Obstacle' (2004) 18(1) Research in International Business and Finance 115.

of coordination between law enforcement organs and the rampant culture of secrecy entrenched in institutions and public servants. Advocate Gerrie Nel suggested that it was difficult to obtain evidence that he knew existed from some government departments.[55]

Implications and Concluding Remarks

Through the lens of legal culture, this chapter has shown that the challenges that Botswana faced during the implementation of the AML/CFT regime arise out of the structural, cultural and substantive components of her legal culture. These components of her legal culture acted as constraints to implementation by causing hesitation, delays and in some cases, resistance to implementing recommendations of the MERs. Aspects of this legal culture constrain the DPP's attempts to prosecute perpetrators of ML crimes.

Whilst Botswana has addressed most of the strategic deficiencies in her AML/CFT regime, Botswana is not yet out of the woods. In order to overcome these challenges, Botswana needs to address components of her legal culture that act as constraints on the investigation and prosecution of AML/CFT cases. Firstly, Botswana needs to cultivate a culture of policy and law revision. The AML/CFT international regime is ever-changing and one of the fastest developing regimes in the world. Its successful implementation requires a vigorous and vigilant policy review, monitoring and evaluation. This can be achieved by establishing a law review commission. Secondly, there is an urgent need to revise curriculum in education to ensure that financial crimes and money laundering are taught at schools so that they become part of the legal consciousness of the population. This must also be accompanied by developing relevant research apparatus. Thirdly, there is need to safeguard the independence of investigative and judicial institutions to ensure that they are protected from presidential control. To avoid lack of coordination amongst the investigative organs there should be laws or policies that regulate their interactions. As Botswana is in the process of reviewing her Constitution, some of these changes can be incorporated in the Constitution.

Legal culture can stall or enhance prospects of legal change. To ensure successful implementation of the AML/CFT it must be woven into the fabric of Botswana's legal culture – or aspects of Botswana's legal culture that act as bottlenecks must be removed.

55 This is what he is alleged to have stated: "It is not my recommendation that there is no evidence to proceed, but it is my recommendation that one should not proceed with prosecution if all of the evidence is not submitted when we know it is there and cannot get our hands on it." Seretse (n 53).

7 Barriers to Implementing New Technologies for AML/CFT Functions

The Case of Nigeria

Ehi Eric Esoimeme

Introduction

New and innovative methods for electronic funds transfer are emerging globally. These new payment tools include extensions of established payment systems as well as new payment methods that are substantially different from traditional transactions.[1] The global real-time payments transactions volume was valued at over USD 100 billion in 2022.[2] In Nigeria, the volume of mobile and internet banking transactions is increasing at a regular rate.[3] Data released by the Nigeria Inter-Bank Settlement System (NIBSS) shows that bank customers in Nigeria transferred a total of N19.4 trillion via mobile payments in 2022. This shows an increase of 142% year on year compared to N8 trillion of transactions in 2021.[4]

The adoption of new digital and faster payment methods brings immense benefits for account holders as it compresses the time from request to settlement, but it requires banks and other FIs to apply anti-money laundering

1 Financial Action Task Force, 'Report on New Payment Methods' (*FATF*, 13 October 2006) <www.fatf-gafi.org/en/publications/Methodsandtrends/Reportonnewpaymentmethods.html> accessed 13 May 2023.

2 Grand View Research, 'Real-Time Payments Market Size, Share & Trends Analysis Report By Enterprise Size (Large, SME), By Payment Type (P2B, P2P), By End-use Industry, By Component, By Deployment, and Segment Forecasts, 2023–2030' (*Grand View Research*, 1 May 2021) <www.grandviewresearch.com/industry-analysis/real-time-payments-market> accessed 12 May 2023.

3 The National (Money Laundering & Terrorist Financing) Risk Assessment Forum, 'National Inherent Risk Assessment of Money Laundering in Nigeria' (*NRA Forum* 2022) <www.nfiu.gov.ng/Home/NiraReports> accessed 14 May 2023.

4 Nigeria Inter-Bank Settlement System, 'Bank Customers Transfer N19.4 Trillion Over Mobile in 2022' (*NIBSS*, 2023) <https://nibss-plc.com.ng/bank-customers-transfer-n19-4-trillion-over-mobile-in-2022/> accessed 1 June 2023; Adeyemi Adepetun, 'Nigerians pay N2.8tr Bills Electronically, Transfer N19.4tr with Mobile Phones' (*The Guardian*, 16 January 2023) <https://guardian.ng/business-services/nigerians-pay-n2-8tr-bills-electronically-transfer-n19-4tr-with-mobile-phones/> accessed 2 June 2023.

DOI: 10.4324/9781003253808-9

(AML) safeguards at the same speed.[5] When money transfer is instantaneous, FIs may find it difficult to rely on legacy technologies and manual intervention to combat money laundering.[6] A legacy system is defined as any information system that significantly resists changes and modifications.[7] Legacy systems are updated with new algorithms and manually inputted information, generating matrixes for risk interpretation and action, but these very rarely offer a real-time overview of customer transactional or institutional risks.[8] In addition, the quality of the data obtained by legacy systems varies and may not offer the accuracy and detail required to comply with anti-money laundering and combatting the financing of terrorism (AML/CFT) standards.[9]

The best solution will be for banks to deploy machine learning (ML)-based technologies capable of orchestrating a variety of inputs on huge volumes of transactions in a much shorter period of time, using broader sets of data because of the absence of face-to-face interaction in the digital ecosystem.[10] ML is commonly used to enable other categories of artificial intelligence (AI), such as natural language processing (NLP; the meaning of words), computer vision (the meaning of images and videos) and automated speech recognition (the meaning of sounds).[11] Such tools can also offer an alternative means of identifying risks – in effect acting as a semi-independent check on the conclusions of traditional risk analysis.[12] Available evidence suggest that some banks

5 SAS Institute, 'Real-Time Payments Market Size, Share & Trends Analysis Report By Enterprise Size (Large, SME), By Payment Type (P2B, P2P), By End-use Industry, By Component, By Deployment, and Segment Forecasts, 2023–2030' (*SAS* 2019) <www.sas.com/content/dam/SAS/documents/briefs/solution-brief/en/payments-fraud-110795.pdf> accessed 12 May 2023.

6 Nick White, 'How Legacy and Multiple Systems Create Barriers to Effective Fraud Prevention' (*Cifas*, 1 June 2017) <www.cifas.org.uk/insight/fraud-risk-focus-blog/legacy-multiple-systems-create-barriers-effective-fraud-prevention> accessed 25 May 2023.

7 ML Brodie, M Stonebraker Migrating Legacy Systems, Morgan Kaufmann Publ, San Francisco (1995); Zahir Irani, Raul M. Abril, Vishanth Weerakkody, Amizan Omar and Uthayasankar Sivarajah, 'The Impact of Legacy Systems on Digital Transformation in European Public Administration: Lesson Learned from a Multi Case Analysis' (2023) 40(1) Government Information Quarterly 101784, https://doi.org/10.1016/j.giq.2022.101784.

8 International Banker, 'Addressing the Problems of Legacy Banking Systems' (*International Banker*, 26 October 2020) <https://internationalbanker.com/technology/addressing-the-problems-of-legacy-banking-systems/> accessed 25 May 2023; Financial Action Task Force, 'Opportunities and Challenges of New Technologies for AML/CFT' (*FATF*, July 2021) <www.fatf-gafi.org/en/publications/Digitaltransformation/Opportunities-challenges-new-technologies-for-aml-cft.html> accessed 13 May 2023.

9 Financial Action Task Force (n 8).

10 Ian Holmes, *Leveraging Analytics to Combat Digital Fraud in Financial Organizations* (International Institute for Analytics, April 2019) <www.sas.com/en_be/offers/iia-combat-digital-fraud-financial-organizations-2400914/overview.html> accessed 12 May 2023.

11 Shannon England, '6 Technologies Behind AI' (*CODEBOTS*, 11 May 2018) <https://codebots.com/artificial-intelligence/6-technologies-behind-ai> accessed 25 May 2023.

12 Financial Action Task Force (n 8).

are already experimenting with AI and digital identity technologies applicable to their AML compliance programs.[13] These innovations and technologies can strengthen AML compliance approaches and enhance transaction monitoring systems.[14] Unlike rules-based systems, which are easy for fraudsters to test and circumvent, AI and ML adapt to changing behaviours in a population through automated model building.[15] With every iteration, the algorithms get smarter and deliver more accurate results.[16] It is easy to see the value of ML to keep pace with the emerging risks of new payment channels.[17]

Despite the acknowledged benefits, the use of big data and advanced analytics, such as AI for AML/CFT comes with challenges or obstacles to their effective use. This includes analysing structural challenges, such as issues of data quality, inadequate staffing and resources in information technology (IT) departments and the lack of explicit regulatory requirements and guidance.[18] For example, FIs could leverage advanced analytics to more accurately identify suspicious activities, screen their customers and manage risks. Since the accuracy of advanced analytics largely corresponds to the size, quality and relevancy of the data set, the efficacy and efficiency of these tools may depend on the ability of FIs (within and outside of financial groups) to share information.[19] Therefore, this research intends to explore the following questions:

1. What are the underlying technologies that are being used to perform AML/CFT functions?
2. What are the possible challenges facing banks in the implementation of new technology for AML/CFT?
3. How can banks overcome the challenges they face in the implementation of new technology for AML/CFT?

13 Daniel Faggella, 'AI in Banking – An Analysis of America's 7 Top Banks' (*Emerj*, 14 March 2020) <https://emerj.com/ai-sector-overviews/ai-in-banking-analysis/> accessed 25 May 2023.

14 The Board of Governors of the Federal Reserve System, the Federal Deposit Insurance Corporation, the Financial Crimes Enforcement Network (FinCEN), the National Credit Union Administration, and the Office of the Comptroller of the Currency (collectively, the Agencies), 'Joint Statement on Innovative Efforts to Combat Money Laundering' (Financial Crimes Enforcement Network, 3 December 2018) <www.fincen.gov/news/news-releases/joint-statement-innovative-efforts-combat-money-laundering> accessed 13 May 2023.

15 Maija Palmer, 'How Artificial Intelligence is Changing the Game for Banks' (*Sifted*, 13 March 2020) <https://sifted.eu/articles/ai-fintech-eigen> accessed 25 May 2023.

16 Kelvin Dickenson, '4 Ways Artificial Intelligence is Transforming Compliance for Banks' (28 March 2019) <https://bdtechtalks.com/2019/03/28/artificial-intelligence-kyc-aml-compliance/> accessed 25 May 2023.

17 SAS Institute, 'Managing Fraud Risk in the Digital Age: People, Processes and Technologies to Address the Emerging Risks of Online and Mobile Payments' (*SAS* 2020) <www.sas.com/en/whitepapers/managing-fraud-risk-digital-age-109846.html> accessed 12 May 2023.

18 Financial Action Task Force (n 8).

19 Financial Action Task Force, 'Stocktake on Data Pooling, Collaborative Analytics and Data Protection' (*FATF*, July 2021) <www.fatf-gafi.org/en/publications/Digitaltransformation/Data-pooling-collaborative-analytics-data-protection.html> accessed 14 May 2023.

This research will identify the challenges or obstacles to the effective use of innovative technology by banks in Nigeria under three distinct headings of national barriers, legal barriers, and institutional and operational barriers.

To effectively address these barriers, this chapter will identify key recommendations that, if implemented, will provide banks and other FIs with the tools needed to enhance the overall capabilities of technological innovation. The chapter also includes practical recommendations, directed toward the regulatory authorities, to improve data sharing mechanisms and encourage a strong culture of compliance.

The remainder of the chapter is organised as follows. The next section provides a background on AML/CFT requirements. Then the various new technologies that facilitate advanced AML/CFT analytics within regulated entities or collaborative analytics between FIs are summarised. The next section identifies challenges and obstacles that FIs may encounter while developing or deploying these technologies. The final section outlines potential solutions so that commercially available or emerging technologies may be fully utilised to strengthen AML/CFT compliance, consistent with national and international frameworks.

AML/CFT Requirements

Banks and other FIs are required to develop and implement written AML programs reasonably designed to assure and monitor compliance with the Nigerian Money Laundering (Prevention and Prohibition) Act, 2022. In particular, banks are required to implement an AML program that, at a minimum, provides for (1) procedures for using all available information to determine and verify name, address, social security or taxpayer identification number, and other identifying information for a person, to the extent determining and verifying the information is otherwise required under the Money Laundering (Prevention and Prohibition) Act, 2022; (2) procedures for using all available information to determine the occurrence of any transactions or patterns of transactions required to be reported as suspicious; (3) procedures for using all available information to determine whether any records must be made and maintained pursuant to the Money Laundering (Prevention and Prohibition) Act, 2022; (4) independent testing of the Bank's AML program; (5) training of personnel; and (6) the designation of an individual or individuals responsible for assuring day-to-day compliance.[20]

20 Money Laundering (Prevention and Prohibition) Act, 2022, s. 10; Central Bank of Nigeria (Anti-Money Laundering, Combating the Financing of Terrorism and Countering Proliferation Financing of Weapons of Mass Destruction in Financial Institutions) Regulations, 2022, Regulation 14.

Requirement to Develop and Implement an Adequate Customer Identification Program

As part of its AML compliance program, a bank must implement a written customer identification program appropriate for its size and type of business. The program must include risk-based identity verification, record keeping, and retention procedures. In general, the minimum information a bank must obtain prior to opening an account is the customer's name, date of birth, and a residential or business street address.[21] A customer identification program helps a bank determine the risks posed by a particular customer, allowing the institution to ensure that it has the proper controls in place, including suspicious activity monitoring procedures, and to monitor and report on the risks of a particular client.[22] This will be explained in more detail in the next section.

Requirement to Report Suspicious Transactions

The Nigeria Money Laundering (Prevention and Prohibition) Act, 2022 and its implementing regulations impose an obligation on banks to report any suspicious transaction relating to money laundering and terrorist financing.[23] A transaction is deemed to be suspicious if it involves a frequency which is unjustifiable or unreasonable[24] or is surrounded by conditions of unusual or unjustified complexity.[25] It is also deemed suspicious if it appears to have no economic justification or lawful objective[26] or in the opinion of the Bank involves terrorist financing or is inconsistent with the known transaction

21 Money Laundering (Prevention and Prohibition) Act, 2022. S. 4; Central Bank of Nigeria (Anti-Money Laundering, Combating the Financing of Terrorism and Countering Proliferation Financing of Weapons of Mass Destruction in Financial Institutions) Regulations, 2022, Regulations 19–27.

22 Ehi Eric Esoimeme, *The Risk-Based Approach to Combating Money Laundering and Terrorist Financing* (Eric Press 2015).

23 Nigeria Money Laundering (Prevention and Prohibition) Act, 2022, s. 7 (2); Central Bank of Nigeria (Anti-Money Laundering, Combating the Financing of Terrorism and Countering Proliferation Financing of Weapons of Mass Destruction in Financial Institutions) Regulations, 2022, Regulation 37.

24 Nigeria Money Laundering (Prevention and Prohibition) Act, 2022, s. 7 (1) (a); Central Bank of Nigeria (Anti-Money Laundering, Combating the Financing of Terrorism and Countering Proliferation Financing of Weapons of Mass Destruction in Financial Institutions) Regulations, 2022, Regulation 38(1)(a).

25 Nigeria Money Laundering (Prevention and Prohibition) Act, 2022, s. 7 (1) (b); Central Bank of Nigeria (Anti-Money Laundering, Combating the Financing of Terrorism and Countering Proliferation Financing of Weapons of Mass Destruction in Financial Institutions) Regulations, 2022, Regulation 38(1)(b).

26 Nigeria Money Laundering (Prevention and Prohibition) Act, 2022, s. 7 (1) (c); Central Bank of Nigeria (Anti-Money Laundering, Combating the Financing of Terrorism and Countering Proliferation Financing of Weapons of Mass Destruction in Financial Institutions) Regulations, 2022, Regulation 38(1)(C).

pattern of the account or business relationship.[27] The report required to be filed is called a suspicious transaction report (STR).[28]

Banks are also required to file currency transaction reports.[29] This will be explained in more detail in the next section.

Requirement to File Currency Transaction Reports

The Nigeria Money Laundering (Prevention and Prohibition) Act, 2022 and its implementing regulations impose an obligation on banks to report a transfer to or from a foreign country of funds or securities by a person or body corporate including a money service business of a sum exceeding USD 10,000 or its equivalent.[30] The report is to be filed within one day from the date of the transaction.[31] The law also requires a bank to report in writing any single transaction, lodgement or transfer of funds in excess of 5 million naira or its equivalent in the case of an individual or 10 million naira or its equivalent in the case of a body corporate.[32] The report required to be filed is called a currency transaction report (CTR).[33]

Banks are also required to implement procedures for using all available information to determine whether any records must be made and maintained pursuant to the Money Laundering (Prevention and Prohibition) Act, 2022.[34] This will be explained in more detail in the next section.

27 Nigeria Money Laundering (Prevention and Prohibition) Act, 2022, s. 7 (1) (d); Central Bank of Nigeria (Anti-Money Laundering, Combating the Financing of Terrorism and Countering Proliferation Financing of Weapons of Mass Destruction in Financial Institutions) Regulations, 2022, Regulation 38(1)(d).

28 Nigeria Money Laundering (Prevention and Prohibition) Act, 2022, s. 7; Central Bank of Nigeria (Anti-Money Laundering, Combating the Financing of Terrorism and Countering Proliferation Financing of Weapons of Mass Destruction in Financial Institutions) Regulations, 2022, Regulation 39.

29 Ehi Eric Esoimeme, *Deterring and Detecting Money Laundering and Terrorist Financing: A Comparative Analysis of Anti–Money Laundering and Counterterrorism Financing Strategies* (DSC Publications Ltd. 2018).

30 Nigeria Money Laundering (Prevention and Prohibition) Act, 2022, s. 3 (1); Central Bank of Nigeria (Anti-Money Laundering, Combating the Financing of Terrorism and Countering Proliferation Financing of Weapons of Mass Destruction in Financial Institutions) Regulations, 2022, Regulation 40(2).

31 Nigeria Money Laundering (Prevention and Prohibition) Act, 2022, ss. 3 (1), 11 (1).

32 Nigeria Money Laundering (Prevention and Prohibition) Act, 2022, s. 11 (1); Central Bank of Nigeria (Anti-Money Laundering, Combating the Financing of Terrorism and Countering Proliferation Financing of Weapons of Mass Destruction in Financial Institutions) Regulations, 2022, Regulation 40(1).

33 Nigeria Money Laundering (Prevention and Prohibition) Act, 2022, s. 11; Central Bank of Nigeria (Anti-Money Laundering, Combating the Financing of Terrorism and Countering Proliferation Financing of Weapons of Mass Destruction in Financial Institutions) Regulations, 2022, Regulation 40.

34 Ehi Eric Esoimeme, *The Risk-Based Approach to Combating Cross-Border Financial Crimes in the African Continental Free Trade Area* (DSC Publications Ltd. 2022).

Record Keeping Requirements

Banks must keep all records of the identification data obtained through the customer due diligence process (e.g., copies or records of official identification documents such as passports, identity cards, driver's licenses and similar documents, account files and business correspondence, including the results of any analysis undertaken such as inquiries to establish the background and purpose of complex and unusual large transactions), for at least five years after the business relationship is ended, or after the date of the occasional transaction.[35] The rationale for record keeping is to facilitate the reconstruction of individual transactions and provide, if necessary, evidence for the prosecution of criminal activity.[36]

A bank is also required to conduct independent testing of the bank's AML program.[37] This will be explained in more detail in the next section.

Independent Testing

Banks are required to conduct an independent compliance testing commensurate with the AML risk profile of the bank to monitor and maintain an adequate program.[38] By not conducting the required independent review, a bank will be unable to identify vulnerabilities in its compliance program and properly monitor the account activity of its customers to detect suspicious activity going through the bank.

Independent testing of the bank's AML program should be conducted annually, unless the bank does not execute transactions for customers or otherwise hold customer accounts or act as an introducing broker with respect to customer accounts, in which case independent testing must be conducted biennially.[39]

Banks are also required to provide for education and training of personnel regarding their responsibilities under the AML program.[40] This will be explained in more detail in the next section.

Training

A bank's AML program must provide for education and training of personnel regarding its responsibilities under the program, including the detection of

35 Nigeria Money Laundering (Prevention and Prohibition) Act, 2022, s. 8; Central Bank of Nigeria (Anti-Money Laundering, Combating the Financing of Terrorism and Countering Proliferation Financing of Weapons of Mass Destruction in Financial Institutions) Regulations, 2022, Regulations 35 and 36.

36 Esoimeme (2022) (n 34).

37 Esoimeme (2022) (n 34).

38 Nigeria Money Laundering (Prevention and Prohibition) Act, 2022, s. 10 (1) (d); Central Bank of Nigeria (Anti-Money Laundering, Combating the Financing of Terrorism and Countering Proliferation Financing of Weapons of Mass Destruction in Financial Institutions) Regulations, 2022, Regulation 15.

39 Esoimeme (2015) (n 22).

40 Esoimeme (2022) (n 34).

suspicious transactions.[41] A bank's training program must provide AML staff with adequate job-specific training. This training program should not only focus on general AML requirements but also include topics on risks specific to the bank.[42]

Banks must designate an individual or individuals responsible for ensuring day-to-day compliance with AML requirements.[43] This will be explained further in the next section.

Designation of a Compliance Officer

A bank is required to designate an individual or individuals responsible for ensuring day-to-day compliance with AML requirements.[44] The requirement extends beyond the actual designation of a person to fulfil this role. Appointing an AML officer is not sufficient to meet the regulatory requirement if that person does not have sufficient authority, resources or time to satisfactorily complete the job.

Banks must provide the necessary level of authority, independence and responsibility to its AML compliance officers to ensure day-to-day compliance with AML requirements. The bank's compliance officer and the compliance staff should be empowered with sufficient authority and autonomy to implement the Bank's AML program.[45]

New Technologies Identified to Comply With AML/CFT Requirements

ML technology has found its way into the financial industry, aiming at optimising system performance using massive training data sets.[46] ML models are built off of algorithms that analyse the training data set, classify the inputs and outputs, then analyse it again.[47] In ML, data sets are split into three subsets:

41 Nigeria Money Laundering (Prevention and Prohibition) Act, 2022, s. 10 (1) (b); Central Bank of Nigeria (Anti-Money Laundering, Combating the Financing of Terrorism and Countering Proliferation Financing of Weapons of Mass Destruction in Financial Institutions) Regulations, 2022, Regulation 14(4)(b).

42 Esoimeme (2015) (n 22).

43 Ehi Eric Esoimeme, *Deterring and Detecting Money Laundering and Terrorist Financing: A Comparative Analysis of Anti–Money Laundering and Counterterrorism Financing Strategies* (DSC Publications Ltd. 2018).

44 Nigeria Money Laundering (Prevention and Prohibition) Act, 2022, s. 10 (1) (a); Central Bank of Nigeria (Anti-Money Laundering, Combating the Financing of Terrorism and Countering Proliferation Financing of Weapons of Mass Destruction in Financial Institutions) Regulations, 2022, Regulation 13.

45 Esoimeme (2022) (n 34).

46 Yi Hong, Tharaj Thaj and Emanuele Viterbo, *Delay-Doppler Communications: Principles and Applications* (Elsevier 2022).

47 Kirsten Barkved, 'The Difference between Training Data vs. Test Data in Machine Learning' (*Obviously AI*, 11 February 2022) <www.obviously.ai/post/the-difference-between-training-data-vs-test-data-in-machine-learning> accessed 24 May 2023.

training, validation and test sets.[48] The training set is the largest portion of the data and is used to train a model to predict an expected outcome; testing data allows you to assess the progress of the algorithm's training and change or optimise it for better results.[49] The function of training data is different based on the type of model.[50] In supervised learning, the training data consists of input-output pairs, also known as features and labels.[51] Features are the input variables used to make predictions, while labels are the corresponding output variables that the model is trying to predict.[52] The goal of supervised learning is to build an artificial system that can learn the mapping between the input and the output, and can predict the output of the system given new inputs.[53] In unsupervised learning, the training data consists of input features only, without any corresponding labels.[54] The goal of unsupervised learning is to discover hidden and underlying patterns in unlabelled data, without any guidance from output labels.[55] Unsupervised learning algorithms are typically used for tasks such as clustering, dimensionality reduction and anomaly detection.[56] There are also hybrid models that use a combination of supervised and unsupervised learning.[57] The validation set is a smaller portion of the data that is not used during the training phase. It is used to fine-tune the model's hyperparameters, which are not directly optimised during the training process.[58] It helps protect models from overfitting and underfitting.[59]

48 Günter Röhrich, 'Training, Validating and Testing – Successfully Comparing Model Performances' (*Towards Data Science*, 1 September 2020) <https://towardsdatascience.com/train-test-split-c3eed34f763b> accessed 24 May 2023.
49 Ostap Zabolotnyy, 'A Guide to Training and Testing Data in Machine Learning' (*First Bridge*, 2023) <https://firstbridge.io/blog/artificial-intelligence/training-and-testing-data-in-machine-learning> accessed 24 May 2023.
50 Jason Brownlee, 'Train-Test Split for Evaluating Machine Learning Algorithms' (*Python Machine Learning*, 24 July 2020) <https://machinelearningmastery.com/train-test-split-for-evaluating-machine-learning-algorithms/> accessed 24 May 2023.
51 Margaret Rouse, 'Training Data' (*Techopedia*, 8 May, 2023) <www.techopedia.com/definition/33181/training-data> accessed 25 May 2023; Eleonóra Bassi 'Training vs. Testing Data in Machine Learning' (*CoinTelegraph* 2023) <https://cointelegraph.com/learn/training-vs-testing-data-in-machine-learning> accessed 24 May 2023.
52 Bassi (n 51).
53 Q Liu and Y Wu, 'Supervised Learning' in NM Seel (ed), *Encyclopedia of the Sciences of Learning* (Springer 2012). <https://doi.org/10.1007/978-1-4419-1428-6_451>.
54 Amal Joby, 'Unsupervised Learning: How Machines Learn on Their Own' (*G2*, 19 March 2021) <https://learn.g2.com/unsupervised-learning> accessed 1 June 2023.
55 Khadija El Bouchefry and Rafael S de Souza, 'Chapter 12 – Learning in Big Data: Introduction to Machine Learning' in Petr Škoda and Fathalrahman Adam (eds), *Knowledge Discovery in Big Data from Astronomy and Earth Observation* (Elsevier 2020) 225–49.
56 Bassi (n 51).
57 MonkeyLearn, 'What Is Training Data in Machine Learning?' (*Rachel Wolff*, 2 November 2020) <https://monkeylearn.com/blog/training-data/> accessed 24 May 2023.
58 Bassi (n 51).
59 Amal Joby, 'What Is Training Data? How It's Used in Machine Learning' (*TECH*, 30 July 2021) <https://learn.g2.com/training-data> accessed 24 May 2023.

Once your ML model is built, testing data once again validates the progress of the algorithm's training and allows adjustment or optimisation for improved results.[60] Test data provides a final, real-world check of an unseen data set to confirm that the ML algorithm was trained effectively.[61]

ML is commonly used to enable other categories of AI, such as NLP, computer vision and automated speech recognition.[62] This is further explained in the following subsections.

Using Computer Vision With NLP and ML for Customer Due Diligence

The latest technological innovations that combine computer vision with NLP and ML algorithms can help organise data points from digitised customer due diligence forms and identification documents into categories, such as name, date of birth, occupation, permanent address, nationality, type of account and nature of the banking relationship, and then segregate them for authentication and review by due diligence analysts and compliance officers.[63] Traditionally this process was done through manual data entry or optical character recognition technology, both of which are tedious and error-prone.[64] When a document is uploaded to the mobile banking or internet banking system for digital onboarding purposes, the AI technology can automatically identify and understand each type of incoming document and sort them to be sent to the AML group for review and approval.

For the ML model to be effective, it must be trained on tens of thousands of customer due diligence documents,[65] such as a valid means of identification, residence permit (for expatriates), birth certificate, proof of residence and a duly registered power of attorney, where an individual appoints another person to be a signatory to their personal account. Each document should have its data points labelled according to data type.[66]

60 Iryna Sydorenko, 'Machine Learning and Training Data: What You Need to Know' (*Label Your Data*, 17 March 2021) <https://labelyourdata.com/articles/machine-learning-and-training-data> accessed 24 May 2023.

61 David Carty, 'Training Data vs. Validation Data vs. Test Data for ML Algorithms' (*APPLAUSE*, 29 April 2021) <www.applause.com/blog/training-data-validation-data-vs-test-data> accessed 24 May 2023.

62 England (n 11).

63 Ehi Eric Esoimeme, 'Application Programming Interfaces and Artificial Intelligence-Enabled Systems' in Sanction Scanner (ed), *Expected Changes in AML After Covid-19* (Sanction Scanner 2020).

64 Ehi Eric Esoimeme, 'Ehi's Predictions for the Anti-Money Laundering Sector in 2021' in Sanction Scanner (ed), *Expected Anti-Money Laundering Trends in 2021* (Sanction Scanner, 19 February 2021).

65 Alkhalili, Mohannad, Mahmoud H. Qutqut and Fadi Almasalha, 'Investigation of Applying Machine Learning for Watch-List Filtering in Anti-Money Laundering' (2021) 9 IEEE Access 18481–96.

66 YS Hwang and SY Bang, 'A Neural Network Model APC-III and Its Application to Unconstrained Handwritten Digit Recognition' (Processing of International Conference on Neural Information Processing 1994) 1500–5.

This could include customer profile data like account name, date of birth, occupation and residential address. The data scientist should then run this labelled data through the ML algorithm. This would train the software to discern between words, phrases and chains of text that appear to humans as the image of letters and chains of text as shown in banking and customer due diligence documents.

A bank could then run new documents that haven't been labelled into the software. The algorithm could then recognise all the text characters on each document and transcribe them to a digital format. These categories could be names, dates of birth and residential addresses. The software could also mark areas that are left blank or have missing information.

Using Intelligent Automation, NLP and ML to Enhance the Risk Assessment Process

The latest technological innovations that combines intelligent automation, AI and ML with know your business/customer domain expertise can create a holistic view of customer risk and business relationship risk through simulation features that grant integrated access to external data sources for customer risk profile enrichment and AI-enabled predictive customer risk scores for accurate high-risk customer management.[67]

For the risk-scoring AI-enabled system to be effective, it must be trained on tens of thousands of customer reference data,[68] such as general and enhanced due diligence information. Each document should have its data points labelled according to data type.[69] This could include due diligence information such as the nature and duration of the bank's relationship with the customer, source of funds, financial capacity, expected activity and the purpose of the account. The data scientist should then run this labelled data through the ML algorithm. This would train the software to discern between high-risk customers. Once the machine has learned how to distinguish customers, it can then be tested on new data to see how accurately it can identify high-risk, medium-risk and low-risk customers. Using the AI training guide is an ongoing process, and as new data becomes available, machines can be retrained to improve their performance.[70]

67 Esoimeme (2022) (34).

68 Ke Zhang, Jianwu Xu, Martin Renqiang Min, Guofei Jiang, Konstantinos Pelechrinis and Hui Zhang. 'Automated IT System Failure Prediction: A Deep Learning Approach' (2016 IEEE International Conference on Big Data (Big Data) 2016) 1291–300.

69 Y LeCun, Y Bengio and G Hinton, 'Deep Learning' (2015) 521(7553) Nature 436–44; Hwang and Bang (n 66).

70 Robert Koch, 'AI Training Data Guide: Essentials of AI Data Solutions' (*Clickworker*, 10 January 2023) <www.clickworker.com/customer-blog/ai-training-data-guide-essentials-of-ai-data-solutions/> accessed 25 May 2023.

Using Facial Recognition Technology With ML to Enhance Ongoing Due Diligence Measures

Banks can integrate the facial recognition software into their existing databases of customers' faces for verification.[71] This measure can enhance ongoing due diligence measures for internet banking or mobile banking customers and transactions.[72] To be effective, the ML model behind the software must be trained on thousands of images, videos, and photo identification (ID) cards showing human faces from various angles and in various lighting conditions. These images and videos must be labelled with points denoting the locations of facial features, such as eyes, eyelids, cheekbones, and lips.

These labelled images should then be run through the software's ML algorithm. This would have trained the algorithm to discern the sequences and patterns of 1s and 0s that, to the human eye, form the image of a person's face as displayed in a static image or live footage on a camera. In this case, there are internal and external cameras on an automated teller machine (ATM) and remote deposit capture (RDC) for scanning customers' faces and verifying their face from their photo ID card.

The user could then expose the software to faces that are not labelled using a camera attached to a self-service device. The algorithm behind the software would then be able to recognise a customer's face as shown on their ID card. The system can then validate the customer's transaction once their face is recognised. For example, a customer could insert their card into the bank's ATM, and the facial recognition software would verify that the actual account owner is trying to access their bank account with a camera.

Using a Sophisticated, End-to-End AML Solution With Embedded AI and ML Techniques to Spot More Suspicious Activity With Greater Accuracy

Banks in Nigeria can gain comprehensive risk coverage with a hybrid approach to monitoring transactions.[73] This approach combines human-guided supervised ML to detect known risks with advanced analytic techniques (including unsupervised ML) to identify unknown risks and hidden relationships.[74]

71 Niccolo Mejia, 'Facial Recognition in Banking – Current Applications' (*Emerj*, 5 December 2019) <https://emerj.com/ai-sector-overviews/facial-recognition-in-banking-current-applications/> accessed 28 May 2023.

72 Niccolo Mejia, 'Machine Vision in Banking – Facial Recognition and OCR' (*Emerj*, 23 January 2019) <https://emerj.com/ai-sector-overviews/machine-vision-in-banking-facial-recognition-and-ocr/> accessed 28 May 2023.

73 Ehi Eric Esoimeme, 'The FinCEN Files: How Anti-Money Laundering Procedures Can Identify and Reduce the Money Laundering Risks Facilitated Through the Purchase and Sale of Precious Metals, Precious Stones and Jewels' (2021) 23(10) Financial Regulation International <https://papers.ssrn.com/sol3/papers.cfm?abstract_id=3758442> accessed 28 May 2023.

74 Pavlo Tertychnyi, Mariia Godgildieva, Marlon Dumas and Madis Ollikainen, 'Time-aware and Interpretable Predictive Monitoring System for Anti-Money Laundering' (2022) 8 Machine Learning with Applications 100306 <https://doi.org/10.1016/j.mlwa.2022.100306>.

As a result, AML departments can more effectively monitor suspicious activities.[75] To be effective, the ML model behind the software must be trained on thousands of customer reference data and transaction data,[76] including but not limited to currency activity involving multiple transactions greater than \$10,000; currency activity (single and multiple transactions) below the \$10,000 reporting requirement; currency transactions aggregated by customer name, tax identification number or customer information file number; funds transfer records in banks with low funds transfer activity; and records for monetary instrument sales. These transactions must be labelled with points denoting the sender, beneficiary, amount involved, the geographic location, and both common and complex money laundering techniques. These labelled transactions should then be run through the software's ML algorithm. This would have trained the algorithm to discern the sequences and patterns in transactions.

The user could then expose the software to transactions that are not labelled using an automated transaction monitoring system.[77] The algorithm behind the software would then be able to recognise a customer's reference data and transaction data. The system can then detect unusual/uncharacteristic behaviour by customers, and patterns of behaviour that are characteristic of money laundering or terrorist financing, which after analysis may lead to suspicion of money laundering or terrorist financing.

The Challenges of Implementation of New Technologies for AML/CFT in Nigeria

The adoption and implementation of new technologies to the AML/CFT frameworks is not without challenges. Core challenges are national, legal, institutional and operational.

National Barriers

National barriers mostly relate to the absence of reliable, accurate and complete data from the government. This data can be used to train ML models.

Limited Access to Training Data From the National (Money Laundering and Terrorist Financing) Risk Assessment Forum

A money laundering detection system is only as good as its training data. The wide variety of money laundering techniques is ever increasing. To counteract

75 Xingrong Luo, 'Suspicious Transaction Detection for Anti-Money Laundering' (2014) 8(2) International Journal of Security and its Applications 157–66 <https://doi.org/10.14257/ijsia.2014.8.2.16>.

76 Emad Mohammed and Behrouz Far, *Supervised Machine Learning Algorithms for Credit Card Fraudulent Transaction Detection: A Comparative Study* (IEEE Annals of the History of Computing, IEEE, 1 July 2018) <https://doi.ieeecomputersociety.org/10.1109/IRI.2018.00025>.

77 John O Awoyemi et al., 'Credit Card Fraud Detection Using Machine Learning Techniques: A Comparative Analysis' (2017 International Conference on Computing Networking and Informatics (ICCNI) 2017) <https://doi.org/10.1109/iccni.2017.8123782>.

this, decades of records, external data sources and true cases must be collated and referenced to facilitate the identification of possible money laundering activities. It is therefore essential that this data is accessible, either through the bank's own systems or a third-party provider.[78] It is worthy of note that Nigeria does not update the National Risk Assessment (NRA) regularly. The first NRA was published in 2016[79] and the second was published in 2022.[80] The NRA sets out the key money laundering and terrorist financing risks for the country concerned. The NRA also includes the most recent money laundering typologies and case studies that can be used by data scientists to train the ML algorithm.

Absence of Complete and Current Information From the Corporate Affairs Commission

Banks and other FIs may also encounter challenges gaining access to beneficial ownership (BO) information, partially due to the absence of complete and current information kept by the Corporate Affairs Commission (CAC). GIABA's Second Mutual Evaluation Report of Nigeria revealed that company registration documents kept by the CAC are not dependable and current. Contrary to the requirements of the Companies and Allied Matters Act (CAMA), entities that failed to file yearly returns for as long as 13 years are still on the register with no sanctions applied.

Legal Barriers

Legal barriers mostly relate to regulatory requirements and guidance for the use of end-to-end AML solutions. Core challenges include lack of explicit guidance on the use of financial technology, lack of explicit regulatory requirements and guidance for the use of automated monitoring systems, and no provision mandating the public disclosure of the asset details of public officers.

Lack of Explicit Guidance on the Use of Financial Technology for Data Sharing

On 17 February 2021, the Central Bank of Nigeria (CBN), in line with its mandate to promote financial system stability, issued the Regulatory Framework for Open Banking in Nigeria (RFOBN) to foster the sharing and leveraging of

78 Emma Wadey, 'A-Z of Financial Crime in Africa: The What, Why and How to Tackling Financial Crime in Africa' (*Temenos* 2019) <www.temenos.com/wp-content/uploads/2019/08/Financial-Crime-Africa-whitepaper-2019-Aug-21.pdf> accessed 22 May 2023.

79 The National (Money Laundering & Terrorist Financing) Risk Assessment Forum, 'Report of Nigeria National Risk Assessment on Money Laundering and Terrorism Financing' (*NRA Forum* 2016) <www.nfiu.gov.ng/Home/NRAReport> accessed 28 May 2023.

80 The National (Money Laundering & Terrorist Financing) Risk Assessment Forum (n 3).

customer-permissioned data by banks with third-party firms to build solutions and services that provide efficiency, greater financial transparency and options for account holders and to enhance access to financial services in Nigeria.[81] Open exchange of data and services through APIs could generate sufficient training data for the ML algorithm. Since the accuracy of advanced analytics largely corresponds to the size, quality and relevancy of the data set, the efficacy and efficiency of these tools may depend on the ability of FIs (within and outside of financial groups) to share information.[82]

While the RFOBN stipulates, amongst others, data and application programming interface (API) access requirements, principles for API, data, technical design and information security specifications, it does not provide guidance on the steps institutions should consider when managing the primary risks that may arise from service relationships between FIs and foreign-based third parties, and the implications of the relationships within the context of the examination process.

The use of foreign-based service providers is a common business practice that can be a less costly alternative to self-processing or to using domestic service providers. However, this practice raises country, compliance, contractual, reputation, operational (e.g., transactional) and strategic issues in addition to those presented by use of a domestic service provider.[83]

Lack of Explicit Regulatory Requirements and Guidance for the Use of Automated Monitoring Systems

On 20 June 2022, the CBN issued new Regulations, the Central Bank of Nigeria (Anti-Money Laundering, Combating the Financing of Terrorism and Countering Proliferation Financing of Weapons of Mass Destruction in Financial Institutions) Regulations, 2022 (hereinafter CBN AML/CFT/CPF Regulations, 2022) after reviewing the CBN AML/CFT Regulations, 2013 and their amendments to comply with provisions of the Money Laundering (Prevention and Prohibition) Act, 2022, Terrorism (Prevention and Prohibition) Act, 2022, and relevant extant AML/CFT/CPF Regulations. The CBN AML/CFT/CPF Regulations, 2022 were issued by the CBN to promote compliance with AML/CFT laws and regulations and safeguard FIs from being used for financial crimes.[84]

81 Central Bank of Nigeria, 'Regulatory Framework for Open Banking in Nigeria' (*CBNF*, February 2021) <www.cbn.gov.ng/out/2021/psmd/circular%20on%20the%20regulatory%20framework%20on%20open%20banking%20in%20nigeria.pdf> accessed 26 May 2023.

82 Financial Action Task Force (n 19).

83 Federal Financial Institutions Examination Council, 'Outsourcing Technology Services' (*FFIEC*, 15 July 2004) <www.ffiec.gov/press/pr071504.htm> accessed 26 May 2023.

84 Central Bank of Nigeria, 'Circular to all Banks, Other Financial Institutions (OFIs) and Payment Service Providers (PSPs): Central Bank of Nigeria (Anti-Money Laundering, Combating the Financing of Terrorism and Countering Proliferation Financing of Weapons of

While the CBN AML/CFT/CPF Regulations, 2022 stipulate, amongst others, the AML, CFT and CPF institutional policy framework for risk assessment, risk mitigation and independent testing; customer due diligence measures; enhanced due diligence measures; maintenance of records; and monitoring and reporting of suspicious transactions,[85] it does not provide guidance for the use of regulatory technologies with embedded AI and ML techniques. The United Kingdom, on the other hand, has provided explicit guidance for the use of automated monitoring systems.[86] The lack of explicit regulatory requirements and guidance for the use of an end-to-end AML solution with embedded ML techniques to spot more suspicious activity is a challenge for FI data pooling and the use of collaborative analytics.

No Provision Mandating the Public Disclosure of the Asset Details of Public Officers

Banks and other FIs in Nigeria wishing to build a risk-scoring AI-enabled system may encounter challenges gaining access to the asset details of public officers. In a lawsuit marked FHC/ABJ/CS/65/2020, seeking "an order for leave to apply for judicial review and an order of mandamus to direct and/or compel President Buhari, Vice President Osinbajo, 36 state governors and their deputies to make public their summary of assets."[87] The Socio-Economic Rights and Accountability Project (SERAP) went further to seek a mandamus order to compel the Code of Conduct Bureau (CCB) "to make available to the public, specific details of asset declarations submitted to it by successive Presidents, Vice-Presidents, Senate Presidents, Speakers of House of Representatives, state governors and their deputies since 1999."[88] The CCB, which contended that no law empowered it to release to the public the assets declaration forms submitted by public officers, vehemently opposed the suit. The

Mass Destruction in Financial Institutions) Regulations, 2022' (CBN, 20 June 2022) <www.cbn.gov.ng/Out/2022/FPRD/AML%20CIRCULAR%20AND%20REGULATIONS%20MERGED.pdf> accessed 27 May 2023.

85 Central Bank of Nigeria (Anti-Money Laundering, Combating the Financing of Terrorism and Countering Proliferation Financing of Weapons of Mass Destruction in Financial Institutions) Regulations, 2022, Regulations 11, 12, 13, 14, 15, 19, 20, 21, 22, 23, 24, 28, 29, 30, 31, 35, 36, 37, 38, 39, 40.

86 The Joint Money Laundering Steering Group, 'Prevention of Money Laundering/Combating Terrorist Financing: Guidance for the UK Financial Sector' (*JMLSG*, July 2022 (amended May 2023) <www.jmlsg.org.uk/guidance/current-guidance/> accessed 28 May 2023.

87 Premium Times, 'SERAP Asks Court to Order Buhari, Osinbajo, 36 Governors to Publish Their Assets' <www.premiumtimesng.com> accessed 26 January 2020; <www.premiumtimesng.com/news/more-news/374377-serap-asks-court-to-order-buhari-osinbajo-36-governors-to-publish-their-assets.html?tztc=1> accessed 16 August 2023.

88 The Punch, 'Compel Buhari to Make Assets Public, SERAP Urges Court', (https://punchng.com/ 26 January 2020) <https://punchng.com/compel-buhari-to-make-assets-public-serap-urges-court/> accessed 16 December 2021.

court, in an 11 May 2020, judgment by Justice Muslim Hassan, agreed with the CCB and dismissed SERAP's suit.[89]

Institutional and Operational Barriers

Institutional and operational barriers mostly relate to adapting practices to new and sometimes untested systems or technology solutions. Issues relate to cybersecurity, internal fraud, frequency of training, independent testing and information sharing among parents and subsidiaries.

Cyberattack

ML models are often trained, using a large data set of financial transactions from the database of different FIs, to predict the next fraudulent transaction. Cloud storage is required or recommended to store the training input data and output data when the data is larger than the hard drive.[90] As data storage has shifted increasingly to the cloud, cybercriminals have exploited the opportunity to attack vital digital infrastructure in Nigeria.[91] In 2018, commercial banks in Nigeria lost a cumulative N15 billion ($39 million) to electronic fraud and cybercrime. This was a 537% increase on the N2.37 billion loss recorded in 2017.[92] The issue became worse for banks as they have lost credible, talented and tech-savvy executives. This issue cuts across the entire banking sector, as close to 600 of bank employees in the IT sector have relocated abroad.[93]

Internal Fraud

Internal fraud is considered the biggest problem facing banking institutions, with recent research by Temenos putting its influence at 70%.[94] Fraud is

89 The Guardian, 'Transparency in Asset Declaration Regime Still a Long Way Ahead' <https://guardian.ng/> accessed 15 September 2020 <https://guardian.ng/features/transparency-in-asset-declaration-regime-still-a-long-way-ahead/> accessed 8 December 2021.

90 G Yufeng, 'Big Data for Training Models in the Cloud' (*Towards Data Science*, 5 October 2017) <https://towardsdatascience.com/big-data-for-training-models-in-the-cloud-32e0df348196> accessed 22 May 2023.

91 The Guardian, 'Cyber Security in Nigeria – Challenges and Solutions' (*The Guardian*, 28 October 2020) <https://guardian.ng/news/cyber-security-in-nigeria-challenges-and-solutions/> accessed 22 May 2023.

92 Cee Harmon, 'Cybercriminals Inflicting Pain As More Nigerians Embrace e-Payments' (*National Economy*, 29 November 2022) <https://nationaleconomy.com/cybercriminals-inflicting-pain-as-more-nigerians-embrace-e-payments/> accessed 1 June 2023.

93 Adeyemi Adepetun, 'Cybercrimes Raise Concerns for N30.2tr Monthly E-Payments' (*The Guardian*, 29 November 2022) <https://guardian.ng/news/cybercrimes-raise-concerns-for-n30-2tr-monthly-e-payments/> accessed 22 May 2023.

94 Emma Wadey, 'A-Z of Financial Crime in Africa: The What, Why and How to Tackling Financial Crime in Africa' (*Temenos* 2019) <www.temenos.com/wp-content/uploads/2019/08/Financial-Crime-Africa-whitepaper-2019-Aug-21.pdf> accessed 22 May 2023.

usually perpetrated by those with the highest levels of access to IT systems, such as systems and database administrators. These actors are better placed to commit or facilitate the fraud, and they are capable of erasing all evidence of their actions.[95] A pioneer chairman of the Economic and Financial Crimes Commission (EFCC), Nuhu Ribadu, has said money laundering from fraud occurs with the active connivance of banks and their workers. Ribadu stated:

> Our banking system is prone to abuse by corrupt elements. As investigations reveal every now and then, almost no case of corruption occurs without the involvement of banks and bankers.[96]

Employee fraud and money laundering could have a negative effect on the productivity of AI-enabled monitoring systems to identify and review sufficient information on the internet banking blockchain for suspicious transactions. The EFCC has in recent times investigated, detained and prosecuted several bank executives for allegedly mismanaging customers' funds.[97] On 16 June 2021, a Lagos State High Court convicted a former managing director of the defunct Bank PHB, Francis Atuche, for defrauding the bank of N25.7bn.[98] A former managing director of the defunct Oceanic Bank, Cecilia Ibru, was also convicted and ordered to repay $1.2bn.[99] Also, a former chairman of Skye Bank (now Polaris Bank), Tunde Ayeni, and a former managing director of the defunct Intercontinental Bank, Erastus Akingbola, are facing corruption charges.[100] The current EFCC chairman, Abdulrasheed Bawa, speaking on

95 Frank Eleanya, 'Cyber Fraud Rises 534% as Nigerian Banks Lose N3.5bn' (*BusinessDay*, 16 February 2021) <https://businessday.ng/banking-finance/article/cyber-fraud-rises-534-as-nigerian-banks-lose-n3–5bn/> accessed 22 May 2023.

96 Wale Odunsi, 'How Nigerian Banks Aid Money Laundering – Nuhu Ribadu' (*Daily Post*, 13 December 2017) <https://dailypost.ng/2017/12/13/nigerian-banks-aid-money-laundering-nuhu-ribadu/> accessed 28 May 2023.

97 Eniola Akinkuotu, Jesusegun Alagbe, Alexander Okere, Omobola Sadiq and Amarachi Orjiude, 'Asset Declaration: EFCC Issues Final Warning, Targets Over 120 Bank MDs, Top Executives' (*The Punch*, 20 June 2021) <https://punchng.com/asset-declaration-efcc-issues-final-warning-targets-over-120-bank-mds-top-executives/> accessed 28 May 2023.

98 Agency Report, 'N25.7bn Fraud: How Nigerian Banker, Francis Atuche, Begged for Mercy after Conviction' (*The Premium Times*, 17 June 2021) <www.premiumtimesng.com/news/top-news/468223-n25-7bn-fraud-how-nigerian-banker-francis-atuche-begged-for-mercy-after-conviction.html> accessed 23 June 2021.

99 Olusola Joshua Olujobi, 'Recouping Proceeds of Corruption: Is There Any Need to Reverse Extant Trends by Enacting Civil Forfeiture Legal Regime in Nigeria?' (27 May 2021) Journal of Money Laundering Control, ahead-of-print <https://doi.org/10.1108/JMLC 09-2020-0107>.

100 Vanguard, 'EFCC Indicts Tunde Ayeni in N29.5bn Fraud, Exonerates Capt Hosa Okunbo from Alleged Corruption' (*Vanguard* 2021) <www.vanguardngr.com/2021/01/efcc-indicts-tunde-ayeni-in-29-5bn-fraud-exonerates-capt-hosa-okunbo-from-alleged-corruption/> accessed 23 June 2021; Agency Report, 'Alleged Money

Channels TV's *Sunrise Daily* said on 15 June 2021 that bankers usually aid corrupt officials in laundering public funds, even as he alleged that a former Minister of Petroleum Resources delivered $20m in cash to a bank executive to purchase a $37.5 million property a bank manager put up for sale.[101]

Failure to Add New and Updated Information to Improve the ML Algorithm

Data training is a process that never ends. Banks must constantly add new and updated information to improve the ML algorithm, obtain better insights and more accurately predict outcomes.[102] GIABA's Second Mutual Evaluation Report of Nigeria revealed that large banks have automated systems for monitoring transactions of customers and identifying unusual transactions. However, these monitoring systems are not frequently updated, which reduces their effectiveness to identify suspicious transaction reporting.[103]

Failure to Undertake Independent Testing of the AML/CFT Functions

AML testing (audit) improves the integrity and accuracy of the ML technology used in the AML compliance program.[104] International standards require that the automated account monitoring system's programming methodology and effectiveness should be independently validated to ensure that the models are detecting potentially suspicious activity.[105] GIABA's Second Mutual Evaluation Report of Nigeria further revealed that larger FIs have set up internal control structures that ensure an independent unit reviews their AML/CFT system. Forex dealers, microfinance banks and insurance brokers do not

Laundering: EFCC Re-Arraigns Ex-Intercontinental Bank Chief, Erastus Akingbola' (*Premium Times*, 13 March 2019) <www.premiumtimesng.com/news/more-news/320012-alleged-money-laundering-efcc-re-arraigns-ex-intercontinental-bank-chief-erastus-akingbola.html> accessed 28 May 2023.

101 Akinkuotu, Alagbe, Okere, Sadiq and Orjiude (n 97).

102 Carlos Melendez, *Data is the Lifeblood of AI, But How Do You Collect It?* (IDG Communications, Inc., 8 August 2018) <www.infoworld.com/article/3296044/data-is-the-lifeblood-of-ai-but-how-do-you-collect-it.html> accessed 22 May 2023; Clickworker, 'The Process of AI Training' (*Clickworker*, 2 September 2021) <www.clickworker.com/customer-blog/process-of-ai-training/> accessed 22 May 2023.

103 Inter-Governmental Action Group against Money Laundering in West Africa (GIABA) 'Anti-money Laundering and Counter-Terrorist Financing Measures – Federal Republic of Nigeria, Second Round Mutual Evaluation Report' (*GIABA*, August 2021) <www.giaba.org/reports/mutual-evaluation/nigeria.html> accessed 1 June 2023.

104 Federal Financial Institutions Examination Council, 'BSA/AML Examination Manual' (*FFIEC*, 27 February 2015) <https://bsaaml.ffiec.gov/manual/AssessingCompliance-WithBSARegulatoryRequirements/04> accessed 2 June 2023.

105 Financial Action Task Force, 'International Standards on Combating Money Laundering and the Financing of Terrorism & Proliferation' (*FATF*, 16 February 2012 as amended February 2023) <www.fatf-gafi.org/en/publications/Fatfrecommendations/Fatf-recommendations.html> accessed 2 June 2023.

undertake independent testing of the AML/CFT functions. They consider their operations small and maintain conducting independent testing of AML/CFT function may increase their operation cost.[106] Failure of banks to independently validate the ML model will negatively affect the automated account monitoring system's ability to identify patterns of unusual activity.

Ineffective Information Sharing Among the Parent and Subsidiaries

According to GIABA, financial groups have AML/CFT policies that apply to all entities within the group. However, FIs interviewed did not demonstrate effective information sharing among the parent and subsidiaries for AML/CFT purposes.[107] Ineffective information sharing among the parent and subsidiaries may negatively affect the size, quality and relevancy of the data set as the efficacy and efficiency of the ML technology depends on the ability of FIs (within and outside of financial groups) to share information.

Implementing National, Legal, Institutional and Operational Reforms to Create an Enabling Environment for the Use of New Technologies in AML/CFT

The opportunities and challenges of using new technologies for AML/CFT may depend more on the national, legal, institutional and operational framework than additional technological development, as discussed in the previous section. This section outlines potential reforms so that commercially available or emerging technologies may be fully utilised to strengthen AML/CFT compliance consistent with national and international frameworks.

National Reforms

This section outlines the national reforms to enhance the overall capabilities of technological innovation.

Implementing Policies That Encourage Regular Updates of the NRA

Nigeria should update its NRA regularly to reflect the risk profile of the country. Nigeria can adopt the approach of the United Kingdom. The United Kingdom published its first NRA in 2015, the second in 2017 and the third in 2020. The NRA sets out the key money laundering and terrorist financing risks for the country concerned.

Implementing Policies That Promote Timely, Adequate, Accurate and Up-to-Date BO Information

The CAC should maintain timely, adequate, accurate and up-to-date BO information. The CAC should have a policy of inquiring/prohibiting or otherwise

106 Inter-Governmental Action Group against Money Laundering in West Africa (GIABA) (n 103).
107 Inter-Governmental Action Group against Money Laundering in West Africa (GIABA) (n 103).

becoming aware of foreign companies that are shareholders in local companies and that have issued bearer shares. This policy is particularly relevant for identifying the ultimate BO of local companies which can impede effective law enforcement investigations involving foreign companies. The CAC should also have a strong monitoring and sanctioning regime. According to GIABA's Second Mutual Evaluation Report on Nigeria, existing monetary sanctions are not dissuasive enough to guarantee compliance to make disclosures, including the BO of foreign partners and shareholders.

Legal Reforms

This section outlines the legal reforms to enhance the overall capabilities of technological innovation.

Review of RFOBN by the CBN

The CBN should review its RFOBN by providing guidance on the steps institutions should consider when managing the primary risks that may arise from service relationships between FIs and foreign-based third parties, and the implications of the relationships within the context of the examination process. This approach was adopted by the United States Federal Financial Institutions Examination Council in its 2004 guidelines titled "Outsourcing Technology Services."[108]

Review of the CBN AML/CFT/CPF Regulations, 2022

The CBN should further review the CBN AML/CFT/CPF Regulations, 2022 by providing guidance for the use of regulatory technologies with embedded AI and ML techniques. This approach was adopted by the United Kingdom's Joint Money Laundering Steering Group in its 2022 guidelines titled "Prevention of Money Laundering/Combating Terrorist Financing: Guidance for the UK Financial Sector."[109]

Enacting a Law Empowering the CCB to Release to the Public the Assets Declaration Forms Submitted by Public Officers

The Nigerian National Assembly should enact a law empowering the CCB to release to the public details of declared assets by public officers.

Institutional and Operational Reforms

This section outlines the institutional and operational reforms to enhance the overall capabilities of technological innovation.

108 Federal Financial Institutions Examination Council (n 83).
109 The Joint Money Laundering Steering Group, 'Prevention of Money Laundering/Combating Terrorist Financing: Guidance for the UK Financial Sector' (*JMLSG*, July 2022 (amended May 2023) <www.jmlsg.org.uk/guidance/current-guidance/> accessed 28 May 2023.

Adequate Staffing and Resources

Banks and other FIs should ensure adequate staffing for the proper monitoring of day-to-day compliance with cybersecurity and process automation to mitigate cyberattacks. FIs should dedicate sufficient human and technological resources to minimise the risk of cyberattacks.

Monitoring of Employee Conduct

Once a business relationship has been established with an employee using the pre-employment background screening process, FIs must conduct ongoing monitoring of the business relationship in accordance with the assessed level of risk. FIs must ensure that they monitor their employees' accounts for potential signs of fraud and money laundering.[110] FIs should subject employees' accounts to the same AML/CFT procedures as applicable to other customers' accounts.[111] Due diligence and account monitoring procedures should be performed on employees' accounts under the supervision of the AML/CFT Chief Compliance Officer, and the account of this officer should in turn be reviewed by the Chief Internal Auditor or a person of adequate and similar seniority.[112]

FIs should have a policy that mandates that a lie detector test should be taken once in five years by all staff of the FI. For staff in very sensitive positions, the lie detector test should be taken every three years. This will enable the lie detector policy to be more effective. Let us take, for example, a person who passes the lie detector test genuinely without any influence of corruption; there is still a possibility that the person may change over time. The temptation to follow current employees to collect bribes is very high. But if the FI put a policy in place that mandates all personnel take the lie detector test every five years starting from the first five years after recruitment, the cankerworm called corruption may be curbed effectively. Imagine if every employee knew that they were going to be asked by an examiner, five years after working, to confirm if they ever collected a bribe during the time they worked in the institution. In such a situation, most employees would desist from taking bribes or engaging in corrupt acts. The above measure would ensure that current employees who are chosen as examiners for the lie detector tests are fit and proper persons for the job.

Regular Updates of Automated ML Systems for Monitoring Transactions

Automated systems for monitoring transactions of customers and identifying unusual transactions should be updated more frequently.

110 Central Bank of Nigeria (Anti-Money Laundering and Combating the Financing of Terrorism in Banks and Other Financial Institutions in Nigeria) Regulations, 2013, Regulation 38(1).

111 Central Bank of Nigeria (Anti-Money Laundering and Combating the Financing of Terrorism in Banks and Other Financial Institutions in Nigeria) Regulations, 2013, Regulation 38(2).

112 Central Bank of Nigeria (Anti-Money Laundering and Combating the Financing of Terrorism in Banks and Other Financial Institutions in Nigeria) Regulations, 2013, Regulation 38(3).

External Independent Reviewer

FIs should engage and retain an independent, external, qualified, and experienced external auditor (the "third-party reviewer"), not subject to any conflict of interest, to examine their compliance program and to conduct risk-based independent testing of their AML/CFT program. Independent testing will include program governance, compliance structure and staffing; risk assessments; compliance with all record keeping and reporting requirements, including currency transaction reporting, suspicious activity reporting, and know your customer policies, procedures and controls; transaction monitoring; and training and communications.

Using Technology-Driven Applications for Information Sharing and Crime Reporting

Banks should deploy technology driven application for information sharing and crime reporting among the parent and subsidiaries for AML/CFT purposes. The technology application will complement the existing measures for promoting open banking. The data elicited from information sharing technologies will go a long way in aiding investigations into potential money laundering activities and improving the quality of suspicious activity reporting.

Concluding Remarks

This chapter offers a high-level overview of the opportunities and challenges of implementing AI-enabled technologies for AML/CFT in Nigerian banks and other FIs. This chapter addressed the implementation of new technologies known as regulatory technology (RegTech), such as AI, ML, big data and advanced cognitive analytics/algorithms targeting customer identification and verification requirements, and broader AML/CFT compliance obligations. The research also identified challenges or obstacles to their effective use. This includes analysing structural challenges, such as issues of data quality, inadequate staffing and IT resources and the lack of explicit regulatory requirements and guidance. Technological innovation offers great potential for the effectiveness of AML/CFT. However, its adoption and implementation to the AML/CFT frameworks is not without challenges. Core challenges as identified in this chapter are national, legal, institutional and operational. The chapter outlines potential reforms so that commercially available or emerging technologies may be fully utilised to strengthen AML/CFT compliance consistent with national and international frameworks. FIs and regulatory authorities are encouraged to adopt and implement these reforms to enhance the overall capabilities of technological innovation.

8 Anti-Money Laundering Compliance Challenges Within Nigerian Financial Institutions

Emmanuel Oluwasina Sotande

Introduction

Anti-money laundering and counter-terrorist financing (AML/CFT) standards require ongoing reviews that match the evolving threats posed to the formal financial system of an economy. Ideally, AML/CFT measures should be in line with Financial Action Task Force (FATF) Recommendations. The FATF is the international standard setter in the fight against money laundering and terrorist financing (ML/TF) and provides a forum for an effective global response to the threats posed. Since February 2012, the FATF Recommendations have been the recognized global AML/CFT standard. The Recommendations set out the essential measures that countries should have in place to identify the risks they face, apply preventive measures, develop policies to facilitate domestic cooperation, establish powers and responsibilities of competent authorities, enhance transparency and availability of beneficial ownership information and facilitate international cooperation.

Jurisdictional peculiarities are the major determinants of the areas of emphasis for legal, institutional and regulatory requirements. Hence it is necessary that for countries to be able to determine commensurate AML/CFT measures, it is expected that they carry out an assessment to enable them identify, assess and understand the risks to which they are exposed. Nigeria's national ML/TF risk assessment exercise in 2016 revealed the deficiencies of the country. The ML threat and vulnerability levels were both rated medium high in the course of the assessment, giving rise to a medium high-risk rating of money laundering (ML) in Nigeria. The assessment further revealed that bureau de change (BDC) and real estate are the first and second most vulnerable sectors to ML risk. Within the financial sector, the banking sector ranked highest while the insurance sector ranked the least. The least vulnerable sectors to ML risk are development finance institutions, microfinance banks (MFBs), primary mortgage banks and finance companies.[1]

1 The National (Money Laundering & Terrorist Financing) Risk Assessment Forum, 'National Inherent Risk Assessment of Money Laundering in Nigeria' (*NRA Forum* 2022) <www.nfiu.gov.ng/Home/NiraReports> accessed 14 December 2023.

DOI: 10.4324/9781003253808-10

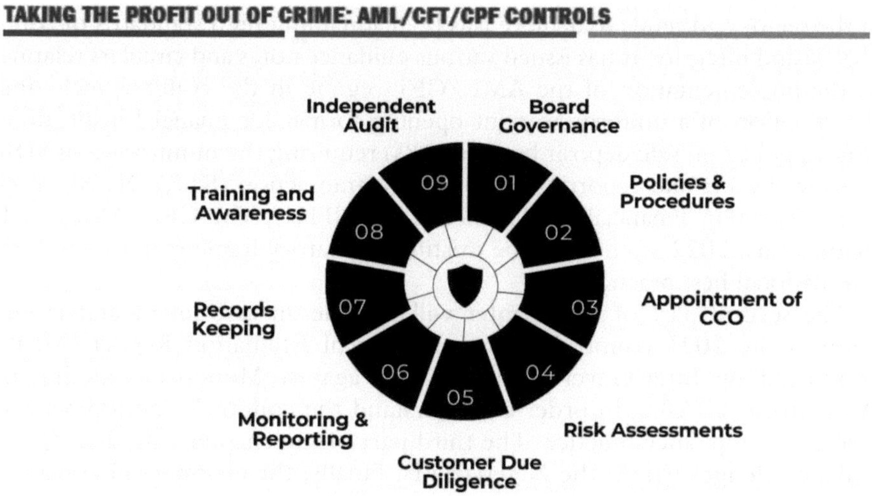

Figure 8.1 AML/CFT controls for financial institutions in Nigeria.

Source: P Boleigha (2023). Challenges and Priorities for AML'CFT Compliance: Developing a Culture of Compliance

To successfully elevate compliance management to a strategic advantage, compliance must be embedded in an organization's culture taking into the consideration the enlisted AML/CFT controls in Figure 8.1. These controls are independent audit, board governance, policies and procedures, appointment of ML reporting officer, risk assessments, customer due diligence (CDD), monitoring and reporting, record keeping, and training and awareness.

A positive culture of compliance entails encompasses enterprise risk management; addresses the risks that arise in each strategic area; establishes control points for the risk elements; ensures controls are well documented for internal and external purposes; and identifies the specific people responsible for managing each compliance element. Without a commitment to compliance, even the best policies and procedures will be useless. Therefore, FIs that lack a robust compliance culture may have a difficult time adapting to the current regulatory environment.[2]

For instance, the banking sector accounts for 95% of the financial system assets.[3] The sector is under the regulatory purview of the Central Bank of Nigeria (CBN), which provides banking services to the government and operators

2 P Boleigha, *Challenges and Priorities for AML/CFT Compliance: Developing a Culture of Compliance* (2023).

3 The National (Money Laundering & Terrorist Financing) Risk Assessment Forum (n 1).

in the sector and tends to achieve this by maintaining high standards of compliance and integrity. It has issued various guidance notes and circulars relating to the implementation of the AML/CFT regime in the country, including the adoption of a uniform account opening format for financial institutions (FIs), a policy on safe deposit boxes (SDBs) requiring the monitoring of SDB activities by FIs and reporting of suspicious transaction (STR)-related issues to the Nigerian Financial Intelligence Unit (NFIU). The CBN AML/CFT Regulations, 2022 strengthen the existing regulatory framework in line with international best practice.

The second part of the chapter will provide an assessment and evaluation of the 2021 country's follow-up Mutual Evaluation Report (MER) conducted by Inter-Governmental Action against Money Laundering in West Africa (GIABA) in order to understand the country's development in terms of compliance practice. The third part of the chapter will identify the AML challenges within the Nigerian FIs. Finally, the chapter will conclude by submitting future thoughts on effective AML compliance system within the Nigerian FIs.

GIABA's MER on Nigeria: Evaluation and Analysis

In order to understand the country's development in terms of compliance practice, it is necessary to evaluate the 2023 follow-up MER. Consequently, it is imperative to understand the existing capacity that is deployed to monitor the country ML/TF risks and vulnerabilities in line with the implementation of AML policy and strategic framework. It is equally relevant to explore legal and institutional framework arrangement to ensure compliance with global compliance standards by FIs.

The technical rerating by GIABA reveals that the country is compliant in 7 FATF Recommendations, largely compliant in 14 Recommendations, partially compliant in 17 Recommendations and non-compliant in 2 of the Recommendations. The ratings of the mutual evaluation caused the country to be placed on GIABA's enhanced 'Follow-Up' process and subsequently under the FATF International Cooperation Review Group 2022. Table 8.1 illustrates the country rating for the FATF Recommendations.[4]

The effectiveness of the country's measures to combat ML and TF was equally rated during the mutual evaluation conducted in 2019. According to the report, Nigeria exhibits moderate effectiveness in two immediate outcomes (IOs), which are IO3 on supervision and IO6 on financial intelligence. The other nine outcomes were rated low (see below table).

4 Inter-Governmental Action Group against Money Laundering in West Africa (GIABA), *Anti-money Laundering and Counter-Terrorist Financing Measures – Federal Republic of Nigeria, Second Round Mutual Evaluation Report* (GIABA, August 2021) <www.giaba.org/reports/mutual-evaluation/nigeria.html> accessed 1 June 2023.

Table 8.1 Nigeria 2021 Technical Compliance Ratings on the 40 FATF Recommendations

Compliant	*Largely Compliant*	*Partially Compliant*	*Non-Compliant*
R.4; confiscation and provisional measures	R.5; terrorist financing	R.1; assessing risks and applying a risk-based approach	R.7; targeted financial sanctions related to proliferation
			R.8; non-profit organisations
R.9; financial institutions secrecy law	R.10; customer due diligence	R.2; national cooperation and coordination	
R.13; correspondent banking	R.16; wire transfers	R.3; money laundering offence	
R.14; money or value transfer services	R.17; reliance on third parties	R.6; targeted financial sanctions related to terrorism and terrorist financing	
R.29; financial intelligence unit	R.18; internal controls and foreign branches and subsidiaries	R.11; record keeping	
R.30; responsibilities of law enforcement and investigative authorities	R.21; tipping-off and confidentiality	R.12; politically exposed persons	
R.31; powers of law enforcement and investigative authorities	R.26; regulation and supervision of financial institutions	R.15; new technologies	
	R.27; powers of supervisors	R.19; higher risk countries	
	R.35; sanctions	R.20; reporting of suspicious transactions	
	R.36; international instruments	R.22; designated non-financial business and professions (DNFBPs): customer due diligence	
	R.37; mutual legal assistance	R.23; DNFBPs: other measures	
	R.38; mutual legal assistance: freezing and confiscation	R.24; transparency and beneficial ownership	
	R.39; extradition	R.25; transparency and beneficial ownership of legal arrangements	
	R.40; other forms of international cooperation	R.28; regulation and supervision of DNFBPs	
		R.32; cash couriers	
		R.33; statistics	
		R.34; guidance and feedback	

Table 8.2 Nigeria 2021 Rating on FATF Immediate Outcomes

Immediate Outcome	*Rating*
IO1 – Risk, policy and coordination	Low Effectiveness
IO2 – International cooperation	Low Effectiveness
IO3 – Supervision	Moderate Effectiveness
IO4 – Preventive measures	Low Effectiveness
IO5 – Legal persons and arrangements	Low Effectiveness
IO6 – Financial intelligence	Moderate Effectiveness
IO7 – Money laundering investigation and prosecution	Low Effectiveness
IO8 – Confiscation	Low Effectiveness
IO9 – Terrorist financing investigation and prosecution	Low Effectiveness
IO10 – Terrorist financing preventive measures and financial sanctions	Low Effectiveness
IO11 – Proliferation financial sanctions	Low Effectiveness

Some aspects of the technical rating for Nigeria that affect FIs were poorly rated in the mutual evaluation. The country was rated as partially compliant with Recommendation 6 on targeted financial sanctions related to terrorism and terrorist financing due to several technical deficiencies including a convoluted and unclear process of list dissemination, absence of clear mechanisms to inform the private sector, duplicative freezing measures, and other major gaps. FIs rely on the Nigeria Sanctions Committee for information on individuals and entities designated as terrorist in line with United Nations Security Council Resolutions 1267 and 1373. However, the 'Nigeria List' of designated terrorists is yet to be developed and disseminated to the FIs or competent authorities.

Furthermore, Recommendation 7 on targeted financial sanctions related to proliferation is rated non-compliant as at the time of the on-site visit in 2019. However, major steps have been made in this regard, especially with the enactment of the Terrorism (Prevention and Prohibition) Act, 2022, which provides for an effective, unified and comprehensive legal, regulatory and institutional framework for the detection, prevention, prohibition, prosecution and punishment of acts of terrorism, terrorism financing, proliferation and financing of the proliferation of weapons of mass destruction in Nigeria. Moreso, there is need for an adequate assessment of the nonprofit organization sector. This will produce relevant indicators to guide reporting STRs by FI reporting entities and also aid regulators and supervisors in carrying out their supervisory functions.

FIs, especially banks, have a good level of understanding of ML/TF risks and AML/CFT obligations, but the application of CDD and enhanced due diligence (EDD) measures differ across FIs. For example, FIs establish the beneficial ownership of corporate customers using documentation from the Corporate Affairs Commission (CAC). The MER states that FIs generally apply mitigating measures for ML risks but focus less on terrorist financing risk. Largely, banks have in place rules to detect geographic and transactional red flags. This has given rise to a gradual increase in reporting STRs, though not clearly in keeping with their level of risk.

The understanding of ML/TF risks shown by the other FIs and nonbank sector is lower, especially among MFBs and foreign exchange dealers (BDCs). BDCs do not generally apply risk profiling and controls. Though the BDCs are also regulated and supervised by CBN, the level of supervision does not seem to be consistent with their risk exposure, considering a large number of them are unregistered/unlicensed operators and other risk factors.

There is a correlation between the involvement of both formal and informal currency exchange service (BDC) in the manipulation of the complex ML web for the integration of illicit enrichment from corruption/terrorism. Also, at least 400 suspects including 180 BDC operators were nabbed by security operatives in mid-2021 for alleged links to terrorism financing.[5] Having evaluated and analysed the GIABA's follow-up MER on Nigeria in this section, the next section switches gears and provides in-depth understanding on challenges impeding effective AML compliance within the FIs in Nigeria.

Challenges of the FIs to AML Regimes

The analysis of impediments to combat illicit financial flows including ML/TF are categorized and properly evaluated.[6] Additionally, this chapter throws more light on typical AML challenges within the Nigerian FIs. These are political, operational, social, economic and legal Impediments. Each of these impediments will be discussed in turn in this chapter.

FIs AML Compliance and Political Challenge in Nigeria

The political landscape and corruption are a major vulnerability that impedes AML compliance effectiveness within the Nigerian FIs. In many developing countries, such as Nigeria, where we have an effective AML system, there is a strong correlation to good governance and political accountability that is free of corruption. Corruption is endemic and systemic across all sectors of Nigeria's economy, comprising a threat in itself and enabling other illicit conduct. Nevertheless in Nigeria, high-profile politically exposed persons (PEPs) will set up a company with family or fictional names as directors and apply for tenders, but with the PEP as the final beneficiary and signatory on the bank

5 Abdulaziz Abdulaziz, Chris Agabi, John C Azu and Sunday Michael Ogwu, 'Nigeria: Terrorism Financing – 180 BDC Operators Pay N900m Penalties to CBN' (*AllAfrica*, 7 June 2021) <https://allafrica.com/stories/202106070207.html> accessed 28 May 2023.

6 Emmanuel Sotande, 'Impediments Affecting the Curbing of Illicit Financial Flows of Organised Crime in Developing Economies: Policy Implications' (2019) 26(1) Journal of Financial Crime 5–21 <https://doi.org/10.1108/JFC-11-2017-0108>.

account.[7] Additionally, many of the PEPs in Nigeria are ex-bank executives, therefore circumventing FATF Recommendation 10 on CDD and Recommendation 12 on special measures on transactions of PEPs would be an easy task to achieve in a politically affiliated bank to legitimize proceeds of crime within the FIs. In Nigeria and other global communities, transactions of PEPs are presumed as high-risk transactions; therefore FATF recommendations suggested that enhanced CDD be followed to mitigate affiliated risk associated in the transactions of PEPs and their associates. Consequently, the political godfatherism status that exists with many bank officials and PEPs in Nigeria impedes cooperate governance and financial system integrity in the quest to legitimized illicit enrichment from corruption within the Nigerian context.[8]

According to an expert interview with National Drug Law Enforcement Agency (NDLEA) Investigator 2, the PEPs that are expected to be the role models in Nigerian political environment are the most criminal minded in the country, and some of them were ex-bank executives from the FIs. This makes culture of crime in the country a pleasure, and the punishment of crime is less fashionable[9] as a result of involvement of PEPs using their bankers' associates in crime and political godfatherism a menace to circumvent cooperate governance and FATF recommendations within the Nigeran FIs. This explains the 'symbiotic' relationship between the FI employees and the PEPs, creating a weak link in the Nigerian AML system, and cooperate governance and AML policy to combat crime are compromised.

The prevalence of private sector and/or political corruption within the FIs in Nigeria creates degeneration of measures to secure financial system integrity in the country.[10] The consequential effect of this weak link is witnessed in the overall low effectiveness rating by the GIABA[11] on the country AML system and IO4 – Preventive measures to combat ML/TF in Nigeria.

Having considered FIs' AML compliance and political challenge in Nigeria, the next section will address the operational challenges for AML compliance within Nigerian FIs.

Operational Challenges for AML Compliance Within Nigerian FIs

It has been argued by many scholars that the fight against ML started in developed countries where civilization and sophistication is the norm of the

7 Em. Professor Jackie Harvey, *Tracking Beneficial Ownership and the Proceeds of Corruption: Evidence from Nigeria* (Northumbria University, 31 October 2021) <https://ace.globalintegrity.org/resources/tracking-beneficial-ownership-and-the-proceeds-of-corruption-evidence-from-nigeria-2/> accessed 28 May 2023.

8 Em. Professor Jackie Harvey, *Tracking Beneficial Ownership and the Proceeds of Corruption: Evidence from Nigeria* (Northumbria University, 31 October 2021) <https://ace.globalintegrity.org/resources/tracking-beneficial-ownership-and-the-proceeds-of-corruption-evidence-from-nigeria-2/> accessed 28 May 2023.

9 Sotande (n 6).

10 Sotande (n 6).

11 Inter-Governmental Action Group against Money Laundering in West Africa (GIABA) (n 4).

society.[12] Therefore, implementation of recommendations and standards from developed countries to combat ML within the FIs and reporting entities within developing economy such as Nigeria comes with a great deal of challenges. For instance, developing countries such as Nigeria are applying stringent AML policies and standards in their countries at face value. These countries are not allowed to take specific initiative of their own without applying standard-setter methodology and frameworks. In many countries, FATF recommendations are copied word-for-word in their AML legislation in order to achieve FATF technical compliance during the mutual evaluation assessment of the FATF-style regional bodies. The applied foreign frameworks and recommendations are not best solutions for AML circumstances in many developing countries, thereby limiting the fight against illicit financial flows from a global perspective. The following operational challenges are identified as AML compliance weak links within the FIs in Nigeria: challenge of new technologies; failure to comply with CDD; lack of a robust addressing system; harassment of ML reporting officers by law enforcement agencies (LEAs); an ineffective feedback mechanism between the Nigerian FIs, LEAs and NFIU; and a record keeping deficit within the Nigerian FIs.

This section has evaluated operational AML challenges within Nigerian financial institutions. The next section will look at new technology AML impediment in Nigeria.

Impediment of AML Compliance With New Technologies

FATF Recommendation 15 on new technologies requires countries to be aware of how criminals can abuse the use of new technologies, automated business processes and technological advancements, particularly within the FIs to perpetrate crime. Ability of FIs to stay compliant with R.15 will require very rigorous AML products and customer risk assessment prior to introduction of new products and technologies. This requires both capital and human resources in order to identify the potential risks associated with new technologies. The AML risk assessment process within the FI comes with great deal of operational cost to the Nigerian local banks that are struggling and competing with their counterpart international banks located in developed countries. Major inventors of the AML solutions for monitoring the associated risks and threats of new products and technologies are located in developed countries. Transportation of the AML solutions from developed countries to Nigeria is very expensive to procure, limiting many local banks in Nigeria with the option of partial compliance and non-compliance with R.15 of FATF due to lack of budgetary allocation

12 Terence Halliday, Michael Levi and Peter Reuter, *Global Surveillance of Dirty Money: Assessing Assessments of Regimes to Control Money-Laundering and Combat the Financing of Terrorism* (Center on Law and Globalization, 30 January 2014) <https://orca.cardiff.ac.uk/id/eprint/88168/> accessed 1 June 2023.

to deploy new AML solutions to mitigate inherent risks (Researcher's own experience at the NFIU).

Additionally, the lack of robust regulatory framework to supervise new technologically related products, such as virtual assets, by many FIs regulators in developing economies resulted in poor regulatory frameworks and lack of AML risk-based supervision of the virtual assets; for example, the complexity existence of cryptocurrencies regulation in Nigeria.

This section has looked at new technology AML impediment in Nigeria. The next section will address the failure to comply with the required customer identification programme.

Failure to Comply With CDD

According to GIABA 2021[13] the application of CDD and EDD measures differs across FIs and generally did not reflect Nigeria's risk environment across the board. Again, banks appeared to institute the most far-reaching controls. FIs establish the beneficial ownership of corporate customers using documentation from the CAC. Though Recommendation 10[14] of the FATF on CDD requires reporting institution such as FIs to use reliable sources of information to identify and verify the legitimacy of their customers when conducting transactions in Nigeria, the lack of an ecosystem-related database limits the effectiveness of robust CDD in the countries. The principle of know your customer (KYC) is not effective in Nigeria due to the lack of a centralized database where all relevant identity document can be sorted for the purpose of CDD.

Consequent to the challenges of CDD in Nigeria, the bank verification number (BVN) is a financial reform implemented in February 2014 by the CBN in collaboration with the Bankers' Committee to protect the integrity of the financial system in Nigeria.[15] Whilst the FIs handle the enrolment of customers' BVNs, the Nigerian Inter Bank Settlement System generates a unique BVN for every account enrolled and provides a secure database for them, and the CBN supervises the whole process to enhance financial system integrity.[16] The introduction of BVNs is expected to provide biometrics solution for identity management challenges within the FIs and the banking sector in particular. Experts also believe that implementation of BVN biometrics solution will combat fraud and identity theft threats within Nigeria banks.

13 Inter-Governmental Action Group against Money Laundering in West Africa (GIABA) (n 1).

14 Financial Action Task Force, *International Standards on Combating Money Laundering and the Financing of Terrorism & Proliferation* (FATF, 16 February 2012 As amended February 2023) <www.fatf-gafi.org/en/publications/Fatfrecommendations/Fatf-recommendations.html> accessed 2 June 2023.

15 Adikea Paul, 'The Effect of Bank Verification Number (BVN) in Nigeria Economy' (Entrepreneurship and Small business Management) <www.academia.edu/27579960/> accessed 2 June 2023.

16 Interview with CBN/NFIU (CBN, 12 July 2018).

Having considered failure to comply with CDD as a challenge in this section, the next section will look at the lack of a robust addressing system as an unusual challenge within developing economies.

Lack of Robust Addressing System

In the same vein, addressing system in most developing economies are not organized.[17] For instance, in Nigeria, the postcode addressing system does not exist for the use of FIs to verify the actual location of their potential customer for the purpose of preventive measures to combat ML and other related crimes. The absence of a robust addressing system in Nigeria further increases the operational cost of the FIs. Consequently, the Nigerian banks have to physically conduct visitation of their customer by locating them in their addresses before granting approval for the operation of certain accounts.[18] This further creates an additional AML compliance burden on the operation of the FIs in Nigeria. Nevertheless, in developed countries such as the United Kingdom and the United States, where robust addressing system exist, the FIs in those countries need not conduct physical verification at the residing locations of their customers before onboarding them into FIs.[19] This could further limit the success of financial inclusion strategy in the country, whereby customers without suitable address are discourage to operate bank accounts in the country. Many houses are not serially numbered; consequently, winning the war against ML and terrorism is uncommon to locate potential money launderer and terrorist offenders during LEA investigation activities.[20]

This section has looked at the lack of robust addressing system as an unusual challenge within developing economies. The next section will evaluate consequence of ineffective cooperation between ML reporting officers and other competent authorities such as LEAs as an impediment of the AML system in Nigeria.

Lack of Effective Collaboration Between Money Laundering Reporting Officers (MLRO) Within the Nigerian FIs and LEAs

It is pertinent to mention the existing collaboration gaps between MLROs of the banks and the Nigerian LEAs. According to the interview with Chief Compliance Officer 2, many MLROs of the banks had been treated like common criminals by some LEAs in Nigeria. This usually happens when the LEAs are not achieving the set-out targeted expectations of their investigational activities. They resort to the use of force and intimidation on the bankers as against the principle of private-public sector collaboration suggested in the

17 Interview with UNODC Expert (UNODC, Nigeria).
18 Interview with Chief Compliance Officer 1.
19 Sotande (n 6).
20 Interview with NDLEA Investigator 1 (NDLEA Nigeria).

FATF Recommendation 2 on national cooperation and coordination[21] for combatting ML. It is noteworthy to mention that informer mechanism and collaborative outreach is deployed by both FIs and LEAs to combat illicit financial flows in many developed economies located in the Global North, where AML standards were developed.

Ineffective Feedback Mechanism Between the Nigerian FIs, LEAs and NFIU

According to the MER of Nigeria by the GIABA, as noted in R.33 on statistics of combatting ML in Nigeria, the NFIU has the mandate to collect statistical information. However, relevant information is often deficient, including on terrorist financing prosecutions and convictions and other relevant issues. Moreover, available formation was often of uncertain provenance and lacked consistency. FIs and designated non-financial business and professions receive little feedback from supervisory authorities, with the CBN, SEC, and the NFIU better at providing broader guidelines on reporting and detecting STRs. These deficiencies and ambiguities limit Nigeria's ability to fully understand and appreciate the complexity and scope of its ML/TF risks within the country AML system and FIs in particular.[22] This report suggested that the lack of feedback, some of which results from a reluctance of the FIs to share information, adversely impacts the ability of the NFIU to improve guidance to reporting entities and to enhance its analytical efforts. At least some of this, it was indicated, resulted from a reticence to share information.[23]

Deficit of Record Keeping Within the Nigerian FIs

Recommendation 11 on record keeping indicated Nigeria was rated partially compliant due to the improper manner of preservation of information and truncations record by some FIs, the inability of some sectors in meeting record keeping requirements, and the inconsistency and the inadequate number of on-site examinations of the financial sector by the competent authorities.[24] The following are major identified deficiencies highlighted by the GIABA in its MER of Nigeria published in 2021.

- There is no requirement for FIs to keep records of the results of any analysis undertaken.
- There is no time frame within which FIs should make records available to competent authorities.
- The scope of competent authorities that can request for records kept by FIs is limited.

21 Financial Action Task Force (n 14).
22 Inter-Governmental Action Group against Money Laundering in West Africa (GIABA) (n 1).
23 Inter-Governmental Action Group against Money Laundering in West Africa (GIABA) (n 1) 15.
24 Inter-Governmental Action Group against Money Laundering in West Africa (GIABA) (n 1) 15.

Socio-economic AML Challenges Within the Nigerian FIs

This section reviews the following social-economic challenges that impede the Nigeria AML system within the FIs. They are misuse of cash transactions to divert and launder government funds within the FIs; abuse of internal bank accounts to shield the true beneficial ownership of ill-gotten funds within the FIs; vulnerability of banking relationship practices amongst the Nigerian FIs; abuse of position to circumvent AML policy to commit personal economic gain; and the social deficit employed consequence of AML compliance on financial inclusion.

Abuse of Cash Transaction

Operations of cash transaction are predominant within the financial sector in Nigeria and create a vulnerability to the abuse of cash transactions for the purposes of ML/TF. It is evident in the analysis of STRs that are linked to some public accounts, especially state governments. Cash transactions are more prevalent during election years. This may include the use of cash to bribe party officials in order to secure party nomination during the party primaries, payment of cash for vote-buying on election day, payment of cash to thugs and security agents to violently obtain and divert ballot boxes for votes rigging, cash bribery to electoral officers to ensure winning during and after the election, and finally, dollar-denominated cash budgets to finance anticipated post-election judicial process.[25] Therefore, illegality and/or illicit financial flows emanating from elections present reasonable ML/TF vulnerabilities.

SANITIZED CASE STUDY 1: SYPHONING PUBLIC FUNDS THROUGH THE USE OF BANKS' INTERNAL ACCOUNTS AND ABUSE OF CASH TRANSACTION BY GOVERNMENT OFFICIALS[26]

A financial intelligence unit received 35 mandatory disclosures filed on 11 bank accounts that are linked to the HT state government in Nigeria. Over a certain period of time, the accounts received a total deposit of N132,234,827,567.11, which is equivalent to US$289,354,108.46. The source of the funds is federal government allocation and internally generated revenue, and the purpose was for socio-economic development of the state including providing security, universal basic education, infrastructure and rural development. Analysis of utilization of funds

25 The United Nations Office on Drugs and Crime and UK Aid, *Corruption in Nigeria: Patterns and Trends: Second Survey on Corruption as Experienced by the Population* (UNODC, December 2019) <https://nigerianstat.gov.ng/elibrary/read/1031> accessed 15 June 2023.

26 **Assessment of Money Laundering Typologies from Corruption in Nigeria. A Publication of the Nigerian Financial Intelligence Unit. May 2023.**

from the account revealed a likelihood of ongoing high-level corruption by HT state government officials who are linked to the accounts either as signatories or cashiers or through BVN. The signatories were seen to be engaged in frequent multiple and structured cash withdrawals. This was especially observed in accounts that are linked to the executive arm of the government. About $48,535,740 was withdrawn in cash during the reviewed period. Another tool employed by corrupt officials to syphon public funds is the use of banks internal accounts. Funds meant for the state government are diverted into internal accounts operated by the bank. Since transactions from internal accounts are not subject to AML/CFT controls, such transactions are not reported. The account provides potential anonymity for both the source and beneficiary of transactions. The total amount withdrawn through internal accounts amounted to US$7,066,969.90.

ML/TF Features of the Case:

- Abuse of cash transaction.
- Use of bank internal account.
- Frequent structured cash withdrawal by account signatories.

Source: Assessment of Money Laundering Typologies from Corruption in Nigeria. A Publication of the Nigerian Financial Intelligence Unit. May 2023.

Abuse of cash transactions is compounded by the deficit of financial inclusion within a state government's business process. There is lack of adequate financial services and financial inclusion systems among the states. For the period of 2015 to June 2020,[27] 80% of STRs filed on accounts linked to the 36 state governments were cash transactions. The north-east, where there is prevalence of terrorism and insecurity, accounts for the highest value of the reported STRs. This is a high-risk zone, where states have to utilize cash originating from security votes to counter-insurgency. Nevertheless, it is estimated that these secretive, unaccounted-for cash expenditures and corruption of security votes add up to over $670 million (N241.2 billion) annually.[28] This is affirmed by a strong correlation in financial inclusion at the financial centre where the state with high presence of FIs account for the highest level of electronic transactions. Lagos State is where the headquarters of most FIs

27 Nigeria Financial Intelligence Unit database from the GoAML solution.

28 Matthew T Page, 'Camouflaged Cash: How "Security Votes" Fuel Corruption in Nigeria' (*Transparency International*, May 2018) <https://ti-defence.org/wp-content/uploads/2018/05/DSP_Nigeria_Camouflage_Cash_Web2.pdf> accessed 15 June 2023.

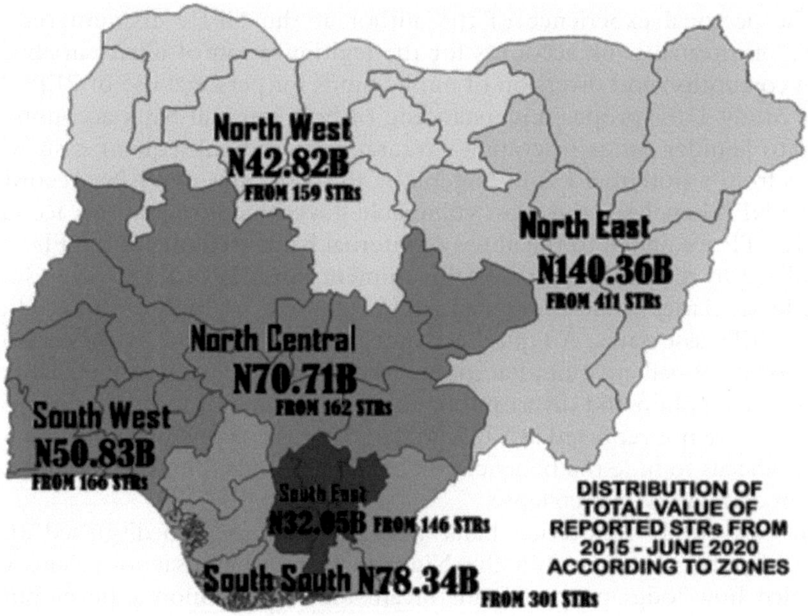

Figure 8.2 Distribution of total value of reported cash-related suspicious transactions by financial institutions from January 2015 to June 2020 according to the Nigerian geopolitical zones.

Source: Nigerian Financial Intelligence Unit.

are situated and accounts for 15% of the total value of electronic transfer–related STRs.

The fist category of the social-economic challenge is the abuse of cash transaction as elucidated in typological Case Study 1 of this section. The next category will focus on the abuse of internal bank account to shield the true beneficial ownership of ill-gotten funds.

Abuse of Internal Bank Account to Shield the True Beneficial Ownership of Ill-Gotten Funds

Another critical challenge that impedes effective AML compliance system within the Nigerian FIs is the deliberate use of internal bank accounts to shield sensitive transactions of high-profile and valued net-worth customers away from the AML raider. Internal bank accounts are the usual self-owned operational and suspense accounts of the FIs. Most of the operational and internal bank accounts of the FIs in Nigeria are classified as low risk. Therefore they are not usually subjected to STR reporting and the AML monitoring framework within the banks.

The personal experience of the author at the NFIU encountered the abuse of internal bank accounts for the legitimization of illicit enrichment from corruption and diversion of public funds for personal use of PEPs. See Case Study 1 for proper understanding of how internal bank accounts are used to launder funds in complex transactions and subsequent cash withdraws from a potential FIs in Nigeria by the associates of PEPs. According to the NFIU analysis, the most vulnerable government operations accounts to ML/TF are linked to the abuse of internal bank accounts of the FIs. This is utilized to receive and transfer government funds in order to disguise the true beneficiaries while using shell companies and multiple cash withdrawals by PEPs associates. A typical account that was analysed by the author is the Covid-19 palliative fund account, where the PEP utilized internal bank account to syphon and divert public funds and frequent multiple cash withdrawals were not reported as STRs. When there is a deliberate collusion with bank officials to hide the beneficiaries of certain funds, the AML compliance system of a nation will collapse.

In Case Study 1, internet bank accounts were used to disguised direct theft of public funds within the Nigerian financial transactions. This case revealed how lodgement of funds meant for socio-economic development in a particular state was being syphoned using multiple cash withdrawal. In this case, a total of US$289 million was concealed using internal bank accounts of a prominent FI in Nigeria and subsequently, the signatories to the accounts structured and withdrew the total sum of US$48 million in multiple cash transactions within the review period. The ML feature of this case suggests abuse of multiple cash transaction and abuse of internal bank accounts to syphon funds meant for the socio-economic development of a state, and major conduits in this laundering process are the state government officials and associates of PEPs who are the signatories to the state government accounts in this transaction.

This section illustrates how the abuse of internal bank account can be used to shield the true beneficial ownership of ill-gotten funds in ML scheme. The next section will focus on the abuse of corresponding banking to launder proceeds of funds.

Abuse of Corresponding Banking to Launder Proceeds of Funds

In Case Study 2, a front company was used by a PEP to launder the proceeds of corruption originating from Nigeria with the abuse of correspondent banking relationship. The total sum of USD 7.7 million was laundered through an illegal currency exchange service operation, also known as BDC in Nigeria, and the total sum involved in the case was transferred to banks located in tax haven countries. The features of this cases suggested that vulnerability of correspondent banking relationship is a critical tool to legitimize proceeds of crimes originating from illicit enrichment and corruption by PEPs.

SANITIZED CASE STUDY 2: ABUSE OF CORRESPONDENT BANKING RELATIONSHIP TO LAUNDER PROCEEDS OF CORRUPTION[29]

XZ Trust Company Ltd is linked to a PEP in Nigeria. It is operated in proxy by nominee shareholders including the PEP's son. On 14 February 2019, XZ Trust Company Ltd transferred US$3,000,000 to T&A Company Ltd. Furthermore, through the use of two other entities that are linked to the nominee shareholders, another sum of $4,900,000 was also transferred to T&A Company Ltd. The recipient entity is registered in Nigeria, and their line of business is given as production and marketing of dairy products. However, the entities financial transactions suggest that they are engaged in providing illegal currency exchange service and illegal international money transfer operation. It is also revealed that the promoters of T&A are linked to the ownership of several BDC licenses.

Analysis of utilization of funds from T&A Company Ltd's account showed that upon receipt of funds, a substantial amount was transferred to UT Bank London, MT Bank Germany and WT Bank, Isle of Man. Also, several transactions were carried out in favour of multiple BDCs, shipping companies and other companies with oil and gas interests.

The source of fund to XZ Trust Company is mostly from a bank account domiciled in SB Bank UK. The account in SB Bank has received funds from entities incorporated in Isle of Man that are linked to the nominee shareholders.

The report was forwarded to a competent law enforcement authority and is under investigation.

ML/TF Features of the Case:

- Use of correspondent banking relationship.
- Illegal currency exchange service operation.
- Illegal international money transfer service operation.
- Huge fund transfer to banks in tax havens.
- Use of bank accounts linked to multiple currency exchange service providers.
- Use of entities that are registered in tax havens.

The key vulnerable sectors that were used in this case are illegal and legal currency exchange service operators and FIs. In addition, presence of banking secrecy in many international financial centres, in particular the Isle of Man,

29 **Assessment of Money Laundering Typologies from Corruption in Nigeria. A Publication of the Nigerian Financial Intelligence Unit. May 2023.**

is also a key feature that facilitated the movement of this ill-gotten fund out of Nigeria.

Vulnerability of Banking Relationship Practices Amongst the Nigerian FIs

According to Sotande (2019), the low profitability status of many FIs in developing economies forced good banking culture.[30] The current banking practices in Nigeria suggested that FIs now recruit marketers and they are usually promoted based on level of banking businesses they are able to attract to their banks. Therefore, targets are set for them to scout for money deposits in order increase the profitability ratio of the recruiting FIs.[31] Consequently, the banker who meets their targets are promoted while those who do not attained their targets are usually sacked and disposed of their duty. Therefore, in the quest to meet required deposit targets set out by the FIs, many desperate marketing bankers will approach customers with illicit funds and even help them to clean dirty money during the placement process within the Nigerian FI. According to the interview with the National Crime Agency Expert in Nigeria, a critical challenge against the fight on illicit financial flows in Nigeria is the practice of relationship banking, whereby account officers can tip off their customers during the investigation activities of the LEAs and relevant competent authorities (CAs).[32]

The Investigator 2 in the Economic and Financial Crime Commission (EFCC) also affirmed that relationship officers to bank customers sometimes participate in the process of cleaning the dirty money to legitimized and shield the proceeds of crime. This is illustrated in the following box:

The Role of Relationship Officer in Legitimized Proceeds of Crime Within Nigerian FIs

The offenders often called their account officers, which are also known as relationship officer, by phone to come and pick the illicit funds in their home. Most of the time a bullion van could be used to pick up cash worth $ *3,000,000.00* USD from the offender's home. The account officers would then open an account for the offender with the collected proceeds of crime. The interesting aspect of it that the mandate card that is expected to be filled by the customer will be filled by the relationship officer on their behalf. The officer also assists in the structuring of the withdrawals of the ill-gotten funds into amounts to evade ML transaction reporting by the FIs.

30 Sotande (n 6).

31 Interview with the Chief Compliance Officer 1 and 2.

32 Expert Interview with the Nigeria Liaison officer of the National Crime Agency, United Kingdom.

This scenario enumerates the illegal role of the relationship officer when abusing the vulnerability of the FI in the quest to achieve the set-out money deposit targets within their banks. This practise impedes the fight against ML and financial system integrity within many developing economies.

Abuse of Position to Circumvent AML Policy to Commit Personal Economic Gain

In most cases where AML police and cooperate governance of the FIs are weak, many employees of the banks will explore this vulnerability to facilitate and commit crime. This crime could be committed locally and internationally. In Case Study 3, we can see the role of a Nigerian bank's offender in the facilitation and commission of international crime of business email compromise (BEC) while collaborating with his foreign counterpart, the main initiator and mastermind of the crime in the United States. It will only take a robust AML policy and sound AML and prudential audit to detect the abuse of position in circumventing AML compliance within the Nigerian FIs.

SANITIZED CASE STUDY 3: LAUNDERING PROCEEDS OF BEC THROUGH FRONT COMPANIES, BDCS AND MULES

Following a petition received from the United States, the US Federal Bureau of Investigation (FBI) through the Legal Attache, United States Consulate, Lagos, agents of Agency B arrested a couple, Mr. and Mrs. X, for their alleged involvement in BEC fraud and ML to the tune of $1.49m .

Investigations revealed that Mrs. X met one Mr. Z in the United States sometime in 2016 and he introduced her to foreign exchange business. Through this encounter, Mrs. X and her husband Mr. X, who is a banker, turned their two registered companies, U General Services Ltd and OP Limited, to conduits for the dispersal of funds wired by Mr. Z, who allegedly owns Q Investment Network.

Mr. Z wires dollars to the accounts of U General Services Ltd and OP Limited. Mrs. X makes cash withdrawals from the company accounts and sells them to BDC operators for Naira equivalents. She then pays the Naira equivalent to various accounts on the instruction of Mr. Z. The scheme is done with the involvement of Mr. X, who is a former assistant general manager of the bank and was relieved of his appointment on his involvement in the scheme.

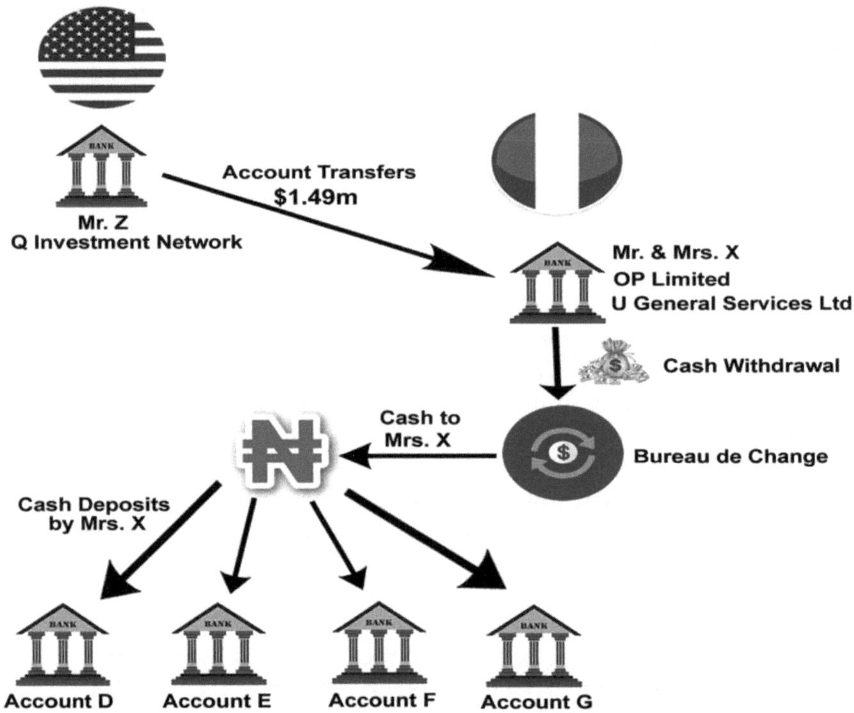

Figure 8.3 Sanitized case study 3: laundering proceeds of BEC through front companies, BDCs and Mules.

ML Features of the Case:

- Use of front companies.
- Cash withdrawals followed by the use of currency exchangers.
- Cash deposits into various accounts not related to the subject (use of mules).
- Use of cash to transact rather than a FI.

Source: Economic and Financial Crimes Commission.

Case Study 3 illustrates mistrust and abuse of office by a senior banker who facilitated the laundering of proceeds originating from BEC fraud emanating from the United States as reported by the FBI to the EFCC in Nigeria. A major offender residing in the United States committed the crime and used a couple, particularly the husband who is a senior banker, to legitimize the proceeds of crime to the tune of US$1.49 million in Nigeria. The fund is deposited in the couple's company account, and subsequently the foreign currencies are withdrawn by the banker and exchanged for local currency (naira) in the unregulated underground currency exchange service market. The ML features of this case suggest the use of front companies, followed by withdrawal of foreign currency and use of money mules to make cash deposits into various accounts not related to the main offender in the United States on his instruction. This approach of ML completely shields the identity of the main offender located in the United States.

SANITIZED CASE STUDY 4: ALLEGED CRIMINAL BREACH OF TRUST, IMPERSONATION, ABUSE OF OFFICE, FRAUD BY SENIOR BANK OFFICIAL

Based on a petition, a former managing director of a bank, Mr. J, was arrested by Operatives of Agency A for alleged criminal breach of trust, impersonation, abuse of office and fraud for using his position as the Bank's managing director to pay XXE Company Ltd a total sum of N1,368,000,000 ($2,993,435.40) between 2011 and 2013.

Investigations revealed that the suspect incorporated a company XXE Company Ltd and listed non-existent persons and others without their consent as directors, and proceeded to grant loans to the companies under the pretence that the directors of the company applied for and are the beneficiaries of the loan. The suspect used his position to waive the required due process for award of such loans including obtaining of collateral, hence the loan has remained for unpaid years. The suspect has also been mentioned in other ML schemes through real estate that involved a high-ranking government official.

Mr. J has been relieved of his appointment and the case has been charged to court.

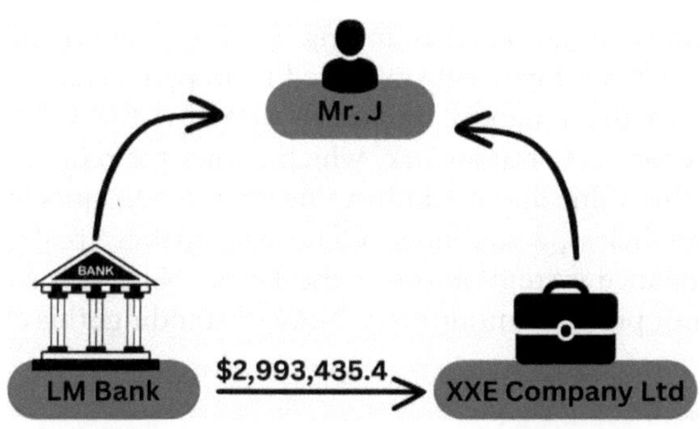

Figure 8.4 Sanitized case study 4: alleged criminal breach of trust, impersonation, abuse of office, fraud by senior bank official.

ML/TF Features of the Case:

- Use of front company.
- Use of fictitious customer identification.
- Abuse of office.
- Forgery.

Source: Economic and Financial Crimes Commission.

Case Study 4 illustrates the abuse of position by a senior bank official to circumvent AML compliance in committing crime locally in Nigeria. In this case, the senior banker incorporated a shell company of which he is the beneficial owner. He then went ahead to make fictitious loan requests from the bank and used his position as a senior bank director to grant the loans to the tune of US$2.9 million for the incorporated shell company. The ML features of this case include abuse of office to circumvent CDD process, the use of fictitious names as company directors, and the use of a front company to award loan to himself. This further impedes the principle of KYC and the AML compliance system within the Nigerian Bank.

Social Justice Deficit: Consequence of AML Compliance on Financial Inclusion

It is pertinent to note that AML compliance within the Nigerian FIs had limited the financial inclusion within the rural areas of Nigeria. This was reemphasized in the expert interview conducted by the author in the CBN.[33] In Kama and Adigun (2013), financial inclusion is defined as the ability to access formal FIs by the members of the society.[34] That is, financial inclusion should provide equal rights to the rich, the poor, the disabled and other excluded populations in the rural areas to free access to financial services and products. The African Development Bank suggested that among the 56.3 million adult population of Nigerian, 64.1 % are financially excluded from patronage of FIs.

Consequent to the Financial Inclusion Strategy, the CBN issued a simplified, three-tiered KYC framework, which allows for reduced due diligence obligations for low-value and medium-value savings accounts within the Nigerian FIs.[35] Nevertheless, a simplified CDD will further create a weak link to the AML compliance system amongst the FIs in Nigeria if such category of transactions is not properly monitored. Notwithstanding, this chapter suggests

33 Interview with the Central Bank Regulator 2.

34 U Kama and M Adigun, *Financial Inclusion in Nigeria: Issues and Challenges* (Central Bank of Nigeria Occasional Paper No. 45. August 2013). <www.scirp.org/(S(lz5mqp453edsnp55rrgjct55.))/reference/referencespapers.aspx?referenceid=2536791> accessed 15 June 2023.

35 Inter-Governmental Action Group against Money Laundering in West Africa (GIABA) (n 1).

introduction of a robust financial inclusion products risk framework to help mitigate unforeseen inherent future vulnerabilities associated with this product. It is noteworthy to state that customer profile and risk could change in the future after being onboarded as three-tiered customer. Therefore, there should be an indicator for the modification of three-tiered customer when there is change in status. This will enhance and future complexity that may be associated with simplified CDD within the Nigeria FIs.

This section discussed the consequence of AML compliance on financial inclusion in Nigeria. The next section will evaluate the legal impediment against AML compliance within the Nigerian FIs.

Legal Impediment Against AML Compliance Within the Nigerian FIs

The recently published MER of Nigeria by GIABA in 2021 recognized that:

> Nigeria has convincingly identified its most material ML threats in terms of predicate offences, and in some sectors evinced a clear understanding of the nature of risk, for example in connection with forex dealers. The authorities also recognize a wide range of vulnerabilities and mitigating factors in reaching conclusions on risks. Yet Nigeria did not show itself to have a thorough ongoing understanding of the modes, methodologies, and typologies of how its ML threats manifest themselves in terms of key ML risks, with respect to corruption, especially with respect to PEPs and the oil sector. Moreover, Nigeria, in many cases did not meaningfully weigh various factors in arriving at its conclusions for overall and sectoral risk levels. Frequently, for example, Nigeria placed undue weight on a single factor, such as the AML legal framework, as a mitigating element to reach an ultimately inaccurate description of risk.

Consequently, rule-based approach for combatting ML within the Nigerian FIs is not sufficient since lawmakers and the PEPs themselves are the 'law-breakers'. The interview with the GIABA Expert 2 suggested that ineffective criminal justice witnesses in some member states in West African regions impede compliance with FATF recommendations. The PEPs will purposely amend stringent laws to weaken the effectiveness of the legal framework in order to maximize the concealment of their ill-gotten funds originating from ground corruption. As a result, legal framework without political will, strong AML policy and cooperate governance to pursue the NRA's overall assessment of Nigeria's ML risks amongst the Nigerian FIs will amount to poor AML system.

Discussion on the Future Thoughts Toward Effective AML Compliance Within the Nigerian FIs

The foregoing strategic policy needs to be put in place before overcoming the numerous challenges facing the effective AML compliance within FIs in developing economies such as Nigeria. Having analysed the revealed challenges to combat ML using the expert interviews and author's experience at the NFIU, there are questions requiring the attention of the standards setters, implementing countries, competent authorities and the private sector (financial intuitions). The concept of cost benefit to ML is of significance and need to be addressed by both international and national actors.[36] Critical questions include the following. First, what is going to be the cost benefit of AML standards as against prudential, profitability ratio and IFFs leakages from the Nigerian FIs? It is pertinent to emphasize that the cost of compliance with anti-ML obligations of the reporting institutions in Nigeria is enormous; consequently, part of their running cost has to be dedicated for conduct of their AML reequipments such as customer visitations for CDD due to lack of a robust addressing system and centralized databases for the use of FIs in the country.

What AML monitoring framework exist within the FIs supervisory authorities in Nigeria? If these questions are addressed by the anti-ML actors in Nigeria, then the wall against illicit financial flows in Nigeria will be significantly surmounted. It has been said that when the measures for remedy are costlier than the problem at hand, it will amount to 'collateral damage' in the long run.[37] A typical collateral damage amongst the FIs in Nigeria pushed the profitability ratio of many national banks to the limit, thereby errant FIs employed unethical ways to circumvent AML standards and sometimes bankers themselves facilitate the ML process. The analysis of the AML challenges among the FIs revealed that transported and domesticated AML policies and instruments to curb proceeds of crime via the FIs should be flexible enough to accommodate the peculiar circumstances of Nigeria. There are great compliance threats when countries are not allowed to fashion out their own anti-ML regime in accordance to their specific economic circumstances. Therefore, localizing the AML system within developing countries where cash-based economies are the norm will require countries like Nigeria to drive their situational AML compliance rather than being compelled to ratify recommendations that are not comparable to their economy (Levi & Halliday, 2014). If cash-based economies are susceptible to the successful implementation of the regimes of ML, then the standard setters such as FATF should provide incentive for AML compliance in developing countries like Nigeria. This chapter call for AML Incentive Regimes as against the usual naming and shaming list such as the European Union and FATF greylist. A great deal of incentive requires the West to develop a dedicated automated online real-time AML solution for the use of their countries' FIs to help flag dirty money originating from developing countries into developed economies, and such dirty funds should be

36 Halliday, Levi and Reuter (n 12) 24.

37 N Passas, 'Cross-Border Crime and the Interface between Legal and Illegal Actors' in BS Fisher and M Gill (eds), (2003) 16(1) Security Journal 19–37.

repatriated back to the origin of IFFs in developing economies like Nigeria. It is estimated that Africa lost up to US$1.8 trillion between 1970 and 2008.[38] More than 70% of these ill-gotten gains were hidden in many global financial centres located in the developed countries. Therefore, Africa will appreciate automatic repatriation of her illicit financial flows into developed countries as an incentive to combat proceeds of crime. This is preferred than the usual overseas official development assistance, the aid originating from developed into developing economies as incentive for the deficit of IFFs in many countries. In Levi and Halliday, standard setters had failed to provide a scientific mechanism to measure the efficiency and success of implemented programmes of regimes of ML. The foregoing analysis affirmed the argument of Passas that the implication of monetary policies and controls of supranational and international organizations of the West narrowed the gaps of economy in the Third World countries, leaving them with preserve asymmetric growth and development.

The collaboration against crime has serious implication for tackling the identified challenges confronting the governance of crime in a developing economy and Nigeria in particular. Though there exist collaboration efforts among the numerous actors creating orders in the governance of crime in Nigeria, the inter-agency rivalry witnessed in the Nigeria criminal justice system needs to be addressed. The LEAs need to see the private sector as a partner in progress (Levi & Osofsky, 1995). In the same vein, effective collaboration is expected from civil societies. According to Levi and Osofsky (1995), their role is inevitable in the evaluation of policy implications to fight crime in any society. The gaps that exist in the prosecutions of cases in Nigerian courts have to be addressed (NDLEA Investigator 2). The courts should expedite actions on the hearing of the hearing of serious crime. If this war is to be won, the symbiotic relationship that impedes the success of war against crime must be eradicated to the bare minimum amongst the developing countries. Furthermore, the limitation to symbiotic relationships between legal and illegal actors will enhance effective collaboration to combat organized crime in Nigeria's environment.

In addition, increasing the risk of commission of organized crime in one country has negative impacts in other jurisdictions. Offenders may transport criminal activities to weaker states within the regional jurisdictions. This has serious implication for policies. The regional actors have to collaborate together by building mechanisms around the governance of crime. There should be focus on increasing the cost of crime in order to make it less attractive within

38 African Union Commission/United Nations Economic Commission for Africa (AUC/ECA), 'Illicit Financial Flows: Report of the High-Level Panel on Illicit Financial Flows from Africa' (AU/ECA Conference of Ministers of Finance, Planning and Economic Development, 8 July 2021) <https://au.int/en/documents/20210708/report-high-level-panel-illicit-financial-flows-africa> accessed 15 June 2023.

the region. This can also be complemented with a robust mechanism and database to label criminal offenders from one jurisdiction to another (EFCC Investigator 1). The effective cooperation will monitor the criminal offender who is on the run from the labelling state to a new state when displacing crime in a global context. Finally, though, there appear to be problematic statistics and empirical studies in the global governance of crime.[39] This problem is more visible within developing economies because capable guardians that are criminal sympathizers and offenders themselves will not make funds available for research and development in the Third World countries. This has major implications in designing robust policies to curb organized crime and ML in developing countries. Therefore, winning the war against the impediments of success of the fight against organized crime and ML in Nigeria requires a critical analysis of the aforementioned policy implications. They are the 'dark side' against winning the war on organized crime in developing economies.

CBN and NFIU should enhance the regulatory framework for BDC operators in the country. This can include a new reporting regime for the BDC to account for any transactions linked to government operational activities within their operations. This is in line with the application of commensurate measures on the identified ML/TF risks that BDCs pose to the integrity of financial system in Nigeria. It is noteworthy to emphasize that most of the cash withdrawn from the government accounts is converted to foreign exchange for illicit enrichment, corruption and ML through both formal and informal currency exchange service operators.

39 J Van Dijk, *The World of Crime* (Sage 2008).

9 The Challenge of Money Laundering by Nigeria PEPs

Beyond the Transplantation of FATF Standards

Chinelo Bob-Osamor

Introduction

Money laundering (ML) involves disguising assets so that they can be used without detecting the illegal activity that produced them.[1] It is an essential part of criminal activities.[2] An analysis of Nigeria AML challenges first requires a good understanding of the predicate crimes that fuel ML in Nigeria. The most prevalent ML predicate crime[3] in Nigeria is corruption. It is the most troubling issue in Nigeria,[4] having held the country in thrall for a very long time.[5] It "undermines the institution of critical infrastructure and development in the country and has also earned the country the title of poverty capital of the world with over 80 million extremely poor people."[6]

In the Corruption Perception Index (CPI) 2021,[7] Nigeria ranks 154 out of 180 countries and territories; it fell back five places from 149 in 2020.[8]

1 United States Department of the Treasury Financial Crimes Enforcement Network, 'What Is Money Laundering' <www.fincen.gov/what-money-laundering> accessed 13 January 2023.

2 Peter Lilley, *Dirty Dealing: The Untold Truth about Global Money Laundering, International Crime, and Terrorism* (Kogan Page Publishers 2006) xiii.

3 A predicate offence or a predicate crime means a crime which is connected to a larger and serious crime. In our context, a predicate offense would mean any crime that generates monetary proceeds, leading the criminal to commit larger crimes such as money laundering and terrorist financing.

4 HEDA Resource Centre, *A Compendium of 100 High Profile Cases in Nigeria* (3rd edn, MacArthur Foundation 2019).

5 Dan Agbese, 'Voices of History 2: Corruption is Good' (*The Blueprint*, 2 June 2022) <www.blueprint.ng/voices-of-history-2-corruption-is-good> accessed 9 June 2022.

6 Olanrewaju Suraju, 'HEDA to Present 4th "Compendium on 100 High Profile Corruption Cases" ' (*News Express*, 8 December 2020) <www.newsexpressngr.com/news/112373-HEDA-to-Present-4th-Compendium-on-100-High-Profile-Corruption-Cases> accessed 10 January 2023.

7 Corruption Perception Index ranks countries based on how corrupt their public sectors are perceived to be. See Transparency International, 'Corruption Perception Index 2020' <www.transparency.lt/en/corruption-perception-index> accessed 5 January 2023.

8 Dennis Erezi, 'Nigeria Ranks Five Places Worse on 2021 Corruption Perception Index' *The Guardian*, 25 January 2022).

DOI: 10.4324/9781003253808-11

Transparency International's 2022 CPI placed the country 150 out of 180 countries.[9]

Corruption and ML offences are inextricably linked[10] and can justifiably be said to be like Siamese twins.[11] Corruption not only generates illicit proceeds of crime but fuels the commission of ML.[12] Grand corruption, which is the abuse of public office for personal gain,[13] involves the misuse of power by PEPs such as Heads of States, Ministers, and top officials for pecuniary profit.[14] PEPs are individuals who are entrusted with prominent public offices, and because of their positions they are presented with higher risks of potential involvement in ML and other predicate offences such as bribery and corruption, as well as engaging in activity related to terrorist financing.[15]

At independence in 1960, Nigeria was believed to be destined for great prosperity. However, decades of corrupt and ineffectual leadership squandered that dream.[16] Nigeria's ex- military leader, Sani Abacha, the poster boy of PEP's ML activities, stole and laundered up to $5 billion of public money according to Transparency International.[17] PEPs remain a higher risk in Nigeria. In a total of 100 high-profile corruption cases considered in Nigeria by the Human and Environmental Development Agenda (HEDA Resource Centre),[18] 41% involved former Governors, 39% involved Government officials, 12% of the

9 Cyril Okonkwo, 'Nigeria Responds to Transparency International's 2022 Corruption Index' (*Voice of Nigeria*, 1 February 2023) accessed 28 February 2023.

10 Norman Mugarura, 'Uncoupling the Relationship between Corruption and Money Laundering Crimes' (2016) 2(1) Journal of Financial Regulation and Compliance 74.

11 Ejike Ekwueme, 'Dampening Corruption and Money Laundering: Emissions from Soft Laws' (2021) 24(4) Journal of Money Laundering Control 848–59.

12 Norman Mugarura, 'Uncoupling the Relationship between Corruption and Money Laundering Crimes' (2016) 2(1) Journal of Financial Regulation and Compliance 74.

13 HEDA Resource Centre, *A Compendium of 100 High Profile Cases in Nigeria* (3rd edn, MacArthur Foundation 2019).

14 Mugarura (n 12) 74.

15 PEPs include Heads of State or government, senior politicians, senior government officials, judicial or military officials, senior executives of state-owned corporations or important political party officials, they also include family members and close associates of such individuals, See FATF Guidance, *Politically Exposed Persons* (Recommendation, 12 and 22 June 2013) <www.fatf-6gafi.org/media/fatf/documents/recommendations/Guidance-PEP-Rec1> accessed 6 December 2022; Walter Pazos, 'How to Assess the Risk of Politically Exposed Persons' 20 September 2017 <www.dnb.co.uk/perspectives/corporate-compliance/politically-exposed-persons-guide.html> accessed 14 October 2020.

16 Chibundu Onuzo, 'How Nigerian Corruption is a Cautionary Tale for the UK' (*The Guardian UK*) <www.theguardian.com/commentisfree/2021/apr/29/nigerian-corruption-cautionary-tale-uk> accessed 5 August 2022.

17 Reuters and CNN, 'US to Return $23 Million Looted by Late Dictator Abacha to Nigeria-Official' <https://edition.cnn.com/2022/08/24/africa/us-returns-abacha-loot-intl/index.html> accessed 5 January 2022.

18 Established in 1999, the Human and Environmental Development Agenda Resource Centre is a Nigerian non-profit human rights and development organisation. <www.macfound.org/grantee/heda-resource-centre-43988> accessed 9 December 2022.

cases involved former ministers and special Assistants to the Presidents and 5% and 2% involved senators and judges, respectively.[19] Nigeria loses about $15 to $18 billion annually because of illicit financial flow (IFF),[20] comprising mostly proceeds of corruption by PEPs.[21]

International Conventions and PEPs

ML is transnational organised crime which involves a number of jurisdictions.[22] The need for international cooperation in combatting ML has been recognised by many governments, and several agreements have been reached in international fora.[23] In 1988, the United Nations established the first international definition of ML in the Convention Against Illicit Traffic in Narcotic Drugs and Psychotropic Substances of the Vienna Convention.[24] The Convention, with its main focus on drug trafficking, obliged States to deprive persons engaged in illicit traffic of drugs of the proceeds of their criminal activities and thereby eliminate the main incentive for so doing.[25] Signatories were also required to criminalise the laundering of drug proceeds.[26]

On the financial front, the Committee on Banking Regulations and Supervisory Practices[27] issued the Basel Statement of Principles on the prevention of criminal use of the banking system for the purpose of ML in December 1988.[28]

19 Robert Osamor, 'Plea-Bargaining in Nigeria: When Crime Pays' (2022) 3(1) Law and Social Justice 35.

20 Chris Onuoha, 'Corruption: Nigeria Loses Over $15 Billion to Illicit Financial Outflows Annually – HEDA' (*Vanguard* 2021) <www.vanguardngr.com/2021/04/corruption-nigeria-loses-over-15-billion-to-illicit-financial-flow-annually-heda> accessed 5 January 2023.

21 Chris Onuoha, 'Corruption: Nigeria Loses Over $15 Billion to Illicit Financial Outflows Annually – HEDA' (*Vanguard* 2021) <www.vanguardngr.com/2021/04/corruption-nigeria-loses-over-15-billion-to-illicit-financial-flow-annually-heda> accessed 5 January 2023.

22 Selina Keesoony, 'International Anti-Money Laundering Laws: The Problems with Enforcement' (2016) 19(2) Journal of Money Laundering Controls 130.

23 Bank of England Quarterly Bulletin, 'Countering Money Laundering' <www.bankofengland.co.uk/quarterly-bulletin/1992/q4/countering-money-laundering> accessed 31 July 2022.

24 David Stewart, 'Internationalizing the War on Drugs: The United Nations Convention against Illicit Traffic' in Narcotic Drugs and Psychotropic Substances' (1989–1990) 18 Denver Journal of International Law and Policy 387.

25 Jeffrey Robinson, *The Laundrymen: Inside Money Laundering, the World's Third Largest Business* (New York Arcade Publishing 1996).

26 Nicholas Ryder, *Money Laundering an Endless Cycle? A Comparative Analysis of the Anti-Money Laundering Policies in the United States, the United Kingdom, Australia, and Canada* (Routledge 2012) 12.

27 The Committee comprises representatives of the central banks and supervisory authorities of Belgium. Canada, France, Germany, Italy. Japan. Ryder (n 26).

The Committee comprises Luxembourg, the Netherlands, Sweden. Switzerland, the United Kingdom, and the United States.

28 Bank of England Quarterly Bulletin, 'Countering Money Laundering' <https://www.bankofengland.co.uk/quarterly-bulletin/1992/q4/countering-money-laundering> accessed 31 July 2022.

The frameworks established by the Vienna Convention and the Basle Statement of Principles have been developed by FATF.[29]

Established in 1989 by the G7[30] and the European Commission, FATF has as its original purpose to co-ordinate a global effort that will tackle ML related to drug trafficking.[31] Though not legally binding, FATF recommendations are recognised and adopted by many countries and international bodies[32] and have assumed a quasi–hard law status.[33]

The central norms of FATF are its recommendations.[34] The first set of recommendations drawn up in 1990 has as its main objective to combat the misuse of the financial systems by persons laundering drug money.[35] In 1996, the recommendations were revised to reflect evolving ML typologies,[36] and efforts shifted from laundering of drug money to proceeds of all serious predicate offences.[37] Corruption became one of the predicate offences, because the stolen assets of a corrupt public official are useless unless they are integrated into the global financial network in a manner that does not raise suspicion.[38]

Global efforts to combat ML continued in 2001 when the Basel Committee on Banking Supervision coined the term ***politically exposed persons*** (PEPs) in its Customer Due Diligence for Banks Guidance.[39] It defined PEPs as individuals who are or have been entrusted with prominent public functions, including heads of state or of government, senior government, judicial or military officials, senior executives of publicly owned corporations and important political party officials.[40]

29 Bank of England Quarterly Bulletin, 'Countering Money Laundering' <https://www.bankofengland.co.uk/quarterly-bulletin/1992/q4/countering-money-laundering> accessed 31 July 2022.

30 G7 is an intergovernmental organisation of the world's seven largest industrialized countries: the UK, US, France, Germany, Canada, Italy, and Japan. See World Atlas, 'G7 Countries' <www.worldatlas.com/articles/group-of-seven-g7-countries.html> accessed 24 January 2023.

31 Nicholas Turner, 'The financial Action Task Force: International Regulatory Convergence through Soft Law' (2014) 59(3) New York Law School Law Review.

32 CFATF, '40 Recommendations' <www.cfatf-gafic.org/home/public-statements/227-articles/fatf-40-recommendations-test-category> accessed 28 July 2022.

33 Georgious Pavlidis, 'Financial Action Task Force and the Fight against Money Laundering and the Financing of Terrorism: *Qua Vadimus?*' (2021) 28(3) Journal of Financial Crime 765.

34 Georgious Pavlidis, 'Financial Action Task Force and the Fight against Money Laundering and the Financing of Terrorism: *Qua Vadimus?*' (2021) 28(3) Journal of Financial Crime 765.

35 FATF, 'The Forty Recommendations' <https://www.fatf-gafi.org/en/publications/Fatfrecommendations/The40recommendationspublishedoctober2004.html#:~:text=The%2040%20Recommendations%20provide%20a,%2C%20and%20international%20co%2Doperation> accessed 8 January 2024.

36 FATF, 'The Forty Recommendations' <https://www.fatf-gafi.org/content/dam/fatf-gafi/recommendations/FATF%20Standards%20-%2040%20Recommendations%20rc.pdf> accessed 8 January 2020.

37 Nicholas Turner, 'The Financial Action Task Force: International Regulatory Convergence through Soft Law' (2014) 59(3) New York Law School Law Review 5.

38 FATF Report, 'Laundering the Proceeds of Corruption' <www.bing.com/search?q=FATF+Report%2C+%60Laundering> accessed 16 December 2022.

39 Basel Committee on Banking Supervisors, *Customer Due Diligence for Banks* (Bank for International Settlements, October 2001) <www.bis.org/publ/bcbs 85.pdf> accessed 2 December 2022.

40 Basel Committee on Banking Supervisors, Customer Due Diligence for Banks (Bank for International Settlements, October 2001) <www.bis.org/publ/bcbs 85.pdf> accessed 2 December 2022.

During the 2003 review and revision of its 40 recommendations, FATF included for the first time the specific term PEP,[41] along with the definition of that term and an explicit recommendation that financial institutions (FIs) establish appropriate risk management procedures to determine the PEP status of their customers and to take special measures during business relationships with foreign PEPs, their family members, and close associates.[42] FATF special measures include obtaining senior management approval for establishing business relationship with such customers, taking reasonable measures to establish the source of wealth and source of funds and conducting enhanced ongoing monitoring of the business relationship.[43] FATF later expanded this mandatory requirements to domestic PEPs and PEPs of international organisations.[44] By 2022, FATF proudly proclaimed that "over 200 jurisdictions around the world have committed to FATF Recommendations."[45]

Nigeria Anti-ML Framework and PEPs

The Nigeria AML journey can best be described as a "roller coaster," with the country constantly making efforts to comply with FATF regulations and international conventions. Nigeria ratified the UN resolution on ML in 1989 and promulgated its first decree on ML, the National Drug Law Enforcement Agency (NDLEA) Decree 1989.[46] However, Okpala avers that Nigeria got it wrong from the start because the primary typology of ML in Nigeria is proceeds of corruption laundered by PEPs and not the proceeds of drugs.[47]

The Nigeria Money Laundering Act of 1995 criminalised ML, the first country in Africa to do so.[48] The focus, however, remained proceeds of drug trafficking. In 2001, Nigeria was included in the list of Non-Cooperative Countries and Territories (NCCTs) by FATF. The NCCT includes countries with poor anti-money laundering and counter-terrorist financing (AML/

41 Daniele Canestri, 'Politically Exposed Entities: How to Tailor PEP Requirements to PEP Owned Legal Entities' (2019) 22(2) Journal of Money Laundering Control.

42 FATF 40 Recommendations 2003, Recommendation 6 <https://www.fatf-gafi.org/content/dam/fatf-gafi/recommendations/FATF%20Standards%20-%2040%20Recommendations%20rc.pdf> accessed 7 December 2022.

43 FATF 40 Recommendations 2003, Recommendation 6 <https://www.fatf-gafi.org/content/dam/fatf-gafi/recommendations/FATF%20Standards%20-%2040%20Recommendations%20rc.pdf> accessed 7 December 2022.

44 FATF Guidance, 'Politically Exposed Persons (Recommendations 12 and 22)' 2013 <https://www.fatf-gafi.org/content/dam/fatf-gafi/guidance/Guidance-PEP-Rec12-22.pdf> accessed 7 December 2022.

45 FATF Website <www.fatf-gafi.org/countries> accessed 6 January 2022.

46 NDLEA Act 1989.

47 Chinedum Okpala, 'An Evaluation of the role of Prosecutorial Discretion in the Anti-money laundering Regime of Nigeria'. A thesis submitted in partial fulfilment of the requirements of Nottingham Trent University, for the Degree of Doctor of Philosophy. Nottingham Trent University (United Kingdom ProQuest Dissertations Publishing 2020) 37.

48 Ehi Eric Esoimeme, 'Nigeria Money Laundering Bill 2016: A Critical Appraisal' (2017) 20(1) Journal of Money Laundering Control 79.

CFT) regimes.[49] Nigeria was blacklisted for "obvious unwillingness or inability to co-operate with the FATF in the review of its system."[50]

The implication of this blacklisting is reflected in the FATF warning to the international community to deal cautiously with Nigeria.[51] Thereafter, the Money Laundering Decree of 1995 was repealed and replaced with the Money Laundering (Prohibition) Act (MPLA) 2003. Drug trafficking was replaced with predicate offences which covered a wide range of criminal conducts including proceeds of crime and corruption.[52]

Subsequently, the Economic and Financial Crimes Commission (EFCC) was formed in April 2003 in response to pressure from FATF on Nigeria to tackle its ML challenge.[53] The EFCC Act mandates the commission to eradicate all financial crimes through prevention, enforcement and coordination.[54]The MPLA 2003 was further amended through the Money Laundering Prohibition (Amendment) Act 2004 to give the AML agencies more power to investigate, institute cases and prosecute offenders.[55] Nigeria was removed from the FATF blacklist in 2006, following this series of legislative and financial sector reforms that included the establishment of the Nigerian Financial Intelligence Unit (NFIU). The MPLA 2004 was later repealed and replaced with the MPLA 2011.

The MPLA 2011 for the first time paid particular attention to public officers.[56] Just like FATF Recommendations 12 and 22,[57] the MPLA 2011 requires the FIs and designated non-financial institutions (DNFIs) when dealing with public officers to put in place appropriate risk management systems, obtain senior management approval before establishing business relationships with public officers and ensure ongoing monitoring of business relationships.[58] The Money Laundering (Prohibition) Act 2011 addressed the legal weaknesses in the Nigerian AML/CFT regime as contained in the country's Mutual

49 FATF, 'One Step Forward: Nigeria Gets FATF List of High- Risks Jurisdictions' (*Teingo* 2013) <https://tennygee.wordpress.com/2013/10/31/one-step-forward-nigeria-gets-off-financial-action-task-force-fatf-list-of-high-risk-jurisdictions/> accessed 5 March 2023.

50 Babajide Komolafe, 'Inside NFIU and the New Regime Stopping States from Messing with Local Government Funds' (*Vanguard* 2019) <www.reportnaija.ng/2019/05/19/inside-nfiu-and-the-new-regime-stopping-states-from-messing-with-local-govt-funds> accessed 27 February 2022.

51 FATF (n 49).

52 Ehi Eric Esoimeme, 'Nigeria Money Laundering Bill 2016: A Critical Appraisal' (2017) 20(1) Journal of Money Laundering Control 79.

53 Nigerian Finder, 'History of EFCC (Economic and Financial Crimes Commission)' <https://nigerianfinder.com/history-of-efcc-economic-and-financial-crimes-commission> accessed 19 April 2022.

54 EFCC, 'Mission' <www.efcc.gov.ng/efcc> accessed 28 February 2023.

55 Nlerum Okogbule, 'Official Corruption and the Dynamics of Money Laundering in Nigeria' (2007) 14(1) Journal of Financial Crimes 49.

56 Money Laundering (Prohibition) Act (MPLA) 2011, S.3(8).

57 FATF Guidance, Recommendations 12 and 22.

58 MPLA 2011, S.3(8) 1 and 2.

Evaluation Report (MER) conducted by the Inter-Governmental Action against Money Laundering in West Africa (GIABA).[59]

Notably, Markovska et al. opine that rolling out relevant legislations has never been the challenge; the real problem is that those AML regulations exist as mere paper rules in Nigeria[60] because of lack of political will that should drive the process.[61] Good legislation can be meaningless if not properly enforced.[62]

Expectedly, when GIABA reviewed Nigeria's Money Laundering (Prohibition) Act (MLPA) 2011 and identified more deficiencies that include non-compliance in customer due diligence (CDD), supervision and monitoring, suspicious transaction reporting (STR) and international cooperation,[63] Nigeria in the same year once again dropped in the ratings of FATF and was reincluded in the FATF blacklist.[64]

In 2013, FATF removed Nigeria from its blacklist again because it had taken steps to improve its ML regime by enacting AML/CFT legislation and has commenced supervision across all sectors.[65] The country's Money Laundering (Prohibition) (Amendment) Act 2012 amended the MLPA 2011 and expanded the scope of ML offences and enhanced CDD.[66] However, what was experienced in practice was quite different from what is on paper.[67]

In 2017, Nigeria AML took another hit as the Egmont group suspended the membership of NFIU over concerns about the NFIU's lack of independence from the EFCC.[68] In September 2018 the decision was rescinded and

59 Inter-governmental Action Group against Money Laundering in West Africa (GIABA) is an FATF styled regional body (FSRB) for West Africa that conducts Mutual Evaluation Reports <www.giaba.org> accessed 9 December 2022.

60 Anna Markovska, Nya Adams, Bill Tupman and Zabyelina Yuliya, 'Political Corruption and Money Laundering: Lessons from Nigeria' (2015) 18(2) Journal of Money Laundering Control 169.

61 Anna Markovska, Nya Adams, Bill Tupman and Zabyelina Yuliya, 'Political Corruption and Money Laundering: Lessons from Nigeria' (2015) 18(2) Journal of Money Laundering Control 169.

62 Nlerum Okogbule, 'Combating Money Laundering in Nigeria: An Appraisal of the Money Laundering (Prohibition) Act 2004' (2007) 28(2) Statute Law Review 156.

63 Inter- governmental Action Group against Money Laundering in West Africa (GIABA) MER 2012.

64 Omoh Gabriel, 'The Vanguard, FATF Blacklist: Failure of Nigeria's Banking Reform and War againstCorruption'(*Vanguard*2012)<www.vanguardngr.com/2012/02/fatf-blacklist-failure-of-nigerias-banking-reform-and-war-against-corruption> accessed 27 February 22.

65 Babajide Komolafe, 'Inside NFIU and the New Regime Stopping States from Messing with Local Government Funds' (*Vanguard* 2019) <www.reportnaija.ng/2019/05/19/inside-nfiu-and-the-new-regime-stopping-states-from-messing-with-local-govt-funds> accessed 27 February 2022.

66 Law Nigeria, 'Money Laundering (Prohibition) (Amendment) Act 2012' <https://lawnigeria.com/2020/01/money-laundering-prohibition-amendment-act-2012> accessed 26 December 2022.

67 John Hatchard, *Combating Corruption -Legal Approaches to Supporting Good Governance and Integrity in Africa* (Edward Elgar Publishing Ltd UK 2014) 45.

68 John Hatchard, *Combating Corruption -Legal Approaches to Supporting Good Governance and Integrity in Africa* (Edward Elgar Publishing Ltd UK 2014) 45.

membership of NFIU restored after the group "concluded that legislative changes in Nigeria has addressed the issues that led to its suspension."[69]

Nevertheless, in February 2019, less than six months after the Egmont group rescinded its decision against the NFIU, the European Commission placed Nigeria in the expanded 23 "dirty money" blacklist, due to strategic deficiencies in the country's AML/CFT frameworks.[70]

The recently enacted Money Laundering (Prevention and Prohibition) Act 2022 (MLPPA) has repealed the MPLA 2011. The Act changed the term "public officers" to PEPs[71] but retained similar provisions on PEPs as the repealed act.[72] Today, Nigeria is on FATF's greylist, having been placed under increased monitoring by FATF in February 2023,[73] after it committed to resolve swiftly the identified strategic deficiencies within agreed time frames.[74]

Enforcement Challenges

Arrests Without Diligent Prosecution

The Nigerian anti-corruption agency, the EFCC appears to be trivialising its assignment by not following up arrests with prosecutions. The spate of arrests by the EFCC and how suspects are released without prosecution leaves much to be desired.[75] The membership of the Nigerian Senate is replete with former political office holders who had been guests of the EFCC with little or no prosecution.[76] Also, eight ex-Governors who were arrested on corruption and ML charges between 2015 and 2021 gradually had their cases swept under the carpet.[77]

Available records show that the EFCC secured a total of 2,220 convictions across the country in 2021, mostly cybercrime related, while the high-profile

69 John Hatchard, *Combating Corruption -Legal Approaches to Supporting Good Governance and Integrity in Africa* (Edward Elgar Publishing Ltd UK 2014) 45.

70 Bassey Udo, 'Why European Commission Included Nigeria among 23 "Dirty Money"' (*Premium Times*, 20 February 2019) <www.premiumtimesng.com/business/business-news/314106-why-european-commission-included-nigeria-among-23-dirty-money-blacklist.htm> accessed 28 February 2022.

71 Money Laundering (Prevention and Prohibition) Act 2022, S. 7.

72 Money Laundering (Prevention and Prohibition) Act, S. 8 (a)–(c).

73 FATF, 'Black and Grey List' (24 February 2023) <www.fatf-gafi.org/en/countries/black-and-grey-lists.html> accessed 28 February 2023.

74 FATF, 'Black and Grey List' (24 February 2023) <www.fatf-gafi.org/en/countries/black-and-grey-lists.html> accessed 28 February 2023.

75 Luke Onyekakeyah, 'Does EFCC Joke with Arrests?' (*The Guardian*, 21 April 2022) <https://guardian.ng/opinion/does-efcc-joke-with-arrests>accessed 2 March 2023.

76 Luke Onyekakeyah, 'Does EFCC Joke with Arrests?' (*The Guardian*, 21 April 2022) <https://guardian.ng/opinion/does-efcc-joke-with-arrests>accessed 2 March 2023.

77 Sahara Reporters, 'Eight ex-Governors Whose Over 500 Billion Corruption Cases with EFCC Have Been Swept under the Carpet' 16 April 2021 <https://saharareporters.com/2021/04/16/revealed-eight-ex-governors-whose-over-n500-billion-corruption-cases-efcc-have-been-swept> accessed 2 March 2023.

arrests made by the agency amount to nothing.[78] Only 3.75% of cases investigated by EFCC were filed in court, and the bulk of the 23% convictions obtained were on low and mid-level crimes rather than high-profile corruption.[79]

The occasional high-profile cases that are commenced are not diligently prosecuted. A case in point is the case of the accountant general of the Federation Ahmed Idris who was arrested in May 2022 on charges of diverting public funds and ML to the tune of 80 billion naira ($193 million).[80] The EFCC alleged that he used "proxies, family members and close associates" in deals to defraud the government and laundered the proceeds through investment in real estate in Abuja and his home state of Kano.[81]

Characteristically, the trial of Ahmed Idris was stalled on 1 March 2023 because an important statement he made to the EFCC during their investigation was missing from both the court records and the EFCC file.[82] This is a familiar pattern and may well signify the beginning of the end of the trial.

Constitutional Immunities

Nigeria has major difficulties in holding some public officers to account because the constitution cloaks them with immunity while in office.[83] The serving President, Vice President, Governors of the 36 states and their Deputies are all beneficiaries of immunity from prosecution.[84] Immunity from prosecution frustrated the trial of a Nigerian Governor even in the UK. In 2004, Governor Joshua Dariye of Plateau State was arrested and questioned by London Metropolitan Police for ML. While on bail, he returned to Nigeria and thereafter refused to answer any further questions from the London Metropolitan Police relying on constitutional immunity.[85]

Similarly, in 2005, Governor Diepreye Alamieyeseigha of Bayelsa state was arrested in UK and charged with laundering of £1.8 million. Again,

78 Luke Onyekakeyah, 'Does EFCC Joke with Arrests?' (*The Guardian*, 21 April 2022) <https://guardian.ng/opinion/does-efcc-joke-with-arrests>accessed 2 March 2023.

79 Camillus Eboh, 'Accountant General Faces Corruption Charges after Arrest' (*Reuters*, 17 May 2022) <www.reuters.com/world/africa/nigerias-accountant-general-faces-corruption-charges-after-arrest-2022–05–16> accessed 1 March 2023.

80 Camillus Eboh, 'Accountant General Faces Corruption Charges after Arrest' (*Reuters*, 17 May 2022) <www.reuters.com/world/africa/nigerias-accountant-general-faces-corruption-charges-after-arrest-2022–05–16> accessed 1 March 2023.

81 Camillus Eboh, 'Accountant General Faces Corruption Charges after Arrest' (*Reuters*, 17 May 2022) <www.reuters.com/world/africa/nigerias-accountant-general-faces-corruption-charges-after-arrest-2022–05–16> accessed 1 March 2023.

82 Ameh Ejekwonyilo, 'Alleged N109 bn Fraud: Former Accountant General Ahmed Idris' Trial Stalled' (*Premium Times*, 1 March 2023) <www.premiumtimesng.com/news/top-news/585589-alleged-n109bn-fraud-former-accountant-general-ahmed-idris-trial-stalled.html> accessed 2 March 2023.

83 Constitution of the Federal Republic of Nigeria 1999, S.308.

84 Constitution of the Federal Republic of Nigeria 1999, S.308.

85 David Chaikin and JC Sharman, *Corruption, and Money Laundering: A Symbiotic Relationship* (Palgrave Macmillan 2009) 89.

while on bail he escaped to Nigeria.[86] Although section 308 of the Nigerian Constitution, which grants immunity from prosecution to State Governors in Nigeria, was held to have no effect in the United Kingdom,[87] Alamieyeseigha could not be extradited from Nigeria to the UK to face trial.[88]

Furthermore, because he was immune from prosecution, a federal high court struck out the name of the sitting Governor of Delta State, Dr Emmanuel Uduaghan, from a suit seeking to compel the EFCC to investigate an allegation that he conspired with the immediate past Governor of the State, Chief James Ibori, to divert over 120 billion naira in public funds into their private accounts.[89] Indeed the provisions of the immunity clause in the constitution has become a shield which protects corrupt public officials while in office.

EFCC Officials Questionable Conduct

The EFCC has not only grown weaker by the day but has since degenerated into a cesspool of corruption.[90] In 2020 the former Acting Chairman of EFCC Ibrahim Magu appeared before a Presidential Probe Panel. Magu was accused of 21 infractions bordering on corruption and abuse of office[91] that included discrepancies in the reconciliation records of EFCC and the Federal Ministry of Finance on recovered funds; declaration of N504 billion instead of N539 billion recovered.[92] He was also alleged to have frustrated the extradition of former Minister of Petroleum Diezani Alison-Madueke to Nigeria to face trial by refusing to cooperate with anti-corruption agencies in the United Kingdom.[93] Magu was also accused of having "directed designated operatives not to investigate" the allegations of corruption against the three former Governors and one sitting Governor.[94] Despite this litany of offences, Magu was not prosecuted, which questions the sincerity of anti-corruption and anti-ML crusade of the government.

86 Rory Carroll, 'Nigeria State Governor Dresses up to Escape £1.8m Charges in the UK' (*The Guardian*, 23 November 2005) <www.theguardian.com/world/2005/nov/23/hearafrica05.development> accessed 24 January 2023.

87 *R (Alamieyeseigha) v Crown Prosecution Service* [2005] All ER (D) 348; [2006] Crim LR 669.

88 Chaikin and Sharman (n 85) 89.

89 Ise-Oluwa, 'Court Strikes Out Uduaghan's Name from 120bn Naira Fraud Suit' (*Vanguard*, 6 June 2007) <https://allafrica.com/stories/200706050018.html> accessed 3 January 2023.

90 The Vanguard, 'Corruption, Police Destroyed the EFCC' <www.vanguardngr.com/2020/07/corruption-police-destroyed-the-efcc> accessed 19 April 2022.

91 Zainab Suleiman Okino, 'Diezani, Malami, Magu: Shame of a Nation' (*Premium Times*, 16 September 2020) <https://opinion.premiumtimesng.com/2020/09/16/diezani-malami-magu-shame-of-a-nation-by-zainab-suleiman-okino> accessed 5 March 2023.

92 Zainab Suleiman Okino, 'Diezani, Malami, Magu: Shame of a Nation' (*Premium Times*, 16 September2020)<https://opinion.premiumtimesng.com/2020/09/16/diezani-malami-magu-shame-of-a-nation-by-zainab-suleiman-okino> accessed 5 March 2023.

93 Nicholas Ibekwe, 'How Malami Frustrated the Extradition of Diezani, Other Fugitives – Magu' (*Premium Times*, 21 July 2020) <www.premiumtimesng.com/news/headlines/404211-exclusive-how-malami-frustrated-extradition-of-diezani-other-fugitives-magu.html> accessed 5 March 2023.

94 Sahara Reporters, 'Former Anti-Corruption Chief Crushed Cases against Ex-Governor Amosun, Kwnkwaso-Salami Panel' (7 July 2021) <https://saharareporters.com/2021/07/07/former-anti-corruption-chief-magu-crushed-cases-against-ex-governors-amosun-kwankwaso> accessed 5 May 2023.

Dubious Plea Bargain

In the first ten years of existence of the EFCC, only four PEPs were successfully prosecuted through dubious plea bargain deals.[95] In January 2008, the EFCC arraigned former Governor of Edo State, Lucky Igbinedion,[96] for corruption, ML and embezzlement of 2.9 billion naira. Pursuant to a plea bargain, the sundry charges of corruption against the ex-Governor were reduced to one count of failure to declare his interest in a bank account in the declaration of assets form of the EFCC.[97] The sentence thereafter, was so light that it made mockery of the conviction.[98]

Similarly former bank chief executive Cecilia Ibru,[99] and former governor of Bayelsa State Diepreye Alamieseigha & Ors[100] all got a slap on the wrist through plea bargain after laundering huge sums of money.[101] The most damning one is John Yakubu Yusuf,[102] who was charged with embezzling and ML of 27.2 billion naira, property of the Police Pensions Fund. Upon a successful plea bargain, he was sentenced to 2 years' imprisonment with an option of 750,000 naira fine. He promptly paid the fine and went home.[103]

Political Interference and Weak Judiciary

The EFCC is also subject of political interference as it is usually an extension of the incumbent government.[104] Such political interference was manifested in the case of Timipre Sylva, a former Governor who was arraigned on a 42-count charge of ML of 19.2 billion naira in 2013.[105] In 2014 he defected from the PDP to the All Progressives Congress (APC) which eventually won

95 ACE- SOAS Consortium, 'The Politics and Effectiveness of Nigeria's Economic and Financial Crimes Commission. How Can Nigeria's Watch Dog Avoid Political Capture and Prevent Corruption' <https://cddwestafrica.org/the-politics-and-effectiveness-of-nigerias-economic-and-financial-crimes-commission-efcc/> accessed 19 April 2022.

96 *FRN v Lucky Igbinedion*, Charge No FHC/EN/6C/2008; Sahara Reporters, 'Igbinedion Gets Easy Plea Bargain, No Jail Time, Keeps Billion Stolen Funds Keeps Vast Properties' <http://saharareporters.com/2008/12/30/igbinedion-gets-easy-plea-bargain-no-jail-time-keeps-billions-stolen-funds-keeps-vast> accessed 19 December 2022.

97 Robert Osamor, 'Plea-Bargaining in Nigeria: When Crime Pays' (2022) 3(1) Law and Social Justice 32.

98 Daniel Agbiboa, 'As It Was in the Beginning: The Vicious Cycle of Corruption in Nigeria' (2013) 4(3) Studies in Sociology of Science 10–21.

99 *Federal Republic of Nigeria v Dr. (Mrs) Cecilia Ibru* FHC/L/297C/2009.

100 *Federal Republic of Nigeria v Diepreye Alamieseigha & Ors* (2006) 16 NWLR Pt. 1004.

101 Osamor (n 97) 32.

102 *F R N v EsaiDangbar and 5 Ors.* (2012) LPELR-19732(CA).

103 Osamor (n 97) 32.

104 ACE- SOAS Consortium (n 95).

105 Sahara Reporters, 'EFCC Blames Justice Muhammed and Adeniyi Ademola, Ex-Gov Sylva Recovered Properties' (*Sahara Reporters*, 4 September 2017) <http://saharareporters.com/2017/09/04/efcc-blames-justice-ar-muhammed-and-adeniyi-ademola-ex-gov-sylva-recovered-properties> accessed 29 July 2020.

the 2015 presidential elections.[106] The same year all the charges against him were dropped without taking a plea.[107] The 48 properties he forfeited as part of the trial were returned to him by the EFCC in 2016.[108] Timipre Sylva is currently Nigeria's Minister of State for Petroleum.[109]

Political interference was also evident in Danjuma Goje's case in 2019, when the Attorney General of the Federation (AGF) in the exercise of his prosecutorial discretion,[110] discontinued the prosecution of Danjuma Goje.[111] Remarkably, the discontinuance, closely coincided with the withdrawal of Senator Goje[112] from contesting for the seat of the Senate President in favour the President's and the ruling party's preferred candidate.[113] Danjuma Goje was charged with the misappropriation and laundering of 25 billion naira while in office for eight years as governor of Gombe State.[114]

Even when the EFCC manages to secure a conviction, a presidential pardon is granted the convicts. In April 2022, President Buhari granted pardon to two former Governors who were previously convicted for corruption and ML offences filed by the EFCC.[115] Jolly Nyame was serving a 12-year jail sentence for diverting 1.64 billion naira during his tenure as governor of Taraba, while Joshua Dariye was serving 10 years' imprisonment for 1.126 billion naira fraud and ML.[116] The grant of presidential pardon to

106 Seun Adeyeye, 'Ex-Gov Sylva Denies Dumping APC for PDP' (*The Pulse*, 25 October 2018) <www.pulse.ng/news/politics/ex-gov-sylva-denies-dumping-apc-for-pdp/1srcr99> accessed 29 July 2019.

107 Sahara Reporters, 'EFCC Blames Justice Muhammed and Adeniyi Ademola, Ex-Gov Sylva Recovered Properties' <http://saharareporters.com/2017/09/04/efcc-blames-justice-ar-muhammed-and-adeniyi-ademola-ex-gov-sylva-recovered-properties> accessed 29 July 2020.

108 Eniola Akinkuotu, 'Why ex-Governor Sylva Recovered 48 Seized Houses- EFCC' (*The Punch*, 4 September 2017) <https://punchng.com/why-ex-gov-sylva-recovered-48-houses-efcc/> accessed 19 December 2022. See also News Agency of Nigeria, 'EFCC Returns 48 Houses to Timipre Sylva' (*The Herald*) <www.herald.ng/efcc-returns-seized-48-houses-timipre-sylva/> accessed 19 December 2022.

109 Ministry of Petroleum Resources <https://petroleumresources.gov.ng/about/hon-minister-of-state> accessed 20 December 2022.

110 Pursuant to the Constitution of the Federal Republic of Nigeria 1999 (as amended) s 174.

111 NAN, 'Court Quashes Remaining 2 Charges Filed Against Senator Danjuma Goje' (*New Mail*, 5 July 2019) <https://newmail-ng.com/court-quashes-remaining-2-charges-filed-against-sen-danjuma-goje/> accessed 7 July 2020.

112 Osamor (n 97) 32.

113 J Ameh, 'Goje Withdraws Endorses Lawan as Next Senate President' (*The Punch*, 7 June 2019) <https://punchng.com/goje-withdraws-endorses-lawan-as-next-senate-president/> accessed 7 July 2020.

114 Adejumo Kabir, 'EFCC Withdraws from Goje's Corruption Trial' (*Premium Times*, 7 June 2019) <https://petroleumresources.gov.ng/about/hon-minister-of-state> accessed 20 December 2022.

115 Solmon Odeniyi, 'Presidential Pardon: Dariye, Nyame and Three Others Regain Freedom' (*Punch*, 9 August 2022) <https://punchng.com/presidential-pardon-dariye-nyame-three-others-regain-freedom> accessed 20 December 2022.

116 Solmon Odeniyi, 'Presidential Pardon: Dariye, Nyame and Three Others Regain Freedom' (*Punch*, 9 August 2022) <https://punchng.com/presidential-pardon-dariye-nyame-three-others-regain-freedom> accessed 20 December 2022.

these convicts is a mockery of the fight against corruption and ML.[117] Especially when one recalls that the same government enacted the MLPPA 2022 which further fine-tuned the AML regulations against PEPs, then one will understand that passing a new law seem to be a cost-free way of appearing to act while changing little.[118]

One of the goals of anti-ML policy is to catch money launderers and convict them.[119] The Nigerian judiciary is weak, and the independence of the judiciary is a fluke.[120] The judicial arm remains susceptible to pressure from the executive, legislative arms, the business sector, and political leaders.[121] For instance, James Ibori managed to evade justice for many years based on judicial pronouncements.[122] In 2009, a federal high court sitting in Asaba, Delta State, discharged and acquitted Ibori of all 170 charges brought against him by EFCC.[123] Also, Ibori had managed to get every case preferred against him thrown out of court including that in the country's Supreme Court.[124] However, the same Ibori was convicted of fraud and ML in the UK in 2012 on similar facts[125] and UK returned $5.8m stolen by Ibori to Nigeria in 2021.[126]

The line of enquiry here looks beyond the presence of rules, whether they meet defined FATF standards or whether they firmly comply and ask whether the rules work.[127] The rules have failed to curtail ML by PEPs because those

117 This Day, 'Editorial' (17 April 2022) <www.thisdaylive.com/index.php/2022/04/21/the-pardon-for-dariye-and-nyame> accessed 20 December 2022.

118 Jeremy Pope, 'Parliament and Anti-Corruption Legislation' in Rick Stapenhurst et al. (eds), *The Role of Parliament in Curbing Corruption* (World Bank Institute 2006) 51.

119 Ioana Deleanu and Joras Ferwerda, 'Effectiveness: Threat and Policy Response' in B Unger, J Ferwerda, BM Van Den and I Deleanu (eds), *The Economic and Legal Effectiveness of European Union's Anti-Money Laundering Policy* (Edward Elgar Cheltenham 2014).

120 Wale Odunsi, 'Onnoghen: United Nations Lambast Buhari Government' (*Daily Post*, 11 February 2019) <https://dailypost.ng/2019/02/11/onnoghen-un-lambasts-buhari-govt/#:~:text> accessed 21 April 2022.

121 Tayo Oke, 'Financial Crime Prosecution, Legal Certainty, and Exigency of Policy: Case of Nigeria EFCC' (2014) 21(1) Journal of Financial Crime 56.

122 Sahara Reporters, 'Toothless Bulldog, EFCC Celebrates Ibori's Conviction' (17 April 2012) <https://saharareporters.com/2012/04/17/toothless-bulldog-efcc-celebrates-ibori%E2%80%99s-conviction> accessed 6 January 2023.

123 Daniel Agbiboa, 'As It Was in the Beginning: The Vicious Cycle of Corruption in Nigeria' (2013) 4 Studies in Sociology of Science 1.

124 Tayo Oke, 'EFCC Growing Crisis of Confidence' <https://niyisunmonu.blogspot.com/2012/06/efccs-crisis-of-growing-confidence-by.html> accessed 13 January 2023.

125 Mark Tran, 'Former Nigeria State Governor James Ibori Receives 13-Year Sentence' (*The Guardian*, 17 April 2012) <www.theguardian.com/global-development/2012/apr/17/nigeria-governor-james-ibori-sentenced> accessed 20 December 2022.

126 BBC News, 'James Ibori: UK Returns $5.8m Stolen by Ex-governor to Nigeria' (18 May 2021) <www.bbc.co.uk/news/world-africa-57161645> accessed 20 December 2022.

127 Roland Pol, 'Anti-money Laundering Effectiveness: Assessing Outcomes or Ticking Boxes?' (2018) 21(2) Journal of Money Laundering Control 215.

in political power control the controls,[128] and ensure that corruption and ML prosecutions do not proceed without their approval.[129]

Our case studies consistently show lack of political will on the part of successive governments in Nigeria to enforce AML standards. Absence of political will is the reason Abubakar Bagudu, the kingpin of Abacha ML operations has not been prosecuted in Nigeria. The illicit operations Abubakar Bagudu managed on behalf of Abacha are well documented in suits filed in the United States and the Bailiwick of Jersey.[130]

In 2003 Bagudu was arrested in the United States, where he had lived for three years; he was kept in federal detention for six months while awaiting extradition to Jersey to answer charges of ML.[131] To avoid extradition to Jersey, Bagudu negotiated a deal with the US and Jersey authorities to return $163 million of the laundered assets to Nigeria in exchange for Jersey's withdrawal of the extradition request.[132] Subsequently, Bagudu was repatriated to Nigeria to face trial and the evidence collated in Jersey and Switzerland were sent to Nigeria's Attorney-General (A-G).[133] He is yet to be questioned, rather he was cleared to contest three different elections: one for the Senate and two for Governorship. He is currently the Governor of Kebbi State.[134]

The various settlement deals reached by successive governments and the Abacha family also reflects lack of political will. In July 2002, President Obasanjo announced that a settlement had been reached with the Abacha family under which they would keep $100 million if they returned $1 billion.[135] As a result Mohammed Abacha was released from prison after three years of awaiting trial for corruption and ML.[136] Mohammed Abacha later denied making any such

128 John Hatchard, *Combating Corruption: Legal Approaches to Supporting Good Governance and Integrity in Africa* (Edward Elgar Law 2014) 279.

129 John Hatchard, *Combating Corruption: Legal Approaches to Supporting Good Governance and Integrity in Africa* (Edward Elgar Law 2014) 280.

130 Nicholas Ibekwe, 'How Kebbi Governor Abubakar Bagudu Was Arrested in America' (*Premium Times*, 21 September 2019) <www.premiumtimesng.com/news/headlines/353583-how-kebbi-governor-abubakar-bagudu-was-arrested-in-america.html> accessed 7 January 2023.

131 Nicholas Ibekwe, 'How Kebbi Governor Abubakar Bagudu Was Arrested in America' (*Premium Times*, 21 September 2019) <www.premiumtimesng.com/news/headlines/353583-how-kebbi-governor-abubakar-bagudu-was-arrested-in-america.html> accessed 7 January 2023.

132 Nicholas Ibekwe, 'How Kebbi Governor Abubakar Bagudu Was Arrested in America' (*Premium Times*, 21 September 2019) <www.premiumtimesng.com/news/headlines/353583-how-kebbi-governor-abubakar-bagudu-was-arrested-in-america.html> accessed 7 January 2023.

133 Nicholas Ibekwe, 'How Kebbi Governor Abubakar Bagudu Was Arrested in America' (*Premium Times*, 21 September 2019) <www.premiumtimesng.com/news/headlines/353583-how-kebbi-governor-abubakar-bagudu-was-arrested-in-america.html> accessed 7 January 2023.

134 Nicholas Ibekwe, 'How Kebbi Governor Abubakar Bagudu Was Arrested in America' (*Premium Times*, 21 September 2019) <www.premiumtimesng.com/news/headlines/353583-how-kebbi-governor-abubakar-bagudu-was-arrested-in-america.html> accessed 7 January 2023.

135 BBC News, 'Abacha's Son Fights Back' (19 November 2002) <http://news.bbc.co.uk/1/hi/world/africa/2492425.stm> accessed 7 January 2023.

136 BBC News, 'Abacha's Son Fights Back' (19 November 2002) <http://news.bbc.co.uk/1/hi/world/africa/2492425.stm> accessed 7 January 2023.

deal and his trial has been stalled ever since.[137] Similarly, President Jonathan also entered a secret deal with the Abacha family in 2014, in which the family was to return part of their loot in exchange for perpetual immunity from prosecution.[138]

Partial political will to combat ML in Nigeria is often exhibited by the government in the prosecution of members of the opposition parties. The recent resurrection of the charges and prompt prosecution and conviction of the spokesperson of the opposition Labour Party, Dr Doyin Okupe,[139] smacks of a political witch hunt because the principal offender in that case, the former National Security Adviser Sambo Dasuki has not been prosecuted.[140]

Recommendations

The authority of any other agency or person to institute criminal proceedings in Nigeria is subject to the overriding constitutional powers of the Attorneys-General to institute, take over, or discontinue criminal proceedings against any person before any court of law, except a Court Martial.[141] In the exercise of the powers vested in him by the constitution the A-G is unchallenged and unchallengeable.[142]

Meanwhile, in Nigeria the AGF who doubles as the chief law officer and Minster of Justice[143] is an appointee of the President and can be removed from office by the President without recourse to any other authority. Therefore, the AGF is prone to act in the interest of his appointor, and that is why there is no history of an A-G that was removed for abuse of prosecutorial discretion in any matter.[144] Consequently, in Nigeria where the government lacks the political will to prosecute corrupt PEPs, the A-G will either fail to prosecute them or decline the prosecution of pending cases by entering a *nolle prosequi*. In this regard, recently the AGF was accused of not cooperating with anti-corruption agencies in their bid to bring corrupt PEPs to justice.[145]

137 BBC News, 'Abacha's Son Fights Back' (19 November 2002) <http://news.bbc.co.uk/1/hi/world/africa/2492425.stm> accessed 7 January 2023

138 Bassey Udo, 'Abacha: Inside the Secret Deal Jonathan Authorised to Shield Ex- Dictator's Family from Prosecution' (*Premium Times*, 15 May 2015) <www.premiumtimesng.com/investigationspecial-reports/183028-abacha-loot-inside-the-secret-deal-jonathan-authorized-to-shield-ex-dictators-family-from-prosecution-2.html> accessed 7 January 2023.

139 Chris Ewokor, 'Nigeria Election: Peter Obi Campaign Chief Doyin Okupe Convicted of Money Laundering' (*BBC News*, 19 December 2022) <www.bbc.co.uk/news/world-africa-64030970> accessed 13 January 2023.

140 Fadehan Oyeyemi, 'Court finds Doyin Okupe Guilty of N240m Money Laundering Charges' (*Daily Post*, 19 December 2022) <https://dailypost.ng/2022/12/19/court-finds-doyin-okupe-guilty-of-n240m-money-laundering-charges/> accessed 14 January 2023.

141 *The State v Okpegboro* 1980 (2) N.C.R. 291.

142 Robert Osamor, 'Administration of Criminal Justice in Nigeria and Plea Bargaining: Motions without Movement' (2022) 6(2) African Journal of Law and Human Rights 124–25.

143 S. 150(1) of the Constitution of the Federal Republic of Nigeria, 1999 <http://www.nigeria-law.org/ConstitutionOfTheFederalRepublicOfNigeria.htm>.

144 Benjamin Igwenyi, 'Jurisprudential Appraisal of *Nolle Prosequi* in Nigeria' (2016) 4(2) Global Journal of Politics and Law Research 19.

145 The Chairman of Presidential Advisory Committee Against Corruption in Nigeria Prof. Itse Sagay (SAN), had accused the current Attorney General of the Federation, Abubakar

Therefore, to ensure that a compromised A-G does not abuse the exercise of the overarching prosecutorial authority vested in his office by the Constitution, a prosecution review commission is proposed for Nigeria. This will provide a check on the exercise of prosecutorial discretion by the A-G. A prosecution review commission is uniquely a Japanese institution. "In Japan if a public prosecutor decides not to indict a suspect, the victim of the crime, or a suitable proxy, may demand a hearing regarding the prosecutor's decision."[146] They have the power to review, upon request of a victim or the victim's proxy, a prosecutor's decision not to indict a suspect in a criminal case."[147] The verdict of the commission binds the A-G. Without such powers there can be no check on capricious actions by prosecutors.[148]

For Nigeria, the proposed Prosecution Review Commission should be solely for economic and financial crimes offences committed by PEPs. In terms of the membership, it should be presided over by a retired judge of the Court of Appeal or the Supreme Court, other members should include representatives of the Nigerian Bar Association, other professional associations, and civil society associations. The victims who are eligible to request a review of the AGF's decision not to indict are members of the society who are the real victims of economic and financial crimes because monies that are syphoned from Nigeria are taken from the public sector.[149]

Furthermore, in Nigeria, the immunity clause in section 308 of the Constitution ensures that the President, his Vice, States' Governors, and their Deputies are immune from prosecution while in office. This gives corrupt politicians endless possibilities of embezzlement of state resources and affords them ample time to cover up their tracks while in office.[150] Therefore, there is need to curtail the constitutional immunities enjoyed by these PEPs.[151] I propose that the immunity should be limited to civil cases for the obvious reason that the likely avalanche of such cases will cripple the executive functions of these offices. However, immunity should not be extended to criminal cases because apart from the enormity of criminal allegations the consequences of political corruption, especially ML, is deleterious to the corporate well-being and

Malami of frustrating the war against corruption cited in Eniola Akinkuotu, 'Malami Has Power to Stop Corruption Cases -Aide' (*The Punch*, 20 July 2020) https://punchng.com/malami-has-power-to-stop-corruption-cases-aide/ accessed 4 March 2023.

146 Mark D West, 'Prosecution Review Commissions: Japan's Answer to the Problem of Prosecutorial Discretion' 1992 92(3) Columbia Law Review 685.

147 Mark D West, 'Prosecution Review Commissions: Japan's Answer to the Problem of Prosecutorial Discretion' 1992 92(3) Columbia Law Review 694.

148 Mark D West, 'Prosecution Review Commissions: Japan's Answer to the Problem of Prosecutorial Discretion' 1992 92(3) Columbia Law Review 702.

149 Markovska, Adams, Tupman and Yuliya (n 60) 169.

150 Markovska, Adams, Tupman and Yuliya (n 60) 169.

151 John Hatchard, *Combating Corruption: Legal Approaches to Supporting Good Governance and Integrity in Africa* (Edward Elgar Law 2014) 332.

existence of Nigeria.[152] The enormity of criminal matters is further emphasised by the constitutional provisions which prohibits any person who has been convicted of a criminal offence from holding any public office either by election or appointment.[153]

In conclusion, the establishment of a Prosecution Review Commission to check abuses of the exercise of prosecutorial discretion by the AGF and the limitation of the immunity clause to only civil matters will ensure the prosecution of corrupt PEPs, even where the government lacks the political will to enforce AML regulations.

152 L Adeleke, 'The Practice of Plea Bargaining in Nigeria: Antithesis of the Broken Windows Theory of Corruption Abstract' (2019) 6 <www.researchgate.net/publication/335524123_THE_PRACTICE_OF_PLEA_BARGAINING_IN_NIGERIA_ANTITHESIS_OF_THE_BROKEN_WINDOWS_THEORY_OF_CORRUPTION_ABSTRACT>; PE Echewija, 'Plea Bargaining and the Administration of Criminal Justice in Nigeria: A Moral Critic' (Autumn 2017) 41(3) IAFOR Journal of Ethics, Religion & Philosophy 44.

153 Constitution of the Federal Republic of Nigeria 1999 (as amended) ss 66(1)(c), 107(1)(c), 137(1)(d) and (e), 147(5), 182(d) and (e), 192(4).

10 The Vulnerability of Politically Exposed Persons (PEPs) in Africa

Towards Transparency in Beneficial Ownership

John Hatchard

Introduction

The laundering of the proceeds of crime by politically exposed persons (PEPs) through companies, trusts, and other entities (hereinafter collectively referred to as 'legal persons') remains the focus of considerable international attention, not least because of the revelations from the Panama Papers and the Pandora Papers. The Financial Action Task Force (FATF) has noted that due to their position and influence, many PEPs 'are in positions that can be abused for the purposes of committing money laundering offences and related predicate offences, including corruption and bribery'.[1] It means that combatting money laundering by PEPs is a unique challenge for they possess the ability to 'control the AML controls'. The key is to target the vulnerabilities of PEPs. One potential vulnerability is transparency in the beneficial ownership of legal persons. It is commonplace for PEPs to launder their proceeds of crime through offshore financial centres, which allow them to establish legal entities through which nominee directors may effectively provide anonymity to the true beneficial owner(s).

Action to enhance transparency of beneficial ownership is therefore a central focus for combatting money laundering for when this secrecy is removed, PEPs become vulnerable to disclosure of their illegal activities. Accordingly, this chapter critically reviews recent moves towards enhancing beneficial ownership transparency both within Africa and in the United Kingdom and its associated jurisdictions. The introduction leads to a discussion of the problem of PEPs. Next, the chapter considers the concealing of beneficial ownership by PEPs and then reviews the ongoing work of the FATF in setting international standards designed to enhance beneficial ownership transparency. The following section provides an African perspective by considering recent development in the offshore financial centre of Seychelles. Thereafter, the chapter provides a more global perspective by providing a case study of the United Kingdom and its 'secrecy jurisdictions' through which numerous African PEPs have laundered their proceeds of corruption. The conclusion offers a consideration of possible future developments.

1 FATF, *Guidance: Politically Exposed Persons* (FATF 2013), at [1] (hereinafter FATF PEPs paper).

DOI: 10.4324/9781003253808-12

The Problem of PEPs

PEPs are 'individuals' who are or have been entrusted domestically with prominent public functions, family members and close associates.[2] The term also includes members of ruling royal families.[3] 'Close associates' are individuals who are closely connected to a PEP, either socially or professionally.[4] In practice this is an incomplete list, a point reflected in South Africa where the Financial Intelligence Centre Act 2001 (as amended) refers to prominent influential persons (PIPs) instead of PEPs, a term that is designed at the domestic level to also include private sector individuals who have business dealings with public sector officials and elected officials in the public services.[5] This is particularly relevant to the notion of state capture as highlighted in the Gupta case in South Africa.[6]

The problem of PEPs is that they 'pose a high risk of money laundering by the very nature of their position'.[7] This demands a recognition that they are the most powerful political entities in any society with unique access to state assets and influence over state institutions. This includes control over the anti-money laundering (AML) safeguards, for example by undermining the development and/or effectiveness of national AML laws and institutions.

Even so, PEPs remain vulnerable to detection when the AML safeguards are effective, not only domestically but also globally where PEPs are unable to 'control the controls'. One such vulnerability is through establishing transparency in the beneficial ownership of legal persons.

Concealing Beneficial Ownership, PEPs, and Money Laundering

The term 'beneficial owner' means

> one or more natural persons who ultimately own or control a customer or the natural person or persons on whose behalf a transaction is

2 See the FATF, *The International Standards on Combating Money Laundering and the Financing of Terrorism and Proliferation* (FATF 2012) General Glossary (hereinafter the FATF Recommendations).

3 Intergovernmental Action Group against Money Laundering in West Africa (GIABA), *Corruption – Money Laundering Nexus: An Analysis of Risks and Control Measures in West Africa* (GIABA 2010) 54.

4 FATF PEPs paper, at [11]. Persons who are or have been entrusted with a prominent function by an international organisation are also included in the FATF definition. These are 'members of senior management i.e. directors, deputy directors and members of the board or equivalent functions'.

5 See Schedule 3A.

6 See generally *The Commission of Enquiry into State Capture Report* (the Zondo Commission Report) 2022. For a helpful review of the report see the Corruption Watch analysis <www.corruptionwatch.org.za/zondo-report-a-summary-of-the-first-four-parts-and-who-it-implicated/>.

7 FATF, *Laundering the Proceeds of Corruption* (FATF 2011) 12.

> being conducted and includes those natural persons who exercise ultimate effective control over a legal person or a legal arrangement.[8]

Reflecting the often complex ownership and control structures of legal persons, the FATF Recommendations add that:

> Reference to 'ultimately owns or controls' and 'ultimate effective control' refer to situations in which ownership/control is exercised through a chain of ownership or by means of control other than direct control.[9]

Inevitably the last tier of control is a natural person(s). Yet identifying such person(s) has proved almost impossible for, as the FATF has highlighted, the 'lack of accurate information on the ultimate owner of legal persons and arrangements on a timely basis is a significant vulnerability' for money laundering.[10]

The FATF has usefully categorised the misuse of beneficial ownership into three broad methods, thus highlighting the range of the practical challenges in addressing the problem:

- Generating complex ownership and control structures though the use of legal persons and legal arrangements, particularly when established across multiple jurisdictions (e.g., shell companies: see below).
- Using individuals and financial instruments to obscure the relationship between the beneficial owner and the asset, including bearer shares,[11] nominees, and professional intermediaries.
- Falsifying activities through the use of false loans, false invoices, and misleading naming conventions.[12]

Money Laundering by PEPs: The Domestic Context

In the African domestic context, there are numerous examples where PEPs have used such mechanisms to conceal their beneficial ownership of stolen property. A good example is the so-called 'Cashgate' case in Malawi. Between 2009 and 2014, government ministers and senior public officials conspired to manipulate the government payment control system. As a result, they were able to draw a

8 Beneficial Ownership Act 2020, section 3 (Seychelles). This is based on the definition found in the FATF Recommendations, General Glossary.

9 FATF Recommendations, General Glossary.

10 FATF, *Report to G20 Finance Ministers and Central Bank Governors* (FATF 2018) at 16.

11 Bearer shares are the shares that are issued in the name of unnamed bearers. Issuing companies of bearer shares do not know about the identity of the owner. As they provide almost complete anonymity, most jurisdictions now ban such shares.

12 FATF/Egmont, *Concealment of Beneficial Ownership* (FATF 2018) at 53.

series of fraudulent Government of Malawi cheques, the proceeds from which were either laundered through the purchase of real estate, expensive vehicles, and other property in Malawi or paid in favour of numerous private contractors on the pretext that they had supplied goods and services to the government. In reality, none had been supplied. Some US$365 million was stolen and laundered.[13] In order to facilitate the laundering of these assets, numerous businesses and companies were registered just a few months or days before being used by the PEPs through which to launder their stolen proceeds.[14] The case neatly illustrates how huge sums of money can be looted from state coffers or acquired through other abuse of office and then laundered by PEPs.[15]

Several reports highlight the problem of the abuse of beneficial ownership. For example, as regards car dealerships, Nigeria has reported that it 'remains very difficult to identify the beneficial ownership of [such] businesses thus posing a very high threat of money laundering'.[16] Similarly, real estate remains a particularly vulnerable sector because the legal ownership of land registered in a company register may be used to conceal the identity of the beneficial owner.[17] The use of microfinance banks through which to conceal the beneficial ownership of funds lodged with commercial banks is also a likely vehicle for money laundering. A serious and growing threat is the use of mobile money (i.e., the use of cell phones) to credit, send, receive, and transfer money and virtual value.[18]

Money Laundering by PEPs: The Global Context

The case of Mahmoud Thiam illustrates the problem of the laundering of stolen assets globally. As the Minister of Mines and Geology in Guinea, Thiam oversaw the signing of an agreement with a Chinese conglomerate, CIF, which was highly disadvantageous to the Republic of Guinea.[19]

13 Figure provided by Victor Chiwala of the Malawi Anti-Corruption Bureau in a presentation to the Global Expert Group Meeting on Corruption involving Vast Quantities of Assets, 2018

14 See also Zambia Financial Intelligence Centre, *Money Laundering Trends and Terrorist Financing Trends Report 2018* (Zambia Financial Intelligence Centre 2018) section 5.

15 For a detailed account of such activity see Tom Burgess, *The Looting Machine* (William Collins 2015).

16 The National (Money Laundering & Terrorist Financing) Risk Assessment Forum, 'Report of Nigeria National Risk Assessment on Money Laundering and Terrorism Financing' (*NRA Forum* 2016) 30. For another example, see United States Department of State *International Narcotics Control Strategy Report* Volume II 'Money Laundering' 2022 report on Seychelles at p 168 (hereinafter the DOS report).

17 For a full discussion on PEPs in Africa and the money laundering process see John Hatchard, *Combating Money Laundering in Africa: Dealing with the Problem of PEPs* (Edward Elgar 2020) 12–29.

18 See, for example, the DOS report on Kenya (pp 123–24); Mozambique (p 141) and Senegal (p 167).

19 The joint venture was via a private company, African Development Corporation Pte Ltd, incorporated in Singapore. CIF owned a total of 85% of the company with the Republic of Guinea owning the remaining 15%.

Shortly before the signing of the agreement, US$3 million was placed into a Hong Kong bank account in Thiam's name, which Thiam had opened the day before, and a further US$5.5 million was later transferred to the same account. Thiam then set about laundering some of the proceeds from this bank account by making wire transfers to shell companies incorporated in Malaysia and Mozambique with the latter being used to purchase the Dutchess County Estate in New York for US$3.75 million. This enabled him to conceal the fact that he and his wife were the beneficial owners of the property. Some of the bribe proceeds were then used to make 'high-end renovations to the Dutchess County Estate'[20] and provide tuition for his children at two private preparatory schools in Manhattan,[21] a ski vacation and skiing lessons, and the purchase of a Steinway grand piano.[22]

Money Laundering by PEPs Through Offshore Financial Centres

The Panama Papers and Pandora Papers have highlighted the role offshore centres play in enabling African PEPs (amongst others) to establish legal persons through which to launder their proceeds of crime. As Nicholls et al. have pointed out, there has been

> persistent criticism of the offshore financial sector . . . since there exist jurisdictions in which legal frameworks and practices [deliberately] obscure the identity of beneficial owners by, for example, placing ownership in the hands of nominee directors and shareholders.[23]

Establishing shell companies is often the key to schemes designed to conceal or disguise beneficial ownership.[24] These are defined by the Organisation for Economic Co-operation and Development (OECD) as 'entities established not to pursue legitimate business activity but solely to obscure the identity of their beneficial owners and controllers' and which function as a corporate veil, providing an effective screen separating criminals from illicit financial activities.[25] As Findlay has observed: 'Shell companies that can-

20 Costing approximately US$250,000.

21 Costing approximately US$88,767.

22 Costing approximately US$46,375. It was also reported that he had transferred some US$560,000 to a foreign minister of another (unnamed) West African state.

23 Colin Nicholls et al., *Corruption and Misuse of Public Office* (3rd edn, OUP 2017) 23.04.

24 FATF/Egmont Group, *Concealment of Beneficial Ownership* (FATF/Egmont Group 2018) 5.

25 OECD Steering Committee on Corporate Governance, *Behind the Corporate Veil: Using Corporate Entities for Illicit Purposes* (OECD 2001) 17. The FATF/Egmont Group consider shell companies as 'companies that are incorporated but which have no independent operations, significant assets, ongoing business activities, or employees'. FATF/Egmont Group, *Concealment of Beneficial Ownership* (FATF/Egmont Group 2018) 11.

not be linked back to the real individuals in control create near-insuperable obstacles for regulators and law enforcement officials'.[26] Similarly a 'shelf company' is an incorporated company that has inactive shareholders, directors, and a secretary and is left dormant for a longer period even if a customer relationship has already been established'.[27] They also pose particular money laundering challenges as they enable PEPs who ultimately own or control the company to remain concealed behind a nominee director(s) and nominee shareholder(s).[28]

This raises the key issue for consideration in the next part of the chapter: how to 'persuade' countries and territories to introduce beneficial ownership transparency requirements.

FATF and Beneficial Ownership Transparency: 'Know Your Beneficial Owner'

The FATF describes itself as an inter-governmental policymaking body whose objectives are to 'set standards and promote effective implementation of legal, regulatory and operational measures for combating money laundering'.[29] The FATF was established with the mandate to:

> assess the results of co-operation already undertaken in order to prevent the utilisation of the banking system and financial institutions for the purpose of money laundering, and to consider additional preventive efforts in this field, including the adaptation of the legal and regulatory systems so as to enhance multilateral judicial assistance.[30]

In order to ensure a global response and outreach, FATF membership comprises 37 states and two regional organisations, which represent most of the major global financial centres. South Africa is the only African member, but to complete the global 'family' the FATF has developed a series of FATF-style regional bodies (FSRBs). In the African context, there are currently four such

26 Michael Findlay, Daniel Neilson and Jason Sharman, *Global Shell Games: Testing Money Launderers' and Terrorist Financiers' Access to Shell Companies* (Centre for Governance and Public Policy 2012) 5 <www.gfintegrity.org/wp-content/uploads/2014/05/Global-Shell-Games-2012.pdf> accessed 20 July 2018.

27 FATF/Egmont Group paper 'Concealment of Beneficial Ownership' 2018, at 65–67.

28 The Conference of State Parties to the United Nations Convention against Corruption, *Report of the International Group Meeting on Beneficial Ownership* (CAC/COSP/2017/CRP.5) 32, also notes that corruption schemes increasingly use new sophisticated types of corporate vehicles with so-called tax havens or secrecy jurisdictions being used to facilitate the criminality.

29 Introduction to the FATF Recommendations 2012.

30 Introduction to the FATF Recommendations 2012.

regional bodies. The result is that over 200 countries and jurisdictions are members of the FATF and/or of a FSRB and have committed to implementing the FATF Recommendations. As Raol helpfully explains, FSRBs

> are viewed as 'local chapters' that follow the FATF Recommendations, with mentions of regional socio-economic issues in their guidelines. The FSRBs work more at a regional level to raise awareness and offer technical aid in spreading FATF guidelines via peer pressure and mutual evaluations. Though FATF is the only anti-money laundering/combating terrorist financing standard-setting body, it depends heavily on FSRBs for inputs that affect FATF guideline amendments.[31]

In 2012 the FATF published the International Standards on Combating Money Laundering and the Financing of Terrorism and Proliferation (the 2012 Recommendations).[32] This is a set of 40 Recommendations together with detailed Interpretive Notes (INs) and a General Glossary. The 2012 Recommendations 'set' out the essential measures that countries must have in place in order to combat money laundering. Two such measures are to enhance the transparency and availability of the beneficial ownership of legal persons and arrangements and to facilitate international cooperation.[33]

As regards beneficial ownership, the FATF has highlighted that the 'lack of accurate information on the ultimate owner of legal persons and arrangements on a timely basis is a significant vulnerability' for money laundering.[34] This concern led to the revision in March 2022 of FATF Recommendation 24, which now sets out the following:

- Countries should assess the risks of misuse of legal persons for money laundering or terrorist financing and take measures to prevent their misuse.
- Countries should ensure that there is adequate, accurate, and up-to-date information on the beneficial ownership and control of legal persons that can be obtained or accessed rapidly and efficiently by competent authorities, through either a register of beneficial ownership or an alternative mechanism.

31 Jay Raol, 'The Role of FATF Style Regional Bodies (FSRBs) in Combating Money Laundering and Financing of Terrorism' (*IDM Merit Blog* 2022) <www.idmerit.com/blog/the-role-of-fatf-style-regional-bodies-fsrbs-in-combating-money-laundering-and-financing-of-terrorism/#:~:text=FATF%20Style%20Regional%20Bodies%20%28FSRBs%29%20are%20viewed%20as,FATF%20guidelines%20via%20peer%20pressure%20and%20mutual%20evaluations>.

32 For a background to the development of the FATF Recommendations see William Gilmore, *Dirty Money: The Evolution of Money Laundering Countermeasures* (2nd edn, Council of Europe Publishing 1999) 79.

33 Introduction to the 2012 FATF Recommendations.

34 FATF, *Report to G20 Finance Ministers and Central Bank Governors* (FATF 2018) at 16.

- Countries should not permit legal persons to issue new bearer shares or bearer share warrants, and take measures to prevent the misuse of existing bearer shares and bearer share warrants.
- Countries should take effective measures to ensure that nominee shareholders and directors are not misused for money laundering or terrorist financing.

On the face of it, these are non-mandatory requirements which FATF members may choose whether or not to implement. Indeed, this is implied in the term 'Recommendations'. However, hidden in the General Glossary to the 2012 Recommendations is the following:

> For the purposes of assessing compliance with the FATF Recommendations, the word *should* has the same meaning as *must*.

In other words, 'Recommendations' is FATF-speak for 'Requirements', and members of the 'FATF family' are required to implement them.

'Competent authorities' in Recommendation 24 refer to 'all public authorities with designated responsibilities for combating money laundering'.[35] Such authorities must be able to 'obtain, or have access in a timely fashion to, adequate, accurate and current information on the beneficial ownership and control of companies and other legal persons (beneficial ownership information) that are created in the country'.[36] At a minimum this must include information about the legal ownership and control structure of the company, its shareholders and directors. All companies created in a country must be registered in a company registry. Accurate and up-to-date information on the beneficial ownership must be held by that company or have mechanisms in place to enable a competent authority to determine the beneficial ownership in a timely manner.

In addition, countries must take steps to prevent the misuse of nominee directors and nominee shareholders, for example by requiring them to disclose the identity of their 'nominator' and for this information to be included in the company register.[37] To reflect the development of new entities, this now applies to virtual asset service providers (VASPs).[38]

35 See FATF Recommendations General Glossary. This includes the FIU, investigative and prosecutorial authorities, and authorities with AML supervisory or monitoring responsibilities.

36 IN to FATF Recommendation 24 [1]. A note adds that 'References to creating a legal person, include incorporation of companies or to any other mechanism that is used'.

37 IN to FATF Recommendation 24 [15].

38 Defined in the FATF Recommendations General Glossary as meaning any natural or legal person . . . and as a business conducts . . . operations for or on behalf of another natural or legal persons: i) exchange between virtual assets and fiat currencies; ii) exchange between one or more forms of virtual currencies; iii) transfer of virtual assets; iv) safekeeping and/or administration of victual assets or instruments enabling control over virtual assets; and v) participation in and provision of financial services related to an issuer's offer and/or sale of a virtual asset. See generally FATF Guidance, *Virtual Assets and Virtual Asset Service Providers* (FATF Guidance 2019).

FATF Recommendation 25 further states that countries 'should ensure that there is adequate, accurate and timely information on express trusts, including information on the settlor, trustee and beneficiaries that can be obtained or accessed in a timely fashion by competent authorities'.[39] Similar provisions should apply to foundations, Anstalt, and limited liability partnerships.

As regards international cooperation, the FATF requires countries to 'rapidly, constructively and effectively' provide basic and beneficial ownership information. This may include facilitating access by foreign competent authorities to basic information held by company registries and using their domestic powers to obtain beneficial ownership information on behalf of foreign counterparts.[40]

Based on these Recommendations, in assessing the adequacy of beneficial ownership transparency provisions in a country or territory, three key questions are raised, as explained in the following sections.

Are Legal Persons Required to Maintain a Register of Beneficial Ownership?

This is fundamental to transparency. Kenya provides a helpful example. Here a 2017 statutory amendment requires every company to 'keep a register of its members which shall include information relating to beneficial owners of the company, if any'.[41] Companies risk a fine of KSh500,000 for failure to update their registers.

Is There a Central Register of Beneficial Ownership of Legal Persons?

A useful example comes from Zambia, where the Companies Act 2017 contains extensive provisions regarding beneficial ownership transparency including requiring the disclosure of beneficial ownership in the public company registry to a Registrar of Beneficial Ownership.[42]

In practice, some African countries face a major challenge in implementing this requirement effectively. For example, in Kenya companies' records at

39 In 2014 the FATF published its *Guidance on Transparency and Beneficial Ownership*. This requires States to ensure that measures are in place to: prevent legal persons or arrangements from being used for criminal purposes; make legal persons/arrangements sufficiently transparent; and ensure that accurate and up-to-date basic and beneficial ownership information is available on a timely basis.

40 IN to FATF Recommendation 24 [19].

41 Section 8 Companies (Amendment) Act 2017 amending section 93 Companies Act 2015.

42 This highlights a frequent issue where beneficial ownership registration is limited to certain legal persons. In Zambia there is a now a proposal that this is extended to other forms of business entities such as trusts and cooperatives 'to ensure transparency across the regime': see Zambia Financial Intelligence, *Centre Money Laundering and Terrorist Financing Trends Report 2018* (Zambia Financial Intelligence 2018) 13.

Companies Registry are reportedly out of date, and there is no mechanism by which a company can compel shareholders to reveal the beneficial ownership of shares being held.[43] This is likely to be the position in other African countries. Further, in some countries, the problem is exacerbated by the sheer number of companies registered. For example, the Seychelles Financial Services Authority reported in 2020 that there were 224,525 international business companies (IBCs), 918 foundations, and 849 international trusts registered.[44]

Can Such Information Be Shared With the National Financial Intelligence Unit and Law Enforcement Agencies as Well as Through International Cooperation?

This highlights the challenge for Africa countries of having the legal tools available, backed up by the political will, to make the system effective so as to break through the veil of secrecy offered to PEPs and thus enable national and international investigative bodies to obtain accurate information as to the ultimate beneficial owner of the legal person.

Action towards beneficial ownership transparency in African countries remains extremely limited. For example, a 2020 study by the Tax Justice Network (the TJN study) identified only five African states with beneficial ownership laws[45] – that is, where all types of companies are required to register and update their beneficial ownership information. This situation was not unique.[46] It follows that enhancing the transparency of legal persons remains work in progress. This is emphasised by GIABA, which has noted the significant shortcomings with most of the company registries in the region failing to have a comprehensive understanding of their FATF obligations and thus to implement effectively beneficial ownership requirements at the national level.[47]

43 See Daly & Imander Legal Alert 'Impact of the new Companies (Amendment) Act 2017': <www.dalyinamdar.com/wp-content/uploads/2017/10/impact-of-the-new-companies-amendment-act-2017.pdf>.

44 DOS report 169.

45 Moran Harari, Andres Knobel, Markus Meinzer and Miroslav Palanský, 'Ownership Registration of Different Types of Legal Structures from an International Comparative Perspective State of Play of Beneficial Ownership – Update 2020' <https://deliverypdf.ssrn.com/delivery.php? ID=631024088114107118117069093099082030097033001017049013093124094124025096066029088067106004003004103059109065001072113123067072019040011087093004029027089077080003026049041083093107081019072023119117104121010028109118025120073070080126125006088013121071&EXT=pdf&INDEX=TRUE> accessed 20 July 2022.

46 This was a global study, and the vast majority of the 133 jurisdictions covered did not have effective beneficial ownership registration provisions.

47 See GIABA press release 'GIABA organizes Regional Workshop on Beneficial Ownership Requirements' December 2019 and GIABA, *Annual Report 2018* (GIABA 2018) at 284.

The FATF Recommendations do not address a further question:

Is there a public register of beneficial ownership of legal persons?

As noted below, very few countries globally have done so, yet even here, significance is being made in this respect.

The next two sections consider the application of these questions in relation to the offshore world.

Towards Beneficial Ownership Transparency in the Offshore World 1: An African Case Study

Obscuring the money laundering trail often involves PEPs and their accomplices establishing shell companies[48] and other legal persons located in a variety of offshore jurisdictions. These are the 'facilitating states' which offer the secrecy and anonymity which PEPs demand in order to further their money laundering schemes. In exchange, facilitating states enjoy significant economic benefits. This has long resulted in a lack of the political will to address the need for transparency in the offshore world. This section explores the African offshore world through a case study of the Seychelles. Given their significance as facilitating money laundering by African PEPs, a later section explores the role of British Overseas Territories (BOTs) and Crown Dependencies (CDs) and the ongoing efforts by the UK to develop beneficial ownership transparency there.

Seychelles is one of the best known offshore financial centres in Africa.[49] The country was named in the Pandora Papers as one of the main destinations for establishing offshore companies and they provide unprecedented details as to the ownership of shell companies including PEPs from Angola, Chad, Mozambique, and Zimbabwe. Indeed the notoriety of the country meant that until 2021 Seychelles was on the European Union blacklist of tax havens.[50]

The Beneficial Ownership Act 2020 (BOA 2020) is therefore of considerable interest as it highlights a commitment towards at least partial beneficial ownership transparency.

48 A shell company is defined in the DOS report (p 8) as 'An incorporated company with no significant operations, established for the sole purpose of holding or transferring funds, often for money laundering purposes'. The attraction of shell companies is that only the legal ownership is revealed, thus enabling the PEP to conceal their identity as the beneficial owner of the company and its assets.

49 The others are Botswana, Mauritius, and Namibia.

50 See further International Consortium of Investigative Journalists 'Massive money-laundering probe heartens anti-corruption activists but fails to lift Pandora Papers' pall over Seychelles' <www.icij.org/investigations/pandora-papers/massive-money-laundering-probe-heartens-anti-corruption-activists-but-fails-to-lift-pandora-papers-pall-over-seychelles/> accessed 20 July 2022.

Are Legal Persons Required to Maintain a Register of Beneficial Ownership?

Here section 5(1) of the BOA 2020 provides as follows:

> Every legal person and legal arrangement shall maintain a register, to be known as a register of beneficial owners, at the principal place of business of its resident agent, containing the following information in respect of every beneficial owner of such legal person or legal arrangement –.
>
> (a) the name, residential address, service address, date of birth and nationality of each beneficial owner;
> (b) details of each beneficial owner's beneficial interest, as may be prescribed by regulations;
> (c) the date on which a person became a beneficial owner;
> (d) the date on which a person ceased to be a beneficial owner;
> (e) where a nominee holds interest on behalf of the beneficial owner –
>
> (i) the name, residential address, service address, date of birth and nationality of each nominee holding the interest on behalf of the beneficial owner and the particulars and details of the interest held by the nominee; and
> (ii) the identity of the nominator, and where the nominator is a legal person, the identity of the natural person who ultimately owns or controls the nominator.

The scope of the Act is also noteworthy. Section 9(1) provides: 'Every legal person or legal arrangement, as the case may be, shall identify and verify its beneficial owners'.

This covers certain types of domestic and non-domestic companies, trusts, partnerships, and foundations.[51] The inclusion of trusts is important as in most countries there is no legal requirement to register trusts or at least to identify the beneficial owner of the trust.[52]

51 Legal persons in the non-domestic category comprise an international business company incorporated or continued or converted under the International Business Companies Act; a protected cell company incorporated under the Protected Cell Companies Act; and a company incorporated under the Companies (Special Licences) Act. A resident trustee of an international trust under the International Trusts Act; a general partner of a limited partnership under the Limited Partnerships Act; and a foundation established under the Foundations Act.

52 South Africa also has a similar provision. For a scathing report about the lack of registration requirements for both trusts and foundations see Tax Justice Network, *Financial Secrecy Index: Key Financial Secrecy Indicator 2: Trust and Foundation Register* (Tax Justice Network 2020) <https://fsi.taxjustice.net/PDF/2-Trusts-Foundations-Register.pdf>.

The threshold for reporting beneficial ownership is seen as being an 'Achilles heel' due to the ability of PEPs to avoid being identified.[53] Here the regulations made under the BOA 2020 provide that the controlling ownership interest threshold of at least 10% applies for the identification of the beneficial owners in the case of legal persons except for foundations. In the case of legal arrangements and foundations, all beneficial owners must be identified regardless of the threshold of controlling ownership interests.[54] Indeed it begs the question as to why there is any threshold requirement for beneficial ownership at all.

Is There a Central Register of Beneficial Ownership of Legal Persons?

Here section 5(7) of the BOA 2020 provides that the 'registerable particulars of the register of beneficial owners maintained under subsection 5(1) shall be submitted to the Financial Intelligence Unit in such form and manner as may be specified by the Financial Intelligence Unit'. A financial intelligence unit (FIU) 'serves as a national centre for the receipt and analysis of: (a) suspicious transaction reports; and (b) other information relevant to money laundering, associated predicate offences and terrorist financing, and for the dissemination of the results of that analysis'.[55] As a former FATF President has emphasised, the 'effective use of financial intelligence is a critical factor in identifying and tracking criminals, including through the exchange of information at the domestic and international levels'.[56]

Can Such Information Be Shared With Other Financial Intelligence Unit and Law Enforcement Agencies Through International Cooperation?

This is a vital requirement and it is noteworthy that the role of the Seychelles FIU includes

- Establishing cooperation with domestic and international institutions and foreign counterparts, entrusted with the responsibility for organising an effective AML/CFT regime.
- Exchanging information with foreign FIUs based on partnership principles in accordance with the Statute of the Egmont Group of Financial Intelligence Units and in accordance with the Memoranda of Understanding.

53 See Andres Knobel, *The Achilles Heel of Effective Beneficial Ownership Registration: Why Is Everyone Fixed on 25%?* (Tax Justice Network 2017) </www.taxjustice.net/2017/05/11/achilles-heel-effective-beneficial-ownership-registration-everyone-fixed-25/>.

54 *Beneficial Ownership Guidelines* issued by the Financial Services Authority and Financial Intelligence Unit 2020 5.

55 FATF Recommendation 29.

56 See "Remarks by FATF President Marshall Billingslea" at the FATF Ministerial Meeting, Washington, DC, 12 April 2019 <www.fatfgafi.org/publications/fatfgeneral/documents/speech-fatf-ministerial.html>.

The Egmont Group[57] describes itself as is a 'united body of 166 Financial Intelligence Units'[58] whose role is to provide a forum for FIUs around the world in order to

> improve cooperation in the fight against money laundering and financing of terrorism and to foster the implementation of domestic programs in this field, especially in the areas of information exchange, training, and the sharing of expertise.[59]

Is There a Public Register of Beneficial Ownership of Legal Persons?

The BOA 2020 makes no provision for a publicly accessible registry of beneficial ownership. The issue of public beneficial ownership records is discussed below. However, the lack of such a provision in the BOA 2020 suggests a reluctance to go further than making such information available to law enforcement authorities in case this causes companies to move to jurisdictions which offer greater protection.

Towards Beneficial Ownership Transparency in the Offshore World 2: The UK, BOTs, and CDs

The Panama Papers and Luanda Papers have highlighted that numerous African PEPs have used offshore jurisdictions allegedly through which to launder their proceeds of corruption. Of particular importance are the BOTs with the British Virgin Islands (BVI) being the jurisdiction of choice for the incorporation of many offshore companies named in the Panama Papers.[60]

The use of such companies to purchase high-end real estate for PEPs in safe-haven states is highlighted in a 2018 study by Global Witness which found that 'Over 87,000 properties in England and Wales valued at an excess of US$132.4 billion are owned by anonymous companies registered in tax havens'.[61] This reflects the findings of a 2014 study by Transparency International that 9.3% of properties in the City of Westminster, 7.3% in Kensington and Chelsea, and 4.5% in the City of London were owned by shell companies registered in an offshore 'secrecy' jurisdiction.[62] The study further revealed that London properties were held by offshore companies with the vast majority

57 Named after the location of its first meeting at the Egmont Palace in Belgium.

58 See Egmont Group "About the Egmont Group" <https://egmontgroup.org/en/contentabout>.

59 See the Egmont Charter 6. For a full discussion on the work of the Egmont Group and FIUs based in Africa see John Hatchard, 'The Role of Financial Intelligence Units in Combating Money Laundering: An African Perspective' 2022 (2) Journal of International and Comparative Law 103–30.

60 The Panama Papers disclosed that nearly 1,000 offshore companies were linked to more than 330 politicians, with 656 being located in the British Virgin Islands.

61 Global Witness press release, 17 March 2017.

62 Transparency International, *Corruption on Your Doorstep: How Corrupt Capital Is Used to Buy Property in the UK* (Transparency International 2014) 16.

being registered in the BOTs and CDs.[63] Not surprisingly, the use of offshore companies for the purchase and sale of property for PEPs in London has been described as 'prolific'.[64] The UK National Crime Agency has calculated that £90 billion is laundered through the UK each year and that 'this laundering can only be done, by and large, through British Overseas Territories [BOTs], which are central to this nefarious activity'.[65] This makes a case study of moves to enhance beneficial ownership transparency in the BOTs all the more significant in addressing money laundering by African PEPs.

In doing so, it must be emphasised that the use of such entities through which to purchase real estate and other property is perfectly legal. However, given the danger that they can be used to facilitate money laundering by PEPs, it is not surprising that the need to identify the beneficial ownership of such legal entities is now of international and national significance in the fight against money laundering by PEPs. Here the key is developing the political will to do so. The United Kingdom provides a helpful illustration of the point.

Law Enforcement Cooperation Between the UK, BOTs, and CDs

In 2016 the then British Prime Minister, David Cameron, proposed greater compliance by the BOTs and CDs to provide UK tax and law enforcement authorities with access to company ownership records. The proposal was made having regard to FATF and G20 initiatives and the UK Government's decision to introduce a public central register of beneficial ownership.[66]

This resulted in an Exchange of Notes between the UK Government and each of the key BOTs and the CDs. In each Note, the UK and respective government (referred to as the 'Participants') recognised:

> the importance of the provision of beneficial ownership information for the prevention and detection of corruption, money laundering, terrorism

63 Transparency International, *Corruption on Your Doorstep: How Corrupt Capital Is Used to Buy Property in the UK* (Transparency International 2014) 5. More than one-third of all foreign companies holding London property were incorporated in the British Virgin Islands (13,831 properties), Jersey 14% (5,960 properties), the Isle of Man 8.5% (3,472 properties) and Guernsey 8% (3,280 properties).

64 See *Solicitors Regulation Authority v Sharif*, 2019, unreported, Solicitors Disciplinary Tribunal, at [21]. Mr Sharif, a senior London solicitor, provided this information in mitigation when faced with a charge of failing to comply with AML KYC regulations in relation to the proposed purchase of high-end property in London by two foreign PEPs. For a comment see John Hatchard 'Legal Practitioners as Potential Money Launderers: Beneficial Ownership Transparency and PEPs: *Solicitors Regulation Authority v Sharif*' (2019) 31(1) Denning Law Journal 189.

65 Andrew Mitchell MP in the House of Commons debate of the Report Stage of the Sanctions and Anti-Money Laundering Bill, *Hansard,* 1 May 2018, 42. There are 14 BOTs including Anguilla, Bermuda, the British Virgin Islands, Cayman Islands, Gibraltar, Montserrat, and the Turks & Caicos Islands, which each offer a range of offshore financial services. The Crown Dependencies comprise the Bailiwick of Guernsey, the Bailiwick of Jersey, and the Isle of Man.

66 See Technical Protocol, at 3.

financing, financing of the proliferation of weapons of mass destruction and other serious and organised crime.[67]

Each individual Note focuses on three key commitments by each of the Participants:

1. To provide the law enforcement authorities of the other Participant with beneficial ownership information for corporate and legal entities incorporated in their respective jurisdictions.
2. To hold adequate, accurate and current beneficial ownership information for corporate and legal entities incorporated in their own jurisdictions.
3. To give law enforcement authorities of the Participants the 'automatic' right to the provision of unrestricted and timely (within twenty-four hours or, where urgently required, within an hour) beneficial ownership information held in the other jurisdiction.[68]

This is a significant development, especially given the fact that previously, as each BOT and CD is a separate jurisdiction for the purposes of international cooperation, such information could only be requested by the UK via the potentially lengthy and complex mutual legal assistance process.

The Exchange of Notes therefore provides for the 'timely, safe and secure access for law enforcement [and tax] authorities to beneficial ownership information', with the security of the request and information being specifically provided for in each Note.[69] The Notes are a neat example of the manner in which the political will can bring about a fundamental improvement in AML action. Perhaps not surprisingly, the new arrangements did not meet with universal approval with accusations that the UK government had 'managed to strong-arm the Crown Dependencies and a number of Overseas Territories into signing [the Exchange of Notes]'.[70]

Since then, the BOTs and CDs have reportedly made 'significant progress in implementing the commitments by introducing legislation and establishing, where they did not already exist, central registers or similar effective systems'.[71] This represents a major step forward in assisting law enforcement agencies and tax authorities identify the ultimate beneficial ownership of companies registered in the BOTs and CDs.

67 See *Exchange of Notes between the Government of the United Kingdom and the Government of the Cayman Islands in respect of the sharing of beneficial ownership information*, at 2.

68 A Technical Protocol is attached to each *Exchange of Notes* setting out the practicalities of the arrangements (Technical Protocol).

69 See Technical Protocol, at 7(vi).

70 See Fillipo Noseda, 'Too Much Information: When the UK Gets it Wrong' (2017) 21(2) Jersey and Guernsey Law Review 182, 193–94.

71 See statement to the House of Commons by Sir Alan Duncan, Minister for Europe and the Americas, HC Deb 1 May 2018, vol. 640.

Towards a Public Registry of Beneficial Ownership: the United Kingdom, BOTs, and CDs

Whilst making beneficial ownership information available to law enforcement authorities is a major step forward, the Panama Papers and Pandora Papers disclosures have increased pressure on countries to introduce a public registry of beneficial ownership.

The UK is the first G20 country to introduce such a register. Section 81 of the Small Business, Enterprise and Employment Act 2015 amended the Companies Act 2006 and requires companies to keep a 'register of people who have significant control over the company'. The annual returns by companies (known as 'confirmation statements') must contain beneficial ownership details. The register is accessible to the public free of charge.

At that point, the UK Government resisted the idea of imposing similar provisions on the BOTs or CDs, although Bermuda (1981) and Jersey (2018) already had already established central registers of beneficial ownership, with Montserrat having committed to doing so. However, all-party parliamentary pressure led to the UK Government agreeing to require all BOTs to introduce a public beneficial register. Section 51 of the Sanctions and Anti-Money Laundering Act 2018 is headed 'Public registers of beneficial ownership of companies registered in British Overseas Territories' and provides as follows:

> (1) For the purposes of the detection, investigation or prevention of money laundering, the Secretary of State must provide all reasonable assistance to the governments of the British Overseas Territories to enable each of those governments to establish a publicly accessible register of the beneficial ownership of companies registered in each government's jurisdiction.[72]

The register must be broadly in line with the UK provisions, noted earlier.[73]

Not surprisingly, the reaction from some OTs was highly critical. The key argument was that public beneficial ownership registers would have a significant deleterious financial impact on them as legal persons would relocate to more secretive locations. Thus, they should only be introduced if and when public registers become a global standard.[74] This has proved an unsustainable position, and Andrew Fahie, the Premier of the British Virgin Islands, has

72 Section 49(3) provides that 'Money laundering' has the meaning given by the Proceeds of Crime Act 2002, section 340(11).

73 Section 22(7) provides that 'a "publicly accessible register of the beneficial ownership of companies" means a register which, in the opinion of the Secretary of State, provides information broadly equivalent to that available in accordance with the provisions of Part 21A of the Companies Act 2006'.

74 See DS Smith, *Statement by Premier on the Royal Assent of the Sanctions and Anti-Money Laundering Bill* (Government of the Virgin Islands, 23 May 2018).

announced that the territory will adopt a publicly accessible register of beneficial ownership for companies, in line with international standards by 2023. The Government of the Cayman Islands has followed suit.[75]

During the parliamentary debate on the Act, a clause requiring the introduction of a similar provision for the CDs was withdrawn. This was in recognition of the very different constitutional relationship between the UK and the CDs. However, in June 2019 the CDs made a joint commitment to establish a public beneficial ownership register.[76]

The introduction of public beneficial registers in the UK, BOTs, and CDs is extremely welcome and is part of an international move towards beneficial ownership transparency.

This action is reinforced by the introduction of the 5th EU Anti-Money Laundering Directive which entered into force on 9 July 2018. The Directive (which was partly influenced by the publication of the Panama Papers) requires all states to allow 'any member of the general public' access to beneficial ownership registers to obtain information concerning the beneficial owner's month and year of birth, country of residence, and nationality, as well as the nature and extent of the beneficial interest held. It means that there is a clear shift towards a global commitment to address the vulnerability of beneficial ownership as a money laundering tool.[77]

Concluding Thoughts and Future Developments

The quality of life in a country does not depend primarily upon its size or resources but on its leadership.[78] Given their political power and influence, the failure of that leadership provides African PEPs with unique money laundering opportunities and the ability to control the AML controls. Even so, as argued in this chapter, they remain vulnerable if AML strategies are utilised effectively, both nationally and transnationally and beneficial ownership transparency is a key strategy. To be effective each country must adhere to the following principles.

Firstly, the establishment of a central beneficial ownership register.

As a GIABA recommendation puts it: 'Authorities of member States should create centralized systems for collecting, maintaining and disclosing/sharing accurate and up-to-date beneficial ownership information in a timely manner'.[79]

75 Statement by the Government of the Cayman Islands dated 9 October 2019.

76 'Joint Commitment by Guernsey, Jersey, and the Isle of Man: Registers of beneficial ownership of companies' Press release dated June 2019. This action is designed to bring the CDs into line with the requirements of the EU 5th Anti-Money Laundering Directive.

77 In another example of the challenge of obtaining the political will to comply with AML obligations, by March 2020 just 5 of the 27 EU member countries had established publicly available centralised registers of beneficial ownership. These were Bulgaria, Denmark, Latvia, Luxembourg, and Slovenia.

78 See the very eloquent view of James F Mitchell in *A Season of Light* 2001, Concepts Publishing, p 173 et seq. Mitchell was a former Prime Minister of St Vincent and the Grenadines.

79 Recommendation from a GIABA Regional Workshop on the 'Implementation of Beneficial Ownership Requirements', Abuja, Nigeria, 3–5 December 2019.

The effectiveness of this depends upon:

- All legal persons and legal entities being required to register beneficial ownership. This includes companies, trusts, foundations, and partnerships.
- The threshold for identifying beneficial ownership being suitably low. As noted earlier, in the case of Seychelles the threshold is very low or non-existent.
- The register to be accurate and updated as necessary. In practice this remains problematic in many African countries.

To enhance information gathering, the GIABA recommendation states:

- Relevant competent authorities should adequately supervise entities obligated to collect and maintain beneficial ownership information, and promptly apply effective, persuasive, and dissuasive sanctions for non-compliance.

Secondly, to provide that beneficial ownership information held in the register is made available to the national financial intelligence unit, and further, that such information can be shared with other national FIUs as well as with local law enforcement agencies. As the GIABA recommendation puts it:

> Member States should strengthen domestic collaboration and co-ordination, as well as international cooperation, relating to exchange of information on beneficial ownership.

The prevalence of money laundering by African PEPs on a global scale emphasises that this requires a global response through maintaining effective international cooperation by means of mutual legal assistance.[80]

Thirdly, to provide beneficial ownership information upon request to law enforcement bodies in other countries or jurisdictions. In practice it is essential for swift and efficient process for requesting beneficial ownership information. The UK/BOT approach provides a helpful model for cooperation between states.

Fourthly, to provide a public register of beneficial ownership. This is the most difficult and controversial issue. Some have argued that the secrecy attaching to such registers is fundamental to the effective operation of the offshore world and the introduction of such registers will lead to companies moving to those jurisdictions that continue to offer secrecy, and further, that they raise significant privacy issues so that effective safeguards are necessary to counterbalance the importance of transparency and the right to privacy. This may mean restricting the amount of personal data that is made available to the public.

80 A discussion on this issue is beyond the scope of this chapter. See generally John Hatchard, *Combating Corruption: Legal Approaches to Supporting Good Governance and Integrity in Africa* (Edward Elgar Publishing 2014) chapter 8.

Yet the introduction of public registers of beneficial ownership is seen by many as a game changer, and this is gathering pace as increasing numbers of states and jurisdictions are committing to their introduction.[81] It should be noted that the focus of the FATF is on law enforcement cooperation and there is no mention in the FATF Recommendations of the need for countries to establish a public register of beneficial ownership of companies and trusts. Indeed, in recognition of the fact that its members could not agree on the point, the FATF has suggested that countries and territories *could* introduce such registers.

The Political Will and Economic Implications

Combating money laundering by PEPs requires the political will not only on the part of 'victim' states and especially in those states that facilitate the laundering to take effective action. Action is facilitating states is especially important as PEPs do not enjoy the controls that they do domestically.

The FATF Recommendations set out the strategy for doing so and, as all African states are members of the FATF or a FSRB, they are required to implement those provisions. If these are done effectively, despite their ability to 'control the AML controls', PEPs will be vulnerable to AML actions.

Work in Progress

A feature of the work of the FATF is its constant review of AML standards and the updating of its Recommendations as a result. The 2022 revision to Recommendation 24 and its Interpretive Note were noted earlier. A review of Recommendation 25 is now underway.

There is also the economic reality to consider for some offshore jurisdictions may refuse to implement the relevant laws for fear of driving away business to other jurisdictions which offer greater secrecy. Accordingly, all financial centres must enjoy a level playing field, and this requires the establishment of a global standard relating to beneficial ownership transparency.

It is remarkable how rapidly the issue of transparency in beneficial ownership has come to the top of the AML agenda. Indeed prior to 2016, the idea of public beneficial ownership registers was unthinkable. Now some of the most notorious secretive offshore financial centres have agreed to establish such registers.

In recent years several African states have introduced legislation providing for limited beneficial ownership transparency. Increased efforts are required to 'persuade' all African countries to implement their FATF obligations.

The message of this chapter is that despite their ability to 'control the controls', PEPs are increasingly vulnerable to having their money laundering activities revealed. The move towards beneficial ownership transparency is certainly a move in the right direction.

81 See, for example, the Economic Crime (Transparency and Enforcement) Act 2022 (UK).

11 Can FATF's Focus on Beneficial Ownership Aid Anti-Corruption Efforts in a 'Low-Capacity' Country?

Challenges From the Front Line in Nigeria

Jackie Harvey, Peter Sproat, Sue Turner and Tony Ward[1]

Introduction

Nigeria has been described as the 'powerhouse' of West Africa[2] and is projected to become the 'third most populous country in the world by 2050'.[3] As a major oil producer for well over half a century, Nigeria should be a wealthy country, instead, its current per capita income places it in the group of lower-middle-income economies.[4] One contributing factor to this state of affairs is corruption, or as the Human Environmental Development Agenda (HEDA) – the Nigerian human rights non-governmental organisation (NGO) – noted recently: 'Corruption has robbed Nigeria of opportunities for development'.[5] Nigeria ranks in the bottom quartile of countries in

1 Chapter drafted by the authors on behalf of the additional project team members including Abdullahi Shehu, Abdullahi Bello, Petrus van Duyne, Sam Sittlington, Alan Doig, Jan van Koningsveld and Sinan Gonul.

2 GIABA, *Mutual Evaluation Report. Anti- Money Laundering and Combatting the Financing of Terrorism: Nigeria* (GIABA 2008) 9 <www.giaba.org/media/f/299_Mutual%20Evaluation%20Report%20of%20Nigeria.pdf> accessed 9 September 2022; GIABA, *Anti-money Laundering and Counter-terrorist Financing Measures – Federal Republic of Nigeria, Second Round Mutual Evaluation Report* (GIABA, August 2021) 3 <www.fatf-gafi.org%2Fmedia%2Ffatf%2Fdocuments%2Freports%2Fmer-fsrb%2FGIABA-Mutual%2520Evaluation%2520Report%2520of%2520the%2520Federal%2520Republic%2520of%2520Nigeria.pdf&usg=AOvVaw3LG3aQ0By5NUyOdgY2gzYw> accessed 9 September 2022.

3 *International Monetary Fund, Nigeria: 2019 Article IV Consultation, Country Report No. 19/92, 5 April (IMF 2019).*

4 World Bank classification; see <https://data.worldbank.org/country/XN>.

5 HEDA, *A Compendium of 100 High Profile Corruption Cases in Nigeria,* November, published by the Human and Environmental Development Agenda, (2020) 9 <https://hedang.org/wp-content/uploads/2020/12/2020-Compendium.pdf> accessed 12 January 2022.

DOI: 10.4324/9781003253808-13

Transparency International's Corruption Perception Index (CPI)[6] and consistently ranks 'low' in the Absence of Corruption section of the World Justice Project's Rule of Law Index.[7]

Corruption in Nigeria is not only a historical phenomenon but appears to be a continuing characteristic of the country's governance and a contributor to its poor GDP per capita. The International Monetary Fund[8] calls for increased attention by the Nigerian authorities to enhance governance transparency, particularly in respect to public sector accountability, while the Inter-Governmental Action Group against Money Laundering in West Africa (GIABA) similarly suggested:

> The corrosive effects of illicit proceeds generation, especially proceeds from large-scale endemic corruption and related [money laundering], have undermined effective and transparent governance and development in Nigeria over many years.[9]

Despite this, corruption itself should not be regarded as a natural situation – it is the 'outcome of the power to make decisions that circumvent existing rules and criteria to gain an advantage'.[10] There are myriad challenges in preventing its occurrence and in pursuing those that are corrupt, and many proposals to reduce or impede corruption have been posited, one of which is the use of the anti-money laundering (AML) and asset recovery policies recommended by the Financial Action Task Force (FATF) – an intergovernmental organisation established by the G7 in 1989.

This chapter considers the prospects for one of the more recently emphasised aspects of the FATF's AML policies, its recommendations on beneficial ownership (BO),[11] and whether greater transparency on BO would enhance anti-corruption efforts in Nigeria. The rationale for this focus was provided by the commitment made at the London international anti-corruption summit in May 2016 that Nigeria would create a public central register of company BO information.[12] The first part of the chapter is this introduction, and the second provides a very brief description of the origins of the FATF and its place in

6 The Corruption Perception Index for 2021 scored Nigeria at 24 out of 100, ranking it 154 out of 180, see <www.transparency.org/en/cpi/2021/index/nga> accessed 9 September 2022.

7 In 2021 Nigeria was ranked at 119/139 countries for the absence of corruption scoring 0.32, in contrast the UK scores 0.82 <https://worldjusticeproject.org/rule-of-law-index/country/2021/Nigeria/Absence%20of%20Corruption/> accessed 9 September 2022.

8 International Monetary Fund, *Nigeria: Selected Issues* (Country Report 19/93) (IMF, 2019).

9 GIABA (n 2) 24.

10 Petrus van Duyne and Jackie Harvey, *Grand Corruption in Nigeria: What Can Be Learned from a Review of Cases?* (GI-ACE Research Programme Working Paper 12, 2021) 3 <https://ace.globalintegrity.org/wp-content/uploads/2021/06/grand-corruption-in-nigeria-harvey-06-2021-1-1.pdf> accessed 12 January 2022.

11 FATF Recommendations 24 and 25.

12 Country Statement from Nigeria, London Anti-Corruption Summit, 12 May 2016 <https://assets.publishing.service.gov.uk/government/uploads/system/uploads/attachment_data/

international law and politics. The third delineates the notion of BO and explains its inclusion in the FATF's AML regime. The fourth considers the usefulness of information on BO in relation to cases of grand corruption in Nigeria. The fifth charts the progress the Nigerian authorities have made in introducing the FATF's Recommendations with respect to BO. The sixth considers some of the practical challenges associated with the creation of a register of BO. This is followed by a discussion and some suggestions on practical changes and modification that could be implemented to improve Nigeria's chances of establishing a useful BO register and concludes with some wider reflections these have prompted on the legitimacy and effectiveness of the AML regime as a whole.

Before considering the origins of the FATF and its place in international law and politics, it is necessary to note the chapter is based on findings from a UK Aid–funded research project that considered BO as part of the global fight against corruption and money laundering.[13] Our project focused on grand corruption in Nigeria with the objective of assessing and proposing improvements to the identification and tracking of BO in Nigeria to increase the likelihood of recovering the proceeds of grand corruption.[14]

The Origins of the FATF and Its Place in International Law and Politics

The FATF was established by the G7 at their meeting in Paris in 1989. The agenda for this meeting contained 11 issues. Money laundering was a subject of the last one, on drugs, of which the last two sections were devoted to criminal assets recovery and the creation of a financial action task force. The 1990 Financial Action Task Force on Money Laundering Report made 40 Recommendations to nation states as to how they might introduce laws and procedures to identify and report suspicions of drug money[15] and ultimately recover these criminal assets. An examination of the document indicates that the approach was always going to be reliant upon collective action. FATF's conclusion drew attention to the importance of political support, that their recommendations should be rolled out globally, and that the process would

file/523799/NIGERIA-_FINAL_COUNTRY_STATEMENT-UK_SUMMIT.pdf> accessed 12 October 2022.

13 The cross-disciplinary research project involved a team of academics and practitioners led by Northumbria University and funded by UKAid as part of the Global Integrity Anti-Corruption Evidence Programme (GI-ACE), Tracking Beneficial Ownership and the Proceeds of Corruption: Evidence from Nigeria.

14 For further information about the project please see <https://ace.globalintegrity.org/projects/benowner/>.

15 FATF, *The Forty Recommendations of the Financial Action Task Force on Money Laundering* (FATF, 1990). It is worth noting that this 'simple' document of 28 pages plus and appendix of six pages for the first version expanded to 134 pages for the 2012 version and was supported by a further raft of legislation, regulations and guidance notes: <www.fatf-gafi.org/publications/fatfrecommendations/documents/internationalstandardsoncombatingmoneylaunderingandthefinancingofterrorismproliferation-thefatfrecommendations.html> accessed 9 September 2022.

be expedited through regular assessment of progress. The wider the range of countries applying their recommendations, 'the greater their efficiency would be'. Nothing was mentioned, however, about how countries would be encouraged to adopt the rules other than by 'political impetus'.[16]

After this somewhat inauspicious start, the FATF has undergone a 'rapid evolution from a fringe institution to a key body of governance'.[17] The focus of its recommendations has moved beyond concern with prevention of laundering the proceeds arising from drug production and trafficking and into other areas. These include the financing of terrorism and proliferation of weapons of mass destruction.[18] The scope of AML thus widened from drugs to all financially motivated crimes via serious or organised crime. The range of financial institutions that perform AML duties has broadened (also bringing within its scope designated non-financial businesses and professions),[19] while the duties themselves have deepened and involve a greater set of tasks than was originally envisioned. This far wider scope is too much for the one intergovernmental body to monitor and supervise, and a series of FATF-style regional bodies (FSRBs) have been created. The relationship between the two was set out by the FATF in 2012.[20] This document notes the pre-eminence of the FATF as 'the only standard-setting body and the guardian and arbiter of the application of its standard', wherein the FSRBs are 'free-standing Organisations'[21] without hierarchy; however, the latter only have 'recognition' by the FATF.

Despite the fact the FATF or any of its FSRBs do not have authority to issue directives to countries, FATF's increasingly detailed 'policy recommendations' have been incorporated and updated by all but a few nation states. Numerous authors have pointed out for many countries compliance with the recommendations is far from voluntary.[22] The widespread acceptance of the

16 FATF, *The Forty Recommendations of the Financial Action Task Force on Money Laundering* (FATF, 1990) 28. It is worth noting that this 'simple' document of 28 pages plus and appendix of six pages for the first version expanded to 134 pages for the 2012 version and was supported by a further raft of legislation, regulations and guidance notes: <www.fatf-gafi.org/publications/fatfrecommendations/documents/internationalstandardsoncombatininternationalstandardsoncombatingmoneylaunderingandthefinancingofterrorismproliferation-thefatfrecommendations.html> accessed 9 September 2022.

17 Mark Nance, 'Rethinking FATF: An Experimentalist Interpretation of the Financial Action Task Force' (2018) 69 Crime, Law & Social Change 132.

18 Susan Turner and Jonathan Bainbridge, 'An Anti-Money Laundering Timeline and the Relentless Regulatory Response' (June 2018) 82 The Journal of Criminal Law.

19 DNFBP is a classification introduced by the FATF to include economic sectors deemed to pose a risk of money laundering. Examples include the accounting profession, estate agents and the legal profession.

20 FATF, *High-Level Principles and Objectives for FATF and FATF-Style Regional Bodies* (FATF, October 2012).

21 FATF, *High-Level Principles and Objectives for FATF and FATF-Style Regional Bodies* (FATF, October 2012) 1.

22 See, for example, Terence Halliday, Michael Levi and Peter Reuter, 'Why do Transnational Legal Orders Persist? The Curious Case of Money-Laundering Controls' in Gregory Shaffer Ely Aaronson (eds) *Transnational Legal Ordering of Criminal Justice* (CUP 2020); Petrus van Duyne, Jackie Harvey and Liliya Gelemerova, *The Critical Handbook of Money Laundering* (Palgrave Macmillan 2018).

FATF's 40 recommendations is in part a consequence of FATF's assertion that failing to implement them could result in a country being ostracised from the international financial system, with far-reaching consequences. In the face of such potentially draconian consequences, Nigeria may have felt that it had few options other than to join their FSRB[23] and that through this membership of GIABA, they 'consent' to the recommendations.

It would no doubt be too simple to attribute FATF's influence solely to this coercive power. In legal terms, FATF benefitted from the degree of formal recognition accorded by the UN Convention against Transnational Organized Crime and UN Convention against Corruption (UNTOC and UNCAC). In both Conventions the 'State Parties are called upon to use as a guideline' the recommendations of FATF and the FSRBs (although neither is mentioned by name in either convention (UNTOC art. 7(3); UNCAC art. 14(4)). More important than this limited, non-binding legal authority is the legitimacy derived from the expertise of FATF and the FSRBs, which lends their recommendations an aura of objectivity. As Hülsse and Kerwer argue,[24] this both avoids the imputation that countries who implement their recommendations are simply bowing to the demands of more powerful states and saves governments the work of devising their own solutions. The danger, however, is that compliance with FATF recommendations will neither be tailored to local conditions nor backed by the political will to make them succeed. We shall see that both these concerns could be argued to apply to Nigeria with respect to BO.

BO and Its Role Within the AML Regime

The FATF's 40 recommendations can be viewed as an attempt to introduce situational crime control to the financial system of every country. The aim is to transform each individual financial gatekeeper into a guardian of the wider financial sector. The belief is this monitoring and reporting of financial activity to the authorities will deter acquisitive criminals – including the corrupt – from using the financial system to launder and – in the case of disguise of BO – hide their ill-gotten gains using legal persons or arrangements fronted by others. Specific recommendations on BO have been part of the FATF's attempts to increase the transparency of national financial systems since proposals on transparency and (arrangements for) BO of legal persons were first introduced into the 40 recommendations in 2003 as recommendations R33 and R34, subsequently renumbered as recommendations R24 and R25[25] in the 2012 version.

23 Jackie Harvey, Susan Turner, Tony Ward, Peter Sproat and Jonathan Bainbridge *Transnational Criminal Law: A Case Study of the International Anti-Money Laundering Framework as Applied in Nigeria, a Case of Smoke and Mirrors* (2021) <https://ace.globalintegrity.org/wp-content/uploads/2021/03/Jackie_Harvey-Smoke_Mirrors-1.pdf> accessed 12 January 2022.

24 Rainer Hülsse and Dieter Kerwer, 'Global Standards in Action: Insights from Anti Money-Laundering Regulation' (2007) 14(5) Organization 625.

25 The topic is also explored through dedicated publications by FATF: 'Concealment of Beneficial Ownership', July 2018; Guidance for a Risk-based approach for legal professionals, June 2019; and Best Practices on Beneficial Ownership for Legal Persons, October 2019.

Here it should be noted that a beneficial owner is the natural person (or one of the persons) who ultimately owns or controls a legal person or arrangement or the natural person(s) on whose behalf a transaction is conducted. It also includes those persons who exercise ultimate effective control over a legal person or arrangement, considering shares, voting rights and influence, including both direct and indirect interests. While the FATF do not note a figure, a widely used disclosure threshold for ownership or control of a company or trust is 25% , a level used in a wide range of jurisdictions, including the UK[26] and the US.[27]

Having the requisite legal framework in place to enable disclosure to take place is assessed under technical compliance; how well the framework works in practice is assessed under effectiveness.[28] Under the recommendations, a country is required to maintain adequate, accurate and timely information on BO and to ensure access to that information. The effectiveness of a jurisdiction's BO framework is assessed under Immediate Outcome 5. As set out in the FATF's 2013 methodology, country assessors consider, firstly, whether a country's legal persons and arrangements could be misused for criminal purposes (including availability of appropriate sanctions in the event that they are), and secondly, whether information on their beneficial owners is readily available to the relevant authorities (including basic information being in the public domain). Further, R24 and R25 are framed in expectation of information-sharing amongst agencies within a single jurisdiction and between different jurisdictions.

Given the salience of BO, FATF is currently undertaking a public consultation[29] regarding amendments to these recommendations to 'strengthen the international standard' to 'ensure greater transparency'.[30] There can be little

26 The UK HM Treasury is currently undertaking a consultation to assess *'the Overall Effectiveness of the* [Regulatory and Supervisory] *Regimes*' <www.gov.uk/government/consultations/call-for-evidence-review-of-the-uks-amlctf-regulatory-and-supervisory-regime> accessed 9 September 2022.

27 In the US, the Corporate Transparency Act, 2021 has established a (non-public) register of BO.

28 FATF, *FATF Methodology for Assessing Compliance with the FATF Recommendations and the Effectiveness of AML/CFT Systems* (2013) <www.fatf-gafi.org/publications/mutualevaluations/documents/fatf-methodology.html> accessed November 2020.

29 See FATF 'Revisions to Recommendation 24 and its Interpretative Note – Public Consultation' <www.fatf-gafi.org/publications/fatfrecommendations/documents/public-consultation-r24.html> accessed 9 September 2022.

30 FATF updated R24 in Match 2022 to further strengthen the approach to the collation, retention and sharing of up-to-date information on BO in a timely manner with the competent authorities. The update requires countries to follow a risk-based assessment of national legal persons and of foreign created ones that are linked to their country. Further that public authorities should have access to BO information of legal persons during public procurement. See FATF, 'Public Statement on Revisions to R.24' <www.fatf-gafi.org/publications/fatfrecommendations/documents/r24-statement-march-2022.html#:~:text=Paris%2C%204%20March%202022%20%2D%20The,to%2Ddate%20information%20on%20the> accessed 11 October 2022.

doubt that this requires huge compliance costs in time and staff.[31] The mandated system presupposes an extensive national resource base (within both the police authorities and the regulated sector) to effectively operate the FATF standards. This then begs the question as to whether the availability of BO information in a country such as Nigeria would provide a useful additional tool to the authorities in their attempts to combat corruption, making the resource burden worthwhile.

Will Disclosure of BO Be Useful?[32]

Posing a question about the potential usefulness of BO disclosure for a country such as Nigeria may appear a little strange. However, some academics have argued that the FATF's guidelines are ethnocentric and designed to work in G7-like developed economies which have well-developed structures of governance and sophisticated financial sectors.[33] The FATF has not accepted this charge, although it has acknowledged that some countries might struggle in their attempts to achieve an 'effective prioritisation and implementation of the FATF standards on money laundering and terrorist financing'.[34] These it designates as 'low-capacity countries'.[35] Certainly Nigeria appears to fulfil at least some of the criteria to meet this designation, as less than half of adults have bank accounts and the shadow or informal economy accounts for almost half of GDP.[36] More relevant for the purposes of our discussion is the question whether recommendations on BO are needed given that grand corruption

31 Petrus C van Duyne, Wouter de Zanger and François HG Kristen, 'Greedy of Crime-money. The Reality and Ethics of Asset Recovery' in PC van Duyne et al. (eds), *Corruption, Greed and Crime Money. Sleaze and Shady Economy in Europe and Beyond* (Wolf Legal Publishers Nijmegen 2014).

32 **Some of this discussion also appears in our working paper Petrus C van Duyne and Jackie H 'Harvey Grand Corruption in Nigeria: What Can Be Learned from a Review of Cases?' (2021) <https://ace.globalintegrity.org/wp-content/uploads/2021/06/grand-corruption-in-nigeria-harvey-06-2021.pdf>.**

33 Van Duyne et al. (n 31); NV Azinge-Agbire, *Regulating and Combatting Money Laundering and Terrorist Financing: The Law in Emerging Economies* (Routledge 2014).

34 FATF, *Guidance on Capacity Building for Mutual Evaluations and Implementation of the FATF Standards within Low-Capacity Countries.* (FATF 2008) 3 <www.fatf-gafi.org/media/fatf/documents/reports/Capacity%20building%20LCC.pdf> accessed 1 February 2022.

35 FATF refrains from identifying countries as falling within this designation. Instead, it sets out criteria for determining a country to be 'low capacity' (FATF, *Guidance on Capacity Building for Mutual Evaluations and Implementation of the FATF Standards within Low-Capacity Countries.* (FATF 2008) 3 <www.fatf-gafi.org/media/fatf/documents/reports/Capacity%20building%20LCC.pdf> accessed 1 February 2022) 4–5:

(i) Competing priorities for scare government resources;
(ii) Severe lack of resources and skilled workforce to implement Government programmes;
(iii) Overall weakness in legal institutions;
(iv) Dominant informal sector and cash-based economy;
(v) Poor documentation and data retention systems; and,
(vi) Very small financial sector.

36 IMF (n 8)

in Nigeria is quite blatant and, in practice, employs less complex forms often involving simple cash withdrawal, misappropriation, diversion or straightforward disappearance of public funds.[37]

It was, therefore, appropriate to look further into how far the concealment of BO does in fact play a part in cases of grand corruption in Nigeria. As part of our project, we analysed over 100 cases of grand corruption, defined for purposes of our study as

> serious or large-scale perversion of a person's integrity in the performance of duty or work by bribery etc., where 'grand' refers to either the scale or the seriousness of the activity, which may include the harm it inflicts.

We recognise that an accurate delineation of the important element 'grand' remains problematic. Setting any financial threshold remains arbitrary: is $1 million enough to classify a case as 'grand corruption'? We consider that there is also another element that delineates 'grand' – the connection with higher levels of political or entrepreneurial decision-making. This may be more decisive because of its association with the ability to exert influence. It was this focus that we applied to our review of the cases of grand corruption.

The starting point for our investigation into the disguise of BO in the hiding of the proceeds of grand corruption was an interrogation of data collected from several sources. The main sources were the compendia of corruption cases produced by the Nigerian civil society organisation HEDA. It produced its first Compendium of *100* High-profile Corruption Cases in Nigeria in 2018, and this has been followed by those of 2019, 2020 and most recently 2021.[38] Their publication constitutes the most detailed secondary source of information on corruption in Nigeria we have found, and in doing so included cases we view as grand corruption. HEDA itself looked for high-profile corruption cases brought to court during the last decade involving public officers and 'substantial' sums and derived its cases from the Economic and Financial Crimes Commission (EFCC), the Independent and Corrupt Practices Commission (ICPC) documents and other sources. Unfortunately, because it is

37 Jackie Harvey, Abdullahi Bello, Alan Doig, Petrus C van Duyne, Sinan Gonul, Jan van Koningsveld, Abdullahi Shehu, Sam Sittlington, Peter Sproat, Susan Turner and Tony Ward, *Tracking Beneficial Ownership and the Proceeds of Corruption: Evidence from Nigeria*, Final Project Report (Northumbria University, October 2021).

38 Our analysis was based on the content of the 2018 and 2019. The 2020 compendium was produced after we had completed our analysis of the 2018 and 2019 data. This version removed some of the older cases that seem to have been 'ongoing' with no further court information available: five cases that we had excluded from our analysis either because the cases had been dismissed (three), charges had been dropped (one) or did not meet our definition (one). In addition, this version of the report removed four cases that we had included in our analysis (one convicted, one pending due to hospital admission with no further information, another ongoing with no update and a final one removed without record). The 2020 version introduced 59 new cases that do not show any fundamental differences to those included in our analysis. The 2021 version was published in November 2021.

produced by another, we cannot say anything about the relationship between these 100 cases and the totality of all known cases. What we can say with reasonable confidence is that, given their sources, they are a good sample of detected grand corruption cases.

HEDA's compendia were not the only source from which we extracted information. We also looked at the World Bank's STAR asset recovery database and reports by Transparency International that mentioned Nigeria. Like HEDA itself, we examined the websites of the EFCC,[39] ICPC[40] and Nigeria's Code of Conduct Bureau (CCB), although in the case of the latter we note that apart from three tables of cases handled by the independent Code of Conduct Tribunal, there was no database. In addition to the websites of anti-corruption agencies we also extracted information from that of another Nigerian based NGO – the Cleen Foundation – established in 1998 to promote public safety, security and access to justice by carrying out empirical research. We also made use of news reports to provide additional and/or current information on the cases. From this database we removed cases of low-level corruption, dismissed/acquitted cases, deaths before conviction and cases with a serious lack of information. This left us with some 60 cases that we reviewed.

Our analysis of the information on grand corruption provided clear evidence of the nature and extent of grand corruption and how easy it was to misuse funds for personal gain. While it did not provide a large compendium of BO cases. it was evident that BO was disguised in a significant number of the 60 cases, albeit in ways that were not especially sophisticated. Sixteen of the 60 cases[41] (27%) made use of immediate family, friends or close associates as a means of removing the proceeds. This frequently involved contracts being awarded to companies run by close friends/business associates or family – usually wives and sons acting as front figures for a shell corporation; in five cases relatives were specifically mentioned as co-defendants. In these cases, proceeds were placed in bank accounts in the name of a direct relative

39 Their website provides a PDF 'High Profile, Oil Subsidy, etc. Matters Being Prosecuted' which appears to have been produced in 2015 <www.efccnigeria.org/efcc/images/HIGH%20PROFILE%20CASES%20BEING%20PROSECUTED%20BY%20THE%20EFCC%20FOR%20%20%20%20%20%20%20AG.pdf>. In addition, they have produced an annual report of convictions for the years 2013–2016 relating to all economic crime and fraud convictions. The confiscation and recovery information cannot be connected to a database with information about perpetrators and predicate offences. The group TransparencIT <https://transparencit.com/2018-mid-year-convictions-of-efcc-and-icpc/> refers to the numbers of prosecutions by the EFCC for the period January to June 2018, however, without any details.

40 Databases: (1) records of funds and properties recovered from 2006 to 2019; (2) a cash refund list of two pages; (3) status of criminal and civil cases as at March 2015; (4) the data collection on enforcement and petitions until 2017 consisted of tables that were not suitable for statistical analysis.

41 Note the analysis is based on the 60 cases; most involved many approaches and thus have been coded multiple times.

or close friend. Subsequent follow-up transactions, such as the purchase of assets, namely property (in Nigeria and sometimes overseas) and high-value goods (planes, yachts etc.), were also in the name of relatives or friends. There appears little apparent concern about how straightforward it might be to link the financial traces from these frontmen/women to the criminal perpetrator of the corrupt act.

There are 24 cases (40%) in which Nigerian companies have been specifically mentioned or arraigned as co-defendants. These were either as shell companies or as investments in and of themselves. Often multiple companies were used, all of which were domiciled in Nigeria and had successfully managed to open bank accounts. Eight of the cases make specific mention of banks: seven where the shell companies held accounts and a further one where a bank 'warehoused' funds on behalf of the defendant.

Across the cases, purchase of property was widespread, and 17 of the cases (28%) involved the purchase of property both in Nigeria and elsewhere. There are some high-profile cases of corruption that show the importance of professional enablers.[42] Lawyers featured prominently in the cases of Alison-Madueke[43] and of Ibori,[44] arranging for money to be moved in accordance with their client's instructions. In the case of the former, property was held in trust for the suspect with the lawyer acting on client instructions to disburse the rental receipts; and in the case of Ibori, his lawyer used their own firm's client account to move funds while agents were used to act as nominee directors of companies. Our findings appear consistent with those of the most recent mutual evaluation, which notes: 'Most [money laundering] predicates occur domestically, and their proceeds are laundered in Nigeria. However, large sums, particularly from corruption and other major schemes, are transferred out of Nigeria and laundered abroad'.[45]

Considering the evidence that BO is disguised in cases of grand corruption, how might adoption of BO rules and creation of a registry prevent or, more realistically, reduce opportunity for disguise to occur in practice? Certainly, the intent of the FATF recommendations is, in the first instance, to reduce opportunity for disguise, hence greater transparency is regarded as a deterrent. An additional benefit is that registry creation should speed up investigations by the relevant anti-corruption agencies by making it more straightforward for them to 'uncover who actually benefits from the ownership of an asset – for

42 Olatunde Otusanya, Solabomi Ajibolade and Eddy Omolehinwa, 'The Role of Financial Intermediaries in Elite Money Laundering Practices: Evidence from Nigeria' (2012) 15(1) Journal of Money Laundering Control.

43 Diezani Alison-Madueke, former Minister for Petroleum Resources under Goodluck Jonathan who oversaw Nigeria's state-owned oil company.

44 James Ibori, Governor of Nigeria's oil-rich Delta State from 1999 to 2007.

45 GIABA (n 2) 21.

example a company or real estate that is involved in a corrupt scheme'.[46] However, there are different approaches and ways in which BO information is collected, controlled and shared. For example, not all countries have elected to make the contents of the register open to the wider public, although Open Ownership[47] – an NGO that helps countries generate quality data on company ownership that complies with international standards – argues that public access provides a means not only of reducing opportunity for corruption but also for building trust in governments. This then leads us to consider Nigeria's attempts to introduce legislation on BO.

Nigeria's Progress on AML and the Laws on BO Disclosure

Elsewhere we have set out in detail the development of the AML regime in Nigeria tracking its implementation from the first Money Laundering Decree No. 3 of 1995.[48] The enactment of legislation and associated agency creation was in part driven by Nigeria having been listed as a non-cooperative state (the Non-Cooperative Countries and Territories [NCCT] designation) from 2001 until its removal in 2006.[49] However, the introduction of new laws and institutions guarantees neither compliance with the technical rules of an external organisation nor an AML system that is effective in practice. FATF assesses the effectiveness of a country's AML regime on a periodic basis through a system of peer or mutual evaluation. The country underwent its first mutual evaluation in 2008, carried out on behalf of the FATF by GIABA. As discussed below, this evaluation identified several deficiencies that required attention. As noted by van Duyne et al.[50] in 2011, Nigeria went onto an 'improving list'[51] until its delisting following the sixth follow-up report in May 2013. Since

46 World Bank, *Enhancing Government Effectiveness and Transparency: The Fight against Corruption* (World Bank 2020) 250 <https://documents1.worldbank.org/curated/en/235541600116631094/pdf/Enhancing-Government-Effectiveness-and-Transparency-The-Fight-Against-Corruption.pdf> accessed 15 October 2021.

47 Open Ownership 'What we do' <www.openownership.org/what-we-do/>.

48 Harvey et al. (n 23).

49 See FATF, 'Annual Review of Non-Cooperative Countries and Territories 2006–2007' (2007) Eighth NCCT Review 11 <www.fatf-gafi.org/media/fatf/documents/reports/2006%2020 07%20NCCT%20ENG.pdf> accessed 9 September 2022.

50 Van Duyne et al. (n 31).

51 FATF stopped using the NCCT listing when the last country was removed in 2006 (see www.fatf-gafi.org/publications/high-riskandnon-cooperativejurisdictions/more/aboutthenon-cooperativecountriesandterritoriesncctinitiative.html?hf=10&b=0&s=desc(fatf_releasedate). It replaced this system by a series of 'public statements' about countries with 'strategic deficiencies' and those that were 'improving' these are referred to as 'high-risk and other monitored jurisdictions' (see www.fatf-gafi.org/publications/high-riskandnon-cooperativejurisdictions/?hf=10&b=0&s=desc(fatf_releasedate)).

then, the country has avoided identification as a country with strategic deficiencies in its framework and thus is no longer subject to related international sanctions.

The 2008 mutual evaluation scored against 40 recommendations and an additional nine special recommendations (largely focused on counter-terrorist financing). Despite FATF's removal of Nigeria from the list of NCCTs two years earlier, the review team found Nigeria to be compliant against only 2 of the 49 recommendations. They were, however, partially compliant against 22 and largely compliant against a further 7 of the recommendations. Unfortunately, they were found to be non-compliant on the remaining 18. In summary, the evaluation team found that the country had a comprehensive AML framework but no comprehensive framework against terrorist financing. Despite the apparently comprehensive AML legislative framework, the report noted little evidence that the authorities were able to implement that framework. The evaluation team highlighted five main areas that the authorities needed to address: inadequate resources for dealing with large and complex cases; deficiency in data in respect of prosecutions and convictions and in connection with suspicious transaction reports (STRs); poor controls within designated non-financial businesses and professions (DNFBPs); issues over transparency and of identification of BO; and the need to improve international financial intelligence unit (FIU) cooperation. Following this evaluation, Nigeria was the subject of seven follow-up reports on progress in addressing these deficiencies, with the last report being in May 2015. No further documentation is made available through the GIABA site, and there is no statement of Nigeria's removal from that process.

The most recent second-round evaluation of Nigeria[52] occurred in the autumn of 2019 with the report published in August 2021. This report notes that Nigeria has 'improved its AML/CFT legal and institutional frameworks in line with the FATF standards',[53] which is hardly a ringing endorsement. Indeed, it goes on to comment somewhat tortuously that Nigeria 'has implemented an AML/CFT system that is averagely effective in some respects'.[54] Of course, it could be argued that for a 'low-capacity' country with extensive corruption, managing an 'average' performance is in fact a positive outcome.

52 GIABA refer to their report as the second round (with the first having been in 2008). This round equates to the equivalent fourth round of FATF reviews as it was conducted in accordance with the revised 2012 Recommendations and in compliance with a model under which technical compliance is separated from evaluation of 'effectiveness'. See FATF, *Methodology for Assessing Compliance with the FATF Recommendations and the Effectiveness of AML/CFT Systems* (2013) <www.fatf-gafi.org/publications/mutualevaluations/documents/fatf-methodology.html>.

53 GIABA (n 2) 5.

54 GIABA (n 2) 6.

From the most recent evaluation report (the 2021 Report), it might appear that Nigeria has managed to improve its AML regime. The evaluation of technical compliance found Nigeria to be compliant with seven of the 40 recommendations, largely compliant with 14 and partially compliant with a further 17 of the recommendations. The review team found Nigeria to be non-compliant with only 2 of the recommendations.[55] On paper, this would appear to be an improvement from the review that took place over a decade earlier. However, a legal framework must be operationalised if the AML/anti-corruption regime is to be effective, and the 2021 Report suggests that Nigeria has at times placed 'undue weight on a single factor, such as the AML legal framework, as a mitigating element' in connection with risk assessment.[56] In consequence, many of the deficiencies in regime effectiveness highlighted in 2008 resurfaced in the 2021 evaluation. In brief, the most recent evaluation team identified the need for improvements in agencies' ability to assess money laundering and terrorist financing risks; maintenance of relevant statistics with which to assess regime effectiveness; strengthening international cooperation; enhancing transparency or BO of legal persons and arrangements; and enhancing investigation and prosecution of money laundering and terrorist financing and ultimate asset recovery. Nigeria has made progress with its technical legal compliance, although this may be because it could have been easier to implement a new act and create a new agency rather than address deficiencies in the operation of those already in existence. It has been suggested that this situation was quite deliberate as 'it is rarely in the interests of political elites to establish independent and well-resourced institutions that threaten the networks that sustain their power'.[57] The 2021 Report notes on several occasions that corruption is prevalent and is identified as a major threat, but that there is no clear strategy to identify or respond to the related ML risk, which is, consequently, underestimated.

Addressing the subject of BO specifically, the 2008 mutual evaluation rated Nigeria as largely compliant with the former recommendations R33 and R34 dealing with transparency of legal persons and arrangements.[58] The review

55 These were Recommendation 7 covering targeted financial sanctions related to proliferation and Recommendation 8 about non-profit organisations.

56 GIABA (n 2) 48.

57 Oluwaseum Bamidele, Azeez O Olaniyan and Bonnie Ayodele, 'In the Cesspool of Corruption: The Challenges of National Development and the Dilemma of Anti-Graft Agencies in Nigeria' (2015) 7(1) African Social Science Review 84 <http://digitalscholarship.tsu.edu/assr/vol7/iss1/5> accessed 15 October 2021. Attention is also drawn to weak institutional structures within Nigeria as being contributory to corruption by Otusanya et al. (n 42) and Musa Zakari and Mark Button, 'Confronting the Monolith: Insider Accounts of the nature and Techniques of Corruption in Nigeria' (2022) 3(2) Journal of White Collar and Corporate Crime.

58 *FATF 40 Recommendations* (2003) <www.fatf-gafi.org/media/fatf/documents/FATF%20Standards%20-%2040%20Recommendations%20rc.pdf> accessed 7 October 2022.

team noted the absence of measures that would ensure the relevant authorities were able to access adequate, accurate and timely information on the BO and control of legal persons. At the time, there was no legal requirement for BO information to either be retained by companies or collected by the relevant authorities – which in Nigeria's case would be the Corporate Affairs Commission (CAC).[59] Therefore, the CAC only recorded legal ownership.

The latest FATF Report repeated many of these criticisms when suggesting the CAC did not 'collect and maintain, timely, adequate, accurate and up-to-date BO information impacting on transparency and verification of BO of legal persons'. They repeatedly describe the available information as being unhelpful for reporting entities and supervisors. FATF state that the CAC continued to hold only basic and not BO information; that there was limited sanctioning for non-compliance with CAC requirements; and, that the lack of BO information negatively impacted on the work of law enforcement agencies. However, as already noted, the FATF recently published report was actually based on an evaluation that took place in 2019 and it did not take account of the passage of the Companies and Allied Matters Act, 2020 (CAMA).

This is important because the passage of CAMA in 2020 has provided the legal framework within which the CAC has been able to begin the development of a more comprehensive company register and database for BO of companies. Relevant sections of CAMA are s.119 – 123 (disclosure of persons with significant control) and s.791 (disclosure of significant control in a limited liability partnership); s.868 explains significant control. Under the provisions of CAMA, s. 119 (1) a person who gains significant control over a company (PSC) must, within seven days, disclose to the company details of the shareholding. On receipt of the information (s. 119 (2) CAMA), the company is required to notify the CAC within a period of one month and also include the same information within the next annual return. S. 119 (3) CAMA provides for the updating of the register by CAC. The provisions are enforceable by a fine for company officers (daily during the period of default) that is to be determined by the CAC under its regulations (s. 119 (5) CAMA). The equivalent provisions apply under s. 791 CAMA to limited liability partnerships.

Practical Considerations in Registry Creation

The main elements of BO data that should ideally be included within a register are set out by the World Bank (2020) and summarised in the following table. These standards are also used by Open Ownership, the organisation that has been supporting CAC with the creation of their online register.

59 Relevant legislation was the Companies and Allied Matters Act, 1990.

Table 11.1 Elements of the Beneficial Ownership Data Standard[60]

Data About Individuals	*Data About Companies*	*Data About Relationships*
Name	Name	The type of relationship, e.g., shareholding, voting rights
Official identifiers, like tax ID	Official identifiers, like official registration numbers	The level of interest, e.g., percentage of shares held and whether it is held directly or indirectly through another entity
Nationalities and tax residencies	Jurisdiction in which the company is registered	Start and end date of the relationship
Date and place of birth	Founding and dissolution date	
Place of residency and contact address	Address	
Whether they are a politically exposed person		

On paper the requirements seem to be quite straightforward; however, in practice there are several challenges that they pose for an agency tasked with creating and maintaining an accurate and up-to-date register. Countries underestimate the difficulty of both creating a register and in determining the ultimate beneficial owner, especially in cases of legal entities or arrangements that cross borders of have multiple layers of ownership. Indeed, the World Bank noted 'the need for new legislation, institutions and resources can be significant stumbling blocks for many countries'.[61] Not only has the CAC had to launch a website for the register, but before the BO register can be fully functional, the Commission also faces the monumental task of automating what is still a largely manual record system containing basic information about company ownership – such as registration number, company name, address and date of registration – gathered in accordance with the earlier Act.

As noted earlier, a commonly used disclosure threshold is 25% . Nigeria has elected to disclose at a far lower threshold than many other countries, selecting a much more ambitious threshold of only 5%. This has two serious implications: it creates a far greater number of persons with significant control (PSCs) who will have to report; and it places a far greater burden on the CAC. The burden on the CAC is twofold. Firstly, it must be able to ensure, with some degree of confidence, the accuracy of the data contained therein (avoiding opportunity for misidentification), and secondly, it requires both resources and tools with which to police non-compliant obliged entities and unregistered beneficial owners.

60 World Bank (n 46) 254.
61 World Bank (n 46) 259.

The CAC are aware that they have legacy issues with the quality of some of their records, noting that prior to 2012 there had been no checking of details that were supplied to register a company. Indeed, it was only after 2012 that each director of a company had to submit a formal ID. They realise that data captured prior to 2012 may, therefore, not be correct, and they face restrictions working to the originally designed data capture form. Additionally, there has been little or no effort to verify whether information historically supplied is accurate or whether required updates/annual submissions have been made. Even if not by deliberate deception, errors easily creep in, particularly within free-form fields where spelling mistakes can be common, or information can be incorrectly recorded due to lack of experience by those doing the reporting. For all data, accurate or otherwise, the existing records need updating to include information on the beneficial owners of each company. CAC records are currently searchable provided the company name is known. Other key details about companies (outside of the company name, registration number, and registration address) are behind a paywall and remain opaque. Although the register is 'public', that has currently only been achieved in a limited sense.

The CAC is also challenged by their own limited internal capacity to police the information that is being supplied to them and because the new law provides only administrative sanctions for non-compliance. A penalty fine may not be sufficient to ensure compliance and may restrict its overall effectiveness. Nevertheless, a strength of the law may be that the reporting requirements apply to circumstances in which shares are acquired and subsequently sold within a 14-day notice period (s. 120 (4) CAMA). If enforceable, this could provide a potential flag for further investigation.

Issues of accuracy could be addressed through starting afresh, requiring all companies to re-register; however, in practice this approach is far from realistic. In addition to the challenges facing the CAC we recognise a fundamental tension between the objectives and requirements of those tasked with collection and submission of information (not just government agencies but the entire regulated sector) and those seeking to make use of that information. As always, there is a balance to be struck in terms of reasonableness in expectations placed upon those required to adhere to the provisions and the desire of law enforcement to collect as much information as is possible. An additional consideration concerns capacity and ability to make use of that information. Much of our prior work in the field of AML has been on proportionality[62] advocating 'less is more' – making it simpler and less costly for the private sector will make that sector more likely to comply with requirements. This view

62 Petrus van Duyne, Jackie Harvey and Liliya Gelemerova, 'The Monty Python Flying Circus of Money Laundering and the Question of Proportionality' in Georgios Antonopoulos (ed), *Illegal Entrepreneurship, Organized Crime and Social Control: Essays in Honour of Professor Dick Hobbs'* (Springer 2014) 14; Petrus van Duyne, Jackie Harvey and Liliya Gelemerova, 'A "Risky" Risk Approach: Proportionality in ML/TF Regulation' in Clive Walker and Colin King (eds), *The Handbook of Criminal and Terrorist Financing Law* (Palgrave 2017).

accords with that of the World Bank which pointed out the benefits of sharing information on a searchable platform from the outset, 'reducing the compliance burden on users and ensuring better data quality'.[63] Our observation is that it is critical to get the basics right and not set aims that are overly complex or ambitious. It is better to have less information that is accurate, verifiable, and accessible than a lot of worthless data.

Some Practical Suggestions and Wider Reflections

A few small but significant decisions and changes now could assist the CAC considerably in successfully delivering a useful register. First, it must be acknowledged that this agency has a huge task on its hands and needs proper resourcing if information is to be verified and historic data cleaned when transferred to the online portal.[64] Second, in populating the data on PSC, the CAC should start with the largest shareholdings and concentrate on ensuring accuracy of the information that is provided to make the best use of the available resources. Third, it should enable public access to the register details of BO to enable civil society organisations to add an additional level of checking of accuracy of data. Finally, amendment of the AML/CFT Regulations (2013 ss. 13–16) should be considered to require the regulated sector to report discrepancies between PSC information available through CAC and the information that they obtain through independent checks when on-boarding new or transacting with existing customers.[65] Although discrepancies are not necessarily a sign of sinister activities or intentional wrongdoing and may be the consequence of a huge range of factors, such as missing paperwork, slow filing systems, lateness or lack of knowledge or understanding of filing requirements among smaller companies, the reporting of discrepancies may help to ensure the accuracy of BO information.

On this latter point it is not without irony that we observe the comment by the evaluation team 'FIs hold BO information suitable for their purposes and present a more reliable information source than the CAC'.[66] It is understood that there may be a negative impact on genuine investors due to increased transaction and business costs of obliged entities and an associated increase

63 *World Bank (n 46) 259.*

64 Records can be accessed from <https://search.cac.gov.ng/home> with the search engine driven by company name; there is a link to 'view persons with significant control of this company', which we did not find populated.

65 The UK recognised problems with the accuracy of the data captured in its registry of company information maintained by the UK companies registry, Companies House. The Money Laundering, Terrorist Financing and Transfer of Funds (Information on the Payer) Regulations 2017 (as amended), now requires the regulated sector to report discrepancies between BO information available at Companies House and the information that they may obtain through their own independent checks.

66 *GIABA (n 2) 176.*

in the time it will take to comply with the requirements.[67] Therefore, any mechanism for reporting discrepancies should be straightforward and simple and lead to rectification of the register to reduce the compliance burden on all parties. The majority will truthfully comply, freeing CAC resources to focus on companies likely to be created for illegal purposes.

Conclusion

There is no 'silver bullet' that we can recommend in connection with ensuring BO transparency, but instead, we have noted several incremental improvements that would help to improve the effectiveness of measures being undertaken in Nigeria to assist in the fight against corruption. The World Bank suggest that to be truly valuable, BO information can be combined with asset declarations, although we note there are problems with this data as well, and small steps towards achieving an accurate and up-to-date company registry are foundational.

Reflecting more broadly, for as long as powerful actors are happy with the status quo, they may continue to drag their feet by failing to properly resource the registries to do their job, and the question whether Nigeria has the political will to implement anti-corruption and AML measures effectively is one that could be asked of many states. As Brinkerhoff has argued, the degree of political will on any country's part to tackle corruption must be suspect when the push for change comes from external actors.[68] This is all the more so when the external actor in question is a body such as FATF, established – on a remarkably informal legal basis for such a powerful institution – by a club of the world's richest countries.

The focus in this chapter has been on the technical aspects of Nigeria's system for the registration of BO, rather than on the global politics of AML regulation, and we have made constructive recommendations because we accept that within the Nigerian regulatory apparatus there are individuals and bodies with a genuine commitment to tackling corruption and money laundering. However, the question of how far the Nigerian system is *designed* to succeed, or to 'look good on paper' while being denied the resources to make much impact in reality, cannot be avoided. In turn, this raises questions about the legitimacy and effectiveness of the global AML regime as a whole.

67 The BO provisions CAMA ss. 119–123 are a small part of a very detailed act on company governance and reporting. A 173-page user guide to company registration is available on the CAC website at <https://pre.cac.gov.ng/assets/docs/crp-user-guide.pdf>.

68 Derick W Brinkerhoff, 'Assessing Political Will for Anti-Corruption Efforts: An Analytical Framework' (2000) 20 Public Administration and Development 239; Derick W Brinkerhoff, *Unpacking the Concept of Political Will to Fight Corruption* (Christian Michelsen Institute 2010) <www.u4.no/publications/unpacking-the-concept-of-political-will-to-confront-corruption> accessed 17 February 2022.

12 Suspect Wealth and the Compliance Willingness of Small States

Dominic Thomas-James

Introduction

Small island jurisdictions that entered into the offshore financial services market as a means of economic sustainability have long been on the receiving end of international criticism. These criticisms typically relate to their knowing or inadvertent receipt of suspect wealth, facilitation of criminality or enabling of fiscal advantage (even if legally permissible) though their products and services.

The fiscal island paradise is a powerful stereotype to which the international community has become well accustomed, and which has become popularly mainstream with events like the Panama and Paradise Papers. Indeed, this image is further fuelled by popular depiction in film, television and literature. As compelling as this is, what is less understood is the extent to which such jurisdiction are, or are not, complying with international standards on money laundering, terrorism financing, corruption and other related anti-economic crime efforts such as transparency and international cooperation. Many international standards presuppose a significant degree of compliance, which has to be considered against domestic backdrops including development challenges and economic over-reliance on financial services.

Building upon earlier research on three specific small island jurisdictions in the Caribbean and North Atlantic,[1] this chapter sets out to consider the anti-money laundering compliance successes and challenges in offshore jurisdictions with particular reference to British Overseas Territories (UKOTs) and the ongoing issue of beneficial ownership (BO) transparency. It provides background overview on important concepts of "suspect wealth" and "offshore", as well as highlighting material aspects of the development journeys of small-island jurisdictions into offshore centres. It also acknowledges some of the more pressing criticisms levelled at them from the international community, broadly defined. With particular reference to corporate ownership registers, but also other closely related recent developments in this field such as

1 D Thomas-James, *Offshore Financial Centres and the Law: Suspect Wealth in British Overseas Territories* (Routledge 2021).

DOI: 10.4324/9781003253808-14

economic substance laws and cooperation with international tax matters, the chapter sets out that there is compliance willingness, but the abilities and likelihood of effective implementation on this particular issue will inevitably vary given the significant and less understood differences between the jurisdictions which seldom acknowledged in international fora.

What Is Suspect Wealth, and Why Are We Concerned About It?

It is first necessary to look at some of the concerns that have manifested internationally about economic crime. Economic crime can include many interrelated types of misconduct,[2] such as corruption, money laundering, terrorism financing, tax crimes, embezzlement, fraud, theft, market abuse and other serious organised crime like drug or human trafficking. Often, many types operate simultaneously, such as drug dealing and laundering the money through a legitimate business, say a restaurant.

Notwithstanding the difficulty of measuring the true costs or extent of economically motivated crime, there are many estimates which carry illustrative value. For example, the United Nations Office on Drugs and Crime estimate that somewhere in the region of $800 billion to $2 trillion are laundered each year. The scale of flight capital fleeing a jurisdiction through misconduct such as tax evasion or embezzlement has become equally concerning from a development standpoint. Kar and Spanjers (2015) estimate that some $1.1 trillion emanating from corruption and tax evasion flowed illicitly from developing nations.[3] Economic crime and its impact on development is firmly visible in various international instruments and initiatives, such as the UN Sustainable Development Goals. Goal 16 (Peace, Justice and Strong Institutions) emphasises that corruption, theft, bribery and tax evasion cost developing countries some $1.26 trillion per year. International concerns about corruption and related conduct are enshrined in the UN Convention Against Corruption, which details that corruption inhibits development and sustains poverty. The foreword describes it as an "insidious plague" with wide-ranging corrosive effects on society. In the UN Convention's General Assembly Resolution, corruption's wide-ranging impact is summarised as follows: "[concern] about the seriousness of problems and threats posed by corruption to the stability and security of societies, undermining the institutions and values of democracy, ethical values and justice and jeopardizing sustainable development and the rule of law".

Money laundering as a facilitative type of crime ensures that crime remains a profitable activity. The laundering process is remarkably straightforward

2 For comprehensive background, see BAK Rider (ed), *Research Handbook on International Financial Crime* (Elgar 2015).

3 D Kar and J Spanjers, *Illicit Financial Flows from Developing Countries: 2004–2013* (Global Financial Integrity 2015) <www.gfintegrity.org/wp-content/uploads/2015/12/IFF-Update_2015-Final-1.pdf> accessed 7 January 2022.

as a concept, yet we continue to see both primitive and complex methods being used – whether absorbing criminal funds into cash-intense businesses or using the expanding and complex digital world of virtual assets. The Financial Action Task Force (FATF) defines money laundering as the processing of criminal proceeds to disguise their illegal origin. As with corruption, concerns about money laundering have become an international priority and are firmly matters of national security and stability. This is due to the risks that money laundering present and the harm it does to economies and societies, institutions and key aspects of a country's development. The International Monetary Fund (2016) has noted money laundering's ability to threaten financial sector stability. Indeed, the integrity objective which underpins financial services legislation in the UK specifically references the concern about the UK financial system not being used for a purpose connected with financial crime, as per section 1D of the Financial Services and Markets Act 2000.

Elsewhere, and outside the perimeters of illegal conduct, tax avoidance is a similar scale concern, and this activity has firmly thrust offshore jurisdictions under a bright spotlight. A study by Cobham and Jansky (2017) found that multinationals' corporate tax avoidance amounts to some $500 billion each year.[4] International efforts aimed at tax cooperation, information exchange and initiatives such as economic substance targeting profit shifting has seen considerable development in recent years. Tax avoidance continues, therefore, to be a focus of the international community through various initiatives such as corporate transparency and tax cooperation, and the targeting of profit shifting.

The more attention we give to interdicting economic misconduct, the more likely it is that those with suspect wealth emanating from malign activity will try to conceal it. Much like targeting the proceeds of crime following the war on drugs from the 1970s onwards, the war on terror necessitated a similar ethos. As President George W. Bush stated following the 9/11 terrorist attacks, the concept is about starving terrorists of their funding (US Treasury Department, 2002). The idea of targeting the proceeds and the operational lifeblood of financial crime is straightforward from an enforcement standpoint. Such enables the disruption of the crime itself while at the same time serve criminological and criminal justice theories such as deterrence if the motivation behind economic crime is ultimately disrupted. Yet, it also affords investigators better knowledge about the scope of operations and thereby assist in intelligence dimensions. While critics are often quick to juxtapose the relatively meagre sums seized by law enforcement efforts relative to the global costs of money laundering, at the coalface the reality is that a cash

4 A Cobham and P Jansky, *Global Distribution of Revenue Loss from Tax Avoidance* (United Nations University World Institute for Development Economics Research 2017) <www.wider.unu.edu/publication/global-distribution-revenueloss-tax-avoidance> accessed 7 January 2022.

seizure of, say, £100,000 from a county lines drug dealing operation might be crucial to the interdiction of the same. Not only is the upside removed, but from the criminal enterprise's position, it may necessitate corners being cut in future operations and thereby potentially exposing operational vulnerabilities.

In response to the risks posed by money laundering and terrorism financing, the global community has, in its varying manifestations, come up with international rules and standards. The principal standard bearer tasked with international AML regulation is the FATF and its regional affiliates. Their anti-money laundering/counter-terrorism financing (AML/CFT) recommendations[5] have become unchallenged and prominent global rules, despite their manifestation as soft law. They are also not set in stone, with updates undertaken in key areas as was seen in 2022 with the update on BO requirements.

Concerns about money laundering at international levels, such as the European Union (EU), have also led to a series of AML/CFT initiatives and Directives, which member states have been obliged to implement as minimum standards. While standardisation is a desirable feature of globalisation in this area, the reality is that the costs of implementing AML/CFT standards and controls are often significant, while yielding little results relative to suspect flows. Interventions of the kind inherent in the global AML regime presuppose a significant degree of compliance, which can be challenging based on regional circumstances or capital and human resource limits. The position of offshore financial centres – the types of jurisdiction this chapter concerns – also present a complex problem, and one which is deeper than the ostensibly effortless activity of enacting and administrating global AML standards. The aforementioned compliance obligations in terms of human resources and financial capacity, can be challenging for micro-population countries – many being small, remote islands. Further, there are considerable differences between such jurisdictions, for example their emphasis or otherwise on financial services, which means that some standards are of greater or lesser relevance or significance depending on the country concerned. There is also the issue of priorities which further compound capacity concerns. When globally influential events like the Panama or Paradise Papers occur which, inarguably, were as much to do with economic crime as aggressive tax avoidance, standards quickly take on the perception of being a "catch-all". In the context of considering the compliance willingness of small island jurisdictions, we have to consider, first, what "suspect wealth" actually means and why it is important in terms of offshore.

Much has been written on financial crime,[6] as well as its proceeds. Suspect wealth as a concept,[7] however, remains under-researched. It is wider in

5 FATF Recommendations 2012.

6 See, for example, Rider (n 2).

7 Such was the focus of this author's doctoral thesis at the University of Cambridge: D Thomas-James, *Suspect Wealth: A Risk to Stability, Development and Sustainability: The Case of Bermuda the TCI, and Anguilla* (University of Cambridge, 2019).

scope than traditional interpretations of the proceeds of crime, despite it also including the same. Suspect wealth as a concept is arguably where the complexity arises when assessing the role played by offshore financial centres in the global financial system. As will be considered later in this chapter, events like the Bahamas leaks and the Panama, Paradise and, most recently, the Pandora Papers demonstrate that the problem as defined by the international community is not simply confined to nefarious and malign activity, but also things like permissible facilitative activity that states are increasingly taking an interest in and condemning, such as tax avoidance through offshore vehicles.

As I have elsewhere defined,[8] suspect wealth can be wealth attributed to criminality, but also wealth attributable to controversial, yet perhaps, legal conduct – for example, wealth fleeing some type of civil or matrimonial injunction. The point about tax avoidance is an important one from both a legal and a moral standpoint. It is, of course, indelibly important to maintain a clear line between conduct that is permitted under law and conduct which is not permitted under law. Lawyers and law students alike will be familiar with the principle of jurisprudential positivism that a law properly so-called and one's duty to comply with it, stands irrespective as to whether the law is a good law or whether it can be justified in moral terms.[9] The well-established legal doctrine of legitimate fiscal planning (*IRC v Duke of Westminster* [1936]), for example, may yet hold strong, yet be seen in a completely different light in times of austerity such as a global health pandemic, whereby the notion of paying one's "fair share of tax" garners increasing weight, even if fiscal planning to limit one's fiscal obligations may be permissible under law. Aggressive or artificial forms of tax avoidance are increasingly being perceived as immoral and treated similarly by international commentators and watchdogs to tax evasion. As far as this chapter is concerned, it is important to consider suspect wealth broadly rather than, for example, just that relating to the proceeds of serious crime.

The role of offshore centres that knowingly or inadvertently receive suspect wealth is of interest in this context. The notion of those that mind other people's wealth – often professionals who are qualified and regulated, and oftentimes acting as fiduciaries – are therefore the gatekeepers to it. Indeed, it is this group who are tasked with due diligence and know your customer requirements which underpin global AML rules, to obviate the risk of becoming inveigled or outright co-conspirators in terms of concealing suspect wealth and thereby facilitating crime. Indeed, the eminent criminological and sociological scholarship of Sutherland, and his work on defining the "white collar criminal" committing crimes in the course of their employment,[10] certainly bears true to this setting. This group is expanding to more and more industries, as the Money

8 Thomas-James (n 7); Thomas-James (n 1).

9 See HLA Hart, 'Positivism and the Separation of Law and Morals' (1958) 71(4) *Harvard Law Review* 593–629.

10 See E Sutherland, 'White Collar Criminality' (1940) 5(1) American Sociological Review 1–12.

Laundering Regulations in the UK demonstrate. The offshore problem, and international interest in reforming offshore financial centres, emphasises the extent to which there may be wilful blindness in such jurisdictions about how problematic their offerings or services may be. Many, such as Russell and Graham (2016), have claimed that they are simply in denial about it.[11]

The Development of Small Jurisdictions as Financial Centres

The development of small jurisdictions as leading financial centres is not an issue confined to island nations but seen across the world. The development of small island nations specifically, however, is an interesting and under-researched area in both development and legal scholarship. It is interesting for many reasons, one such being the development advancement of such jurisdictions into, in some cases, world-leading service providers and market places. However, one has to first consider some of the sober realities that have plagued small island nations during the earliest stages of their development, even right through to today in an age where many, through economic diversification, are now considered "middle income" or wealthy jurisdictions.

Many suffer from the same challenges – including not having higher education institutes in which research into their own economic and social development can occur; talent shortages compounded by "brain drain"; relatively restrictive and protectionist immigration policies; lack of scholarly and research interest about them occurring in overseas research institutions; limited power or influence in the international community; narrow economies including overreliance on tourism; geographical positioning and connectivity – often meaning that basic things such as healthcare are dependent upon neighbouring states; and proneness to natural and environmental disasters such as being located within tropic cyclone zones. The ravages of hurricanes Irma and Maria in the Caribbean in late 2017, which caused severe destruction and hardship in islands like Anguilla, the Turks and Caicos Islands (TCI), and the British Virgin Islands (BVI), is a plain reminder of the challenges that some jurisdictions face regardless of their development as financial centres. These challenges tend to resonate for years after the event, particularly impacting major industries like tourism.

The concept of "brain drain" is an important issue for small islands and particularly concerning for those who have chosen to develop their economies through financial and business services. The phrase was coined in the 1950s by the British Royal Society. It described the outflow of science and technology professionals to the US and Canada (Dodani & LaPorte 2005, 488). For those islands still developing key sectors like finance, business, compliance and reg-tech, including many in the Commonwealth Caribbean, it is as much a challenge to recruit skilled and professional personnel from overseas

11 See D Russell and T Graham, 'The Panama Papers' (2016) 22(5) Trusts and Trustees 481–86.

as it is in terms of keeping local talent from migrating overseas to train and work. During the Covid-19 pandemic, some islands, such as Bermuda, offered remote working visas. This concept was designed to recover from tourism losses wrought by the pandemic lockdowns and travel restrictions. This has to be considered in the context of Bermuda's significant level of development, and could not be achieved in many island jurisdictions – particularly those which are less developed, or whose reliance on tourism is more significant.

Part of the reason that little research has been conducted regarding small island jurisdictions that have entered into the offshore market is that in the case of many there are few or no higher education establishments – thereby precipitating the need for students to travel elsewhere to study, train and potentially remain to work. This is particularly acute in the areas of law, finance and consulting. It is also the case that many islands have strict immigration policies and traditionally protectionist stances on the right to work, obtain residency permits or citizenship, as well as the voting franchise. It remains the case that in many UKOTs, the voting franchise is only available to "Belongers"[12] rather than residents on extended work visas.

A purpose of this chapter is to highlight some of these challenges that small offshore islands face as explanatory bases upon which to consider their true levels of compliance with international AML standards. No matter how developed one's financial and business offerings become, many of the aforementioned development concerns still apply and have the capacity to stunt a country's development. It is important to bear the above context in mind when considering their development as financial centres in a relatively short space of time, but also to contextualise some of the more pressing issues facing them. This is because the ever-changing nature of international standards presupposes a substantial degree of compliance and, more fundamentally, a significant level of both human and capital resources to achieve it. Of course, it is critical to remember that although many challenges are shared – not all small island nations suffer from the same development or capacity-related issues.

Turning now to their development journeys, many islands entered into the offshore financial and business service sectors over previous decades which represented, at least in the Caribbean region, a growing trend. Contrary to the popular belief that this was devised as some secret, nefarious endeavour set against a broader context of onshore financial de-regulation and lax oversight, the move was rather more straightforward and economically minded. Momentum towards greater financial independence and increased autonomy, together with a view towards sustainable development, all became suddenly achievable through economic diversification and the provision of offshore financial and business services. Many small islands – some with complex colonial histories – and many with hazardously narrow, barter-based, consumption

12 While this term can vary depending upon Territory, generally it refers to people of a British Overseas Territory who have "Belonger status" as of right or by grant.

economies, saw the opportunity to diversify. By the mid-1980s, many Caribbean islands had followed similar paths. For example, in 1981, the TCI entered into the offshore services market; Antigua and Barbuda entered into it in 1982; and the BVI followed in 1984. Many small islands have made enormous successes from this transition – including Bermuda, whose world-leading (re)insurance sector is regularly listed in the world's top insurance markets, the BVI with its sizeable incorporation sector; or the Cayman Islands with its significant funds market.

In the context of the dissolving post-war British Empire, small island jurisdictions engaged in rethinking their economic models, and commenced sustainable development strategies modelled on product and service offerings in the financial context. In an international development context, this was set against declining development and bilateral aid programmes from large, developed jurisdictions over the course of the 1980s and 1990s. As educational opportunities for students at the international level developed considerably, so did pressures for small islands from brain drain – particularly in the most remote of islands. Freyer and Morriss (2013), regarding the Cayman Islands' development, observe that the islands established a "financial regulatory system that enabled the territory to achieve more economic development and diversification than its peers".[13] They go on to say that this development brought Cayman into the highest per capita wealth in the Caribbean area, thereby putting it on par with the prosperity of the UK itself. They further advance that the journey was collaborative in terms of policymaking and highlight a crucial role played by UK officials. The combination of tax policy and economic development in the 1950s and 1960s in the UK, as well as post-war decolonisation, led to many jurisdictions – then under British control – to take advantage of fiscal opportunity resulting from increased taxes and capital controls onshore in the UK. This provided considerable momentum toward establishing sustainable futures[14] and led to increased financial independence.

A good example of small jurisdictions in the wider Caribbean engaging in this upward trajectory includes the Bahamas and their establishment of the Society of Trust and Estate Practitioners (STEP), which occurred in the mid-to-late 1990s. Its aim was to provide qualifications and teaching to support the creation and expansion of a professional services infrastructure. This came within a context of significant literacy increases in the Bahamas during the 1970s to the 1990s. STEP enabled the jurisdictions' citizens to obtain valuable training and credentials which proved invaluable as the islands embarked upon diversifying their economies by entering into the business services and offshore market. It is also important to note that contrary to the notion of

13 TA Freyer and PA Morriss, 'Creating Cayman as an Offshore Financial Centre: Structure and Strategy Since 1960' (2013) 45 Arizona State Law Journal 1297–398, 1300.

14 RT Kudrle, 'Tax Havens and the Transparency Wave of International Tax Legalization' (2016) 37(4) University of Pennsylvania Journal of International Law 1153–82, 1155.

"putting up their for sale notices",[15] many jurisdictions embarked upon this journey with significant support from metropolitan powers such as the UK, particularly through the provision of technical assistance and personnel support in the areas of legal and constitutional reform, institution building and legislative drafting.

With a GDP per capita of $116,890, Bermuda – as an example – is one of the world's wealthiest jurisdictions in the company of the likes of the Principality of Monaco and Liechtenstein. Its international financial services and offshore financial centre contributed to 39% of GDP and accounted for 18% of employment in 2016.[16] It has a substantial reinsurance market which dominates its financial and business sector, with 15 of the world's top 40 reinsurers based there.[17] Considering its economic value proposition from this market alone, Bermuda reinsurance provides more than a quarter of capacity for Lloyds of London, and provided some 9% of claims from the 9/11 terrorist attacks and 20% of UK flood losses following the 2016 flooding.[18] Despite this significant sector, and the business services that support it, Bermuda continues – much like many similar island nations – to suffer from development-related challenges, despite its ostensible wealth. There are deep-rooted economic and social challenges in the islands, such as living standards, wage gap, little in terms of social welfare, homelessness and crime. Bermuda has had documented gang crime problems which increased significantly from the late 2000s. There were 35 gang-related homicides between 2009 and 2017 (Bermuda Government 17.11.2017). Many Bermudians struggle on non-professional wages, and there have been prevalent social initiatives such as Bermuda's Coalition for the Protection of Children providing nutritional breakfasts for school children.

Similarly, Anguilla – with its relatively high GDP per capita, at $21,068, low crime rates and a "tax haven" reputation – also continues to suffer various development challenges which often go overlooked by the international community. With the above, Anguilla is too wealthy to receive UK aid.[19] A sobering example which demonstrates the fragility of Anguilla's development was seen during the 2017 hurricanes. The then Attorney General, John McKendrick

15 See Rider (n 2); Thomas-James (n 1) at xii.

16 See Bermuda Government, 'Department of Statistics, Digest of Statistics 2017, Table 6.1' (2017) 2 <www.gov.bm/sites/default/files/2017-Digest-of-Statistics.pdf> accessed 5 December 2021.

17 KPMG '(Re)insurance in Bermuda: View from the Bridge' (2017), 1 <https://home.kpmg/content/dam/kpmg/bm/pdf/2017/03/Charles-Thresh-Mike-Morrison.pdf> accessed 5 December 2021.

18 Bermuda Business Development Agency, 'Bermuda is Different' (2016) <www.globenewswire.com/news-release/2016/04/05/826101/0/en/Bermuda-is-different-BDA-responds-to-Panama-Papers.html> accessed 10 December 2021.

19 DfID, 'UK Secures Change to International Aid Rules: Restrictions to Britain's Aid Support to Countries Affected by Crises and Natural Disasters that Severely Impact their Economy are Lifted' (1 November 2018), Press Release.

QC, recalled in a detailed account having to live in temporary housing without mains power or running water for some 3 months.[20] The Attorney General's portfolio is substantial, as the territory's principal lawyer, who also serves as Director of Public Prosecutions. As one of the most senior appointees in the jurisdiction, it was telling to see just how ravaged the islands' basic infrastructure was, including the ability of government and justice system to function. A few years prior to this, Anguilla's banking sector was placed under the control of its domestic banking regulator, the Eastern Caribbean Central Bank (ECCB). The ECCB Agreement Act 1983 (as amended) stipulates the conditions for this to occur, including where the interests of the financial institutions' depositors or creditors are threatened, or if the institution is unlikely to meet its obligations, or if the financial system of the territory is in danger of disruption. The regulator found all three applied as regards Anguilla's indigenous banks and in 2013 they were deemed insolvent and placed under receivership.[21] With sizeable shortfalls in both banks, in the event of a run, collapse would have occurred.[22] Anguilla further suffers from dependency on neighbouring islands, with no deep ports for large cruise liners and its airport being of insufficient capacity to host large international air traffic. It also relies upon its neighbours for collaboration on healthcare. Notwithstanding both a luxury tourism industry and focus on financial services, Anguilla is said to have one of the least-developed public medical facilities under a UK flag.[23] It also suffers from an outdated constitution, which trickles down to affect the development of jurisprudence in line with modern legislation, which is lacking in key areas such as anti-bribery.

Elsewhere, in the TCI, two Commissions of Inquiry instigated by the UK Government in a period of three decades relating to allegations of ministerial misconduct, led to the territory losing its sovereignty twice during this period. In 1986, a Commission of Inquiry led by Mr Louis Blom-Cooper QC found the Chief Minister to be guilty of unconstitutional behaviour and ministerial malpractices.[24] Further, in 2008–2009, the Commission of Inquiry undertaken by Sir Robin Auld suggested a criminal investigation of the Premier

20 J McKendrick, 'A Tropical Attorney General' (2018–2019) Inner Temple Year Book 134–35.

21 Caribbean Development Bank, 'Loan & Project Summary: Anguilla Bank Resolution – Bridge Bank Capitalisation Loan' (2016) <www.caribank.org/publications-and-resources/resource-library/board-papers/loans-grants-and-projectsummaries/anguilla-bank-resolution-bridge-bank-capitalisation-loan> accessed 10 December 2021.

22 See, for background, *Anguillian*, 'Government Publishes Key Findings on NBA & CCB' (9 November 2015) <https://theanguillian.com/2015/11/government-publishes-key-findingson-nba-ccb/> accessed 10 February 2022.

23 Anguilla Government London Office, 'Anguilla and Brexit: Britain's Forgotten E.U. Border' (2017) <https://westindiacommittee.org/anguillabrexit-britains-forgotten-eu-border/> accessed 10 February 2022.

24 TCI Commission of Inquiry, 'Report of Mr Louis Blom-Cooper QC into Allegations of Arson of a Public Building, Corruption and Related Matters' (1986), 109 <https://turksandcaicosislands.org/CofI1986BlomCooperQC.pdf> accessed 5 January 2022.

who, following his resignation and period of direct rule ensuing in the islands, was arrested in Brazil and returned to TCI charged with offences relating to money laundering and bribery. The trial is, following years of challenges, ongoing at the time of writing. For a jurisdiction which, on the face of it, has developed a financial and offshore business services sector, to have lost its sovereignty twice is an alarming reality and one which has impacted the islands' development.

The above examples relating to Bermuda, TCI and Anguilla show that the islands face continued challenges in many areas, to one degree or another. Whether it is urgently needed constitutional and legal development with a focus on integrity-education; or greater attention placed on the development of legal infrastructure; or whether the necessity of economic diversification to insure against the unfortunate inevitability of environmental crises; there are considerable challenges which are unique to the islands and are sometimes overlooked by international critics. For those jurisdictions which have been implicated in international cases as facilitating economic crime through their services and vehicles, these factors certainly do not justify lack of compliance with international standards; but they could go some way in explaining it, or better still contextualising it. Oftentimes, this key distinction is missed.

Their development as financial centres has, however, trigged a global anti-tax haven narrative that is increasingly powerful. With their status, they are held to the same high standards as other, powerful international players. The concept of the small jurisdiction that has ventured into global big business is an interesting one, not least given that it appears somewhat juxtaposed. If one drops a pin in a major global marketplace such as the City of London, New York, Singapore or Tokyo, for example, one is instantly surrounded by visibly functioning and busy economies, high-rise office blocks, streets of professionals, business support services like law, accountancy and consulting firms, transport infrastructure and other support businesses like cafes, gyms, bars, restaurants and hotels. By contrast, an island hundreds or thousands of miles from other land that operates a sophisticated financial sector seems – as espoused by their critics – as odd as it sounds. It may surprise the reader to learn that even for some of the most developed UKOTs, direct flights to London do not exist. Scholars such as Roberts (1995) have posited that these are small places, for big money. Indeed, the words of author W. Somerset Maugham about the French Riviera being a "sunny place for shady people" springs to mind. Such has become a convenient stereotype over time. However, the question of compliance and, importantly, willingness to comply with international AML standards remains under-researched. The question is inarguably riddled with subconscious bias stemming from the unrelenting adverse media attention placed on the offshore world. The reader may search in vain to find scholarly articles written about offshore jurisdictions in a positive light.

One feature of international standards relating to the interdiction of economic crime, particularly in the areas of AML/CFT regulation, is that they are not immovable or stagnant. They constantly evolve as we develop greater understanding of risk, but ought to carry sufficient flexibility to take account of different circumstances. For example, many international AML standards espoused by the FATF act as minimum best practices with the ability of gold-plating thereafter. Another example of this relates to illicit enrichment – which the United Nations Convention Against Corruption suggest at Article 20 that states should consider criminalising. Many jurisdictions are developing their response to this in real time, with some countries such as the UK and Ireland having instead adopted civil rather than criminal measures – including the unexplained wealth order provisions under the UK Criminal Finances Act 2017. If the goal of the international community is, and should be, to garner participants' compliance with international AML standards, viewing offshore jurisdictions in a one-size-fits-all manner simply because they share commonalities and hold externally imposed labels of "tax haven" is problematic. At the very least, their financial sectors are fundamentally different. It may surprise the reader that Bermuda's incorporation sector pales by comparison in size relative to that in the BVI.

There is another problem, which relates to consistency when it comes to classifying so-called tax havens on international blacklists and greylists. Whether listed by countries, political unions, anti-corruption watchdogs, transparency groups, or AML standard setters, this form of sanctioning is increasingly powerful given the effect it has on a country's reputation and consequent de-risking activities. Blacklisting and greylisting can motivate change and serve as a deterrent for non-compliance. However, as Sharman (2006) has argued for instance, no two lists of tax havens contain the same countries. Then, there is the issue of featuring on one country's list, but not another's; or whether some lists such as the EU's List of Non-Cooperative Jurisdictions for tax, are problematically narrow in their focus.

The "Problem" of Offshore

Whatever one's prejudice about offshore jurisdictions, Palan (1999) framed the position in a way which is perhaps rather difficult to argue against – namely, that these kinds of small island jurisdictions in the mid-Atlantic or Caribbean, which are thousands of miles from major economies or countries – would be the last place one would expect to come across a financial centre.[25] As such, their development into modern business markets is an interesting concept. Offshore financial centres have long been viewed by the global community as uncooperative and harmful actors in the global financial system. Criticisms are well-known and include concerns about being tax neutral (or low-tax), facilitating economic crime through banking secrecy legislation, lax regulation or

25 R Palan, 'Offshore and the Structural Enablement of Sovereignty' in M Hampton and JP Abbott (eds), *Offshore Finance Centers and Tax Havens: The Rise of Global Capital* (Macmillan 1999) at 18–21.

limited oversight, being uncooperative in terms of international engagement, and offering products and services that can be abused by nefarious actors determined to conceal their malign activity and ill-gotten gains. The professionals that work there are also subject to the same type of criticisms and concerns about facilitation and corruption. Quite often, the no-tax or low-tax concern unhelpfully converges with the notion of indirect taxation – a prevalent feature of revenue-building for small islands that rely so heavily on imports.

The fiscal paradise stereotype does not account for how the above problems can adversely affect offshore jurisdictions themselves. Against a narrative of wilful blindness often propagated by the international community and watchdogs alike, it is perhaps more convenient to focus on the more obvious issue of offshore jurisdictions causing or facilitating problems elsewhere. And to an extent this may be true or compelling, as Sharman (2017) avers: seldom is public money looted from archipelagic islands in the Caribbean and stashed in developing Africa – rather the other way around.[26] However, despite sustained popular interest in so-called tax havens, oftentimes their development realities are outright ignored or missed. A good example are the effects of TCI losing its sovereignty on two occasions over allegations of public sector misconduct.

The concept of "offshore" seems, as Orson Welles said of bullfighting, both indefensible and irresistible. The indefensibility is visible through the agendas of global transparency and tax justice campaigners, aiming at global tax harmonisation and the gradual erosion and eradication of offshore jurisdictions. The influence of this is not de minimis, as was seen in the enactment of the public register provisions regarding UKOTs in the UK Sanctions and Anti-Money Laundering Act in 2018 (SAMLA). The irresistibility, however, is something we have long been popularly fascinated by. One only has to consider the role of secret vaults concealing wealth, numbered-bank accounts, or fiscal paradise islands as is seen in Fleming's James Bond stories, or more recently popular television shows and films depicting economic crimes. Fraud is now the crime we are most likely to fall victim to, so is it any wonder why fraud and financial crimes are so frequently depicted and sensationalised in popular culture?

Leaving the fiscal island stereotype aside momentarily, as powerful and influential on law-making it may be, the concept of offshore is a complex one. It certainly appears in today's uncertain world to stand in the very face of globalisation, cooperation and the global tax justice and harmonisation campaigns. Despite the inescapable ease of modern commerce, cross-border trade and international financial transacting, modern global views about international finance appear welded firmly against tax havens. Even Pope Francis recently articulated an adverse perception about them in the context of the Covid-19 pandemic.[27] The traditional anti-tax haven campaigns orchestrated

26 See JC Sharman, *Despots Guide to Wealth Management* (Cornell University Press, 2017).

27 *Tax Watch*, 'Covid-19 – Pope Says Tax Avoiders Have Committed "Murder" ' (25 March 2020) <www.taxwatchuk.org/coronavirus_pope_tax_evasion/> accessed 5 December 2021.

by the OECD has, more recently, been seen firmly on the EU's agenda and has manifested through successive blacklisting and greylisting of non-cooperative jurisdictions in the area of tax. During times of crisis, it is unsurprising that public opinion, as well as government opinion, turns swiftly and indiscriminately unsympathetic towards individuals and entities perceived to be exploiting legislative loopholes for fiscal advantage. Indeed, during the Covid-19 pandemic, public officials in several European countries made announcements targeting companies registered in the EU's relatively narrow list of tax havens based on the EU List. On 19 March 2020, Denmark's government announced that a relief package stipulating that companies based in such tax havens could not receive financial assistance.[28] Elsewhere, Poland's government applied conditions for domestic companies being eligible to seek financial assistance administered by the country's Development Fund, including that companies registered in tax havens would not be eligible for guarantees or financial loans under the scheme.[29] In the UK, Church leaders published a letter criticising the practise of large corporations avoiding responsibility and hiding wealth in tax havens.[30]

Considerably before the ongoing pandemic, back with the OECD-led campaigns from the 1990s onwards, the offshore world has long been recipients of such criticisms. We have seen renewed dis-sentiment in recent years in the wake of data breaches emanating from offshore jurisdictions. In particular, the Panama, Paradise and Pandora Papers shone a bright light on the offshore business world. The influence of these publications is inarguable, particularly in the area of corporate transparency, which shall be considered in the next section.

Compliance Willingness: BO Registers and the UKOTs

Particularly of late, many UKOTs with financial centres have been named in successive offshore data breaches. The territories in the Caribbean and North Atlantic are of particular significance given their involvement in global finance. There are 14 UKOTs across the world, with some operating as research centres and military bases, and some are amongst the most remote or least populated territories on earth. Of the 14, there are several that operate – to one degree or another – sophisticated financial sectors, namely Anguilla, Bermuda, the BVI, Cayman Islands, Gibraltar, Montserrat, and TCI. These jurisdictions

28 Government of Denmark, 'Enige om at justere og udvide hjælpepakker til dansk økonomi' (Translated)> (18 April 2020) <www.regeringen.dk/nyheder/2020/regeringen-og-alle-folketingets-partier-er-enige-om-at-justere-og-udvide-hjaelpepakker-til-dansk-oekonomi/> accessed 6 December 2021.

29 Amendment 301, Law No 2020–289, 23 March 2020, tabled on 21 April 2020.

30 *The Times*, 'Clergy Attack Tax-Haven Firms Seeking Coronavirus Bailouts' (27 April 2020), www.thetimes.co.uk/article/clergy-attack-tax-haven-firms-seeking-coronavirus-bailouts-9x826tp72 accessed 6 December 2021.

are strategically significant in different ways. For example, TCI is one of the Caribbean's fastest growing tourism destinations; Anguilla sits within a shipping superhighway; Bermuda is one of the world's largest reinsurance markets; and BVI operates a significant financial services sector, particularly its incorporation and associated activities.

As part of the broad risk-based approach which underpins the modern AML/CFT framework, the concept of knowing your customer has become a firm part of interdicting economic crime through financial transacting. It is not something simply confined to the banking context but, rather, the idea of knowing who is behind a given entity or transaction, and specifically where the money has come from or is going to, now applies to various other sectors such as real estate sales and lettings, luxury goods and works of fine art over a certain value. This is also given that such sectors might be less familiar with regulation or the risks inherent to their activities.

As mentioned, the FATF process measures both technical compliance with recommendations as well as members' effectiveness in terms of implementation of the same. A country may score highly on technical compliance, but on a follow-up peer-review score poorly in terms of implementation, and vice versa. Naturally, the aim is to secure both cooperation at the international level for FATF initiatives. Part of this process, particularly in terms of preparation for such assessments, includes states' conducting national risk assessments as a means of identifying and addressing risks across sectors. As part of the AML framework, BO information is an area closely linked to knowing your customer in the sense that it is all about enhancing due diligence. There is a well-accepted relationship between, for example, anonymous shell companies and the ability of criminals to utilise such structures and vehicles to launder the proceeds of crime, enjoy their ill-gotten gains, and, most importantly, sustain their illicit operations. In 2016, we saw an unprecedented data breach, the Panama Papers. An investigation of the International Consortium of Investigative Journalists (ICIJ), it emanated from the now-closed offshore law firm Mossack Fonseca (MOSSFON) and their Panama office. Shortly thereafter, we saw the Paradise Papers – in similar fashion – this time emanating out of the Bermuda office of the international law firm Appleby's. In both instances, the fallout was particularly damaging for the offshore world and, in particular, the UKOTs. Serious discussions were raised as to their facilitative role regarding the alleged misconduct within the stories that broke.[31] This prompted not only the usual negative media stories, but, importantly, legislative reform affecting the UKOTs as a means of compelling action in the area of BO transparency.

There were serious allegations raised as a result of the data. Some of note include the impact the Panama Papers had in relation to proceedings against

31 Oxfam, 'Tax Havens Serve No Useful Economic Purpose: 300 Economists Tell World Leaders' (8 May 2016) <www.oxfam.org/fr/node/10540> accessed 6 January 2022.

the former Pakistan Prime Minister, who was convicted and imprisoned for 10 years on corruption-related charges. Data from the leak showed that three of his children were linked to an entity registered in BVI that owned real estate in London. The entities had purportedly been used to channel funds. While the data leak did not name him specifically, its main output was to provide investigative lines of inquiry into close associates.[32] Elsewhere, the then Icelandic Prime Minster resigned following revelations of his interests in a BVI-registered entity that owned bonds in the three main Icelandic banks.[33] Further, revelations in the Paradise Papers alleged that Queen Elizabeth II's estate had made offshore investments in the Cayman Islands, which was heavily criticised in the UK media. Setting aside the obvious fact that the Queen is Head of State of the Cayman Islands, the Duchy of Lancaster stated that it was not aware of any tax advantage relating to the investment.[34] Revelations were also levelled at personalities such as racing driver Lewis Hamilton, who allegedly avoided VAT on a private jet. This was met with one British Parliamentarian suggesting that he should "[hold] his head in shame".[35]

The Panama and Paradise Papers served as considerable influence for the passage of the public register provision of SAMLA. Section 51 places a legislative ultimatum on the UKOTs, compelling them to commit to going public with their registers of BO by 2020, later extended to 2023. Otherwise, the territories would face having them imposed by Orders in Council. One of the amendments' architects, the Rt. Hon. Andrew Mitchell MP, stated:

> the territories may well allow access to law and order agencies, within an hour in the case of terrorism, through closed registers, but that does not allow civil society – charities, NGOs and the media – to expose them to the sort of scrutiny that the Paradise and Panama papers did.[36]

Section 51's other architect, Dame Margaret Hodge MP, had earlier emphasised that "[the] Guardian and Panorama [were] to thank for their brilliant investigative work and for placing the data relevant to us under public scrutiny".[37] Later, the UK Foreign Affairs Committee considered public

32 See *New York Times*, 'How the Panama Papers Changed Pakistani Politics' (28 July 2017) <www.nytimes.com/2017/07/28/world/asia/panama-papers-pakistannawaz-sharif.html> accessed 10 February 2022.

33 See *ICIJ*, 'Iceland Prime Minister Tenders Resignation Following Panama Papers Revelations' (5 April 2016) <www.icij.org/investigations/panama-papers/20160405-iceland-pm-resignation/> accessed 10 February 2022.

34 See BBC, 'Paradise Papers: Queen's Private Estate Invested £10 Million in Offshore Funds' (6 November 2017) <www.bbc.co.uk/news/uk-41878305> accessed 10 February 2022.

35 HC Deb (7.11.17) Vol 630, Col 1441, Dame Margaret Hodge MP.

36 HC Deb, 1.5.2018, Vol 640, Col 203, Rt. Hon. Andrew Mitchell MP.

37 HC Deb, 13.11.2017, Vol 631, Col 55, Dame Margaret Hodge MP.

accessibility to BO information to be a matter of national security and that the public have a right to see it.[38]

Publishing misappropriated and potentially confidential or legally privileged information often hides under the veil of public interest. Notwithstanding some of the very serious allegations emerging from such data breaches – some of which were acknowledged earlier – a closer look at the Panama and Paradise Papers data presents interesting findings from a technical standpoint. Such is important if, as we have seen with the passage of SAMLA, the data leaks are to serve as a benchmark for legislative reform that applies to all UKOTs. The Panama Papers data indicates that some 3,253 Anguilla-incorporated companies were named, yet a sizeable number were not active at the point of publication. This left some 1,868 active entities. The data did not include any additional information pointing to the company's purpose, other than the fact it is, or had been, Anguilla incorporated, with the addition of names and a registered address. By contrast, in the Paradise Papers, Anguilla was named sparingly, with only one Anguilla-registered company mentioned which, at the point of publication, was listed as "closed". Putting this into some context, there are approximately 28,000 limited companies registered in Anguilla. The law firm in question, MOSSFON, was essentially a wholesale company incorporation provider, thereby indicating that Anguilla was a popular jurisdiction to engage in this type of corporate servicing. Elsewhere, the Paradise Papers heavily named Bermuda (unsurprisingly given the target was Appleby's Bermuda office) with some 9,450 Bermuda-registered entities named. Although, much like the case of the Anguilla data, some 6,059 Bermuda entities had already been closed. The island was not, however, implicated in the Panama Papers – the indication being that MOSSFON did not use, incorporate, or manage Bermuda entities for its clients. Bermuda has not traditionally been viewed by the international community as a typical domicile for shell companies,[39] and its incorporation sector is relatively small compared to other UKOTs. Similarly, the TCI was not mentioned in the Panama Papers as being a jurisdiction in which any named companies were registered. It was, by contrast, mentioned in the Paradise Papers – with 26 TCI-registered entities named. Contextually, only 2 of the 26 remained active at the point of publication, with the others listed as closed – with some closing even as far back as the 1990s. TCI was mentioned in this data leak in other contexts. such as registered addresses for intermediaries, yet in circumstances where information relating to some 500,000 entities was published, only two active TCI entities were named.

38 See House of Commons, Foreign Affairs Committee 2019, 3.

39 See IMF, 'Bermuda: Final Detailed Assessment Report Anti–Money Laundering and Combatting the Financing of Terrorism' (2008) <www.imf.org/external/pubs/ft/scr/2008/cr08105.pdf> accessed 10 January 2022.

One conclusion to draw from these data leaks, which perhaps should be obvious but is not, is that not all offshore jurisdictions, or UKOTs, are the same. For example, while the Panama Papers data indicates that the BVI and Panama were favoured jurisdictions for incorporation services from a particular law firm,[40] other jurisdictions within the UKOTs network were implicated to differing degrees.

With the focus of the Panama and Paradise Papers on the offshore world, the issue of international standards on BO is timely. Internationally, uptake on central and public BO registers has been protracted which has not been helped by unaligned international standards on the storage and accessibility of such information, and indeed precisely what information should be subject to such. Vagueness on this noticeably juxtaposes the general nature of the global AML movement which presupposes a level of standardisation. FATF's Recommendations on this under Recommendation 24 stipulated that countries must ensure that there is adequate, accurate and timely information on BO and control of legal entities, accessible by competent authorities. While this stops short of specifying that such should be central or government held, or publicly accessible, it does resemble a central register framework present in numerous offshore jurisdictions, such as Bermuda whose register has been established for decades, and more recently in the BVI with its BO Secure Search System (BOSS). At the country-level, even as recently as 2018, Transparency International reported that only 6 G20 countries operated centrally held registers,[41] and as at March 2020, Global Witness reported that only five member states of the EU had gone completely public.[42] In 2022, FATF concluded a widespread consultation on a new BO standard, designed to update the current Recommendation 24. The amendments advocate further towards setting central registers as a benchmark, but continues to stop short at mandating them. It also states that alternatives may achieve the same underlying principles of providing timely and accurate information to public authorities. Some commentators, such as Open Ownership, have suggested that it would be difficult to achieve compliance without having central registers:

> it is difficult to see how alternative mechanisms could achieve the outcomes FATF require: rapid, efficient access to verified BO information by users

40 LJ Trautman, 'Following the Money: Lessons from the Panama Papers, Part 1: Tip of the Iceberg' (2017) 121(3) Penn State Law Review 807–73.

41 Transparency International, 'G20 Leaders or Laggards? Reviewing G20 Promises on Ending Anonymous Companies' <www.transparency.org/en/publications/g20-leaders-or-laggards#> accessed 7 October 2020.

42 Global Witness, 'Patchy Progress in Setting Up Beneficial Ownership Registers in the EU' (*Global Witness*, 20 March 2020), data includes the UK <www.globalwitness.org/en/campaigns/corruption-and-money-laundering/anonymous-company-owners/5amld-patchy-progress/> accessed 7 October 2020.

including domestic and foreign competent authorities, financial and other regulated institutions, and now also public procurement authorities.[43]

Compliance Willingness in the UKOTs?

The UKOTs have until 2023 to make their registers public. It is an established common law principle that the sovereign has the power to establish constitutions' for the territories, per *Phillips v Eyre* [1870]. As such, the UK government has power to legislate on behalf of the territories via Orders in Council. Convention, however, stipulates that this sort of intervention only should occur in what are deemed exceptional circumstances, for example, matters relating to defence, security or environmental disasters. There are also conventions which stipulate that the UK Parliament should not legislate or intervene on matters which are devolved, except with the express consent of the devolved administration concerned.

The non-optional nature of the SAMLA provision rendered considerable outrage from the UKOTs. Bermuda, for example, overtly resisted with its Premier in 2018, stating that the decision to legislate on behalf of the territories represented a regressive colonial mindset. He said that it showed a "wanton disregard" for Bermuda's unique constitutional position and "[an] egregious breach of well-established constitutional conventions". He averred that his government "rejects this regressive colonial mindset that some in London hold, that a Parliament 3000 miles away can impose anything on Bermuda that does not fall under the areas of defence, internal security, the judiciary, and external affairs" (Bermuda Government, 4.5.18, 3–4). Similarly, the then Opposition Leader of Anguilla and Chair of its Public Accounts Committee noted that there was significant inconsistency in approach between the UKOTs and Crown Dependencies, and warned of the disastrous impact on the financial industry and well-being of the Island (Island Sun 21.6.18). In the BVI over 1000 people protested and its government warned of a legal challenge to the UK Parliament's authority (BVI Beacon 25.5.18). To put this in context, BVI's population is 29,000. In the Cayman Islands, the Finance Minister criticised the UK's ignorance of the jurisdiction's compliance and cooperation with over 100 tax authorities internationally, citing specifically HMRC in the UK (Cayman Compass 1.5.18). In TCI, the Premier called the move destructive and constitutionally regressive, adding that it will cause burden and hardship (TCI Government 4.5.18). Indeed, for an issue so fundamental, it was

43 Open Ownership, 'FATF Recommendation 24: Global Standards on Beneficial Ownership Are Rising' (March 2022) <www.openownership.org/blogs/fatf-recommendation-24-global-standards-on-beneficial-ownership-are-rising/> accessed 10 March 2022.

noticeable that the UK Foreign Affairs Committee devoted so little of its most recent report on Resetting the Relationship with its OTs[44] to it.

Despite this resistance, the UKOTs have, since, made commitments to "going public".[45] It is interesting to note that this commitment has been made by jurisdictions like Bermuda and the Cayman Islands – which are well-known international financial centres with leading markets therein including (re) insurance in Bermuda's case and banking and hedge funds in the Cayman Island's case. By contrast, the commitment also includes jurisdictions like the Pitcairn Islands – the world's least populated country with consequently no presence in offshore or international finance. It also includes Anguilla, which only recently committed to implementing a central register of BO information and who traditionally placed such information with the companies registrar and based requests for the same on a summons procedure, per section 2, Anguilla Companies Registry Act. The landscape is therefore vague despite commitments being made within the timescale allotted by section 51 SAMLA. It is therefore unclear how jurisdictions which have traditionally not required timely or accurate collection, or regular updating of information, or engaged in exchanging the same, will cope in terms of effective implementation of a completely open public register. The BVI gave its commitment, albeit subject to it becoming a global standard.[46]

A legitimate question that must be considered is the extent to which small island jurisdictions, with markedly less resources, can or should be held to the same standards as larger, more influential jurisdictions with better capital and personnel resources? Indeed, the fact that good-faith commitments have been made ought to be seen positively. While transparency laws have been enacted following the Panama and Paradise Papers' fallout, it remains uncertain as to whether the goals of public registers are to tackle corruption, money laundering, tax evasion or tax avoidance, or all of the above.

The very nature of "offshore" will likely remain objectionable to its critics, regardless of transparency commitments and economic substance reforms. However, inherent problems associated with the UK's persons with significant control register, it is unsurprising that FATF has recommended amendments to its BO recommendations to stipulate that information must be verified. Notwithstanding that it provides little guidance beyond this as to how such will be achieved, one has to consider the extent to which compliance commitments are likely to transit into anything meaningful. For example, a commitment

44 House of Commons, Foreign Affairs Committee, 'Inquiry: Global Britain and the Overseas Territories: Resetting the Relationship' (2019) Fifteenth Report of Session 2017–19.

45 *Hansard*, HC Vol. 678, col. 63WS (15 July 2020), 'Publicly Accessible Registers of Company Beneficial Ownership in the British Overseas Territories: Written Statement – HCWS369'.

46 BVI Government 'Premier Reiterates Territory's Commitment to an Appropriate Framework for Publicly Accessible Registers (22 September 2020) <https://bvi.gov.vg/media-centre/bvi-premier-reiterates-territory-s-commitment-appropriate-framework-publicly-accessible> accessed 10 November 2021.

to "go public" might include, at first instance, a public register which is not verified (as the UK's one currently is). There are also considerable shortcomings regarding those functioning public registers such as the UK's, such as with verification, use of technology, errors already present, and the extent to which information is accurate given the necessity of updating through annual confirmation statements.[47] As Sharman recently observed: "A lot of the information fed into registries is junk. Public or private, bad information is bad information".[48] Blind technical compliance, without stringent verification systems, means that the accuracy of information relies on the honesty of users and/or their agents, which is concerning if disrupting criminals is what public registers purport to achieve. For islands that have indicated compliance commitments and that hope to secure their place in the international community in the process, yet may lack some of the human or capital resources mentioned in this section to implement a sophisticated open register, this remains a concern. If information is inaccurate or out of date, then the point of scrutiny is undermined at best.

Other Areas to Monitor

Notwithstanding the focus of this chapter on BO issues, there have been significant developments in AML/CFT in the offshore world that are worth noting. Oftentimes, focus on BO – which has been an inevitable consequence of offshore data leaks – omits consideration of other key areas of international cooperation. As we see with the problems inherent in the UK register, notwithstanding that it is public, this issue will take considerable time to achieve not only technical compliance but effective implementation. It is therefore necessary to consider other areas alongside these commitments.

The first to note is in the area of tax cooperation and, in particular, economic substance requirements. These are now firmly part of the global AML framework which formed part of the EU Code of Conduct Group for business taxation's recent investigation into the tax polices of EU and third countries. The motivation behind economic substance relates to the problematic notion of form over substance which has plagued offshore jurisdictions for decades. Further, it moves to increase momentum against aggressive tax avoidance and profit-shifting strategies. Examples of offshore jurisdictions that have, at the time of writing, implemented economic substance laws are plentiful. For instance, in 2018 Bermuda legislated to create the Economic Substance Act under which each Bermuda-registered entity engaged in "relevant activity"

47 See D Thomas-James, '"Imperfectly Perfect" and Other Concerns about Public Registers' (2021) 42(12) Company Lawyer 402–4.

48 Interview: JC Sharman, 'Missing the Mark? Why the Future of Beneficial Ownership Rules Hangs in the Balance' (*Vistra Insights*, 2 March 2021) <www.vistra.com/insights/missing-mark-why-future-beneficial-ownership-rules-hangs-balance> accessed 15 October 2021.

must maintain substantial economic presence in Bermuda. They must comply with the requirements of having economic substance per section 3(1) of the Act, which includes that the entity must be directed and/or managed in Bermuda, as well as having its core income-generating activities in the jurisdiction. It further stipulates that the entity must have adequate, suitably qualified full-time employees in the jurisdiction and ensure that there is adequate operational expenditure incurred in the jurisdiction relating to such relevant activity. The latter is defined as banking, insurance, fund management, financing, leasing, headquarters, shipping, distribution and service centre, intellectual property, and holding. The legislation places the obligation on the entity to file an annual declaration on economic substance which must be filed with the Registrar. Such legislation is not isolated to Bermuda. For instance, as part of recent company law reforms in the TCI, the Companies and Limited Partnerships (Economic Substance) Ordinance 2018 was enacted to implement EU standards on the same. The Act applies to all domestic companies and limited partnerships as well as foreign companies registered in TCI. The BVI enacted the Economic Substance (Companies and Limited Partnerships) Act 2018. In 2019, Anguilla implemented the same through various pieces of legislation including, but not limited to, the Companies (Economic Substance) Regulations 2019 and Companies (Amendment) Act 2019 (Economic Substance). The Cayman Islands also enacted the International Tax Co-Operation (Economic Substance) Act (2021 Revision). All these commitments place obligations on entities to show that they have sufficient economic substance in order to demonstrate that they should not be taxed elsewhere.

Concluding Thoughts and Outlook

For many of the UKOTs – and, for that matter, similar small island nations elsewhere in the Caribbean or Pacific, financial services are a pillar of their economies. This fact is immovable, notwithstanding efforts of diversification. It is clear that greater economic variety is needed as part of islands' development strategies, which has been painfully visible in the wake of recent hurricanes. Yet, financial services in and of themselves have transformed many small islands from barter-based economies to leading service providers in a matter of decades. Far from the nefarious intent which conveniently fits with common stereotypes, the provision of such services significantly impacts the economic wellbeing and prosperity of these jurisdictions. As such, it is perhaps easy to understand why tension emerges when jurisdictions are seemingly told what to do in a non-optional manner. As such, the commitments that have been made by the territories should be viewed in a positive fashion. It demonstrates willingness to comply with this aspect of the global AML framework that is ever-developing and which, alongside other commitments such as economic substance laws and company law reform as well as tax cooperation, demonstrates significant progress.

What is more complex, however, is the extent to which many territories' systems represent viable alternatives, or indeed whether public registers are the silver bullet that transparency campaigners and legislators alike believe it to be – such as those who can demonstrate a functioning central register of BO, information in which is exchangeable to competent investigative authorities. Such certainly seems to be possible when reading the proposed FATF amendments to Recommendations 24 and 25. Provided that information collected is accurate through verification systems, which is what the new global standards point to, then it is difficult to see how such a framework can be viewed as secretive. As was emphasised in this chapter, several islands in the UKOTs network, such as Bermuda, the Cayman Islands, the BVI and TCI, already have such registers. The fact remains that the international community, at the time of writing, is unaligned on an international standard – be that public, closed, central or government held, accessible freely or accessible for a fee. The most notable absentee of public registers is the US, for reasons relating largely to the nuances between the federal and state systems.

When considering compliance willingness, the islands' development challenges also have to be understood and acknowledged. These provide compelling explanations as to the different stages of their development, but also their progress in implementing certain features of the global AML framework. For example, the findings in relation to Anguilla pertain to a desperate need for constitutional reform and greater emphasis on legal development. This presents potential concerns as to the fact that they have yet to implement a functioning central register, despite making higher-level commitments to implement a public one shortly. As was mentioned, not only is technical compliance (e.g., laws on the books) sufficient, but the international regime presupposes effectiveness in terms of implementation – which in many regards, for the offshore world, will be the distinction between commitments and action, success or failure.

With that said, there are serious, unresolved issues with public registers – including the fact that those benchmarked ones still lack independent verification; and the fact that imposing a compliance deadline in the case of the UKOTs of 2023 may further a race to the bottom for illicit finance to jurisdictions which are darker and in which international cooperation (which jurisdictions such as the UK, US and EU, currently enjoy with the UKOTs through bilateral information exchange, common reporting and mutual legal assistance) are non-existent. While commitments demonstrate compliance willingness, given these shortcomings at large, time will tell if compliance effectiveness is being achieved on the ground, or if the aims that the international community have in regards to public registers will be met.

13 Combatting Terrorist Financing

A War Developing Countries Cannot Win?

Simeon Igbinedion

Introduction

The storm of terrorism is raging and indiscriminately impacting everybody and everything across the globe. Since the 9/11 terrorist attacks on the political and economic edifices of the United States in 2001, which claimed about 3,000 lives,[1] the international community has been urgently seeking the panacea to tame the merchants of terror, death and destruction. But it appears that the more such remedial efforts are taken, the more terrorist organisations proliferate around the world.[2]

With an array of well-armed and resourced murderous merchants of violence on the prowl, there seems to be little hope of the global capacity to curtail the criminal mission of these violent non-state actors (VNSAs) to kill, maim and destroy. Between 2013 and 2017, four of the deadliest terrorist groups – the Taliban, ISIL, Boko Haram and Al-Shabaab – carried out about 13,600 attacks on targets and slaughtered 72,519 people.[3] According to the Global Terrorism Index 2022, although deaths from terrorism fell by 1.2% to 7,142 deaths, the number of attacks globally increased by 17% to 5,226 in 2021.[4] Significantly, about half (3,461) of the deaths took place in sub-Saharan Africa, indicating that the continent is still in the throes of horrific terrorism. In all these, the economic costs of these deadly acts are enormous.[5]

1 'September 11 attacks: What happened on 9/11?' (3 August 2021) <www.bbc.com/news/world-us-canada-57698668> accessed 18 August 2022.

2 E.g., as at 12 February 2022, the number of US-designated Foreign Terrorist Organisations stood at 90. See Department of State, 'Foreign Terrorist Organisations: Bureau of Counterterrorism' <www.state.gov/foreign-terrorist-organizations/> accessed 12 September 2022.

3 Worlddata.info, 'Comparison of the Largest Terrorist Groups' <www.worlddata.info/terrorism/groups.php> accessed 13 October 2022.

4 See 'Global Terrorism Index 2022: Measuring the impact of Terrorism' <https://reliefweb.int/report/world/global-terrorism-index-2022> accessed 18 September 2022.

5 See, e.g., Patrick Lenain et al., 'The Economic Consequences of Terrorism' (OECD Economics Department Working Papers No. 334, 17 July 2002) <www.oecd-ilibrary.org/docserver/511778841283.pdf?expires=1644155212&id=id&accname=guest&checksum=1AE2A25179E2C5000DB57FD8F5CD0688> accessed 15 July 2022.

DOI: 10.4324/9781003253808-15

Available data shows that terrorist attacks occur most in developing countries or emerging economies that are riddled with socio-economic, religious and political instability.[6] VNSAs generally and terrorists particularly are believed to capitalise on the vulnerable points in these countries to wreak havoc and elevate their ideological inclinations over and above everyone else. Incontrovertibly, with the exception of a few entities (such as the Irish Republican Army in Northern Ireland, the Tamil Tigers in Sri Lanka, and Lord's Resistance Army in Uganda), most terrorist organisations pursue an Islamic religious agenda.[7] This chapter focuses on Islamic terrorism.

Finance is the substructure upon which rests terrorists' superstructural capacity to carry out terrorist attacks. By the grace of the huge assets that supporters channel towards terrorism, terrorists are able to spend lavishly to sustain their reign of terror on lives, liberties, livelihoods and institutions.[8] Although terrorism can objectively be condemned, there are persons who invoke the statement "one man's terrorist is another's freedom fighter"[9] to rationalise the conduct. Unfortunately, the maze of ambivalence arising from such characterisation tends to undermine societal moral basis for interrogating the legitimacy or propriety of financing it.

This chapter discusses the capacity or otherwise of developing states to win the war against terrorist financing (TF). Although combatting TF is a war every state aims to win, the anti-money laundering and combatting the financing of terrorism (AML/CFT) legal regime that developing states have adopted does not give room for such optimism because it overlooks the states' local circumstances and the peculiarities of the ideological drive behind TF. The chapter is divided into five sections. The next section considers terrorism and terrorist financing, and their nature. Thereafter the chapter discusses the extant legal regime against TF. The following section examines the capacity of developing states to win the war. It argues, inter alia, that irrespective of the states' formal commitments to the AML/CFT legal framework, they stand no chance to win the war in the foreseeable future. The final section concludes the discussion.

6 Worlddata.info, 'Terrorism by Country' <www.worlddata.info/terrorism/country-comparison.php> accessed 13 September 2022.

7 Worlddata.info, 'Terrorism by Country' <www.worlddata.info/terrorism/country-comparison.php> accessed 13 September 2022.

8 See Worlddata.info, Comparison (3); and 'The Richest Terror Organisations in the World' (24 January 2018) <www.forbes.com/sites/rachelsandler/2022/02/12/heres-who-mackenzie-scott-donated-to-so-far-in-february/?sh=298f685b66c1> accessed 17 October 2022.

9 E.g., see Sami Zeidan, 'Desperately Seeking Definition: The International Community's Quest for Identifying the Specter of Terrorism' (2004) 36(3) Cornell International Law Journal 491–92.

Terrorism and Terrorist Financing

Terrorism

Notwithstanding the fact that the international community has spent almost 90 years on terrorism-related deliberations,[10] it has continuously failed to define the conduct in a manner that is universally acceptable.[11] This is largely because terrorism is one of the very few terms that is plagued by so much indeterminacy, subjectivity and political disagreement.[12] Zeidan attributes such a state of affairs to the privileging of the political value of the term over its legal utility.[13] Consequently, people's appreciation of the problem of terrorism is conditioned by their socio-economic, political and ideological idiosyncrasies.

Terrorism is believed to be caused by a variety of factors including, inter alia, economic difficulties, poor governance, cultural or social alienation, and religious ideology.[14] Nevertheless, almost every state prohibits the conduct in its statute books,[15] as modestly complemented or supplemented by some international instruments. Despite the definitional stagnancy around terrorism, article 2(1)(b) of the United Nations Convention for the Suppression of the Financing Terrorism 1999[16] defines the conduct as any

> act intended to cause death or serious bodily injury to a civilian, or to any other person not taking an active part in the hostilities in a situation of armed conflict, when the purpose of such act, by its nature or context, is to intimidate a population, or to compel a government or an international organisation to do or to abstain from doing any act.[17]

10 Mohammed Salman Mahmood and Ahmad Masum, 'A Quest for Defining Terrorism in International Law: The Emerging Consensus' (2014) 10 Journal of International Studies 79.

11 See, e.g., Henok Kebede Bekele, 'Problem of Defining Terrorism under International Law: Definition by the Appeal Chamber of Special Tribunal for Lebanon as a Solution to the Problem' (2021) 12 Beijing Law Review 619; and Alex Schmid, 'Terrorism – The Definitional Problem' (2004) 36(2) Case Western Reserve Journal of International Law 375.

12 Ben Saul, 'Defining "Terrorism" to Protect Human Rights' (October 2008) <http://ssrn.com/abstract=1292059> accessed 2 August 2022.

13 E.g., see Zeidan (n 9) 491–92; and Jacqueline S Hodgson and Victor Tadros, 'The Impossibility of Defining Terrorism' (Summer 2013) 16(3) New Criminal Law Review 495.

14 E.g., see Alex P Schmid, 'Terrorism Prevention: Conceptual Issues (Definitions, Typologies and Theories)' in Alex P Schmid (ed), *Handbook of Terrorism Prevention and Preparedness* (The Hague: ICCT Press Publication, July 2021) 35; and Hussein Solomon, *Terrorism and Counter-Terrorism in Africa: Fighting Insurgency from* Al Shabaab, Ansar Dine and Boko Haram, (ed) (Palgrave Macmillan 2015) 100.

15 E.g., USA PATRIOT Act 2001; UK's Terrorism Act 2000 & Terrorism Act 2006; and Nigeria's Terrorism Prevention Act (TPA) 2022.

16 Adopted on 9 December 1999 and entered into force on 10 April 2002.

17 See also art. 3(a), AU Convention on the Prevention and Combatting of Terrorism 1999.

The claim that terrorism is an organised crime is usually controversial. Although points of intersection exist between terrorism and organised crime,[18] there are many areas of divergence between both of them,[19] particularly those relating to purpose. Article 2(a) of the United Nations Convention on Transnational Organised Crime (UNCATOC) 2000 defines the purpose of an "organised criminal group" as financial or other material benefit in contrast with that of terrorists. Therefore, the gulf between both crimes is likely to endure.[20] Terrorism could be localised within the state, though it is largely trans-border. Although the conduct possesses the character of an international crime,[21] it is not one because states are yet to form the requisite consensus to make it so.

Terrorist Financing

TF is the mobilisation of valuable resources for the purpose of carrying out terrorist acts. TF is variously defined as the means and methods used by terrorist organisations to finance their activities,[22] the "solicitation, collection and provision of funds with the intention that they may be used to support terrorist acts or organisations,"[23] or the "financing of terrorist acts, and of terrorists and terrorist organisations."[24]

The sponsors of international anti-TF mechanisms employ existing anti-money laundering rules in combatting TF. Money laundering is the handling of funds in order to disguise or conceal their illicit origin, whereas TF is the use of resources to execute a terrorist agenda. This implies that the funds available for laundering necessarily derive from criminal origin, but in TF, the provenance of the assets is immaterial. Therefore, the deployment of AML rules to serve the ends of CFT despite their being at cross-purposes[25] is objectionable.[26]

18 Sam Mullins and James K Wither, 'Terrorism and Organised Crime' (Summer 2016) 15(3) Connections 70–76; and FATF-GIABA, 'Terrorist Financing in West Africa' (FATF Report) (October 2013) 13 <www.giaba.org/media/f/632_TF-in-West-Africa.pdf> accessed 15 July 2022.

19 Sam Mullins and James K Wither, 'Terrorism and Organised Crime' (Summer 2016) 15(3) Connections 66–70; and FATF-GIABA, 'Terrorist Financing in West Africa' (FATF Report) (October 2013) 13 <www.giaba.org/media/f/632_TF-in-West-Africa.pdf> accessed 15 July 2022. 66–70.

20 See Mark Shaw and Prem Mahadevan, 'When Terrorism and Organised Crime Meet' (October 2018) 6/7 Policy Perspectives 4.

21 See Antonio Cassese, 'Terrorism is also Disrupting Some Crucial Legal Categories of International Law' (2001) 12(5) EJIL 994–95.

22 UNODC, 'Combating Terrorist Financing' <www.unodc.org/unodc/en/terrorism/expertise/combating-terrorist-financing.html> accessed 17 September 2022.

23 IMF, 'Anti-Money Laundering/Combating the Financing of Terrorism (AML/CFT)' <www.imf.org/external/np/leg/amlcft/eng/aml1.htm> accessed 10 August 2022.

24 See Legislationonline, 'The Interpretative Notes to the Special Recommendations (SRs) on Terrorist Financing (TF)' <www.legislationline.org/documents/id/4181> accessed 12 September 2022.

25 See FATF-GIABA (n 18) 10.

26 See generally Hamed Tofangsaz, 'Rethinking Terrorist Financing; Where Does All This Lead?' (2015) 18:1 JMLC 116–17.

How then do terrorists generate resources? They licitly derive resources from local business or commercial transactions.[27] The Inter-Governmental Action Group against Money Laundering in West Africa (GIABA) – which is a Financial Action Task Force–style West African sub-regional body – has confirmed that terrorists whose operational bases cut across Senegal, Nigeria, Mali, Niger and Cameroon access funds lawfully from members' sale of goods or trading activities, personal donations of profits from businesses, creation of fictitious companies and importation of used cars,[28] contributions from members, financing through financial institutions and begging for alms, and so on.[29]

On the other hand, terrorists illicitly derive huge assets from criminal activities such as arms trafficking, extortion, illegal oil exploration,[30] credit card and cheque fraud, smuggling, robbery, cattle or livestock rustling, racketeering, kidnapping for ransom, abuse of non-profit organisations and, more importantly, drugs trafficking.[31] GIABA has confirmed many of these crimes as the sources of funds for terrorists whose areas of operation are located in previously enumerated states but has stated further that those sources include misuse of non-governmental organisations (NGOs) for terrorist funding, financial contributions of political leaders and alternative remittances.[32]

From the foregoing, it is apparent that terrorists acquire resources through self-sponsorship, sponsorship by non-state actors (individuals, corporate entities, NGOs), or states.[33] The current mechanism for combatting TF is the subject of the next section.

Combatting Terrorist Financing

The battle against TF rests on the tripod of prevention, criminalisation and international cooperation, but this section will discuss only the preventive and criminal measures.

27 FATF-GIABA-GABAC, 'Terrorist Financing in West & Central Africa' (October 2016) 16 <www.fatf-gafi.org/media/fatf/documents/reports/Terrorist-Financing-West-Central-Africa.pdf> accessed 25 July 2022. On how Al Qaeda obtained resources see Tofangsaz (n 26) 116.

28 FATF-GIABA (n 18) 18–20.

29 On how Boko Haram obtains its resources, see Kangdim Dingji Maza, et al., 'Challenges of Combating Terrorist Financing in the Lake Chad Region: A Case of Boko Haram' (April–June 2020) 3 <https://journals.sagepub.com/doi/pdf/10.1177/2158244020934494> accessed 13 September 2022.

30 See Worlddata.info, Comparison (n 3).

31 See also Tofangsaz (n 26) 115; FATF-GIABA (n 18) 20–23.

32 See also Tofangsaz (n 26) 115; FATF-GIABA (n 18) 20–31.

33 E.g., Iran supports Hezbollah while Qatar and the tax revenues of the Gaza Strip support Hamas: Worlddata.info, Comparison (n 3).

Preventive Measures

Article 8(1) and (2) of the 1999 Convention obligates each state party to take appropriate measures to identify, detect, freeze or seize any funds used or allocated for the purpose of committing TF and the proceeds therefrom. Undoubtedly, financial intermediaries (including banks and non-bank financial institutions) are in a special position to interface with the resources used or earmarked for TF. They are required to exercise due diligence in handling their customers and their assets. Thus, article 18(1)(b) specifically obliges each state party to establish measures requiring financial institutions and other professions involved in financial transactions to utilise the most efficient measures available for the identification of their usual or occasional customers; and to pay special attention to unusual or suspicious transactions and report transactions suspected of stemming from a criminal activity. Similarly, the FATF has updated its 40 Recommendations[34] for, as appropriate, combatting money laundering and TF.[35] Specifically, the FATF designed a set of special recommendations (SRs) targeted at TF.[36]

Criminal Measures

Article 2 of the 1999 Convention states that any person commits an offence if he or she by any means, directly or indirectly, unlawfully and wilfully, provides or collects funds with the intention that they should be used or in the knowledge that they are to be used, in full or in part, in order to carry out the act of terrorism.

In the wake of the horrific terrorist attacks on the US in 2001, the UN Security Council (UNSC) invoked its powers under Chapter VII of the UN Charter 1945 to adopt Resolution 1373 of 28 September 2001 where it, among other things, mandated all states to suppress TF, freeze terrorists funds and prohibit their nationals from raising funds for terrorists. Subsequently, in October 2001, the FATF adopted the IX Special Recommendations (SRs) on Terrorist Financing.[37] Like the UNSC Resolution 1373, the SRs request each

34 See FATF, 'FATF 40 Recommendations (October 2003) (incorporating all subsequent amendments until October 2004) <www.fatf-gafi.org/media/fatf/documents/FATF%20Standards%20-%2040%20Recommendations%20rc.pdf> accessed 25 July 2022.

35 See FATF, *International Standards on Combating Money Laundering and the Financing of Terrorism & Proliferation* (FATF 2012–2021) <www.fatf-gafi.org/recommendations.html> accessed 10 October 2022.

36 FATF, 'IX Special Recommendations' (October 2001) (incorporating all subsequent amendments until February 2008) <www.fatf-gafi.org/media/fatf/documents/reports/FATF%20Standards%20-%20IX%20Special%20Recommendations%20and%20IN%20rc.pdf> accessed 17 October 2022.

37 FATF, 'IX Special Recommendations' (October 2001) (incorporating all subsequent amendments until February 2008) <www.fatf-gafi.org/media/fatf/documents/reports/FATF%20Standards%20-%20IX%20Special%20Recommendations%20and%20IN%20rc.pdf> accessed 17 October 2022.

country to, as relevant, criminalise the financing of terrorism, terrorist acts and terrorist organisations, and designate such offences as money laundering predicate offences,[38] freeze and confiscate terrorist assets,[39] report suspicious transactions related to terrorism,[40] and subject relevant persons to administrative, civil or criminal sanctions.[41] Moreover, SRIX mandates countries to ensure that effective, proportionate and dissuasive sanctions are available to deal with defaulters and, where appropriate, confiscate their assets.

All states (including developing ones) are legally bound by UNSC resolutions and practically obligated by FATF Recommendations and Special Recommendations. In addition, most of them are states parties to the 1999 Convention.[42] They have variously integrated the soft and hard laws from the international and intergovernmental organisations into their domestic legal systems. For example, Nigeria, Senegal, Ghana and so many other African States have enacted anti-TF legislations,[43] implemented AML/CFT regulations, joined the regional GIABA and established their financial intelligence units. In spite of all this, why is there still anxiety over the capacity of developing states to win the war against TF? The next section attempts to unravel this question.

A War Developing Countries Cannot Win?

It could be optimistically asserted that developing states can win the war against TF. But it is unsafe to do so without first assessing the local circumstances of the AML/CFT regime they have adopted and the ideological drive behind TF, as the following discussion will demonstrate.

Predication of CFT Regime on Financial Institutions

The precarious predication of the implementation of the substantial part of the current CFT prescriptions on financial institutions is clearly a recipe for developing states to lose the war against TF. Such predication derives from the assumption that resources intended for TF would necessarily be channelled through the states' formal financial institutions. But this is not necessarily so. Truly, many developing states have formally harmonised their domestic legal systems with the existing international CFT regime. However, the latter appears to take two things for granted, namely, that the banks would act scrupulously and generate credible documents.

38 SRII.
39 SRIII.
40 SRIV.
41 SRVI.
42 See Status of the International Convention for the Suppression of the Financing Terrorism 1999 <https://treaties.un.org/pages/ViewDetails.aspx?src=IND&mtdsg_no=XVIII-11&chapter=18&clang=_en> accessed 20 June 2022.
43 E.g., see s. 21 of Nigerian Terrorism Prevention Act (TPA) 2022; art. 279–3 of the Senegalese Penal Code 2007; and Act 875 of Ghanaian Anti-Terrorism (Amendment) Act 2014.

Bank's Scrupulous Oversight

In entrusting the banks with the gatekeeping role of exercising due diligence in handling the financial resources of clients, the sponsors of the AML/CFT regime impliedly presume that the financial institutions would scrupulously implement the prescriptions in order to deter or detect TF. Such presumption is misplaced. The conscription of banks into the trenches erected against TF ignores the fact that these financial intermediaries are ordinarily private business actors out primarily to make profits in the course of their confidential relationship with customers.[44] But the regime has, arguably for good reasons, been instituted to make the financial institutions monitor persons whose financial secrets they are supposed to keep secret. Yet because societal imposition of such duty does not obliterate the purpose for which the banks are in business, the bankers find themselves entangled in a conflict of interests.

It is submitted that the negative effect of compulsorily using the financial intermediaries to enforce these measures without any form of financial incentive accentuates the bankers' dilemma in clearly resolving such conflict[45] in the interest of the public. Obviously, it is usually said that the fear of fines and loss of reputation may motivate banks to have strong AML/CFT frameworks. But such motivation is quite inadequate especially in climes where, because law enforcement is vulnerable to manipulation, the bank stands a good chance to circumvent the rules and get away with it.

Manipulation of Documents

The international promoters of the AML/CFT regime also overlook the extent to which the endemic corruption in many of these developing states can impact negatively on the work of financial institutions. Basically, the banks source information from clients. But a client who intends to open or operate an account for the purpose of TF will not disclose facts related to that purpose. Rather, he or she will present doctored documents to satisfy the bank's curiosity. Assuming the bank desires to honestly verify the information supplied by the client, it may not be able to go far because publicly reliable database is either non-existent or inadequate. For instance, when the two sons of Abacha (Ibrahim Sani and Mohammed Sani) were opening accounts with Citibank, they did not disclose their familial relationship or nomenclatural association with, or the beneficial ownership of, Sani Abacha, their father, who was then the Nigerian military dictator. They misrepresented their identity and status. Thus, their London Citibank private banker understood them to be "unfailingly charming, polite and, above all, reliable" while their New York

44 Gwendoline Godfrey et al., 'Bank Confidentiality – A Dying Duty but not Dead Yet?' (September 2016) 17(3) Business Law International 186.

45 Mihaela Sandulescu, 'Reconciling the Anti-Money Laundering Compliance Duties and the Commercial Objectives of the Bank' in Petrus C van Duyne et al. (eds), *Corruption, Greed and Crime Money: Sleaze and Shady Economy in Europe and Beyond* (CUP 2013) 185.

Citibank private banker did not know they were the sons of the Nigerian head of State for three years.[46] Such occurrence implies that in as much as the best is expected from the documents generated by the banks, there are real possibilities that they can be falsified and the banks would rely on them and throw their gates wide open to terrorist funds. But those in the vanguard against TF appear to disregard this and create the impression that the banks would seamlessly and faithfully perform their roles. The same banks-related argument applies, *mutatis mutandis*, to para-financial institutions such as designated non-financial institutions (DNFIs) or designated non-financial businesses and professionals (DNFBPs) in so far as they are required to create a paper trail of transactions involving their clients.

Cash and Carry Orientation of the Economies

The international legal regime fails to reckon with the fact that the economies of many developing states (including those in West and Central Africa) are cash oriented or cash intensive. Most transactions in developing states are executed with raw cash in the informal sectors of the economies instead of being consummated in banks or DNFBPs. In fact, apart from the fact that the people are used to such a mode of transaction, they prefer it for its predictability, credibility and convenience.[47] Similarly, they are comfortable with the transactional mode because of difficulties associated with the operation of a cashless economy including poor internet connectivity, illiteracy, lack of information and knowledge about financial matters,[48] and the need to keep such transactions confidential for the purpose of diminishing their tax liabilities (such as charges on card payments and unoperational bank accounts).[49] It is true that there have been attempts by some private investors to capitalise on the opportunities some of these challenges associated with cash-intensive economies pose for the people[50] but their reach is still rudimentary. It is worth noting that such cash orientation reflects the contemporary moderate size or

46 United States, 'Minority Staff Report for Permanent Subcommittee on Investigations Hearing on Private Banking and Money Laundering: A Case Study of Opportunities and Vulnerabilities' (hereinafter *Minority Staff Report*, 9 November 1999) 35 <www.hsgac.senate.gov/imo/media/doc/REPORT-Private%20Banking%20&%20Money%20Laundering%20(Nov%201999).pdf> accessed 6 October 2022.

47 Neetu Kumari and Jhanvi Khanna, 'Cashless Payment: A Behavioural Change to Economic Growth' (2017) 2:2 India Qualitative and Quantitative Research Review 94.

48 See Muftau Adesina Abayomi and David Sunday Oyerinola, 'Implications of Nationwide Implementation of Cash-less Policy for the Nigerian Economy: Challenges and Prospects' (2018) 44 Journal of Resources Development and Management 65.

49 CE Rudresha, 'Cashless Transaction in India: A Study' (February 2019) 4(2) International Journal of Scientific Development and Research (IJSDR) 65. See also Kumari and Khanna (n 51) 94.

50 Kingsley Ighobor, 'Africa's Quest for a Cashless Economy Gains Momentum' (*Africa Renewal*, May–July 2017) <www.un.org/africarenewal/magazine/may-july-2017/africa%E2%80%99s-quest-cashless-economy-gains-momentum> accessed 24 July 2022.

the unsophisticated nature of the economies involved in contrast with the large and more sophisticated economies of developed countries.[51]

Obviously, the transactions carried out with cash in a cash-and-carry economy by people who are comfortable with such transactional practice do not feature in the paper trail that may be generated for the purpose of tracking and trapping terrorist funds. Thus, there is disharmony between the externally induced (hard and soft) legal regime against TF that developing states have introduced to or imposed on their territories on the one hand and the prevailing cash orientation of the economies and the people's consciousness and recognition of its utility on the other. Although developing states are aware of such disharmony, they just made do with formally integrating such international regime into their domestic legal orders in order to avert the disapproval of its sponsors. Specifically, they transplanted AML/CFT standards into their domestic laws not necessarily because their territories are receptive to or suitable for those standards but for a variety of reasons, including demonstrating esprit de corps to those sponsors, attracting foreign investment, integrating their economies into the global economy and avoiding FATF sanctions or blacklisting.[52]

Nevertheless, such formal compliance does not address the contempt with which the imported legal norms (of largely predicating the CFT legal regime on banks) treat the local norms (of cash orientation and the people's cultural and historical consciousness or experiences thereon). According to the Sociological School of Law, law can be used to change people's behaviour or way of life, but it is equally important to recall that notwithstanding attempts to do so, the reality of the "living law," as propounded by Eugene Erlich, cannot be ignored.[53] Similarly, from the perspective of the Historical School of Law, led by Von Savigny, law is a product of the history of the people.[54] The school rails against wholesale importation of laws, rules and regulations that ignores, as appropriate, the people's historical behaviour regarding cash and carry transactions.[55] In designing the international legal regime that makes banks the nerve centre of the battle against TF in developing states, the patrons and their local collaborators fail to be aptly guided by the moral lesson from both schools of

51 But see John Bagnall et al., 'Consumer Cash Usage a Cross-Country Comparison with Payment Diary Survey Data' (European Central Bank: Working Paper Series No. 1685/June 2014) <https://ideas.repec.org/p/dnb/dnbwpp/422.html> accessed 22 September 2022.

52 Navin Beekarry, 'The International Anti-Money Laundering and Combating the Financing of Terrorism Regulatory Strategy: A Critical Analysis of Compliance Determinants in International Law' (2011) 31 Northwestern Journal of International Law & Business 179.

53 Eugen Erlich, *Fundamental Principles of the Sociology of Law* with an intro. by Roscoe Pound, with a new intro by Klaus A. Ziegert (Routledge 2017) 493.

54 See Dias, *Jurisprudence* (5th edn, Butterworths 1985) 378; and Kayode Eso, *Thoughts on Law and Jurisprudence* (MIJ Professional Publishers Limited 1991) 259.

55 Robert E Rodes, 'On the Historical School of Jurisprudence' (2004) 49 The American Journal of Jurisprudence 165.

law. Meanwhile, in demonstrating the incapacity of developing states to win the war against TF, terrorists and their supporters cash in on such unwarranted dependence or over-dependence on banks to unceasingly generate, accumulate and move cash or other resources without any paper trail through the informal sectors of the economies of these states.

Therefore, the current CFT regime is a mismatch for plugging the leakages in transactions conducted outside the financial institutions in developing states because there is a socio-cultural and historical misfit between the so-called international standards on the one hand and local conditions on the other. The international norms' expectation that its prescriptions would immediately change the transactional behaviour of the people is largely misplaced. Although such behavioural change may be helpful in the long run, it cannot happen overnight because old habits die hard. In view of the foregoing, the superstructure of TF prohibition or regulation, which heavily relies on financial institutions, is erected on a faulty substructure.

Lack of the Political Will to Enforce the Law

The lack of the political will to enforce the existing regime against TF definitely points to the incapacity of developing states to win the war. By and large, there are laws, rules and regulations validly put in place by states in the developing world to check TF. But it is not enough to institute a legal regime. The incidence of endless flow of financial resources to terrorists despite the existence of measures against TF validates Kelsen's proposition to the effect that efficacy or effectiveness of the law is more important than its validity.[56]

The law is not self-enforcing because it does not have a life of its own. Similarly, the state is an abstraction on behalf of which organs or agents must act. These organs and agents are vested with the power to enforce the law. Unfortunately, in most if not all developing states, institutions are weak and appointed "strong" men and women superintend over them. The institutions rise with the rise and fall with the fall of these appointees. The appointees bring their charisma and discretion to bear on the way of doing government business, including law enforcement. In effect, even where the law is clear on a matter, the ultimate law enforcer who is subordinate in the pyramidal chain of command must factually confirm that the "strong" man or woman occupying the relevant highest rungs of the ladder is comfortable with such enforcement before he or she can safely embark on actual enforcement.

It is within this context that political will to enforce the law is implicated. Political will is the desire to do something irrespective of whose ox is gored.

56 Graham Hughes, 'Validity and the Basic Norm' (1971) 59 California Law Review 697–98; and Luka Burazin, 'Efficacy as a Condition of Validity in Kelsen's General Theory of Norms' (2021), 7–8 <https://papers.ssrn.com/sol3/papers.cfm?abstract_id=3791918> accessed 15 September 2022.

Therefore, lack of political will is declining to do a thing because of the vested, political and narrow interests that would be affected in so doing. The repository of political will are those officials occupying high profile positions and embodying the directing will and mind of the state, including the President, the Prime Minister, Head of Government, Heads of the Armed Services, Inspector General of Police, their privies or proxies, persons who de facto hold the lever of power, and so on. If, as is the case in many developing states, there is no political will to enforce the law against TF, it is because any or a combination of these high-level office holders have something to gain or promote in failing to give the necessary instructions to relevant law enforcement agents to enforce the law and, most importantly, to confirm that there are positive outcomes therefrom. It is against this background that violent elements in Nigeria (including terrorists and their supporters) can extort money; kidnap, negotiate and collect huge ransoms in cash;[57] engage in mining activities in places like Zamfara State[58] (against the clear provisions of the law that vests such endeavour exclusively in the Federal Government), smuggle contraband items including arms and ammunition, and so on, while those vested with legal authority (and political will) simply use their positions to compromise the capacity of the law enforcement agents and ipso facto the state to investigate and bring them to justice.

The political will to tackle Boko Haram terrorists and their financiers has suffered a similar fate in the hands of those entrusted with the legal power to secure Nigeria. In addition to its failure to invoke the provisions of the Terrorism Prevention Act 2022 to investigate, arrest or prosecute offenders and their accomplices, the government has been lukewarm towards weaponising the AML/CFT regime to trace or track terrorists' financiers, and to cripple the terrorists' financial capability. The government's lethargy in dismantling the financial capacity of terrorists can be contrasted with the vigour with which the United Arab Emirate (UAE) Federal Appeals Court in November 2020 upheld the convictions and sentence of six Nigerians to prison terms of ten years to life imprisonment for wiring $782,000 from Dubai to Boko Haram terrorists.[59]

However, five long months later (in April 2021), the Nigerian government security apparatus – in a bid to save its face from the embarrassment

57 'Insecurity: Nigerians Pay Over N7 Billion Ransom to Kidnappers in Nine Years – Report' (28 May 2020) <www.premiumtimesng.com/news/headlines/394899-insecurity-nigerians-pay-over-n7-billion-ransom-to-kidnappers-in-nine-years-report.html> accessed 20 October 2022.

58 'How Illegal Gold Mining Fuels Violent Crimes in Zamfara – ICPC' (3 November 2021) <www.premiumtimesng.com/news/top-news/493226-how-illegal-gold-mining-fuels-violent-crimes-in-zamfara-icpc.html> accessed 25 September 2022.

59 '6 Nigerians Sentenced for Funding Boko Haram Terrorist Group' (10 November 2020) <www.voanews.com/africa/6-nigerians-sentenced-funding-boko-haram-terrorist-group> accessed 26 September 2022. Although as recently as March 2022 FATF still regarded the UAE as a jurisdiction with strategic deficiency, the country's action against the convicts can be understood as reflecting its zero tolerance for terrorism or its financing.

of deliberately declining to take steps against financiers – managed to launch a nationwide crackdown on suspected financiers and collaborators of Boko Haram and other criminal groups in Nigeria[60] and arrested dozens of offenders, including bureau de change operators, gold miners and sellers, and other businessmen. The realisation that the crackdown is the only lame attempt that Nigeria has made against TF in non-bank sectors since the advent of Boko Haram in 2009 symbolises the deplorable state of the national political will to undermine TF. As the government appears to have perfected the act of making a hype or hoax of the fight against TF,[61] nobody takes it seriously anymore.[62]

Islamic Religious Ideology

Out of the various causes of terrorism,[63] this chapter adopts Islamic religious ideology to explain how Islamic terrorists and their financiers undermine the existing CFT legal regime. Erikson and Tedin[64] define (political) ideology as a "set of beliefs about the proper order of society and how it can be achieved."[65] According to Ahmed, loyalty to an ideology is often so total that it allows for or even encourages violence for the purpose of total complete compliance.[66] The European Commission's Expert Group gives an example of the Jihadi Salafist which projects the ideology of hardcore violence laced with the propaganda of creating new caliphates and reclaiming territories which were once under Muslim rule in ancient times in order to knit willing Muslims together. It is from such radicalised pool that terrorists and their supporters-cum-financiers emerge.[67] Incidentally, such ideology largely influenced the expansionist ambitions of ISIL in Iraq and Syria, Boko Haram in Nigeria, and ISWAP in West Africa, and so on.

The ideological conviction of the terrorists and their supporters is strengthened by some Islamic elites and government officials who capitalise on their

60 'Terrorism Financing: Dozens Arrested In Nationwide Crackdown' (19 April 2021) <https://dailytrust.com/terrorism-financing-dozens-arrested-in-nationwide-crackdown> accessed 20 September 2022.

61 'FG Uncovers 96 Terrorist Sponsors, Arrests 45 Suspects' <https://dailytrust.com/just-in-fg-uncovers-96-terrorist-sponsors-45-suspects-arrested-lai-mohammed> accessed 3 October 2022.

62 'Terrorism financing: Name, prosecute suspects, Nigerians tell Buhari' <https://guardian.ng/news/terrorism-financing-name-prosecute-suspects-nigerians-tell-buhari/> accessed 5 October 2022.

63 Adopted (n 16).

64 Robert Erikson and Kent Tedin, American Public Opinion: Its Origins, Content, and Impact (Routledge 2019).

65 Cited in John T Jost, et al., 'Political Ideology: Its Structure, Functions, and Elective Affinities' (2009) 60 Annual Review of Psychology 309.

66 Ranya Ahmed, *How Ideology Influences Terror* (Cambridge Scholars Publishing 2020) 10.

67 Rogelio Alonso, et al., 'Radicalisation Processes Leading to Acts of Terrorism (a concise Report prepared by the European Commission's Expert Group on Violent Radicalisation) (15 May 2008) <www.clingendael.org/sites/default/files/pdfs/20080500_cscp_report_vries.pdf> accessed 25 September 2022.

sharing the same Islamic faith and/or ethnic affinity with the terrorists to make statements or conduct themselves in a manner intended to rationalise or even justify terrorist activities so as to help the terrorists evade the legal consequences of their conduct. For example, a renowned Islamic scholar, Sheikh Abubakar Gumi – while reacting to the outcry of Nigerians over the activities of Nigeria-based VNSAs such as bandits and militant herdsmen[68] who have routinised kidnapping of school children (especially girls)[69] for ransom – downplayed the seriousness of the atrocities and described the perpetrators simply as persons seeking their means of survival.[70] Similarly, the Governor and Chief Law Officer of Bauchi State, Bala Mohammed, justified the non-state actors' possession of dangerous weapons to terrorise or brutalise their compatriots contrary to constitutional provisions.[71] Also, the President of the country failed to relieve the incumbent Minister of Communications and Digital Economy, Isa Patami, of his duties despite being found to have had radical pro-Taliban or Al-Qaeda views or connections.[72] Moreover, the Attorney General of the Federation (AGF), Abubakar Malami, did not hide his sympathy towards the violent actors when – while responding to southern governors' ban on open grazing as a measure to prevent the terrorists' continued bloodshed – he firmly defended their constitutional right to move their cattle from one part of the country to another amidst their ceaseless and massive extra-judicial killings of non-Fulanis notwithstanding the fact that the same constitution frowns upon taking the law into one's hands.[73]

In the midst of such official defence of terrorist activities, there is hardly any serious prosecution of terrorists or their financiers. Apart from motivating

68 They exist alongside Boko Haram (BH). Although they are not known to be affiliated to BH, their modus operandi is largely similar to that of BH. See SA Igbinedion, 'When Jungle Order Rocks the Boat of Legal Order: Inevitability of State Stability for the Peace and Security of Mankind in Africa' (Proceedings of the 15th International RAIS Conference on Social Sciences and Humanities, 6–7 November 2019) 135.

69 Apart from the ransom payments they receive from such criminal activity, the abductors target girls because of their warped indoctrination that education is abominable, particularly where the beneficiaries are girls whom they consider to be of lesser status than boys and candidates for sexual exploitation or pleasure.

70 'Bandits are ethnic militants seeking survival – Gumi' (24 February 2021) <https://thenationonlineng.net/bandits-are-ethnic-militants-seeking-survival-gumi/amp/> accessed 22 September 2022.

71 'Bauchi Governor defends Ak-47 carrying Fulani herdsmen, blasts Ortom, others' (12 February 2021) <https://pmnewsnigeria.com/2021/02/12/bauchi-governor-defends-ak-47-carrying-fulani-herdsmen-blasts-ortom-others/> accessed 7 September 2022.

72 'DSS informed FG of Pantami's extremist views before ministerial appointment, says ex-director, Amachree' (22 April 2021) <www.vanguardngr.com/2021/04/dss-informed-fg-of-pantamis-extremist-views-before-ministerial-appointment-says-ex-director-amachree/> accessed 20 September 2022.

73 'Southern Governors Ban on Open Grazing Is Dangerous, Malami Warns' (20 May 2021) <https://guardian.ng/news/southern-governors-ban-on-open-grazing-is-dangerous-malami-warns/> accessed 24 September 2022.

terrorists to intensify their activities, such utterances or conduct presents a huge opportunity for sections of the communities to donate their resources personally or through their foundations to meet the pecuniary needs of terrorists.

Conclusion

This chapter discussed whether or not developing states cannot win the war against TF. The discussion considered the concept and scope of terrorism and TF. Thereafter, it examined some of the laws, rules and regulations that sponsors of international CFT regime have designed for implementation by states, including developing states. By and large, many developing states have faithfully implemented the international legal regime albeit formally or uncritically.

It is against such domestic implementation that the chapter examined the likelihood of developing states winning the war. The chapter argued that these states cannot win the war as yet because the AML/CFT regime adopted does not reflect their local peculiarities or circumstances. Realistically, developing states currently lack what it takes to win the war.

It is earnestly hoped that appropriate remedial measures would be adopted and implemented so that in the near future the question of whether the developing states can win the war against TF could be emphatically answered in the affirmative.

14 Asset Recovery in Developing Countries

Assessing Successes and Failures and Overcoming Challenges

Jean-Pierre Brun and Anastasia Sotiropoulou

Introduction

According to UN estimates, the global cost of corruption represents a significant percentage of the world's GDP.[1] At the same time, huge amounts of money are diverted illegally from public and social services and are transferred out of developing countries for the personal use of corrupt elites.[2] Proceeds derived from grand corruption committed are often hidden and invested in financial centres around the world. These cross-border transactions strip resources from developing countries and involve practices such as bribery, embezzlement, misappropriation of funds, and money laundering.[3] The cost of corruption is more than the value of stolen assets. Corruption weakens accountability, reduces investment and growth, increases poverty, erodes confidence in public institutions, and diverts resources much needed for developing infrastructure, providing public health services, and guaranteeing access to education.[4] As a result, the recovery of stolen assets is key to economic development and to promoting the interests of the society as a whole.

Asset recovery, defined as the process by which proceeds of corruption are recovered and returned to a foreign jurisdiction, is filled with legal and

1 United Nations, *Global Cost of Corruption at Least 5 Per Cent of World Gross Domestic Product, Secretary-General Tells Security Council, Citing World Economic Forum Data* (10 September 2018) <https://press.un.org/en/2018/sc13493.doc.htm> accessed 13 November 2022); United Nations, The World Bank, *Stolen Asset Recovery (StAR) Initiative: Challenges, Opportunities, and Action Plan* (The World Bank 2007) 1.

2 OECD, *Illicit Financial Flows from Developing Countries: Measuring OECD Responses* (OECD 2014) at 15.

3 OECD, *Illicit Financial Flows from Developing Countries: Measuring OECD Responses* (OECD 2014) at 15, 16.

4 Tanzi Vito, *Corruption Around the World, Causes, Consequences, Scope, and Cures,* IMF Staff Papers, vol. 45, no. 4 (IMF 1998) at 585–86; Gretta Fenner Zinkernagel and Roth Anja, 'Practical Hurdles to Effective International Recovery of Stolen Assets' (2012) 11(1) Jurnal Opinio Juris at 90.

DOI: 10.4324/9781003253808-16

practical difficulties.[5] Since 2005, the year when the United Nations Convention against Corruption (UNCAC) entered into force, efforts to recover stolen assets have met both successes and failures; in some cases progress has been made, while in others, failure and stagnation disappointed the public demand for the repatriation of assets.

Building on the experience acquired in the asset recovery process, this chapter aims to draw lessons from almost two decades of successes and failures, and to take a closer look at the strategical and operational challenges that frequently arise when countries pursue stolen assets. In particular, the first section of this chapter takes stock of the progress of asset recovery efforts since the adoption of the UNCAC, focusing on the underlying rationale of asset return, the significance of the Convention in promoting cooperation while discussing cases that have helped in raising awareness regarding asset recovery. The second section is oriented towards the strategic choices that need to be made by developing countries in terms of selecting the proper legal avenue for the return of stolen assets. The third section addresses the operational challenges that practitioners may encounter at each stage of the asset recovery processes and suggests possible ways to overcome them based on previous best practice examples.

Asset Recovery: Overview of the Progress Thus Far

Depriving criminals of their illicit earnings has been acknowledged as a very effective method in fighting and preventing crime, as it hits them at their supposedly most vulnerable sport: their assets.[6] Since profit is the motive, eliminating criminal gains can help in deterring financial crime.[7] This approach is not new in addressing crime and its consequences. It can be traced back to Beccaria's famous *Dei delitti e delle penne*, where the confiscation of assets coupled with the banishment of the convicted person was considered as a greater punishment that banishment alone.[8] Ever since, the "follow the money approach" is a widely accepted trend in criminal justice policy and is based on the general premise that criminals must not profit from their crimes.[9]

5 Gray Larissa et al., *Few and Far: The Hard Facts on Stolen Asset Recovery* (The World Bank, UNODC, 2014) 9; Vlasic Mark and Gregory Cooper, 'Beyond the Duvalier Legacy: What New "Arab Spring" Governments Can Learn from Haiti and the Benefits of Stolen Asset Recovery' (2011) 10(1) Northwestern Journal of International Human Rights at 19.

6 Hans Nelen, 'Hit Them Where it Hurts Most? The Proceeds-of-Crime Approach in the Netherlands' (2004) 41 Crime, Law & Social Change at 517.

7 RT Naylor, 'Wash-Out: A Critique of Follow-the-Money Methods in Crime Control Policy' (1999) 32 Crime, Law and Social Change at 1.

8 Ligeti Katalin and Michele Simonato (eds), *Chasing Criminal Money: Challenges and Perspectives on Asset Recovery in the EU* (Hart Publishing 2017) at 27.

9 Boucht Johan, *The Limits of Asset Confiscation: On the Legitimacy of Extended Appropriation of Criminal Proceeds* (Hart Publishing 2017) at 1.

When it comes to corruption, identifying the perpetrators and punishing them with deprivation of liberty is certainly a priority. However, given that corrupt acts aim at personal enrichment, with criminals being prepared to even serve prison sentences and later enjoy their profits, tracing and recovering illicit proceeds should also be the focus of law enforcement efforts.[10] A system that permits criminals to retain their criminal gains would signal that crime pays after all.[11] Recovering stolen assets by corrupt leaders, officials, and their associates can serve various purposes: it provides countries with resources that can be devoted to growth and development; it deters potential criminals from committing new crimes as they understand that crime simply doesn't pay given that their criminal proceeds will be traced; and it restores public confidence by signalling that justice has been served.[12]

The recovery and repatriation of stolen assets has been encouraged by various international anti-corruption instruments, most notably the UNCAC, the only legally binding anti-corruption convention with universal application. The UNCAC was adopted on 31 October 2003, went into effect on 14 December 2005, and counts at the moment 189 parties.[13] One of the major breakthroughs of the Convention was the insertion of an entire chapter on asset recovery, chapter V. But beyond chapter V, the recovery of stolen assets is one of the priorities of UNCAC identified in its preamble referring to the vast quantities of assets constituting a substantial proportion of the resources of states that threaten their political stability and sustainable development. Thus, asset recovery is one of the purposes of the UNCAC, with article 1(b) noting that the Convention aims among others "to promote, facilitate and support international cooperation and technical assistance in the prevention of fight against corruption, including asset recovery". The Convention requires states parties to take measures to restrain, confiscate, recover and return the proceeds of corruption, and includes a comprehensive framework for the return of stolen assets.[14] In this regard, the Convention requires from states parties to afford one another the widest measure of cooperation and assistance.[15]

Without doubt, the UNCAC provides a robust framework that supports asset recovery efforts and presents a unique opportunity for states parties to make progress. Since its adoption and its quick pace of ratification, the return of ill-gotten gains to their rightful owners has become a priority with the

10 Basel Institute on Governance, *International Center for Asset Recovery, Tracing Illegal Assets, A Practitioner's Guide* (Basel Institute on Governance 2015) at 19.

11 Boucht (n 9) at 10.

12 OECD (n 2) at 87.

13 UNCAC <www.unodc.org/unodc/en/corruption/uncac.html> accessed 13 November 2022.

14 UNCAC, chapter V, articles 51–59, adopted with United Nations, General Assembly, Fifty-Eight Session, Resolution 58/4, 31 October 2003.

15 See UNCAC, article 51: "The return of assets pursuant to this chapter is a fundamental principle of this Convention, and States Parties shall afford one another the widest measure of cooperation and assistance in this regard."

Convention offering a path to repatriate the amounts recovered.[16] In parallel, countries aware of the benefits of asset recovery have amended their legal frameworks to strategically equip their anti-corruption arsenal. Such efforts were supported by the international organizations such as the UN Office on Drugs and Crime (UNODC) and World Bank's StAR Initiative, as well as multilateral efforts through the UNCAC's Asset Recovery Working Group, the Financial Action Task Force, the G20 Anti-Corruption Working Group, and the G8 Deauville Partnership, which set new standards, develop policies, and promote best practices on asset recovery and related topics.[17]

Among the most significant asset recovery results are the recovery of USD 1.8 billion by the Philippines hidden by Ferdinand Marcos, of an amount of approximately USD 1.9 billion stolen by Sani Abacha in Nigeria, and USD $250 million recovered by Vladimiro Montesinos in Peru, with efforts initiated even before the adoption of UNCAC.[18] Malaysia and Tunisia have also recovered significant amounts during the period 2010 to 2021.[19] These cases played a significant role in raising awareness of the importance of the asset recovery process, mobilized the international community, and gained support.[20] Delays, costs, frustrations, inadequate tools, and cooperation hardships associated with these cases gave incentives to come up with new and more effective mechanisms that would facilitate asset recovery.[21]

Still, the practice of recovering stolen assets has yielded contrasted results. For many other countries, success was limited, or required decades to reach significant outcomes, while in others, initial success was followed by years of disappointing and unfruitful efforts.[22] For some others, asset recovery efforts produced no result at all.[23] For example, very few jurisdictions have taken enforcement action against foreign companies or individuals who have bribed their public officials. Such cases mostly continue to be prosecuted by developed jurisdictions, while among developing countries only a few, such as Nigeria, Costa Rica, and Lesotho, have concluded cases.[24] Such failures may

16 Lohaus Mathis, *Asset Recovery and Illicit Financial Flows from a Developmental Perspective: Concepts, Scope, and Potential* (CMI, U4 Anti-Corruption Resource Center 2019) at 1.

17 Gray et al. (n 5) at 34.

18 Vlasic and Cooper (n 5) at 21.

19 See for Malaysia, U.S. Department of Justice, 'United States Reaches Settlement to Recover More than $49 Million Involving Malaysian Sovereign Wealth Fund' (*Press Release*, 6 May 2020) <www.justice.gov/opa/pr/united-states-reaches-settlement-recover-more-49-million-involving-malaysian-sovereign-wealth> accessed 13 November 2022).

20 UNODC, World Bank, *Stolen Asset Recovery, Towards a Global Architecture for Asset Recovery* (UNCAC Conference Edition 2010) 4.

21 UNODC, World Bank, *Stolen Asset Recovery, Towards a Global Architecture for Asset Recovery* (UNCAC Conference Edition 2010) 4.

22 Gray Larissa et al. (n 5) at 61.

23 OECD (n 2) at 87.

24 Oduor Jacinta et al., *Left Out of the Bargain, Settlements in Foreign Bribery Cases and Implications for Asset Recovery* (StAR Initiative, The World Bank, UNODC 2014) at 18.

be linked to numerous barriers to asset recovery which have been identified, such as deficient resources, legislative gaps, ineffective law enforcement, lack of political will, lack of asset recovery policies, lack of effective coordination, immunity laws, short statutes of limitations, and unreasonable delays in MLA responses.[25] These past successes and failures highlight the need for an analysis of the strategic and operational challenges that have been encountered during the asset recovery process in order to inform the efforts undertaken by developing countries. The following sections discuss such challenges and suggest ways to address them drawing on existing experience.

Strategic Challenges: Navigating the Legal Avenues to Asset Recovery

Strategic challenges often arise at an early stage of the asset recovery process when competent authorities must choose the proper legal avenue for pursuing the return of corrupt proceeds. These decisions must be based on an in-depth analysis of the facts and the circumstances of the case to better understand its main parameters and develop a plan.[26] Different strategic choices must be made at the outset of a case and need to be regularly reassessed during the process. Strong and effective leadership is needed to analyse the advantages and the disadvantages of different strategic options, based on the aspects of each case. This section focuses on the main legal avenues that can be selected or combined by practitioners and explains their advantages and limitations.

Strategic Overview: Combining Legal Avenues to Achieve Asset Recovery

In the context of asset recovery, practitioners in developing countries may consider five venues for the return of assets from foreign jurisdictions.[27] The first is the recovery through the criminal route, with the initiation of a criminal prosecution on the domestic level. Apart from the conviction of the perpetrator, this avenue will aim at the confiscation of the illegal proceeds followed by a mutual legal assistance (MLA) request to foreign jurisdictions to enforce the judgment. The second legal avenue which is gaining a lot of attention lately throughout the world is the confiscation without conviction, non-conviction-based confiscation (NCB), which will be followed by an MLA request to enforce orders in foreign jurisdictions. The third legal avenue seeks to recover stolen assets by bringing private civil actions claiming either compensation from damages or ownership of assets. Administrative confiscation,

25 For a comprehensive analysis of these barriers see StAR Barriers to Stephenson Kevin et al., *Barriers to Asset Recovery, An Analysis of the Key Barriers and Recommendations for Action* (StAR Initiative, The World Bank, UNODC 2011).

26 Brun Jean-Pierre et al., *Asset Recovery Handbook: A Guide for Practitioners, Second Edition, StAR Initiative, The World Bank* (UNODC 2021) at a38.

27 Brun Jean-Pierre et al., Asset Recovery Handbook: *A Guide for Practitioners, Second Edition, StAR Initiative, The World Bank* (UNODC 2021) at 11–20, 202.

typically carried out by an authorized agency, is the fourth legal avenue that may be considered. Finally, the jurisdiction seeking redress can consider joining asset recovery actions launched by foreign jurisdictions.

A multidimensional approach based on conducting these legal actions in parallel or successively is often necessary to achieve significant recovery in grand corruption cases. Indeed, asset recovery efforts generally involve several defendants, various criminal offenses, and assets located in different jurisdictions. As a result, avenues that work for some crimes or some jurisdictions may not be effective for others. While criminal law mechanisms are often necessary, the circumstances of a case often require using remedies beyond the realm of criminal law.[28] Thus, pursuing the recovery of illicit proceeds through the use of civil and administrative measures offer the promise of additional success.[29] These mechanisms do not replace criminal ones but do provide useful complements or alternatives.[30]

Using the right combination of avenues instead of blindly applying the same mechanism for different situations can be challenging for relevant authorities.[31] However, more integrated strategic approaches significantly increase the chances for both successful convictions and successful recoveries.[32] For instance, in the case of Diepreye Alamieyeseigha, the Nigerian authorities decided to bring civil proceedings in the UK and simultaneously pursue criminal proceedings in Nigeria. Parallel to these proceedings, NCB proceedings were brought against real estate property in Cape Town by South African authorities. The combination of various asset recovery mechanisms allowed Nigeria to recover USD 17.7 million through domestic and foreign proceedings.[33]

The choice of the legal avenue, either domestically or in a foreign jurisdiction, depends on the legal framework that is in place as well as on international or bilateral instruments, such as anti-corruption conventions and MLA treaties, that will need to be used as the basis for international cooperation. In countries where the framework is not complete, introducing new legislation or procedures to diversify the legal tools available to relevant authorities is not easy. For example, the effectiveness of criminal proceedings often depends on laws authorizing plea bargaining agreements, which allow peripheral defendants to plead guilty to lesser charges in exchange of cooperation with prosecutors in locating evidence relating to more important suspects. Vladimiro Montesinos, personal adviser of Peru's President Alberto Fujimori and de facto Head of Peru's Intelligence Service, was involved in illegal activities such as bribery

28 Kroeker Robert, 'The Pursuit of Illicit Proceeds: From Historical Origins to Modern Applications' (2014) 17(3) Journal of Money Laundering Control at 274.

29 Kroeker Robert, 'The Pursuit of Illicit Proceeds: From Historical Origins to Modern Applications' (2014) 17(3) Journal of Money Laundering Control at 275.

30 Kroeker Robert, 'The Pursuit of Illicit Proceeds: From Historical Origins to Modern Applications' (2014) 17(3) Journal of Money Laundering Control at 277.

31 UNODC, World Bank (n 19) at 20.

32 UNODC, World Bank (n 19) at 19.

33 Brun (n 26) at 27.

and embezzlement of public funds and had deposited his illegal assets in several jurisdictions. Peru strategically introduced legislation permitting guilty pleas in return for reduced criminal sentences or dismissal of proceedings. Several million dollars were recovered following such guilty pleas.[34] Similarly, Brazil allowed investigators and prosecutors to leverage reduced sentences in exchange of disclosure of information pertinent to the Lava Jato (Car Wash) case.[35] Because ex post facto legislation or procedures will likely face legal or constitutional scrutiny, it is important that developing countries consider at the outset potential legal challenges to such laws and act proactively.[36]

Other challenges in developing countries are linked to the need for coordination with agencies and counterparts in multiple jurisdictions with different legal systems and procedures and the capacity to launch and conduct legal proceedings in domestic and foreign courts.[37] Hence, case management issues should be discussed as early as possible, while investigative and legal teams need to benefit from sufficient human and financial resources. Significant capacity building to train practitioners assigned with conducting these tasks, such as law enforcement officials, prosecutors and judges, are also key to the successful conduct of asset recovery.[38]

Finally, strong strategic leadership and political support are required as a prerequisite for long periods of time while, while at the same time, flexibility is crucial to effectively adapting to new circumstances as they arise. This strong leadership is crucial to enable strategic changes when it appears that legal avenues initially chosen are not going to be successful.

The Legal Avenues for Asset Recovery: Advantages and Limitations

Each one of the legal avenues previously mentioned has specific advantages and limitations. Therefore, the choice of one of them should be based on various legal, practical, or operational considerations as discussed in the following sections.

Criminal Prosecution and Conviction-Based Confiscation

Criminal confiscation is often the primary option that is considered by most countries.[39] In this context, practitioners initiate a criminal prosecution against an individual or a legal entity, obtain a conviction, as well as an order for

34 Referred to as the "Efficient Collaboration Act" (Law 27.378).

35 Federal Prosecution Service, *Caso Lava Jato, Resultados* (Results, Car Wash Case, in Portuguese) <www.mpf.mp.br/grandes-casos/lava-jato/resultados>, where 209 collaboration agreements are mentioned, accessed 13 November 2022.

36 The retroactivity of NCB confiscation laws has been raised in cases in Liechtenstein, the United States, and Thailand.

37 UNODC, World Bank (n 20) at 21; Brun et al. (n 26) at 2.

38 UNODC, World Bank (n 20) at 31.

39 Brun Jean-Pierre et al., *Public Wrongs, Private Actions, Civil Lawsuits to Recover Stolen Assets, StAR Initiative* (The World Bank, UNODC 2015) at 1.

the confiscation of assets held by the defendant.[40] The context of criminal proceedings allows investigators to use more coercive and intrusive means of gathering information and intelligence than civil proceedings. These measures include the use of data from government sources and financial intelligence units (FIUs), provisional measures, such as freezing assets, searches, electronic surveillance, examination of financial records, or access to documents held by third parties.[41]

Criminal penalties including imprisonment, fines, and confiscation are well adapted to the criminal nature of corruption. They satisfy the need to hold the perpetrator accountable by depriving from his or her liberty and the proceeds of crime. They also have a deterrent effect on potential offenders.[42] For many jurisdictions, criminal proceedings also are the only basis for the provision of formal or informal MLA to jurisdictions requesting measures to identify, trace, and secure assets.[43]

However, choosing the criminal route often means encountering significant barriers because insufficient evidence to obtain a conviction beyond reasonable doubts, immunities, or statutes of limitations render criminal proceedings inefficient.[44] In addition to proving that the defendant is guilty, prosecutors may have to show that assets are linked to criminal activity under stringent standards of proof.[45] Moreover, they need legislation ensuring that immunities do not shield public officials beyond the limits prescribed by international law and jurisprudence.[46] Where statutes of limitation have expired, especially when asset recovery efforts are conducted in the context of a regime change happening many years after the corrupt activities, practitioners should consider prosecuting related offenses.[47] For instance, where a bribery act has become statute-barred, practitioners could consider launching proceedings for money laundering or possession of stolen assets. This would avoid being barred from prosecution if the limitation period for "continuous offenses" is suspended until the criminal activity has ceased.

Non–Conviction-Based Confiscation

NCB confiscation does not require a criminal conviction, but only confiscation proceedings against the assets based on evidence that they are derived

40 Brun et al. (n 26) at 14.
41 Brun et al. (n 26) at 15.
42 Brun et al. (n 26) at 15.
43 See UNCAC, article 54(1)(a) that requires States Parties to take measures to give effect to foreign confiscation orders.
44 Brun et al. (n 26) at 15.
45 Stephenson et al. (n 25) at 62.
46 Stephenson et al. (n 25) at 73.
47 Stephenson et al. (n 25) at 75.

from the commission of criminal offenses.[48] Hence, NCB is pursued outside the criminal justice framework and is detached from any prior or parallel criminal proceedings.[49] NCB targets the illicit assets in question and not the individual, hence it is considered to be in rem and not in personam.[50] In many jurisdictions, NCB confiscation can be ordered based on a lower standard of proof such as "balance of probabilities" or "preponderance of evidence", thus easing the evidentiary burden that applies to criminal proceedings.[51] However, in some jurisdictions, a higher standard of proof, "beyond a reasonable doubt" may also be required for a NCB confiscation, as in the case of obtaining a conviction.[52] NCB confiscation proves useful in cases where the criminal confiscation is impossible to achieve, such as when the offender has died, or has escaped the jurisdiction, or is immune from prosecution, when the asset is found and the owner is not known, where there is insufficient evidence to seek a criminal conviction, or when the defendant has already been acquitted.[53]

Although international best practices clearly favour the use of NCB confiscation,[54] the main limitation of this legal avenue is that it is not available in some jurisdictions that only recognize conviction-based confiscation.[55] Such jurisdictions may object to placing confiscation proceedings outside the criminal law realm, as it is believed that they do not offer the constitutional protections and due process rights that are available in criminal proceedings.[56] International enforcement of a domestic NCB confiscation order may be impossible in these jurisdictions, unless their authorities accept to recognize

48 Brun et al. (n 26) at 16.

49 Boucht (n 9) at 67, 68.

50 Boucht (n 9) at 68.

51 Brun et al. (n 26) at 16.

52 Brun et al. (n 26) 16.

53 Brun et al. (n 26) 189; Stefan Cassella, *Civil Asset Recovery: The American Experience*, in *Research Handbook on International Financial Crime*, Barry Rider (ed) (Edward Elgar Publishing 2015) at 500–2.

54 FATF, *Best Practices on Confiscation (Recommendations 4 and 38) and a Framework for Ongoing Work on Asset Recovery* (FATF 2012) at 6.

55 In various countries, such as Czechia and France, non-conviction-based confiscation remains internal to the criminal justice system and are sometimes even embedded in the same criminal proceedings concerning the predicate offence. This is the case in Czechia and France in particular. In others, such as Germany and Switzerland, non-conviction-based proceedings offer an alternative to an impossible prosecution or conviction. Although they are part of the criminal justice system, they have more autonomous format. See analytically United Nations, Conference of the States Parties to the United Nations Convention against Corruption, *Asset Recovery, Challenges, Good Practices and Lessons Learned, and Procedures Allowing the Confiscation of Proceeds of Corruption Without a Criminal Conviction from States Parties That Have Implemented Such Measures in Accordance with Article 54 para. 1(c) of the Convention*, Ninth Session, Sharm el-Sheikh, 13–17 December 2021, CAC/COSP/2021/15, paras. 20–21.

56 Boucht (n 9) at 69; Ligeti and Simonato (n 8) at 35 who provide an overview of ECtHR case law on the treatment of confiscation; also Cassella (n 53) at 502.

the NCB order as the equivalent of a criminal confiscation.[57] Hence, in order to be able to use NCB, developing countries need to ensure that their legal framework provides for such a tool and that the enforcement will be requested in a jurisdiction that also has a relevant provision, or recognizes it as the equivalent of a criminal conviction-based confiscation.

Civil Action

Civil actions may also be an option worthy of consideration. Relevant authorities may initiate proceedings in domestic or foreign civil courts to claim compensation for damages caused by corruption based on tort, breach of contract or illicit enrichment, or to bring proprietary claims.[58] For example, in 2004 the Attorney General of Zambia initiated a civil suit in tort in the UK against the former President of Zambia from 1991 to 2002 and 19 of his associates in order to recover assets transferred to London to fund his expensive lifestyle. The action was brought in London because most of the defendants and most of the assets were located in Europe and especially in London.[59] The civil proceedings were launched in addition to the ongoing criminal proceedings in Zambia.[60] The civil court found the defendants liable for the value of the misappropriated assets and also awarded damages.[61] Civil remedies are useful in addressing the financial consequences of corruption in cases where the highest standard of proof applicable in a criminal trial may be difficult to meet. In addition, civil remedies may be used against legal entities which may not be held criminally liable in certain jurisdictions and have the potential for broadening the scope of potential defendants, including those with "deeper pockets" which facilitated the commission of the offense (including banks, lawyers, or other intermediaries).[62] The initiation of a civil action, however, requires the collection of evidence to prove the misappropriation of assets or liability on the basis of breach of contract or tort or to demonstrate that the claimant is the legitimate owner.[63]

For developing countries, the principal challenge of litigating as a civil party, especially in a foreign jurisdiction, is the cost of tracing the assets without the benefit of investigative tools provided in the context of criminal proceedings and the high legal fees required to obtain relevant court orders.[64] However,

57 Brun et al. (n 26) at 16.
58 Brun et al. (n 39) at 49.
59 *Attorney General of Zambia v Meer Care & Desai & Others* [2007] EWHC 952 (Ch.) (United Kingdom).
60 E. Ryder Katherine, *Making Hay While the Sun Shines: Experiences with the Zambian Task Force on Corruption* (U4 2011) 6.
61 *Attorney General of Zambia v Meer Care* [2007] EWHC 952, at § 57.
62 Brun et al. (n 39) at 5.
63 Brun et al. (n 39) at 49, 56, 60.
64 Brun et al. (n 39) at 5.

evidence gathered during criminal proceedings may, in certain circumstances, also be used in a civil trial and the litigant will have the advantage of a lower standard of proof than that is required in criminal law avenues. This often occurs in two ways: either an act of bribery or corruption as a criminal offense may provide the basis for civil liability in separate civil proceedings, or a civil action for damages may be part in criminal proceedings in countries that recognize the participation of the civil party in criminal proceedings.[65]

Administrative Confiscation

Administrative confiscation (or forfeiture) generally involves a non-criminal, sometimes also non-judicial, mechanism for confiscating assets used or derived from the commission of an offense.[66] In practice, administrative confiscation will be imposed by an authorized agency and is generally restricted to certain types of offences, low-value assets, or certain classes of assets and is used in uncontested confiscation cases.[67] Although, some jurisdictions have made innovative use of administrative processes in high-value cases,[68] choosing administrative confiscation as a method to recover assets located in foreign jurisdictions is risky, as the foreign jurisdiction may only accept to enforce court orders made in the context of criminal or civil procedures.

Asset Recovery in the Context of Legal Actions Initiated by Foreign Jurisdictions

Competent authorities in developing countries may seek to benefit from a criminal or NCB confiscation that has been initiated or finalized in another jurisdiction against corrupt foreign officials or identified assets, including in the context of money laundering investigations. At the conclusion of the proceedings, the harmed state may be able to obtain a portion of the recovered assets through orders of the foreign courts, pursuant to national and international legislation or international agreements.[69] The initiation of an action in a foreign jurisdiction may take place in one of two ways. First, authorities in the jurisdiction affected by corruption may ask the foreign authorities to open their own

65 Brun et al. (n 39) at 64, France for instance is a country that provides for "partie civile".

66 Cuba and Italy, for instance, follow what could be considered an "administrative approach" to the recovery of unlawful assets that is independent of the enforcement of criminal law. See United Nations (n 55) at para. 22.

67 In custom smuggling or drug cases the assets could be of high value, such as a yacht or a private plane, but at the same time in some jurisdictions, stocks held in a company cannot be seized through administrative confiscation by the market regulator.

68 In the Siemens case in Germany, the value of the confiscatory component of the administrative fines totalled EUR 594.75 million. *See* OECD, StAR publication, *Identification and Quantification of the Proceeds of Bribery* (OECD 2012) at 51.

69 UNCAC, article 53(b) and (c) requires States Parties to take measures to permit direct recovery.

case by filing a complaint or more spontaneously by sharing the incriminating evidence or the case file. Second, foreign or international authorities may open a case independent of a request from the jurisdiction affected by corruption and may receive information linking a corrupt public official to the jurisdiction affected by corruption.[70] The participation of the affected state in the proceedings initiated by foreign jurisdictions is often accepted. In some civil law jurisdictions, it may be possible for the affected state to participate in the criminal proceedings as a civil party. In both civil and common law jurisdictions, developing countries may be possible to recover assets in civil proceedings through court-ordered compensation, restitution, or damages, as a party affected by corruption, or as the legitimate owner of recoverable assets.[71]

This avenue is an interesting option, if the jurisdiction seeking redress does not have an adequate legal basis, capacity, or evidence to pursue an international asset recovery action on its own. Some countries (including the US and the UK) apply NCB proceedings in foreign money laundering cases and can accept to return to the affected country all or parts of the confiscated assets pursuant to court orders or asset sharing agreements.[72] For instance, the "1 Malaysia Development Berhad" (1MDB) case involved a state investment fund whose officials and associates had allegedly diverted USD 4.5 billion through complex transactions and the use of fraudulent shell companies. The US government had returned over USD 1 billion to Malaysia by 2020.[73] The downside of choosing this avenue is that the jurisdiction affected by corruption does not have full control over the proceedings. Success depends to a large extent on the capacity and the willingness of the foreign authorities to advance the case and facilitate the participation of the harmed state which will also be dependent on asset sharing agreements or on the ability of the foreign government to return the assets on a discretionary basis.[74]

Operational Challenges in the Asset Recovery Process

The practice of recovering stolen assets is complex. Practitioners must collaborate with domestic agencies as well as with foreign ones in multiple jurisdictions with different legal systems and procedures. Special investigative techniques and skills to "follow the money" beyond national borders are needed, while acting promptly is imperative in order to avoid any dissipation of assets.[75] As seen in the previous section, practitioners may seek to recover assets through a variety of methods, such as by a going after a criminal, civil, administrative. or non-conviction-based confiscation by launching a civil action or by

70 Brun et al. (n 26) at 37.
71 Brun et al. (n 26) at 20.
72 Brun et al. (n 26) at 20.
73 US Department of Justice (n 19).
74 Brun et al. (n 26) at 21.
75 Brun et al. (n 26) at 2.

participating in proceedings initiated by a foreign jurisdiction. The process for recovering stolen assets may vary in form, but its main content and goals remain almost the same.[76] The first stage of the asset recovery process requires the collection of intelligence and evidence and the tracing of assets; at the second stage, practitioners will focus on securing the assets that may be found either on the domestic level or in another jurisdiction; the third stage usually involves court proceedings depending on the legal avenue that is selected; the fourth stage will enforce the orders made at the third stage; and the fifth and last stage will aim at the return of assets to the requesting jurisdiction. Operational challenges are generally encountered in the conduct of the different stages of the asset recovery process, as will be discussed in this section.

Identifying and Tracing Assets: Overview

Law enforcement agencies in developing countries first need to identify stolen or recoverable assets, prove that they are controlled by a corrupt official, and demonstrate that they derive from corrupt activities. To identify and trace assets, competent authorities can gather open-source intelligence and intelligence from government databases, such as databases held by FIUs, land registry records, company registers, and tax records.[77] Depending on the type of the investigative technique, practitioners need to be aware that they may or may not need a prior approval. For instance, when an intrusive technique is necessary, such as in the case of electronic surveillance, search and seizure orders, or production orders, a prior authorization by a prosecutor, a judge, or a senior officer, depending on the given framework, will be needed. More simple investigative techniques, such as physical surveillance and witness interviews, may not require prior approval.[78]

Recoverable assets are often concealed in foreign jurisdictions. For instance, corrupt leaders such as Haiti's Jean-Claude Duvalier, Nigeria's Sani Abacha, and the Philippines' Ferdinand Marcos, had hidden their corrupt gains in countries with strong banking secrecy provisions while they made use of shell companies, false names, and bank accounts, frustrating the efforts of successor governments and law enforcement officials in tracing stolen assets.[79] This is a major challenge for practitioners as they may need to conduct investigations by requesting the assistance of foreign jurisdictions where assets are hidden. In this context, two avenues, informal and formal, are used to obtain information and collect evidence. Informal assistance is the primary tool to gather information and intelligence during the first steps of the investigation and

76 Brun et al. (n 26) at 7.
77 Brun et al. (n 26) at 7.
78 Brun et al. (n 26) at 7.
79 Vlasic and Cooper (n 5) at 19.

may lead to a more rapid identification of assets.[80] It includes the exchange of information between law enforcement, FIUs, and judicial counterparts as permitted by relevant laws and regulations, and helps counterparts build trust, learn about and understand formal requirements regarding the submission of MLA requests.[81] Formal MLA is conducted by issuing written requests to obtain evidence admissible in court, grant provisional measures, and seek enforcement of domestic orders in a foreign jurisdiction. The formal avenue is indispensable for securing evidence through coercive means or judicial orders in another jurisdiction.[82]

Challenges at the Domestic Level

For developing countries, the challenges of asset tracing are often linked to lack of capacity and insufficient resources to conduct very complex cross-border investigations that demand ability to analyse complicated data and unravel complex transactions as well as knowledge regarding how to navigate different jurisdictions where assets are traced.[83] Acquiring expertise in the area of asset recovery is crucial but at the same time possible given the growing number of resources available by international organizations such as the UNODC, the World Bank StAR Initiative, and the International Center for Asset Recovery, among others.[84] Mobilizing available resources from the beginning through a whole of government approach to fighting financial crime and recovering assets is crucial. Incentivization models may be considered to allocate resources to law enforcement bodies. For example, in the UK, assets recovered under the Proceeds of Crime Act (POCA, 2002) are distributed to operational law enforcement agencies under the Asset Recovery Incentivization Scheme (ARIS) and are used to fund future asset recovery efforts.[85]

Asset recovery in grand corruption cases requires collecting information and evidence from various government databases and multiple agencies, including FIUs, tax and customs administrations, anti-corruption and asset disclosure agencies, supervisory bodies, central banks, law enforcement authorities, and the private sector. Gaining allies among various agencies is important in securing continuous support for the case.[86] However, a key

80 Brun et al. (n 26) at 228.

81 International Centre for Asset Recovery, *StAR, Swiss Federal Department of Foreign Affairs, Guidelines for the Efficient Recovery of Stolen Assets* (International Centre for Asset Recovery 2017) 26.

82 Brun et al. (n 26) at 9.

83 U4 Brief, *The Recovery of Stolen Assets: A Fundamental Principle of the UN Convention Against Corruption* (U4 Brief 2007) 2.

84 U4 Brief, *The Recovery of Stolen Assets: A Fundamental Principle of the UN Convention Against Corruption* (U4 Brief 2007) 2.

85 Home Office, *Asset Recovery Statistical Bulletin, 2011/12–2016/17, Statistical Bulletin 15/17* (Home Office, September 2017) at 9.

86 Brun et al. (n 26) at 48.

challenge in this context is the absence or insufficiency of interagency domestic coordination. To address this challenge, authorities in developing countries should consider establishing an effective framework for cooperation with clear guidance regarding the role of each authority, the way in which information will be exchanged and used, and the key contact points involved to avoid confusion, duplication of efforts or even competition among different agencies and to facilitate national coordination.[87]

The mobilization of all available information through an interagency mechanism will also reinforce the efficiency of strategic planning and boost informal exchange of information with counterparts in foreign jurisdictions. This is crucial at the outset in order to find leads, launch the investigation, and consider the right combination of legal avenues as indicated earlier. A good practice example in this context is the establishment by the Tunisian authorities of a national committee to facilitate investigation for corruption, domestic exchanges of information and legal action and to coordinate the conduct of cases in foreign countries, following the fall and flight of President Ben Ali in 2011. The committee comprised officials from the Ministries of Justice, Finance and Foreign Affairs; the Central Bank of Tunisia; the Tunisian FIU; and the Financial Analysis Committee and Customs.[88]

International Challenges

International cases usually involve multiple jurisdictions. For instance, Sani Abacha's case involved at least six jurisdictions apart from Nigeria, namely the Bahamas, Jersey, Liechtenstein, Luxembourg, Switzerland, and the UK.[89] This results in extremely long proceedings and stresses the need for collaboration among different jurisdictions. Lack of timely responses to requests for assistance, insufficient use of informal exchange of information, lack of trust, and difficulties in identifying beneficial owners of assets are common challenges encountered by practitioners.

Lack of timely responses to requests for assistance is often a main issue. When they receive international requests for assistance, some financial centres too often provide little or no response as they often prioritize domestic cases. When requesting authorities do receive a response, it often arrives months or years after the submission of the request. Lack of clear political will in requested jurisdictions to prioritize asset recovery requests also can be a serious issue. Sometimes, however, the reason behind the absence of response or delays may be the lack of "storytelling" from requesting jurisdictions resulting

87 Stephenson et al. (n 25) at 39.

88 See Decree-Law No. 2011–15, 26 March 2011, on the Creation of a National Committee for the Recovery of Ill Gotten Assets Existing Abroad <https://legislation-securite.tn/fr/node/43750> accessed 13 November 2022.

89 Fenner Zinkernagel and Roth (n 4) at 91.

in vague or imprecise requests.[90] For example, when requests are sent hastily at an early stage of the investigation and before the collection of sufficient preliminary information, the link between the corrupt activities and the assets may not appear clearly to the relevant authorities in the requested jurisdiction and they will be unable to proceed with an investigation for both legal and factual reasons. In addition, the discretion given to the competent authorities, including grounds on which an MLA request "may" be refused, is often interpreted broadly and is used as a basis to deny requests.[91] To address these challenges, MLA requests should be complete and straightforward in order to ensure the desired results and avoid the possibility of refusal.[92] Practitioners in developing countries also need to be proactive and involve foreign authorities at the outset of the investigation especially when numerous countries are involved.[93] For instance in the Lava Jato case, Brazilian authorities collaborated with many countries to expose the scandal, using more than 269 MLA requests submitted to 45 countries.[94]

Understanding the requirements for obtaining formal assistance is crucial to prevent refusal. Informal contacts may help in clarifying laws and procedures in the foreign jurisdiction and differences in legal traditions so as to inform strategic choices.[95] However, requesting countries often do not sufficiently combine informal and formal international cooperation requests. Informal assistance allows authorities to benefit from first investigative leads and verifications without being slowed by the MLA process. This flexibility is key to focusing on the scope of the investigations and developing a case theory. Informal assistance also allows relevant authorities to have contacts or conversations with their foreign counterparts on what investigative steps are allowed in their jurisdiction, and under which constraints.[96] For example, developing countries often encounter barriers to MLA because the requested jurisdiction does not recognize the alleged criminal offense for which assistance is sought and as a result refuses on the grounds of lack of dual criminality.[97] The use of early contacts helps requesting countries to consider and anticipate such legal and practical obstacles. A good case example on the combination of informal and formal channels of assistance is the Peruvian prosecutor's personal communication with the Swiss investigating magistrate conducting the Montesinos case both by phone and by person in Zurich. Establishing a productive

90 Stephenson (n 25) at 42.
91 Stephenson (n 25) at 83.
92 Basel Institute on Governance, International Center for Asset Recovery (n 10) at 58.
93 Brun et al. (n 26) at 220.
94 Brazilian Federal Prosecution Service, A Lava Jato em números no Paraná, <www.mpf.mp.br/grandes-casos/lava-jato/entenda-o-caso/curitiba> accessed 13 November 2022.
95 Brun et al. (n 26) at 228.
96 International Centre for Asset Recovery, StAR, Swiss Federal Department of Foreign Affairs (n 81) at 12.
97 Stephenson et al. (n 25) at 81.

personal connection in this case enabled key strategic decisions, clarified MLA requirements, and helped in building and maintaining trust.[98]

Insufficient use of the resources of international bodies that facilitate international cooperation often leads to missed opportunities. A developing country seeking asset recovery should, if possible, become member of the Egmont Group, which facilitates rapid exchange of information between FIUs.[99] Similarly, using communication channels offered by Interpol and other confiscation or asset recovery networks of practitioners, such as the Camden Asset Recovery Inter-Agency Network (CARIN), as well as regional asset recovery interagency networks (ARIN), is often key to reaching out quickly and efficiently to counterparts in foreign law enforcement agencies, communicating and collecting useful investigative information.[100]

Lack of trust can be a major barrier to MLA when the process involves jurisdictions with different political, judicial, or legal systems. Requested authorities in financial centres may hesitate or refuse to provide MLA when they are not certain that the requesting jurisdiction provides defendants with what they consider sufficient guarantees of due process.[101] Refusal to conduct investigations on behalf of developing countries may also be linked to the perception that their legal frameworks provide for disproportionate penalties, including even the death penalty.[102] Building trust despite these differences is key to overcoming the challenges involved in international asset tracing. In this context, having liaison magistrates or legal attaches in diplomatic representations who will be able to provide sufficient detail about domestic proceedings will help developing countries interact with their counterparts beyond official communication at an early stage.[103] Demonstrating strong commitment to the implementation of the UNCAC is another way of building trust, as it can be used as a basis to cooperate in the fight against corruption and in the recovery of stolen assets.[104]

Finally, unravelling the offshore structures used by money launderers is often challenging due to lack of information on beneficial ownership.[105] Failure to identify properties owned or controlled by the suspects in foreign jurisdictions is a major barrier to successful asset recovery. In many grand corruption cases, offshore bank accounts, shares of corporations, real estate properties, luxurious

98 Brun et al. (n 26) at 223; International Centre for Asset Recovery, StAR, Swiss Federal Department of Foreign Affairs (n 81) at 27.

99 Egmont Group of Financial Intelligence Units <https://egmontgroup.org/> accessed 13 November 2022).

100 Camden Asset Recovery Inter-Agency Network (CARIN) <www.carin.network/> accessed 13 November 2022; Asset Recovery Inter-Agency Network Asia-Pacific <www.arin-ap.org/main.do> accessed 13 November 2022; International Centre for Asset Recovery, StAR, Swiss Federal Department of Foreign Affairs (n 82) at 20.

101 Brun et al. (n 26) at 253; Stephenson et al. (n 25) at 20.

102 Brun et al. (n 26) at 254; Stephenson et al. (n 25) at 21.

103 Brun et al. (n 26) at 255.

104 Stephenson et al. (n 25) at 51.

105 Basel Institute on Governance, International Center for Asset Recovery (n 10) at 99.

cars or yachts, and virtual currency wallets are not received or held directly by the corrupt official but are "officially" owned by "corporate vehicles", such as shell companies or by facilitators such as trustees acting for his or her interest.[106] To identify the ultimate "beneficial owner" of assets, investigators need to navigate the complexities of the legal arrangements by which asset ownership is concealed or disguised. For example, a bank account in one jurisdiction may be opened by a company registered in another one, and this company could be owned by entities registered in a third country managed by financial service providers acting secretly on behalf of the ultimate beneficial owner. Even in this (still) simple case, the investigation will need to unravel three offshore layers of concealed ownership and demonstrate the existence of agreements between the apparent owners and the real one. Sending assistance requests to the various jurisdictions involved will cause delays counted in months and years, without guarantees of success. Delays give perpetrators extra time to develop additional layers of anonymity.[107] This challenge is particularly daunting when the concerned jurisdictions do not have in place the legal framework to collect and verify beneficial owner information and the capacity to share such information with other authorities on the national and international level.[108]

Such issues need to be addressed at the global level, making the identification of beneficial ownership part of the customer due diligence process for a wide range of both financial and non-financial institutions and professional intermediaries.[109] Establishing centralized registries and making them available to competent authorities is also key to providing investigators with chances to establish the connection between a natural person and a property, a company, or a legal arrangement.[110] To ensure the collection and sharing of adequate, accurate, and up-to-date beneficial ownership information, countries need to have enabling provisions, enhanced capacity, both in terms of staffing and infrastructure, to

106 Van der Does de Willebois et al., *The Puppet Masters, How the Corrupt Use Legal Structures to Hide Stolen Assets and What to Do about It* (StAR Initiative, The World Bank, UNODC 2011) 33; FATF, *Transparency and Beneficial Ownership* (FATF, October 2014) 3.

107 OECD, *Behind the Corporate Veil, Using Corporate Entities for Illicit Purposes* (OECD 2001) at 15.

108 OECD, *Behind the Corporate Veil, Using Corporate Entities for Illicit Purposes* (OECD 2001) at 42.

109 FATF, *International Standards on Combating Money Laundering and the Financing of Terrorism and Proliferation, The FATF Recommendations* (FATF 2012–2022), see Recommendation 10 on Customer Due Diligence and Interpretive Note to Recommendation 10, at 64.

110 FATF, *International Standards on Combating Money Laundering and the Financing of Terrorism and Proliferation, The FATF Recommendations* (FATF 2012 -2022), see Recommendation 10 on Customer Due Diligence and Interpretive Note to Recommendation 10, at 64. Interpretive Note to Recommendation 24, at 92. *See* UK, *Hajiyeva v National Crime Agency* [2020] EWCA Civ 108, 5 February 2020, where the authorities relied on the appellant's declaration of beneficial ownership of a company, Vicksburg Global Inc., incorporated in the British Virgin Islands, and registered as the sole proprietor of the property in which the appellant resided.

manage and verify data, and enforce clear legal requirements for financial institutions and other designated businesses and professions. Without these features, AML regimes remain vulnerable, and law enforcement agencies are powerless. In cases where the requested jurisdiction does not have in place an adequate a beneficial ownership framework, requesting authorities may directly contact their counterparts for assistance. For instance, the Libyan authorities were unable to establish that Saadi Quaddafi was the sole ultimate beneficial owner of Capitana Seas Limited, a company registered in the British Virgin Islands. With the assistance of the UK Treasury, which intervened and directly contacted the British Virgin Island authorities, Libya was able to be granted a default judgement on a civil action brought in 2011 in the London High Court.[111]

Securing and Restraining Assets

Securing and freezing assets is the second major step of the asset recovery process. Once identified, assets often will need to be secured through provisional measures to avoid dissipation, movement, or destruction.[112] In common law jurisdictions, an order to restrain property often requires judicial authorization. In some civil law jurisdictions, prosecutors, investigating magistrates, or law enforcement agencies may order provisional seizure or restraint of assets, while in others, judicial authorization may be required.[113] In international asset recovery cases, success frequently depends on the capacity to take urgent investigative or provisional measures and short delays can make the difference between a successful and a failed investigation. In this context, failure often comes from lack of ability to freeze assets quickly, if needed prior to investigation of criminal charges, and without carrying a stringent burden of proof in showing a link between property and criminal activity. This challenge is sometimes compounded in foreign jurisdictions by requirements that the requested jurisdiction should provide overly specific information or file charges.[114]

Proper planning is essential for the effective restraint or seizure of assets. Practitioners in developing countries need to identify early in advance the assets that are subject to provisional measures and need to make the necessary arrangements to ensure a suitable timing. If the measures are imposed too early, the target may be tipped off and cease activities, making it difficult to gather evidence and identify other accounts, targets, or the typologies used. However, if the measures are imposed after the target is aware of the investigation, the assets will most likely be dissipated or hidden.[115] When the provisional measures involve a foreign jurisdiction, interaction through informal as well

111 *State of Libya v Capitana Seas Ltd.* [2012] EWHC 602 (Comm).
112 Brun et al. (n 26) at 136.
113 Brun et al. (n 26) at 8.
114 Stephenson et al. (n 25) at 61.
115 Brun et al. (n 26) at 154.

as formal cooperation is important. When foreign authorities have an effective framework in place allowing them to act proactively, assets may be frozen without any delays and even before a formal request. For instance, the Swiss legal framework has facilitated the return of Montesino's assets to Peru by blocking his funds in accordance with the Swiss Money Laundering Act.[116] Assets held in Switzerland by former Egyptian President Hosni Mubarak and Tunisian President Ben Ali were swiftly frozen by the Swiss Federal Council in accordance with the Federal Act on the Freezing and Restitution of Illicit Assets.[117]

Court Proceedings to Seek Confiscation and/or Civil Remedies

Once sufficient evidence is collected, authorities in developing countries need to launch court proceedings to obtain criminal or NCB confiscation, or civil remedies such as compensation or restitution. Confiscation is generally decided by criminal courts following the criminal conviction or guilty plea of the defendant.[118] In some jurisdictions, where NCB confiscation is allowed, courts can order the forfeiture of ill-gotten gains without any judgement convicting the defendant but upon proof that the assets are the proceeds or instrumentalities of crime.[119]

Meeting the burden of proof to obtain a criminal conviction, which requires proof of guilt beyond a reasonable doubt or an intimate conviction, is often challenging when corrupt leaders or officials stay in power long enough to hide their corrupt acts and conceal their assets in foreign jurisdictions. Practitioners in developing countries need to be aware of the challenges in meeting the elements of an offense beyond reasonable doubt.[120] Specific offenses may be easier to prove compared to others. For instance, illicit enrichment, which is based on the fact that government officials cannot explain the increase in their wealth during their mandate, is easier to prove than bribery, which in certain countries may require proof of a corrupt agreement.[121] In such cases, practitioners may consider alternative avenues such as civil ones or NCB.

When the investigation is conducted years or decades after the commission of the crime, obtaining convincing evidence, including documentation or witness statements, is particularly complex. In addition, limitation periods that are too short to permit prosecution of corruption offenses are frequently a significant obstacle to prosecution. Hence, practitioners may seek to recover assets by exploring legal avenues based on the most favourable offenses in terms of statute of limitations. While it will be impossible to initiate criminal or civil proceedings after the conduct has become statute-barred, it is important

116 Brun et al. (n 26) at 154.
117 Brun et al. (n 26) at 142–43.
118 Brun et al. (n 26) at 185.
119 Cassella (n 53) at 499.
120 Brun et al. (n 26) at 66.
121 Brun et al. (n 26) at 66.

to identify offenses with a more favourable limitation period. For instance, when it comes to continuous crimes such as money laundering, the prescription period will be calculated once the illegal activities have ceased.[122]

Legal actions to recover assets are also unsuccessful when they fail to establish that a property is derived from a given offense. The link can be difficult to establish due to lack of evidence or when the assets have been converted, transferred, or comingled with lawful assets, which is often the case.[123] The use of cash transactions and increasing adoption of cryptocurrency exacerbate these challenges. It is even more complicated when illicit profits, such as bribes, are directly received by shell companies in offshore bank accounts, thus leaving no money trail for transactions and wire transfers leading from the jurisdiction harmed by corruption and the one in which the ill-gotten gains are laundered.

To avoid this obstacle, authorities may use value-based confiscation instead of property-based confiscation. Value-based confiscation allows the court to calculate the benefits derived from a crime to order the confiscation of any asset belonging to the defendant up to the value of these ill-gotten gains, even in the absence of any proven link with the prosecuted offense.[124]

Other jurisdictions have legislation that shift the burden of proof or the burden of production of evidence to defendants through so-called "extended confiscation", "lifestyle offenses", "criminal organization", and "unexplained wealth" legislation. Such "enhanced" confiscation generally authorizes prosecuting authorities to make a prima facie case that a defendant's asset shall be considered ill-gotten gains based on their acquisition in a certain period before or after its commission, or on other circumstances, like activities conducted in the context of a criminal organization. Once this prima facie case is made, property owned or acquired by the defendant during the time of the commission of the criminal activities are considered proceeds of crime unless the defendant provides evidence of its legitimate origin.

For instance, the Swiss Federal Act on the Restitution of Assets Illicitly Obtained by Politically Exposed Persons ("Restitution of Illicit Assets Act") has introduced a presumption of illicit origin where the assets have been subject to an extraordinary increase that is connected with the exercise of a public office by the politically exposed person and where the level of corruption in the country of origin is acknowledged as high.[125] Even before this specific legislation, previous Swiss law had allowed courts to shift the burden of proof

122 Brun et al. (n 26) at 54.

123 Boucht (n 9) at 117, 119; Johan Boucht, 'Extended Confiscation: Criminal Assets or Criminal Owners' in Katalin Ligeti and Michele Simonato (eds), *Chasing Criminal Money: Challenges and Perspectives on Asset Recovery in the EU* (Hart Publishing 2017) at 117.

124 Stephenson et al. (n 25) at 65–66.

125 Restitution of Illicit Assets Act (RIAA), article 6, para. 1, <www.admin.ch/gov/en/start/documentation/media-releases.msg-id-37478.html> accessed 13 November 2022.

in the case of the former Nigerian President Sani Abacha and his family, who failed to prove that frozen funds had been obtained legally.[126]

Countries that do not provide for "value-based" or "enhanced" confiscation based on rebuttable presumptions often face a significant barrier to asset recovery. In such circumstances, NCB confiscation, civil proceedings, or joining court processes conducted in the jurisdiction where assets are located may provide alternative avenues.

Enforcement of Confiscation Orders and Asset Return

Once courts have ordered the freezing or the confiscation of assets, steps must be taken to enforce the order. If the assets are located in a foreign jurisdiction, its authorities may enforce the decision by recognizing or registering the foreign order for enforcement in a domestic court.[127] The UNCAC privileges this solution by obliging States to establish a mechanism for direct enforcement, which generally involves the MLA process.[128] Its main advantage is that the foreign court will not need to consider the facts of the case again as its role is only to verify that the order for which enforcement is requested was made in accordance with due process and the rights of the defendants.

The enforcement of a final confiscation order in a foreign jurisdiction should result in the return of assets to the requesting jurisdiction, otherwise, the assets may be transferred to the general treasury or a confiscation fund of the requested jurisdiction.[129] According to the UNCAC, a requested party shall return the confiscated property to the requesting jurisdiction without conditions in cases of embezzlement of public funds or laundering of embezzled funds.[130] For other UNCAC offenses, the requested jurisdiction shall enforce the foreign confiscation order and return the assets when the requesting party reasonably establishes prior ownership, or when the requested State party recognizes damage to the requesting state party as a basis for returning the confiscated property.[131]

In all other cases, the requested party has the obligation to give "priority consideration" to the repatriation of assets to the requesting jurisdiction, the return of assets to their legitimate owners, or the compensation of victims of corruption.[132] The return of assets may depend in this case on the domestic legislation of the requested party, applicable international anti-corruption

126 Federal Department of Foreign Affairs, 'No Dirty Money, The Swiss Experience in Returning Illicit Assets' <www.eda.admin.ch/dam/eda/en/documents/aussenpolitik/voelkerrecht/edas-broschuere-no-dirty-money_EN.pdf> accessed 13 November 2022 at 20.

127 Brun et al. (n 26) at 10.

128 See UNCAC, articles 54 paras. 1(a), 54 para. 2(a), 55 para. 1(b).

129 Brun et al. (n 26) at 10.

130 UNCAC, article 57 para. 3(a).

131 UNCAC, article 57, para. 3(b).

132 UNCAC, article 57, para. 3(c).

conventions, regional agreements, MLA treaties, or special agreements, such as asset sharing agreements. Assets may also be directly returned to the requesting jurisdictions through a court order granting compensation for damages to the victim jurisdiction in the context of a private civil action.[133] In addition, when deciding on confiscation, courts in some jurisdictions may recognize a victim jurisdiction's claim that it is the legitimate owner of the assets.[134]

In practice, asset return is often hindered by a lack of legal frameworks complying with the UNCAC. In addition, several policy issues are likely to arise during any efforts to recover assets in corruption or embezzlement of public funds cases. Requested countries may be concerned that the funds will be siphoned off again due to continued or renewed perception of corruption in the requesting countries, especially if the offender continues to hold office and exerts significant influence.[135] This explains the reluctance of some jurisdictions to repatriate stolen assets without setting up mechanisms to avoid further misuse of these assets in the requesting countries.[136] Problems may arise when the requested jurisdiction attempts to impose, for example, an agreement on how confiscated assets should be managed by the requesting country. Interesting developments in recent years have shown that some forms of asset sharing, or repatriation agreements, can offer solutions. In some cases, international organizations such as the World Bank have been used to facilitate the return and monitoring of recovered funds. For instance, the BOTA Foundation, in Kazakhstan was established in 2008 by the governments of Kazakhstan, Switzerland, and the US, as well as five Kazakhstanis, in order to ensure the transparent return to and use by Kazakhstan of assets alleged to be the proceeds of corruption frozen in Switzerland, and to support vulnerable groups of people in the country. The release of the funds was agreed to be contingent upon the establishment and implementation of the "BOTA Program". The World Bank contracted an international nongovernmental organization to oversee the foundation's operations, offer administrative support, and ensure that the foundation's goals were met.[137]

Conclusion

The recovery of stolen assets has been placed at the top of national anti-corruption agendas of numerous countries, including developing ones which are seriously hit by the theft of public assets. When it is successful, asset recovery can provide much-needed funds, undo the wrongs caused by

133 Brun et al. (n 26) at 11.
134 Brun et al. (n 26) at 11.
135 Brun et al. (n 26) at 11.
136 Brun et al. (n 26) at 11.
137 International Research & Exchanges Board [IREX], 'Returning Stolen Assets: BOTA Foundation Final Report', <www.irex.org/resource/returning-stolen-assets-bota-foundation-final-report> accessed 13 November 2022.

corruption, and help restore public trust. However, practitioners involved in the asset recovery process are not only faced with numerous challenges that require strategic choices in terms of selecting the proper legal avenue for pursuing the stolen assets. They must also overcome operational barriers that arise at each step of the efforts. Successful asset recovery cases have set good examples in addressing obstacles and may support practitioners who can use good practices in similar cases. Drawing on the legacy of successful asset recovery cases, this article aimed to discuss common challenges encountered by practitioners and provide solutions and alternatives to mitigate or avoid risks. Numerous laws, regulations, and legal tools are now in place to overcome possible challenges in the asset recovery process. In parallel, corrupt leaders and officials around the globe are likely exploring or have already come up with new methods and ways that will allow them to escape accountability. In the years to come, successful asset recovery will certainly need commitment and action by all countries and international organizations. As the challenges remain immense, asset recovery needs a collective effort to bring justice to governments and people who have been deprived of their assets.

Part III

Conclusion

15 Strategic Tools for Amplified AML/CFT Compliance in Developing Countries

Nkechikwu Valerie Azinge-Egbiri and Egbiri Egbiri

Introduction

Developed countries have stronger anti-money laundering and counter-terrorist financing (AML/CFT) compliance outcomes.[1] Problems associated with developing countries include endogenous factors which encompass weak laws and institution,[2] abuse of political powers,[3] corruption and failing inter-agency collaborations.[4] Similarly, exogenous factors such as colonialism, neo-colonialism, lack of legitimacy and mismatched transplantation have been implicated in the failings of developing countries to comply with the global standards.[5] Indeed, these factors underscore the underlining conflicts and ambiguities that trail the establishment and operationalization of the Financial Action Task Force (FATF) and the resulting legitimacy crisis that undermines the compliance trajectory of developing countries, while highlighting the internal issues that weaken compliance. Notwithstanding, countries that suffer compliance challenges risks being greylisted or blacklisted by the FATF. Arguably, listed countries encounter setbacks which include a significant reduction

1 Concha Verdugo Yepes, 'Compliance with the AML/CFT International Standards: Lessons from a Cross-Country Analysis' (2011) IMF Working Paper WP/11/117 <www.imf.org/external/pubs/ft/wp/2011/wp11177.pdf> accessed 21 January 2024.

2 NV Azinge-Egbiri, *Regulating and Combating Money Laundering and Terrorist Financing: The Law in Emerging Economies* (Routledge 2022).

3 J Hatchard, 'Know Your Beneficial Owner: PEPs and Beneficial Ownership Transparency' in J Hatchard (ed), *Combating Money Laundering in Africa* (Edward Elgar Publishing 2020) 226–39 <https://econpapers.repec.org/bookchap/elgeechap/19179_5f12.htm> accessed 7 February 2024.

4 J Harvey, *Inter-Agency Mapping – Tackling Beneficial Ownership and the Proceeds of Corruption: Evidence from Nigeria* (Ace Global Integrity 2021) <https://ace.globalintegrity.org/wp-content/uploads/2022/01/Harvey-Nigeria-Project-Interagency-mapping.pdf> accessed 21 January 2024.

5 J Harvey, *Inter-Agency Mapping – Tackling Beneficial Ownership and the Proceeds of Corruption: Evidence from Nigeria* (Ace Global Integrity 2021) 4 <https://ace.globalintegrity.org/wp-content/uploads/2022/01/Harvey-Nigeria-Project-Interagency-mapping.pdf> accessed 21 January 2024.

DOI: 10.4324/9781003253808-18

in their capital flows,[6] development credits,[7] market capitalization and gross domestic product, which triggers a balance of payment crisis.[8]

Noting the significant impact of AML/CFT compliance deficits on the economic outcomes of countries and their ability to combat financial crimes, scholars have offered insights on the factors that undermine compliance and how they can address such challenges. Political will,[9] effective judicial systems, strong compliance culture, rule of law and anti-corruption processes[10] have been promoted as measures to improve compliance outcomes.[11] Likewise, sturdy inter-agency collaboration and a shared understanding of risks are complementary factors for amplified compliance. While these factors are critical, the fractured systems in developing countries often cannot meet the research recommendations which usually provide minimal implementation guidance. This chapter extends existing research by arguing that a contextual adaptation of the quadruplet pillars of understanding,[12] accountability, coordination[13] and capacity (UACC) are critical tools for preparing for mutual evaluations and improving compliance outcomes. While our pillars share some similarities with extant research, it is different. Our chapter deviates from existing research which highlights varied factors as the panacea for failed or amplified compliance but underscores a holistic approach to transforming AML/CFT compliance in a practical way.

Our arguments are made in three parts. The first part highlights the process of mutual evaluation and argues that developed countries have stronger

6 M Kida and S Paetzold, 'The Impact of Gray-Listing on Capital Flows: An Analysis Using Machine Learning' (*IMF*, 27 May 2021) <www.imf.org/en/Publications/WP/Issues/2021/05/27/The-Impact-of-Gray-Listing-on-Capital-Flows-An-Analysis-Using-Machine-Learning-50289> accessed 21 January 2024.
7 L Koker, J de, Howell and N Morris, 'Economic Consequences of Greylisting by the Financial Action Task Force' (2023) 11(5) Risks 81 <http://dx.doi.org/10.3390/risks11050081> accessed 21 January 2024.
8 L Koker, J de, Howell and N Morris, 'Economic Consequences of Greylisting by the Financial Action Task Force' (2023) 11(5) Risks 7 <http://dx.doi.org/10.3390/risks11050081> accessed 21 January 2024.
9 I Idris, 'Political Will and Combating Serious Organised Crime. SOC ACE Evidence Review Paper No. 1. University of Birmingham' <www.birmingham.ac.uk/documents/college-social-sciences/government-society/publications/political-will.pdf> accessed 21 January 2024.
10 A Lenschow, D Liefferink and S Veenman, 'When the Birds Sing. A Framework for Analysing Domestic Factors Behind Policy Convergence' (2005) 12(5) Journal of European Public Policy 797 <http://dx.doi.org/10.1080/13501760500161373> accessed 21 January 2024.
11 S Steinmo, 'Institutionalism' in Nelson Polsby (ed), *International Encyclopedia of Social and Behavioural Sciences Elsevier Science* (2001) <https://faculty.washington.edu/stovel/steinmo.pdf> accessed 21 January 2024).
12 J Ibitola, 'The Role of FATF Recommendations in Shaping Global AML Strategies' (2023) <www.flagright.com/post/the-role-of-fatf-recommendations-in-shaping-global-aml-strategies> accessed 21 January 2024.
13 M Chene, 'Interagency Coordination Mechanisms Improving the Effectiveness of National Anti-Corruption Efforts' in *Transparency International Anti-Corruption Helpdesk Answer* (2019) <https://knowledgehub.transparency.org/assets/uploads/helpdesk/Interagency-coordination-mechanisms_2019_PR.pdf> accessed 21 January 2024.

AML/CFT compliance and effectiveness outcomes in comparison to their developing countries counterparts. It recognizes the exogenous factors that contributes to the challenges faced by developing countries but highlights areas of focus by developed countries that amplified their compliance outcomes. The second part underscores the quadruple pillars as strategic tools for compliance. The third part draws it all together and concludes. The FATF's Mutual Evaluations

A myriad of material, logistical and philosophical bottlenecks impede countries' compliance capacities with the FATF standards. The FATF's mutual evaluation (ME) is poised to unearth these challenges by determining the compliance trajectory of countries and delineating a roadmap for amplified implementation and compliance outcomes. In the ME process, countries, usually via regional bodies, peer-review each other to determine the extent to which their peer has complied with the FATF standards and their extent of effectiveness. While technical compliance requires that necessary laws and frameworks are instituted, effectiveness is focused on ensuring that the laws have their intended effect. Resulting evaluation reports from such assessments provide an extensive description and analysis of a country's AML/CFT system and incorporates recommendations to amplify their framework.[14] The FATF's assessment exercises are usually done by trained assessors,[15] or in cases of joint evaluations, staff of the International Monetary Fund (IMF) and the World Bank.[16] Assessors spend a period of two weeks in countries, assessing their public and private sectors for their technical compliance and effectiveness.[17] In-country assessments are based on prior desk-based research. Such research includes reviews of country's submissions on their technical compliance with law and regulations, followed by a scoping exercise that determines the areas of focus during on-site visits. Countries are ranked on each of the FATF's 40 recommendations[18] and intermediate outcomes,[19] and these results are published within each country's Mutual Evaluation Report (MER). Debatably,

14 FATF, *Mutual Evaluations* (FATF, 2024) <www.fatf-gafi.org/en/publications/Mutualevaluations/More-about-mutual-evaluations.html#:~:text=FATF%20mutual%20evaluations%20are%20in,different%20countries%20assess%20another%20country> accessed 21 January 2024.

15 FATF, *Mutual Evaluations* (FATF, 2024) 14 <www.fatf-gafi.org/en/publications/Mutualevaluations/More-about-mutual-evaluations.html#:~:text=FATF%20mutual%20evaluations%20are%20in,different%20countries%20assess%20another%20country> accessed 21 January 2024.

16 International Monetary Fund, 'Press Release: IMF, World Bank Enhance Efforts at Combating Money Laundering, Terrorist Financing, [Press Release No. 04/70] (2004) <www.imf.org/en/News/Articles/2015/09/14/01/49/pr0470> 21 January 2024.

17 International Monetary Fund, 'Press Release: IMF, World Bank Enhance Efforts at Combating Money Laundering, Terrorist Financing, [Press Release No. 04/70] (2004) 14 <www.imf.org/en/News/Articles/2015/09/14/01/49/pr0470> 21 January 2024.

18 Technical compliance is rated across each of the 40 recommendations, rated as Compliant, Largely Compliant, Partially Compliant, or Non-Compliant.

19 There are 11 outcomes related to effectiveness, rated as either Substantial, Moderate, or Low levels of effectiveness.

these rankings form the basis for decisions on whether the country in question is greylisted or blacklisted.

Many countries have undergone four rounds of MEs,[20] with developed countries leading on compliance and effectiveness outcomes.[21] Most striking is the fourth round of the ME. An analysis of the fourth round of the MERs for 99 countries conducted by the FATF and other assessment bodies revealed that the United Kingdom,[22] Spain[23] and Bermuda[24] had the best compliance outcomes.[25] Expectedly, there were significant correlations across the outcomes of these countries. All three countries were ranked fully compliant on at least 23 recommendations and had zero records of being non-compliant with any recommendation. Crucially, all countries had profound appreciation of their money laundering and terrorist financing (ML/TF) risks and hence instituted appropriate structures to address these risks. Relevant authorities disseminated risk assessment reports to other regulators and regulated entities to facilitate a cohesive approach to mitigating identified risks. These were not one-off activities, rather, any updated risks ratings were equally circulated to relevant stakeholders for required action. Strategic changes made within these countries include legislative amendments, comprehensive supervision for designated non-financial business professionals (DNFBPs), strong national coordination and collaboration, and proactive investigation, prosecution and conviction of a range of ML/TF activities with statistical evidence. The strength of their technical compliance is reflected in their stellar effectiveness outcomes. While these countries still have shortcomings,[26] their remarkable progress cannot be undermined.

20 Financial Action Task Force (FATF), 'Procedures for the FATF Fourth Round of AML/CFT Mutual Evaluations' (February 2023) <www.fatf-gafi.org/en/publications/Mutualevaluations/4th-round-procedures.html> accessed 21 January 2024.

21 Yepes (n 1).

22 Financial Action Task Force (FATF), 'United Kingdom: Mutual Evaluation Report'. (December 2018) <www.fatf-gafi.org/media/fatf/documents/reports/mer4/MER-United-Kingdom-2018.pdf> accessed 21 January 2024.

23 FATF, 'Spain: Follow-Up Assessments' (*FATF*, 2019) <www.fatf-gafi.org/media/fatf/documents/reports/fur/Follow-Up-Assessment-Spain-2019.pdf> accessed 21 January 2024.

24 CFATF, 'Anti-Money Laundering and Counter-Terrorist Financing Measures – Bermuda, Mutual Evaluation Report, January 2020' (*CFATF*, January 2020) <www.cfatf-gafic.org/documents/4th-round-meval- reports/13596-bermuda-4th-round-mer/file> accessed 10 July 2020.

25 Nkechikwu Azinge-Egbiri, Kolawole Ebire and Joy Malala, 'Financial Action Task Force (FATF)'s AML/CFT Standards: An Analysis of Compliance and Effectiveness Status of Assessed Countries under the 4th Round and its FSRB Equivalent' (Global South Dialogue on Economic Crime, 15 August 2022) <https://gsdec.network/wp-content/uploads/2023/05/FATFS-AML-CFT-STANDARD-Analysis-of-the-Compliance-Effectiveness-Status-Original.pdf> accessed 21 January 2024.

26 For instance, with Bermuda, the real estate industry is struggling as many companies have not imbibed the practice of filling the suspicious activity reports and the funds recovered and retained through criminal investigations are considered low given Bermuda's recognised

Developing countries suffered compliance and effectiveness challenges. Generally, these countries performed better on their technical compliance in relation to their effectiveness outcomes, which were significantly low. Such challenge demonstrated that despite efforts to improve their AML/CFT systems, their frameworks have remained largely undeveloped.[27] Ghana's outcome at the time demonstrates this challenge. While Ghana's technical compliance levels improved, its effectiveness remained abysmal.[28] Ghana received substantial ratings on immediate outcome (IO) 2,[29] but recorded low or moderate effectiveness on all other IOs, which was particularly worrying given that countries with weak ratings on IO 4, 5, 6 and 9[30] were susceptible to getting listed. Ghana's situation is reflective of the occurrence across countries in West Africa under the Inter-Governmental Action Group against Money Laundering in West Africa (GIABA), as none of them attained one 'highly effective' rating with regards to the immediate outcomes. Other African countries attained relatively low compliance and effectiveness, with Mauritania, Uganda and Botswana ranking the lowest globally.[31]

The MER analysis demonstrated significant challenges with developing countries. A remarkable weakness amongst developing countries was the failure to conduct comprehensive risks assessments which affected their ability to understand and address their ML/TF risks.[32] Additionally, they had lacklustre frameworks for national cooperation and coordination and had limited transparency of beneficial ownership registers and had limited resources or even expertise to combat ML/TF. For instance, financial intelligence units (FIUs) operated at sub-optimal levels given the absence of financial or human resources to facilitate supervisory oversight, compliance or intelligence gathering.[33] Moreso, while banks predominantly filed suspicious transactions reports, many of them were not actionable. Non-profit sectors failed to adopt a risks-based approach, a challenge that stifled them of necessary resources to execute their objectives with outcomes that disproportionately affected

international financial crime centre status. Additionally, competent authorities such as immigration and customs staff have limited targeted trainings. With the United Kingdom, its financial intelligence unit is limited in its ability to undertake operational and strategic analysis of suspicious transactions reports.

27 Azinge-Egbiri, Ebire and Malala (n 25). Data for 30 April 2020, 99 jurisdictions

28 GIABA, 'Anti-Money Laundering and Counter-Terrorist Financing Measures: Ghana Second Round Mutual Evaluation Report' (*GIABA*, May 2018) <www.giaba.org/Frame/pdf viewer||5fe4bba620263190abef9e8727bd920f15ece780605dd721a9715ca1b62900a0||2NE_MER_GHANA.pdf> accessed 21 January 2024.

29 There are 11 outcomes related to effectiveness, rated as either Substantial, Moderate, or Low levels of effectiveness. Technical compliance is rated across each of the 40 recommendations, rated as Compliant, Largely Compliant, Partially compliant, or Non-Compliant.

30 GIABA (n 28).

31 Azinge-Egbiri, Ebire and Malala (n 25).

32 Azinge-Egbiri, Ebire and Malala (n 25) 31.

33 Azinge-Egbiri, Ebire and Malala (n 25) 32.

women.[34] Fundamentally, international cooperation aimed at facilitating financial intelligence exchange or information request through mutual assistance was also strained due to capacity and resource deficit and the lack of political will to engage in such exercises. Indeed, these vulnerabilities undermined the compliance and effectiveness trajectory of developing countries.

Underlining the weak compliance trajectory of these countries were their belated acquaintance with the FATF standards, data scarcity and lack of understanding of risks alongside the stark absence of necessary preconditions for effective regulations.[35] These pre-conditions, which include legal frameworks, institutional capacity, resources and political will, are usually lacking or erratic. As such, there remains a dearth of human and material resources to strategically position developing countries in the AML/CFT fight. Arguably, these issues placed developing countries at stark disparity with the most compliant jurisdictions that have stellar technical compliance that aligned with their effectiveness outcomes. An appraisal of these better performing countries by an earlier study by Azinge et al.[36] demonstrates a strong correlation between their compliance strategy and compliance outcomes. The running theme in the compliance strategy of stronger performing countries is the unification of 'understanding, accountability, coordination and capacity'. Hence, this chapter argues that developing countries need to unlearn, learn, and apply the UACC approach contextually to improve their compliance outcomes.

An Understanding, Accountability, Coordination and Capacity Approach to Improving Compliance

Scholars recognize the importance of UACC for amplified compliance. While studies have examined contextual factors that undermine or amplify compliance, there are sparse studies on strategic steps that countries can take to prepare for assessments with the goal of improved compliance outcomes. For instance, Neil Jensen and Cheong-Ann Png contended that amplifying political will and resolving capacity deficit are core to developing countries' AML/CFT compliance failings.[37] Joosten et al. conduct a forward stepwise regression analysis of 196 countries to demonstrate that a country's gross domestic product is the most important predictor for compliance.[38] Earlier studies by

34 Azinge-Egbiri (n 2).

35 Azinge-Egbiri, Ebire and Malala (n 25).

36 Azinge-Egbiri, Ebire and Malala (n 25) 35.

37 Neil Jensen and Cheong-Ann Png, 'Implementation of the FATF Recommendations' (2011) 14(2) Journal of Money Laundering Control 110 <http://dx.doi.org/10.1108/13685201111127777> accessed 21 January 2024.

38 Erik Joosten et al., 'Predictors for Compliance with Anti-Terrorist Financing Standards' (2019) 22(2) Journal of Money Laundering Control 257 <http://dx.doi.org/10.1108/jmlc-02-2018-0011> accessed 21 January 2024.

Yepes give more context to Joosten et al.'s findings, as they found that institutional challenges such as inadequate resources, lack of quality regulatory framework and weak inter-agency collaboration contribute strongly to poor compliance outcomes.[39] More recent studies by Mekpor et al. conclude that regulatory quality, technology, the structure of the banking sector, economy size and institution of financial intelligence centre are critical to poor AML/CFT compliance.[40] While these studies problematize the compliance and effectiveness challenges of developing countries, they do not highlight strategic steps these countries can take to enhance their ratings. Drawing lessons from the strategies of the most compliant countries, this chapter fills this gap.

Understanding the FATF's Methodologies and Assessment Processes

For improved compliance outcomes, relevant AML/CFT institutions and sectors must understand the FATF's methodologies and appreciate the country's risks. Such contextual understanding entails an appreciation of their country's threats and vulnerabilities to enable regulators to strategically devote resources to address and mitigate identified risks.

Many developing countries failed on Recommendation 1, which calls on countries to assess risks and apply a risks-based approach. Failures were attributed to their weak or non-existent AML/CFT national risks assessment alongside their failure to involve the private sector in the assessment process. Arguably, such challenges demonstrate that even when risks assessments were done, they were not based on domestic coordination between the public and private sector, thereby undermining the output's robustness. The outcome is that developing countries have bare understanding of their risks, thereby occasioning the misplacement or misapplication of resources or strategies for combatting financial crime. One example pertains to an undisclosed country where top criminal activities generated proceeds of crime which involved corruption, tax evasion, fraud and drug trafficking.[41] Yet the national risks assessments failed to capture these threats, an indication that the risks-based approach (RBA) was not adequately conducted to highlight national and sectoral risks.

39 Yepes (n 1).

40 Emmanuel Senanu Mekpor, Anthony Aboagye and Jonathan Welbeck, 'The Determinants of Anti-Money Laundering Compliance among the Financial Action Task Force (FATF) Member States' (2018) 26(3) Journal of Financial Regulation and Compliance 442 <http://dx.doi.org/10.1108/jfrc-11-2017-0103> accessed 21 January 2024.

41 GSDEC, *Webinar Synopsis – The Financial Action Task Force (FATF)'s Compliant Countries: Lessons for Non-Compliant Jurisdictions* (GSDEC – The Global South Dialogue on Economic Crime Network) <https://gsdec.network/7739/webinar-synopsis-the-financial-action-task-force-fatfs-compliant-countries-lessons-for-non-compliant-jurisdictions/> accessed 22 January 2024.

Various sectors failed to conduct adequate risk assessments. For instance, assessments revealed that relevant authorities struggled to appreciate the risks within the real estate, casino or non-profit sectors, and the risks posed by other actors such as lawyers and accountants.[42] While these lapses are potentially attributed to lack of political will or resources, the failure to understand the risks is costly as countries that need the AML/CFT flexibilities fail to use them. Unintended consequences, such as financial exclusion, usually follow.[43] For instance, the FATF states that low-income countries with large informal financial markets may use simplified customer due diligence (CDD) to curb financial exclusion.[44] Yet, developing countries are reluctant to use these simplifications or exceptions due to fear of negative ME outcomes and challenges with regulatory capacity.[45] As a result, many financial service providers do not take advantage of the RBA's flexibility, which results in suboptimal use of CDD for financial inclusion objectives.[46] These challenges reveal that the RBA is not applied in a proportionate or strategic way within sectors and institutions.[47] Conversely, developed countries utilize the exemptions based on their application of the RBA, which is built on stronger regulatory capacity alongside solid awareness and legal protections.[48]

Assessors also highlight the failings of regulatory bodies and reporting agencies to fully understand the FATF standards, especially the RBA and the MERs. As such, relevant persons are usually unprepared during evaluations, evidencing the lack of a robust national risks assessment. Relevant persons also lack the necessary capacity, expertise or confidence to adequately implement the recommendations.[49] Turning the tide requires continuous capacity building of relevant actors tailored at amplifying the national ML/TF risks of countries – whilst also

42 Azinge-Egbiri, Ebire and Malala (n 25).

43 Kuntay Celik, 'Impact of the FATF Recommendations and their Implementation on Financial Inclusion: Insights from Mutual Evaluations and National Risk Assessments' (*Open Knowledge Repository Beta*, 2 December 2021) <http://hdl.handle.net/10986/36659> accessed 22 January 2024.

44 Kuntay Celik, 'Impact of the FATF Recommendations and their Implementation on Financial Inclusion: Insights from Mutual Evaluations and National Risk Assessments' (*Open Knowledge Repository Beta*, 2 December 2021) <http://hdl.handle.net/10986/36659> accessed 22 January 2024.

45 Kuntay Celik, 'Impact of the FATF Recommendations and their Implementation on Financial Inclusion: Insights from Mutual Evaluations and National Risk Assessments' (*Open Knowledge Repository Beta*, 2 December 2021) <http://hdl.handle.net/10986/36659> accessed 22 January 2024.

46 GIABA's 2018 report about West African countries' use of know your customer (KYC) practices indicated that financial service providers do not take advantage of the flexibility of RBA, which results in suboptimal performance of CDD for financial inclusion goals.

47 Celik (n 43).

48 Financial Conduct Authority, *Understanding the Money Laundering Risks in the Capital Markets* (Financial Conduct Authority | FCA, June 2019) <www.fca.org.uk/publication/thematic-reviews/tr19-004.pdf> accessed 22 January 2024. It is imperative to note that awareness and understanding of risks is not limited to developing countries, as developed countries also face these challenges.

49 Financial Conduct Authority, *Understanding the Money Laundering Risks in the Capital Markets* (Financial Conduct Authority | FCA, June 2019) <www.fca.org.uk/publication/thematic-reviews/tr19-004.pdf> accessed 22 January 2024. It is imperative to note that awareness and understanding of risks is not limited to developing countries, as developed countries also face these challenges.

preparing the country for the MEs. Such capacity building strategy must consider the context of the countries in question to ensure its workability.

The Institutional Culture of Accountability

Accountability within regulatory, judicial and enforcement institutions remain core to amplified compliance. Accountability within such bodies must be systemic and ingrained in their culture to achieve its objectives. Practicalizing this means that such institutions must have the necessary space to implement AML/CFT laws. Such space ought to be accompanied by human, financial and technological resources to facilitate operational autonomy.[50] Many developing countries grapple with an absence of institutional autonomy and capacity, weak competence and continuous political interference that has occasioned agency capture. Additionally, while some agencies have strong systems in place, this is not the case with others. For instance, while investigators and prosecutors may possess a culture of accountability, the judiciary and enforcement officials may lack this, which is problematic. Political interference usually taints the accountability of judicial and enforcement officers alongside unchecked arbitrariness in sentencing and implementation of same, hence the need for sentencing guidelines. Arguably, these issues are interrelated with the developmental concerns of the countries in question. For these reasons, the accountability of focal persons or key actors within institutions is one way to combat financial crime.

The key actors are usually responsible for their institution's action plan and the implementation of same. Such focal persons are expected to possess the capacity to set the institution's tone and influence cultural changes while remaining the go-to persons for the assessment teams and other relevant actors.[51] As such, they must possess strong requisite knowledge and sturdy persuasive and interpersonal skills, which includes the ability to identify key issues and resolve disputes. Indeed, government buy-in is critical to achieving this level of accountability within relevant institutions. Haslett contended that the United Kingdom's compliance outcome was unrivalled due to the involvement of a relevant government minister who was integral to the assessment processes and facilitated information sharing within/and across relevant government agencies.[52]

50 Egmont Group of Financial Intelligence Units, 'Understanding FIU Operational Independence and Autonomy, Toronto, Canada' (2018) <https://egmontgroup.org/wp-content/uploads/2021/09/2018_Understanding_FIU_Operational_Independence_and_Autonomy.pdf> accessed 8 February 2024.

51 Drawing from senior persons reporting in banking law, it is apparent that key stakeholder engagement is key to effectiveness as these persons are involved in decision-making; Ian Carrington and Heba Shams, 'Elements of an Effective AML/CFT Framework: Legal, Regulatory, and Best Institutional Practices to Prevent Threats to Financial Stability and Integrity' in *International Monetary Fund 'Elements of an Effective AML/CFT Framework* 377–413 <www.elibrary.imf.org/downloadpdf/book/9781589067738/ch015.pdf> accessed 8 February 2024; see also FATF, 'Effective Supervision and Enforcement By AML/CFT Supervisors of the Financial Sector and Law Enforcement' (2015) <www.fatf-gafi.org/content/dam/fatf-gafi/guidance/RBA-Effective-supervision-and-enforcement.pdf.coredownload.pdf> accessed 8 February 2024.

52 GSDEC (n 41).

Arguably, the UK's political involvement in its compliance outcome demonstrates the need for observable and solid political will which needs to be transparently demonstrated in terms of institutional outputs. This means that political authorities are to refrain from interfering with the work of relevant institutions with respect to money laundering offences. Rather, their focus would be on channelling resources to relevant institutions to amplify their capacity while ensuring effective coordination, nationally and internationally.[53]

Coordination and Collaboration

As Sprout et al. highlighted in Chapter 11 of this volume, coordination is central to combatting financial crimes. Coordination, however, must be at various levels; nationally (across agencies), internationally and with the FATF or designated assessment institution.

At the national level, the FATF warrants inter-agency collaboration that sees relevant law enforcement actors, supervisors, company registries, private sector and non-profit bodies work together.[54] Research supports the FATF's postulation and demonstrates that robust AML/CFT compliance and regulation cannot be attained by isolated agencies' efforts as interagency collaboration and coordination is essential to ensuring a cohesive fight against economic crimes.[55] Yet, in reality, agencies usually work in silos and have minimal engagements. For instance, the mutual evaluation reports (MER)s of several countries demonstrate that their number of AML/CFT investigations and prosecutions do not result in commensurate sentencing, a challenge that demonstrates the disconnect between the relevant bodies. Addressing such disconnect requires a strategy that trains judges alongside the regulators and prosecutors to understand the intricacies of AML/CFT investigation and prosecution. Fundementally, a standard operating procedures between the relevant actors is also critical to enhance cooperation. Moreso, sentencing guidelines are important to forestall the lack of consistency across AML/CFT judgments. Arguably, such strategy would demonstrate that key actors from relevant bodies have a core role to play in winning the war against financial crime by not only facilitating inter-agency collaboration but using this 'tool' to engineer a comprehensive assessment process. For instance, Bermuda's compliance outcome is largely attributed to its mechanism for cooperation

53 AY Shehu, 'Promoting Financial Sector Stability through an effective AML&CFT Regime' (2010) 13(2) Journal of Money Laundering Control 139–54.

54 FATF, 'Partnering in the Fight against Financial Crime: Data Protection, Technology and Private Sector Information Sharing' (July 2022) <www.fatf-gafi.org/content/dam/fatf-gafi/guidance/Partnering-int-the-fight-against-financial-crime.pdf> accessed 8 February 2024.

55 XiaoTong Loh, 'Suspicious Activity Reports (SARs) Regime: Reforming Institutional Culture' (2021) 24(3) Journal of Money Laundering Control 514–24 <https://doi.org/10.1108/JMLC-07-2020-0078; Isaac Ofoeda Elikplimi K Agbloyor, Joshua Y Abor and Kofi A Osei, 'Anti-money Laundering Regulations and Financial Sector Development' (2022) 27(4) International Journal of Finance & Economics 4085–104 <https://doi.org/10.1002/ijfe.2360>; Ilaria Zavoli and Colin King 'The Challenges of Implementing Anti-Money Laundering Regulation: An Empirical Analysis' (2021) 84(4) The Modern Law Review 740–71 <https://doi.org/10.1111/1468-2230.12628 accessed 22 January 2024.

and coordination. The National Anti-Money Laundering Committee,[56] supported by the Bermudan Monetary Authority, worked closely with the private sector and non-profit actors to improve the country's compliance outcomes. Similarly, the United Kingdom and Spain's successes also hinged on their robust inter-agency coordination. Arguably, inter-agency collaboration and coordination promotes a unified approach to curbing ML/TF while creating mutual trust amongst law enforcement agencies and reporting entities.[57]

Given the cross-border nature of crime, international collaboration and coordination is equally fundamental. Recommendations 37 to 40 require countries to actively cooperate in the fight against financial crime, especially on the freezing and confiscation of assets, and the extradition of criminals.[58] Bermuda, the United Kingdom and Spain have developed frameworks for international cooperation in investigations, prosecution, and asset recovery, and have lessons for less developed countries.[59] FATF-styled regional bodies (FSRBs) promote close cooperation with member states[60] and countries are enjoined to utilize necessary tools such as memoranda of understanding (MOUs) to rapidly detect and recover funds. Yet, the setbacks of these proposed solutions cannot be ignored. For instance, not all countries have efficient FIUs that conduct adequate analysis on suspicious transactions reports, an impediment demonstrable by the variation in the reporting structures across jurisdictions.[61] Hence, FIUs may struggle to exchange information especially given the legal requirement for negotiating and signing MOUs prior to such exchanges.[62] Usually, criminals are able to move funds before MOUs are finalized.[63] Such

56 'The National Anti-Money Laundering Committee – NAMLC' (The National Anti-Money Laundering Committee – NAMLC) <https://namlc.gov.so/> accessed 22 January 2024.

57 Ofoeda, Agbloyor, Abor and Osei (n 55); Zavoli and King (n 55) 740–71.

58 FATF, 'International Standards on Combating Money Laundering and the Financing of Terrorism & Proliferation- the FATF Recommendations' (November 2023) <www.fatf-gafi.org/content/dam/fatf-gafi/recommendations/FATF%20Recommendations%202012.pdf.coredownload.inline.pdf> accessed 22 January 2024.

59 FATF, 'High-Level Principles for the relationship between the FATF and the FATF-Style Regional Bodies' (*FATF*, 2012) updated February 2019 <www.fatf-gafi.org/publications/fatfgeneral/documents/highlevelprinciplesfortherelationshipbetweenthefatfandthefatfstyleregionalbodies.html> accessed 8 February 2024.

60 According to the GIABA: 'We promote close cooperation with member states through the GIABA ad hoc Ministerial Committee, as well as a network of national correspondents. Our technical assistance is therefore targeted at the establishment of strong coordination bodies in the form of inter-ministerial committees, which should be representative of all institutions and stakeholders involved in efforts and actions against ML/TF'.

61 Dionysios S Demetis, 'Technology and Anti-Money Laundering: A Systems Theory and Risk-Based Approach' in Edward Elgar (ed), *Technology and Anti-Money Laundering: A Systems Theory and Risk-Based Approach* (2010) <www.researchgate.net/publication/286036587_Technology_and_anti-money_laundering_A_systems_theory_and_risk-based_approach>.

62 Dionysios S Demetis, 'Technology and Anti-Money Laundering: A Systems Theory and Risk-Based Approach' in Edward Elgar (ed), *Technology and Anti-Money Laundering: A Systems Theory and Risk-Based Approach* (2010) <www.researchgate.net/publication/286036587_Technology_and_anti-money_laundering_A_systems_theory_and_risk-based_approach>.

63 Dionysios S Demetis, 'Technology and Anti-Money Laundering: A Systems Theory and Risk-Based Approach' in Edward Elgar (ed), *Technology and Anti-Money*

challenges demonstrate that tools for collaboration and coordination need to be thoroughly scrutinized to check against unintended consequences.

Collaboration and coordination are also important with regards to the FATF's relationship with countries. The FATF amplified the importance of coordination in its International Co-operation Review Group document, which states that countries' engagement with assessor agencies is a determinant factor for listing.[64] Countries that have adopted a hostile engagement strategy with the FATF have often suffered the backlash of public listing.[65] Hence, it is critical for countries to maintain an amicable and approachable relationship with the FATF and its assessors to avoid listing.

Capacity

Underlining the need for collaboration and coordination is the capacity of the relevant agencies and persons. With lax capacity, countries struggle with implementing domesticated FATF standards.[66] For instance, many developing countries have data shortage on issues central to the FATF assessments, such as the number of convictions, confiscations, the amount involved, the number of supervisory meetings and outcomes decided, amongst others.[67] The challenge with gathering relevant and significant data has occasioned negative evaluation results.[68] Additionally, FIUs' capacity deficit is worsened by the inability of

---

Laundering: A Systems Theory and Risk-Based Approach (2010) <www.researchgate.net/publication/286036587_Technology_and_anti-money_laundering_A_systems_theory_and_risk-based_approach>.

64 FATF, 'High-Risk and other Monitored Jurisdictions' <www.fatf-gafi.org/en/topics/high-risk-and-other-monitored-jurisdictions.html#:~:text=For%20all%20countries%20under%20ICRG,required%20by%20the%20action%20plan> accessed 22 January 2024.

65 Muhammad Idrees, Manzoor Ahmad Naazer and Hashmat Ullah Khan, 'Pakistan and the FATF: Exploring the Role of Diplomacy in Getting off the Grey List' (2020) 4(2) Liberal Arts and Social Sciences International Journal (LASSIJ) 413 <http://dx.doi.org/10.47264/idea.lassij/4.2.32> accessed 21 January 2024. Russia and Malta are key examples.

66 Financial Group Action Task Force, 'Guidance on Capacity Building for Mutual Evaluations and Implementation of the FATF Standards within Low Capacity Countries' (29 February 2008) <www.fatf-gafi.org/content/dam/fatf-gafi/guidance/Capacity%20building%20LCC.pdf.coredownload.pdf> accessed 22 January 2024.

67 GENESIS, 'Implementing FATF Standards in Developing Countries and Financial Inclusion: Findings and Guidelines' Final Report <https://cenfri.org/wp-content/uploads/2009/12/Implementing-FATF-standards-in-developing-countries-and-finacial-inclusion-final-report_Genesis_May-2008.pdf> accessed 8 February 2024; Financial Group Action Task Force, 'Guidance on Capacity Building for Mutual Evaluations and Implementation of the FATF Standards within Low Capacity Countries' (29 February 2008) <www.fatf-gafi.org/content/dam/fatf-gafi/guidance/Capacity%20building%20LCC.pdf.coredownload.pdf> accessed 22 January 2024.

68 GENESIS, 'Implementing FATF Standards in Developing Countries and Financial Inclusion: Findings and Guidelines' Final Report 67 <https://cenfri.org/wp-content/uploads/2009/12/Implementing-FATF-standards-in-developing-countries-and-finacial-inclusion-final-report_Genesis_May-2008.pdf> accessed 8 February 2024; Financial Group Action Task Force, 'Guidance on Capacity Building for Mutual Evaluations and Implementation of the FATF Standards within Low Capacity Countries' (29 February 2008) <www.fatf-gafi.org/content/dam/fatf-gafi/guidance/Capacity%20building%20LCC.pdf.coredownload.pdf> accessed 22 January 2024.

reporting bodies to leverage information from FIUs to combat corruption, tax evasion or other crimes that seek to hide the proceeds of crime. Moreso, the quality of personnel such as banking professionals, prosecutors, investigators, and even supervisory/regulatory bodies have been judged wanting.

FATF country assessors have also reported that even when guided, regulatory bodies do not adopt a RBA when implementing the FATF standards. As previously highlighted, the World Bank, based on the FATF's requirements, advised countries to relax stringent CDD requirements in low-risk situations by allowing the unbanked to hold and use basic banking accounts.[69] Subsequently, the World Bank designed suited products to ensure lower ML/TF risks. Unexpectedly, the relevant authorities in a country with over 60% financial exclusion rate rejected such proposals and products, thereby ousting the RBA. Their concerns, which centred on the probability of getting listed for failing on the CDD requirements, did not take a contextual approach that considered the flexibility offered by the FATF in proven low-risk situations.[70] Such an approach, adopted by several countries contrary to their private sectors' demands, occasions unintended consequences and triggers their listing for non-compliance. Particularly, it unearths the incapacity to appreciate the FATF standards and make suitable judgement calls when required.

Core to amplifying compliance and effectiveness outcomes is the time allocated for preparation. Developed countries with remarkable ratings reportedly prepare for the FATF's assessments long before its due date. Preparedness means that the relevant actors and institutions have a strategy that includes imbibing the FATF standards as part of their ongoing processes towards tackling financial crime, rather than a tick-the-box exercise that is usually rushed.[71] Such strategy inculcates an appreciation of their risks, a plan for risk mitigation and mock assessments. Mock assessments expose countries' weaknesses but allow them time to heighten inter-agency collaboration and enhance procedural familiarity. Moreso, it enables the appreciation that delisting does not necessary mean that countries have attained compliance and effectiveness, but rather have shown deliberate attempts to follow their action plan. Developing countries still struggle with timing and focus so much on getting delisted – and in so doing lose sight of the big picture which is to strengthen their AML/CFT framework and processes.

Recognizing the challenges, the IMF and the World Bank have assisted over 100 countries in building their institutional capacity to fight ML/TF.[72] Specifically, the IMF and the World Bank, alongside the Alliance for Financial Inclusion, have created resource-banks to guide the implementation of the FATF standards. They provide technical assistance focused on enabling countries build their legal and regulatory systems alongside their institutional

69 Celik (n 43).

70 Celik (n 43).

71 A tick-the-box approach also demonstrates limited involvement, planning or strategy devoted to the issue.

72 International Monetary Fund, 'Press Release: IMF, World Bank Enhance Efforts at Combating Money Laundering, Terrorist Financing' (International Monetary Funds, Press Release No. 04/70, 2 April 2004) <www.imf.org/en/News/Articles/2015/09/14/01/49/pr0470> accessed 21 January 2024.

capacity and coordination. Consequently, developing countries are increasingly better able to raise awareness and build regulatory/supervisory capacity for a RBA implementation strategy.[73]

FSRBs also provide technical assistance to states.[74] Like the IMF and World Bank, the FSRBs' technical assistance programs are demand-driven and operate within the parameters of UACC. As such, FSRBs consider political commitment, cooperation, engagement, inter-agency cooperation and coordination as paramount to combatting financial crime.[75] FSRBs also provide mentorship and legal advisory services to countries with the aim of building their FIUs and enabling them to develop and implement national AML/CFT strategies and action plans.

With requisite training, it is expected that relevant actors would be thoroughly prepared for assessments and would potentially have more robust assessment outcomes.[76]

Conclusion

Countries that have attained high AML/CFT ratings have certain traits in common – understanding, accountability, coordination, and capacity. In this chapter, we have highlighted these traits as strategic tools for amplified AML/CFT assessment outcomes for developing countries. We recognize, however, that these tools must be adapted contextually as many developing countries lack the pre-conditions for effective regulation. They compete for scarce government resources and have limited human and financial resources to facilitate implementation.[77] In addition, these countries are predominately cash-based and suffer from data retention and usage issues.[78] Moreso, some recommendations may indeed have paradoxical implications, and the assessment processes may have margins for error that may affect eventual ratings. Still, governments must address financial crime and strengthen their compliance outcomes by devoting budgetary allocations for intellectual and institutional capital to relevant bodies, especially regulatory and enforcement authorities.

73 International Monetary Fund, 'Press Release: IMF, World Bank Enhance Efforts at Combating Money Laundering, Terrorist Financing' (International Monetary Funds, Press Release No. 04/70, 2 April 2004) 69 <www.imf.org/en/News/Articles/2015/09/14/01/49/pr0470> accessed 21 January 2024.

74 Shehu (n 53).

75 Shehu (n 53).

76 Azinge-Egbiri, Ebire and Malala (n 25).

77 Santha Vaithilingam, Mahendhiran Nair and Muthi Samudra, 'Key Drivers for Soundness of the Banking Sector: Lessons For Developing Countries' (2006) 2(1) Journal of Global Business and Technology <https://gbata.org/wp-content/uploads/2013/02/JGBAT_Vol2-1-p1.pdf> accessed 21 January 2024 posits that "intellectual capital play an important role in the well-being of the financial sector and socioeconomic development of a country."

78 Shehu (n 53).

Index

[Note: numbers in **bold** indicate a table. Numbers in *italics* indicate a figure on the corresponding page]